# Phrogram Programming for the Absolute Beginner



Jerry Lee Ford, Jr.

**Course Technology PTR**
*A part of Cengage Learning*

COURSE TECHNOLOGY
CENGAGE Learning™

Australia • Brazil • Japan • Korea • Mexico • Singapore • Spain • United Kingdom • United States

COURSE TECHNOLOGY
CENGAGE Learning™

**Publisher and General Manager, Course Technology PTR:** Stacy L. Hiquet

**Associate Director of Marketing:** Sarah Panella

**Manager of Editorial Services:** Heather Talbot

**Marketing Manager:** Mark Hughes

**Acquisitions Editor:** Mitzi Koontz

**Project Editor:** Jenny Davidson

**Technical Reviewer:** Parker Hiquet

**PTR Editorial Services Coordinator:** Erin Johnson

**Interior Layout Tech:** Value Chain

**Cover Designer:** Mike Tanamachi

**CD-ROM Producer:** Brandon Penticuff

**Indexer:** Sharon Shock

**Proofreader:** Sara Gullion



Library of Congress Control Number: 2007906512

ISBN-13: 978-1-59863-443-3
ISBN-10: 1-59863-443-7

**Course Technology**
25 Thomson Place
Boston, MA 02210
USA

Cengage Learning is a leading provider of customized learning solutions with office locations around the globe, including Singapore, the United Kingdom, Australia, Mexico, Brazil, and Japan. Locate your local office at: **international.cengage.com/region**

Cengage Learning products are represented in Canada by Nelson Education, Ltd.

For your lifelong learning solutions, visit **courseptr.com**
Visit our corporate website at **cengage.com**

Printed in the United States of America
1 2 3 4 5 6 7 11 10 09 08

*To my mother and father for always being there, and to my wonderful children, Alexander, William, and Molly, and my beautiful wife, Mary.*

# FOREWORD

If you are interested in this book, you are one of the many people who want to learn how to create programs for your Windows-based personal computer. Nowadays, knowing how complex PC software has become, one of your biggest challenges can be described by a simple question—where should you begin?

The vision behind Phrogram is to help you answer that question in a way that shows how much fun real programming can really be. Most of what all of us do with today's technologies is use them—both hardware and software; there's nothing wrong with that inescapable fact. But creating our own technology can open up exciting adventures in learning and personal growth. Wholly apart from whether you take up programming as a career, finding the fun in making software that executes commands you have designed, developed, and debugged, is what Phrogram is all about.

Phrogram simplifies many of the more difficult constructs used in modern programming, but it is not a "toy" language, relying on "drag-and-drop" skills or populating worlds with pre-determined objects. Instead, Phrogram challenges you—in a plain-syntax, intuitive, and graphically rich way—to develop the essential mathematical, analytical, and logical skills you will need to truly become a hobbyist, PC game, or "spur-of-the-moment" programmer. Even more, Phrogram provides a solid foundation if you do decide to pursue the broader opportunities that await anyone who becomes highly proficient in information technology. Whether for prototyping, game creation, or simply enhancing your understanding of what computers actually do, Phrogram is powerful enough to offer a gateway into Microsoft's Visual Studio programming languages such as Visual Basic and C#, and the many other complex tools that professional developers turn to every day.

Of course, Phrogram is not your only option for developing PC software, nor is it meant to be the only language you will ever need to create interesting and useful programs. Instead, think of Phrogram as a "stepping-stone" resource on a path toward experiencing the vast and diverse offerings of modern computer programming. This book provides a comprehensive introduction to that resource and will help you navigate the exciting journey on which you now embark.

Now is a great time to try Phrogram, and to get going on your journey into the world of real programming. We on the Phrogram team know that you will enjoy and benefit from it.

David Witus

President
The Phrogram Company

# Acknowledgments

There are a number of individuals to whom I owe many thanks for their help and assistance in the development of this book. I'll start by thanking David Witus, Walt Morrison, and Andy Dunn from the Phrogram Company for taking the time to work with me and provide answers and insights while I was writing this book. I also need to thank Mitzi Koontz who served as the book's acquisitions editor. Special thanks also go out to Jenny Davidson for serving as the book's project editor. I also want to thank Parker Hiquet for all the valuable input and advice. In addition, I would like to thank everyone else at Cengage Learning for all their hard work.

# About the Author

**Jerry Lee Ford, Jr.** is an author, educator, and an IT professional with more than 18 years' experience in information technology, including roles as an automation analyst, technical manager, technical support analyst, automation engineer, and security analyst. He is the author of 24 other books and co-author of two additional books. His published works include *AppleScript Studio Programming for the Absolute Beginner, Microsoft Windows PowerShell Programming for the Absolute Beginner, Visual Basic 2005 Express Programming for the Absolute Beginner, VBScript Professional Projects, Microsoft Windows Shell Scripting and WSH Administrator's Guide, Microsoft Windows Shell Scripting for the Absolute Beginner, Learn JavaScript in a Weekend*, and *Microsoft Windows XP Professional Administrator's Guide*. Jerry has a master's degree in business administration from Virginia Commonwealth University in Richmond, Virginia, and has over five years' experience as an adjunct instructor teaching networking courses in information technology.

# Table of Contents

# Introduction

Welcome to *Phrogram Programming for the Absolute Beginner*! Phrogram is a programming language specifically designed to meet the needs of first-time programmers. Phrogram supports the development of computer games and multimedia programs, as well as music and graphics applications that run on Microsoft Windows. Phrogram consists of a programming language and a friendly and easy to learn integrated development environment, or IDE.

Phrogram started off as the Kid's Programming Language, or KPL, which was created by Jonah Stagner after he decided that he wanted to teach his kids how to program but could not find a programming language that he felt was appropriate for beginner programmers. Originally targeted at children between 10 and 14 years of age, it soon became obvious that the Kid's Programming Language was appropriate for more than just children, and so when version 2.0 was released in 2006, KPL was renamed Phrogram to reflect its broader appeal.

Phrogram runs on computers that use Microsoft Windows. Although Phrogram is capable of producing a wide range of applications, its primary use is on the development of computer games. This book's goal is to teach you everything you need to know to begin programming using Phrogram. To accomplish this goal, this book utilizes a hands-on instructional approach that emphasizes learning by doing, which is accomplished through the development of a series of computer games. As a result, learning to program with Phrogram is both fun and educational.

Phrogram is gaining rapid recognition and popularity as a beginner's programming language. It is being used around the world to introduce middle and high school students to programming and is being taught in a number of universities and colleges. Phrogram is also gaining the attention of many computer enthusiasts and hobbyists who want to learn how to do more with their computers than just surf the Internet.

Phrogram provides first-time programmers with everything needed to get started. Using Phrogram, you can create professional-quality applications and games, which you can then share with your friends or distribute as shareware. So, whether you are a student who has just signed up for an introductory programming class that uses Phrogram or a hobbyist who wants to have some fun, you will find that

Phrogram makes for a perfect first programming language that is capable of developing all kinds of applications, including 2D and 3D computer games.

## Why Phrogram?

Phrogram is very similar to Microsoft Visual Basic but is much easier to learn. Phrogram's IDE is visually very similar to that of Microsoft Visual Studio, the programming environment used to develop Visual Basic, C++, and C+ applications. As such, Phrogram makes for a great starter language, providing everything needed to build a foundation that can then be used to make a speedy transition to business-oriented professional programming languages.

Phrogram supports application development on both 32-bit and 64-bit versions of Microsoft Windows. It provides support for advanced graphics and audio features. Phrogram games can work with the computer's mouse and keyboard as well as with joysticks and many other types of input devices. Although it is not yet supported, Phrogram programmers will eventually be able to develop computer games that can run on the Xbox 360.

Phrogram provides you with everything you need to begin creating computer applications and games. It supports both 2D and 3D graphics and can be used to play digital music and sound effects. Phrogram also supplies tools for debugging, tracking down pesky bugs that prevent your applications and games from working like you want them to.

Phrogram is designed from the ground up with the first-time programmer in mind. At the same time, it is capable of developing robust and powerful applications and games. As such, computer enthusiasts and hobbyists may find that Phrogram is the only programming language they will ever need, while students and aspiring professional programmers will find Phrogram to be a great launching pad from which to begin their programming careers.

## Who Should Read This Book?

*Phrogram Programming for the Absolute Beginner* is designed to teach first-time programmers the fundamental steps involved in creating computer applications and games that run on Microsoft Windows. While previous programming experience is certainly helpful, it is not required. This book does not make any assumptions about your computer background other than that you must have a good working knowledge of computers running Microsoft Windows.

This book is designed to teach you everything that you need to know to get started creating Phrogram applications. It will teach you programming principles and techniques that can be broadly applied to other programming languages, allowing you to quickly and easily transfer what you have learned should you decide to switch to another programming language.

In addition to providing you with a good programming foundation, this book also strives to make your learning experience as fun and interesting as possible. This is accomplished through a games-based approach to teaching Phrogram, which will have you creating computer games starting in the very first chapter. Therefore, if you want to learn how to program and want to have as much fun as possible along the way, this book was designed for you.

## What You Need to Begin

The first thing that you will need to use this book is a copy of Phrogram. Phrogram comes in three different versions: Standard, Academic, and Express. At the time that this book was published, Phrogram Standard was selling for $49.95, Phrogram Academic was selling for $44.95, and Phrogram Express was available for $29.95. Each of these languages is available for online purchase at the Phrogram Company website located at http://www.phrogram.com. If you want to spend a little time working with Phrogram before deciding whether to purchase it, you can download a 30-day trial copy at http://phrogram.com/files/folders/phrogram_installer/entry86.aspx. For your convenience, the 30-day trial copy of Phrogram Standard can be found on this book's companion CD.

**HINT** Every Phrogram example shown in this book was developed using Phrogram Standard. However, everything that you will see also applies to Program Academic. Except for the discussion covering the creation of stand-alone programs, the Class Library Browser, and the use of add-in libraries, everything that this book covers applies to Phrogram Express as well.

Like any programming language, Phrogram has a number of requirements that must be met in order for you to be able to install and run it on your computer. These software and hardware requirements are listed below.

- A computer running Windows Vista, XP, or 2000
- A computer meeting Phrogram's minimum hardware requirements
- Microsoft .NET Framework version 2.0
- Microsoft DirectX 9.0c

### Supported Windows Operating Systems

In addition to a copy of Phrogram, you need access to a computer running one of the following versions of Microsoft Windows.

- Windows Vista
- Windows XP with Service Pack 2
- Windows 2000 with Service Pack 3

All of the figures and examples that are presented in this book will be shown using Phrogram Standard running on a computer using Microsoft Vista. If you work with a different version of Windows, you will notice small differences in the way things look. However, all of the features and functionality provided by Phrogram will work the same and you should not have any problems following along with everything you see in this book.

**HINT** Phrogram only runs on computers using Microsoft Vista, XP, or 2000. If your computer is running an older version of Microsoft Windows, it is probably time for you to consider upgrading your operating system or replacing your computer. However, if this is not an option, you can download a copy of the original Kid's Programming Language from http://www.k-p-l.org, which runs on older Microsoft operating systems.

## Minimum Hardware Requirements

In order to run any of the three available versions of Phrogram, your computer must meet the language's minimum hardware requirements. These requirements are listed in Table A.1.

**Table A.1 Phrogram Minimum Hardware Requirements**

| Requirement | Recommended |
|---|---|
| Processor | 600 MHz |
| Memory | 256 MB |
| Hard Disk | 50 MB |

The requirements shown in Table A.1 represent the minimum hardware requirements that Phrogram needs to operate. However, as is the case with any programming language, you will get better performance if your computer exceeds these minimum requirements. In particular, you will benefit the most from additional memory. While Phrogram will work with 256MB of memory, you will notice much better performance if your computer has at least 512MB of memory.

**HINT** In order to take full advantage of Phrogram's graphics and audio capabilities, you will also want to have a DirectX-compatible graphics and sound card installed on your computer. DirectX has been around for a while now, so any computer meeting Phrogram's minimum hardware requirements most likely has DirectX-compatible hardware.

## Software Requirements

As you will learn in Chapter 1, "Introduction to Phrogram," Phrogram is a .NET programming language. In order to run, your computer must have Microsoft's .NET Framework v2.0 installed. .NET is a free software component provided by Microsoft. If your computer does not have .NET v2.0 installed, the Phrogram installation process will detect its absence and automatically install it.

HINT The version 2 of the .NET Framework requires 280MB of free disk space in order to install.

Phrogram also depends on another Microsoft technology known as DirectX to generate 3D graphics and interact with joysticks and game pads. So, unless you do not plan on working with 3D and game controllers, you will need DirectX version 9.0c installed on your computer. The Phrogram install process ends by providing you with a link to a Microsoft website where you can install DirectX 9.0c, making its installation a snap.

# How This Book Is Organized

*Phrogram Programming for the Absolute Beginner* is organized into four parts. This book is designed to be read sequentially, cover to cover. However, if you have previous programming experience, you may want to jump around, focusing on topics that are of most interest to you.

Part I of this book consists of two chapters that provide an overview of Phrogram and its capabilities and explains how to work with its integrated development environment.

Part II consists of four chapters that are designed to provide a basic Phrogram programming foundation. You will learn how to work with and store data and to apply conditional logic to analyze data and make decisions. You will also learn how to repeat the execution of groups of statements to set up loops that efficiently process large amounts of information and control game play. You will also learn how to organize your program code into procedures in order to improve the overall organization and design of program logic and to make your applications easier to update and maintain.

Part III of this book is made up of four chapters that focus on a variety of advanced topics. These topics include learning basic principles of object-oriented programming and the use of sounds, graphics, and animation in your applications and games. You will also learn how to incorporate support for input devices like joysticks into your games. You will learn how to make sense of errors and error messages that will inevitably occur and to use advanced debugging tools to track down and eliminate nasty programming bugs that prevent your applications from performing like you want them to.

Part IV is made up of two appendices and a glossary. The first appendix reviews the chapter game projects that you will develop as you work your way through this book and explains how to obtain a copy of the book's source code. The second appendix provides a list of online resources that you will want to visit to continue learning more about Phrogram and further your programming knowledge.

The basic outline of the book is as follows.

- **Chapter 1, "Introduction to Phrogram."** This chapter provides a broad overview of Phrogram and its major features and capabilities. You will learn how Phrogram came to be and how it compares to other programming languages. You will also learn about the key components that make up Phrogram and how they work together to simplify application development. This chapter will teach you how to create your first Phrogram application and will show you how easy it is to create a stand-alone copy of your application. You will even learn how to create a distribution package so that you can easily share and distribute your applications with your friends or as shareware.
- **Chapter 2, "Getting Comfortable with the Phrogram Integrated Development Environment."** This chapter provides a guided tour of Phrogram's integrated development environment. You will learn how to work with menus and toolbar buttons. You will learn how to work with different windows and to configure their display. Particular attention will be paid to the features and capabilities provided by the IDE's code editor window.
- **Chapter 3, "Learning How to Work with Data."** This chapter teaches you how to collect and work with different types of data. You will learn how to store and later retrieve data collected during application execution. You will learn about the different types of data that Phrogram supports and how to store and retrieve individual pieces of data as well as groups of related data. You will also learn how to define and create custom data structures of your own design.
- **Chapter 4, "Making Decisions with Conditional Logic."** This chapter teaches you how to apply conditional logic when analyzing data in order to control the logical execution of your applications and games. This will enable you to develop applications and games that can adapt their execution based on the data that they are presented with.
- **Chapter 5, "Using Loops to Process Data."** This chapter explains everything you need to know about how to work with different kinds of loops in order to perform repetitive tasks and process large amounts of input. You will also learn how to use loops to control game animation, which is critical to developing applications that must continuously replay graphic animation sequences and interact with and collect player input during game play.

- **Chapter 6, "Improving Program Organization with Procedures."** This chapter is designed to assist you in writing better and more manageable program code using procedures. You will learn how to define procedures and pass them arguments for processing. You will learn how to return data from procedures back to calling statements. By learning how to take advantage of procedures, you will learn how to develop applications that are easier to update and maintain.
- **Chapter 7, "Getting Comfortable with Object-Oriented Programming."** This chapter will help to cement your understanding of object-oriented programming by providing an overview of Phrogram's support for object-oriented programming. You will learn how to work with objects and to access their methods and properties. You will also take an in-depth look at Phrogram's built-in Class Library.
- **Chapter 8, "Working with Graphics and Animation."** This chapter provides an introduction to graphics and animation programming using sprites. This includes learning how to create sprites and control their movement and interaction with one another. You will learn how to draw shapes, perform collision detection, and get an overview of Phrogram's 3D capabilities.
- **Chapter 9, "Integrating Sound and Working with Input Devices."** This chapter teaches you how to bring your applications to life through the addition of sound effects and audio files. You'll also learn how to develop Phrogram programs that can work with joystick game controls.
- **Chapter 10, "Debugging Your Applications."** This chapter teaches you how to understand and deal with errors that inevitably make their way into most programming projects. You will learn how to work with Phrogram's debugger in order to track down and fix errors. This includes learning how to use the debugger to monitor variable values and to control statement execution within your applications.
- **Appendix A, "What's on the CD?"** This appendix reviews the Phrogram applications developed in this book and made available on the accompanying CD.

- **Appendix B, "What Next?"** This appendix provides additional guidance and advice on how to continue your Phrogram education. Here, you will find information regarding additional reading resources as well as a listing of websites and online forums where you can find Phrogram information.

## Conventions Used in This Book

To help make this book as easy as possible to read and understand, a number of conventions have been applied to help highlight critical information and to emphasize specific points. These conventions are as follows.

- *Italics*. Whenever I introduce an important programming term for the first time, I will highlight the word using italics to give it additional emphasis and to let you know this is a term that you will want to make sure you understand and remember.

**HINT.** Tips on how to do things differently and to point out different techniques that you can apply to become a better programmer.

**TRAP.** From time to time, I will point out areas where you are likely to run into problems and then provide you with advice on how to deal with these situations or better yet to prevent them from occurring in the first place.

**TRICK.** Programming shortcuts that will help to make you a better and more efficient programmer.

**FIND IT ONLINE.** Because Phrogram is constantly growing and evolving, no book can stay fully up-to-date and cover every aspect of the language. To help compensate for this limitation I provide links to online resources at the Phrogram company website that complement and expand upon the information covered in this book.

### Exercises

**To help challenge you as you work through the material presented in this book, I will present you with small programming exercises designed to help you demonstrate your understanding of key programming concepts.**

## Review Questions

**From time to time, I will provide a list of optional questions that focus on important topics to help ensure that you have a good understanding of key concepts.**

## Challenges

**At the end of each chapter, you will find instructions that guide you through the development of a new computer game. Immediately following each game project, you will find a series of suggestions or challenges designed to provide you with ideas to apply to improve the game and further the development of your programming skills.**

# Part I

## An Introduction to Phrogram Programming

CHAPTER 1

# Introduction to Phrogram

Phrogram is a computer programming language developed specifically for first-time programmers. Phrogram is designed from the ground up as a teaching programming language. It supports a very easy to understand syntax and has a relatively short learning curve compared to other programming languages. This chapter will provide you with the basics of how to begin working with Phrogram. It will provide you with an overview of Phrogram and its capabilities. By the time you finish reading this chapter you will have learned how to create and execute your first Phrogram application and how to create a distribution package that serves as an installation program for your new application.

Specifically, you will learn:

- How to install Phrogram
- About Phrogram and what makes it work
- How to create your first Phrogram application
- How to compile and run Phrogram applications
- How to create a distribution package so that you can share your applications

## Project Preview: The Kids Jokes Game

This chapter and every other chapter in this book will end by guiding you through the creation of a computer game. Learning how to program by doing is key to becoming a good programmer and learning how to program by creating games just makes the whole process a lot of fun. Since Phrogram is specifically designed as a learning language that emphasizes graphics, animation, and game development, this book's approach to learning Phrogram programming makes for a perfect match!

This chapter's game project is the Kids Jokes game. When run, this game tells the player a series of three jokes. As shown in Figure 1.1, this game begins by displaying a welcome message. At the bottom of the screen a second message instructs the player to press any key to continue playing.

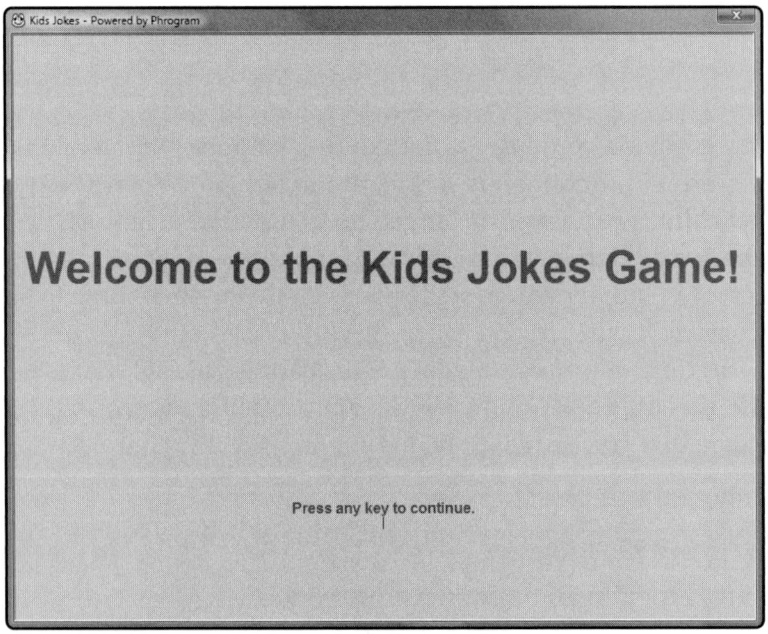


**FIGURE 1.1**

The Kids Jokes game runs and acts like a typical Windows application.

Next, the game displays the opening line of its first joke, as shown in Figure 1.2.

The game then pauses for three seconds to give the player a chance to read the joke before displaying its punch line, as shown in Figure 1.3.

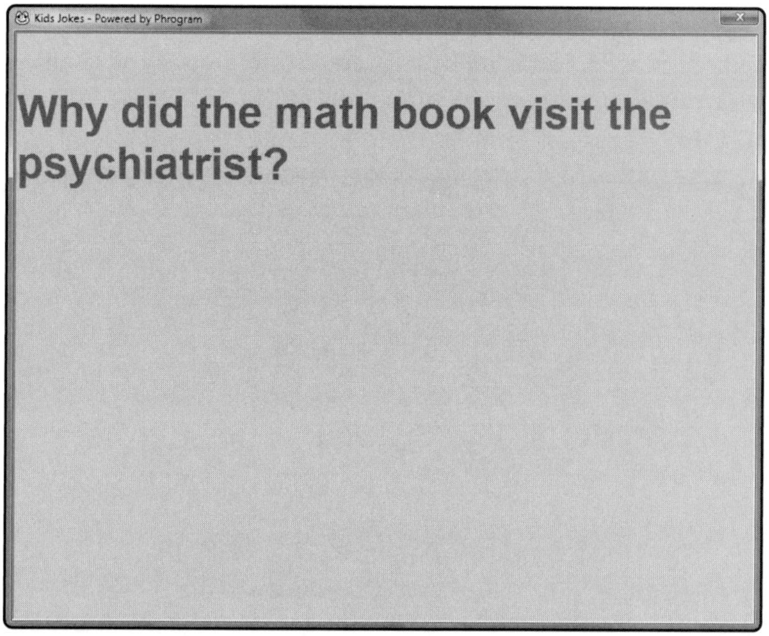


**FIGURE 1.2**

The name of the game displays at the top of the window in the titlebar.

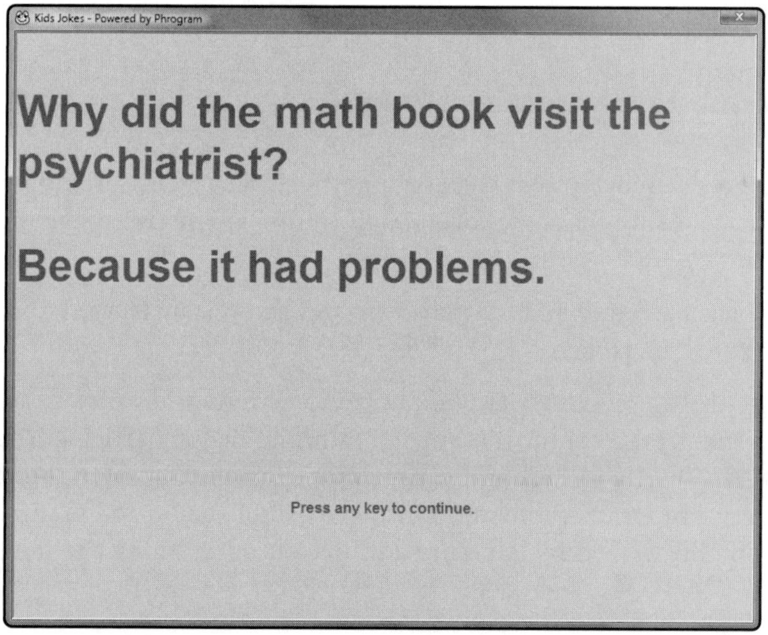


**FIGURE 1.3**

Like any Windows application, you can close the Kids Jokes game at any time by clicking on the close button in the upper-right corner.

To continue on to the next joke, the player must press a key on the keyboard, after which the second joke's opening line is displayed, followed by a three-second pause, and then its joke's punch line displays, as shown in Figure 1.4.

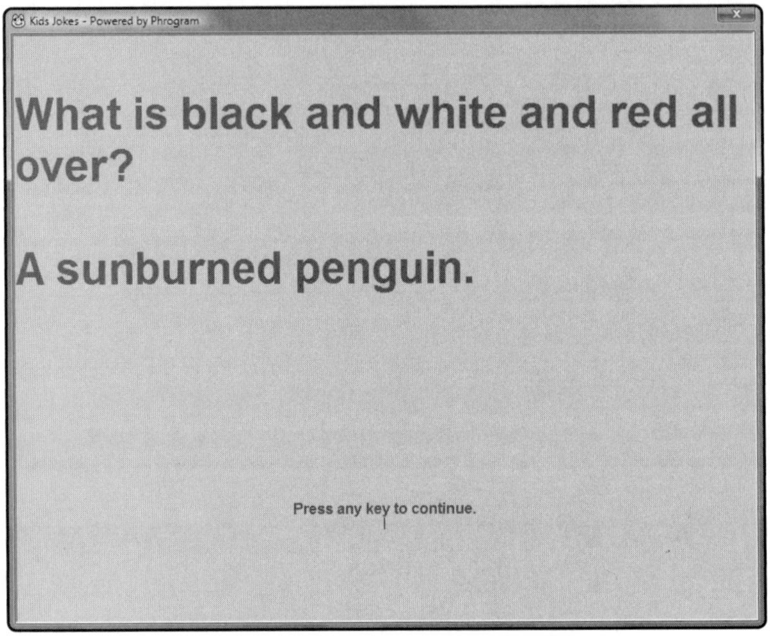


**FIGURE 1.4**

Like many other Windows applications, you can reposition and resize the game's window.

To see the game's final joke, the player must click on a keyboard key again, after which the game's third joke is displayed using the same format and timing as the two previous jokes, as demonstrated in Figure 1.5.

Finally, once the last joke has been told and the player presses a key as instructed, the thank you message shown in Figure 1.6 displays.

After a five-second pause, the game closes its window and ends. As you can see, as far as computer games go, this one is pretty simple, requiring minimal player participation. However, by the time you have finished working on this game you will have learned the basic steps involved in developing any Phrogram game and will have established a foundation from which you can move on and begin working on more advanced programming challenges.

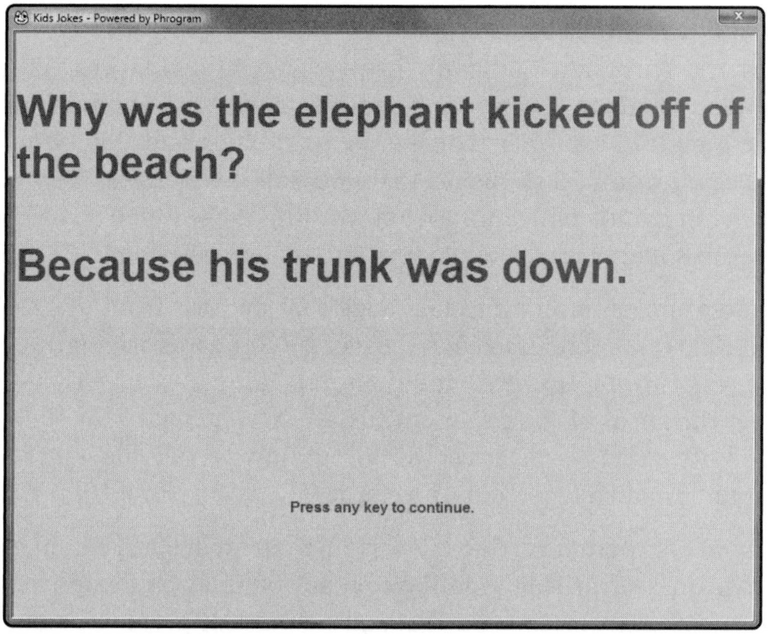


**FIGURE 1.5**

Players can also right-click on the upper-left corner of the game window to access additional commands for controlling the game.

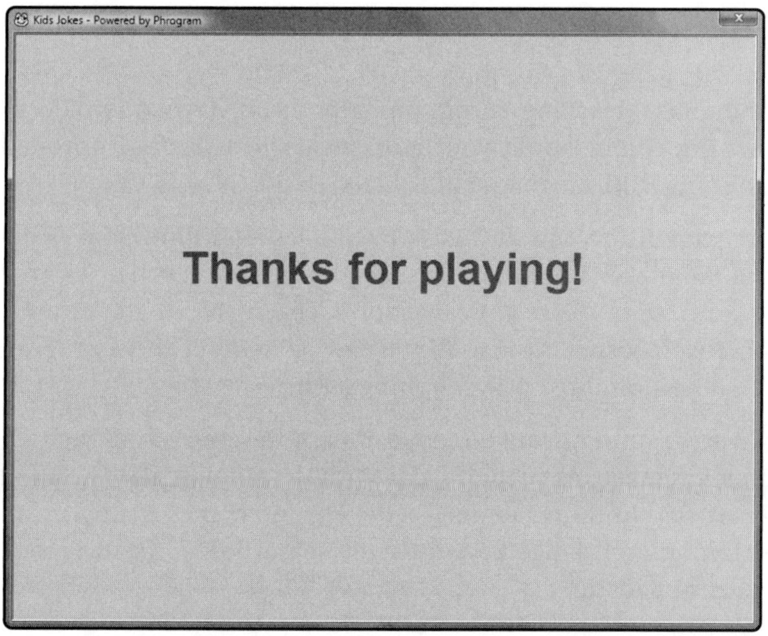


**FIGURE 1.6**

The game thanks the player for taking time to play.

## A Quick Phrogram Overview

Phrogram was created by the Phrogram Company (http://www.phrogram.com). Phrogram provides everything you need to create 2D and 3D computer games and applications of all types. These tools include a built-in compiler that is used to create stand-alone executable copies of your games and applications, a debugger that you will use to track down and fix pesky bugs that keep your games and applications from working the way you want them to, and a code editor with features like syntax color coding and line numbering.

Phrogram is a second generation programming language that evolved from the Kid's Programming Language (KPL). KPL was first released in August of 2005 and was originally targeted at children between the ages of 10–14. However, it did not take long to realize that KPL was equally well suited to meet the needs of computer enthusiasts and hobbyists. As such, when KPL version 2 was released, its name was changed to Phrogram to reflect its wider appeal. Today, Phrogram is being taught at colleges and universities.

As of the writing of this book, Phrogram version 2.2 was just released. For a beginner's programming language, Phrogram is surprisingly similar to many popular professional modern programming languages, emphasizing learning through the use of graphics, sound, and sprite programming. At the same time, Phrogram provides many powerful programming features like 3D graphics development and the ability to support game controllers like joysticks.

As a .NET programming language, learning Phrogram helps to lay down a foundation that helps minimize your learning curve should you later decide to transition to one of the business-oriented programming .NET languages like Visual Basic, C#, and C++.

Despite being remarkably straightforward and easy to understand, Phrogram is designed to resemble programming languages used by professional programmers. For example, the Phrogram IDE is very similar to the IDE used by Microsoft's Visual Studio programming languages, which include Microsoft Visual Basic, C#, and C++. Like all of these programming languages, Phrogram is an object-oriented programming (OOP) language.

Phrogram is the only .NET programming language specifically designed from top to bottom as a teaching programming language. As such, it is ideal for developing basic programming skills. Unlike many modern programming languages, the Phrogram programming language consists of a small collection of English-like keywords whose purpose is easily recognizable and whose syntax is quite minimalistic.

HINT Phrogram is currently being used to teach students in primary and secondary schools as well as in colleges around the world, including the United States, Canada, Mexico, Britain, Sweden, Columbia, Japan, the Czech Republic, China, Brazil, Guam, Russia, New Zealand, Slovakia, and the Philippines.

Phrogram comes bundled with a collection of graphic and sound files that you can incorporate into your applications and is an ideal programming language for developing computer games and just about any type of application you can think of. Although it was not supported at the time this book was published, plans were in the works that would eventually allow Phrogram programmers to create applications that can run on the Xbox 360, allowing Program programmers to leverage their programming skills not just on the world's most popular operating system but also on one of the world's most popular gaming systems.

## Selecting the Right Version of Phrogram

At the time this book was written, Phrogram was available in three different versions as listed here:

- Phrogram Standard
- Phrogram Express
- Phrogram Academic

Phrogram Standard is the commercial version of the programming language. It provides programmers with access to all of Phrogram's features and capabilities and was available (at the time of this writing) for download from the Phrogram Company website (www.phrogram.com) for $49.95.

Phrogram Academic is identical to Phrogram Standard but is licensed for academic use by teachers and students. As such, Phrogram Academic costs less, selling for $44.95.

Phrogram Express is the least expensive option, selling for just $24.95. Each of the versions of Phrogram include a common set of features, as outlined here:

- Advanced code editor
- Integrated debugger
- File input and output support
- 2D and 3D programming support
- Support for game controllers (joysticks)

Phrogram Express lacks several key features found in the other two versions of Phrogram. Most notably, Phrogram Express cannot be used to create stand-alone executable versions of your Phrogram applications, meaning that you are limited to executing your applications from within the Phrogram IDE. Phrogram Express cannot be expanded using optional add-in libraries like Phrogram Standard and Academic can. Phrogram Express also lacks the ability to execute a Phrogram feature known as the Class Library Browser, which you learn about in Chapter 2, "Getting Comfortable with the Phrogram Integrated Development Environment."

Table 1.1 provides a high-level comparison of the different features supported by all three versions of Phrogram. Note that while Phrogram Standard and Phrogram Academic support the same language features, the purchase of Phrogram Academic includes exclusive access to academic forums located on the Phrogram Company website.

**TABLE 1.1 COMPARISON OF DIFFERENT PHROGRAM VERSIONS**

| Value | Express | Standard | Academic |
|---|---|---|---|
| Create stand-alone executable | - | Yes | Yes |
| Class library browser | - | Yes | Yes |
| Basic add-in libraries | Yes | Yes | Yes |
| Advanced add-in libraries | - | Yes | Yes |
| Access to academic forums | - | - | Yes |

**HINT**

Phrogram Academic and Phrogram Express can also be purchased at a discount under an educational value discount licensing (EVDL) program. This program allows students to install Phrogram on their personal computers for as long as they are learning Phrogram in school. When purchased through the EVDL program, schools and classes receive access to private forums set up on the Phrogram Company website for their exclusive access and use. Using these forums, teachers and students can interact and share information as part of their course curriculum.

**FIND IT ONLINE**

One of the best ways to learn about Phrogram is to become acquainted with its user community, which you can do by visiting the forums located at the Phrogram Company website on http://phrogram.com/forums. Once there you can view postings submitted by other Phrogram programmers. To post comments of your own, you must first create a new account, which you can do by clicking on the Join link located in the upper-right corner of the web page. If you have not already done so, take a few minutes to create a new account and then spend a little time reviewing the Beginners Corner forum to see the types of discussions that other beginner Phrogram programmers are having.

## Installing and Activating Phrogram

Like most modern programming languages, Phrogram's installation process is straightforward and easy to perform. Phrogram has several requirements that must be met in order to install and run it. First, it can only be installed on a computer running Microsoft Windows 2000, XP, or Vista. Second, it needs Microsoft .NET Framework 2.0 in order to run. If your computer does not have the .NET Framework installed, the Phrogram install processes will detect its absence and automatically download and install it for you. Finally, Phrogram needs Microsoft DirectX 9.0c.

Even if your computer has a different version of DirectX installed, you are going to need to install DirectX 9.0c anyway. You can download and install Direct X 9.0c before or after Phrogram is installed by visiting http://www.gamesforwindows.com/en-US/AboutGFW/Pages/DirectX10-a.aspx, as shown in Figure 1.7 and clicking on the Get all DirectX Downloads link. Once downloaded, follow the instructions provided by Microsoft to install DirectX 9.0c.

**FIGURE 1.7**
Downloading a copy of DirectX 9.0c.

**TRAP**

Even through Microsoft Vista ships with DirectX 10 pre-installed, this version of DirectX is not backward compatible with earlier versions of DirectX. Phrogram still needs certain DirectX 9.0c components to produce 3D graphics and to interact with game controllers. You can download and install DirectX 9.0c on Microsoft Vista and it will not have any affect on the installation of DirectX 10.

Unless you purchase a license that allows you to install multiple versions of Phrogram off of a CD, typically as part of an educational discount for schools and universities, Phrogram is typically installed by downloading it from the internet and then running its install program. Therefore, you will need an internet connection. Once installed, you will need to register your copy of Phrogram as described later in this chapter.

## Installing Phrogram

When you download Phrogram from the Phrogram Company website, an installation file named PhrogramSetup.exe is downloaded to your computer. The following procedure outlines the steps involved in installing Phrogram. This procedure is the same for all three versions of Phrogram.

> **HINT** For your convenience, a trial version of Phrogram (v.2.2.2906) is also available on this book's companion CD-ROM.

1. Double-click on the PhrogramSetup.exe. A Window similar to the one shown in Figure 1.8 will appear.

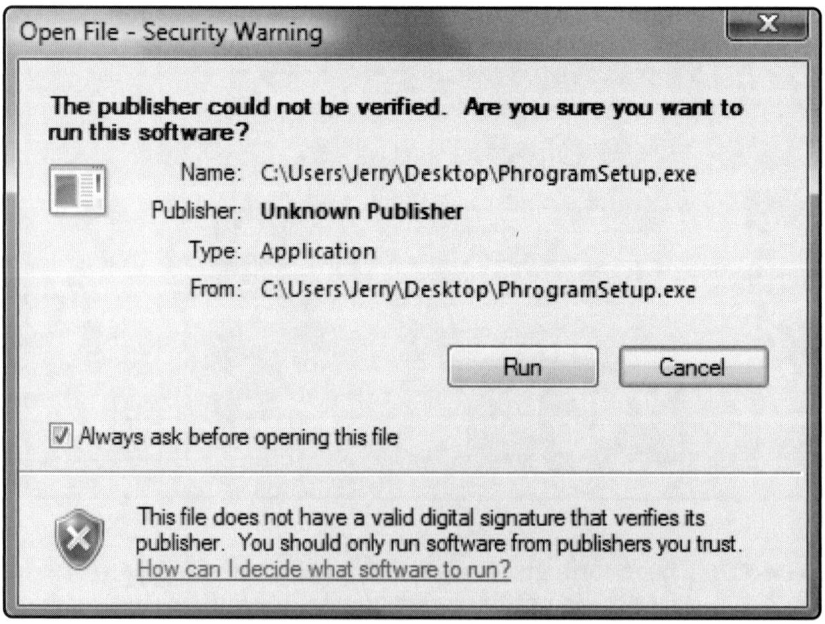


**FIGURE 1.8**

Starting the Phrogram install process.

2. Click on Run. Within a few moments the InstallShield Wizard will appear, as shown in Figure 1.9.

**FIGURE 1.9**

The InstallShield Wizard will guide you through the Phrogram installation process.

3. Click on Next to begin installing Phrogram.
4. You will be prompted to accept the Phrogram License Agreement. Do so by selecting I accept the terms in the license agreement and then clicking on Next.
5. You are then prompted to enter your name and the name of your organization and then to click on Next to continue.
6. You are then prompted to specify the location where you want to install Phrogram's files. Click on Next to accept the default location.
7. Next, you are prompted to click Install to allow the wizard to begin installing Phrogram.
8. Once the installation process has completed, the screen shown in Figure 1.10 displays. This screen reminds you that DirectX is required for Phrogram to be fully functional.

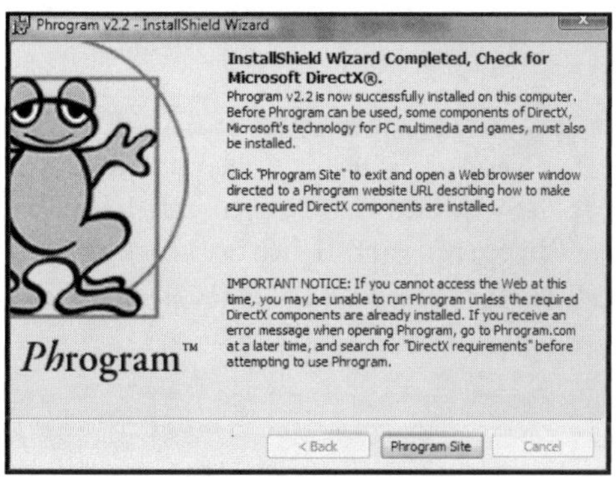


**FIGURE 1.10**

The Phrogram installation process is complete.

9. Click on the Phrogram Site button. In response, the InstallShield Wizard will close and your web browser will start and load a web page located at http://phrogram.com/content/GetDirectX.aspx, as shown in Figure 1.11.

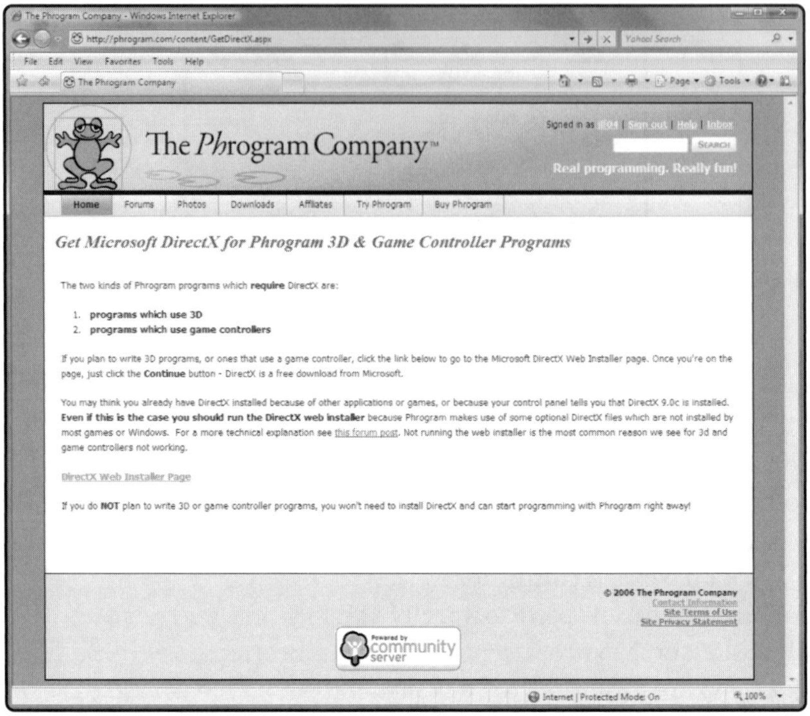


**FIGURE 1.11**

A brief explanation of why DirectX is required.

10. If you have not already installed DirectX 9.0c, then click on the DirectX Web Installer Page link and follow the instructions that are provided to complete the installation of DirectX 9.0c.

> **HINT** Microsoft allows software developers to distribute DirectX along with any application that needs it. However, DirectX is not bundled into the Phrogram installation file in order to reduce the size of its download. This significantly reduces the size of the Phrogram install file and makes for faster downloads. It also allows users that already have DirectX 9.0c to avoid its unnecessary download and re-installation.

## Activating Phrogram

Once Phrogram has been installed, it will run as a free 30-day trial version, after which time you must register it. Doing so changes your Phrogram installation from Phrogram – Unregistered Trial Version to one of the following, depending on which version of Phrogram you purchased.

- Phrogram Academic
- Phrogram Standard
- Phrogram Express

To register your copy of Phrogram, click on the Enter License Code command located on the Help menu. In response, Phrogram displays the Enter Registration Information – Phrogram dialog, as shown in Figure 1.12.

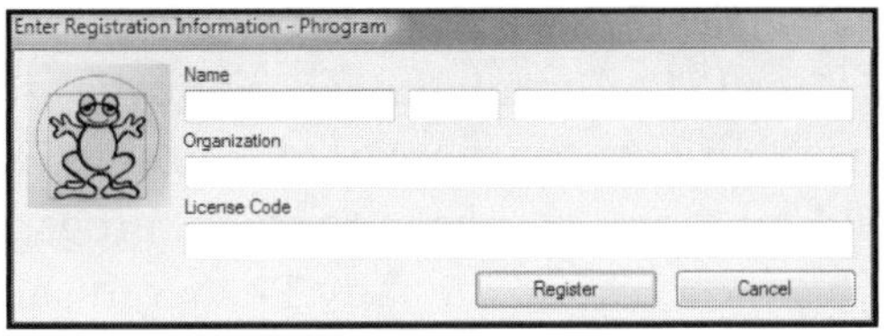


**FIGURE 1.12**

Registering your copy of Phrogram.

If you purchased your copy of Phrogram online, then you will receive an email containing your registration key. The following procedure outlines the steps required to complete the registration process.

1. Enter your first, middle, and last name in the Name field located at the top of the window.
2. If applicable, enter your company or organization name in the Organization field.
3. Enter your Phrogram registration key into the Serial Number field.
4. Click on the Register button. In response, the window shown in Figure 1.13 displays.

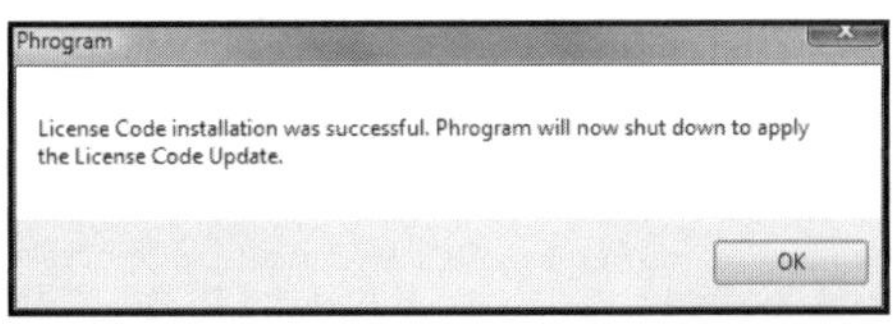


**FIGURE 1.13**

Phrogram must be restarted to complete the registration process.

5. Click on OK.

Once you have completed the registration procedure, Phrogram will shut down in order to apply the registration information.

## Creating Your First Phrogram Application

Now that Phrogram has been installed, let's jump right in and begin working with it. In doing so, you will learn how to create and execute your first Phrogram application. When executed, this program will display a window inside which the words "Hello World!" are displayed. By going through the steps required to develop this program, you will learn the fundamental steps involved in creating a running Phrogram application. These steps include

1. Creating a new Phrogram program
2. Writing the program's source code
3. Saving your program
4. Compiling and testing the execution of the program

Phrogram's *integrated development environment* or *IDE* provides a software development environment equipped with all the tools needed to develop new applications. Using its built-in code editor, you will key in the code statements that make up your applications. Before you can begin working on the HelloWorld program, you need to start Phrogram, which you can do by clicking on Start, All Programs, The Phrogram Company, Phrogram, and then Phrogram. In response, a window similar to the one shown in Figure 1.14 appears.

**HINT** You will learn the ins and outs of working with the Phrogram IDE in Chapter 2.

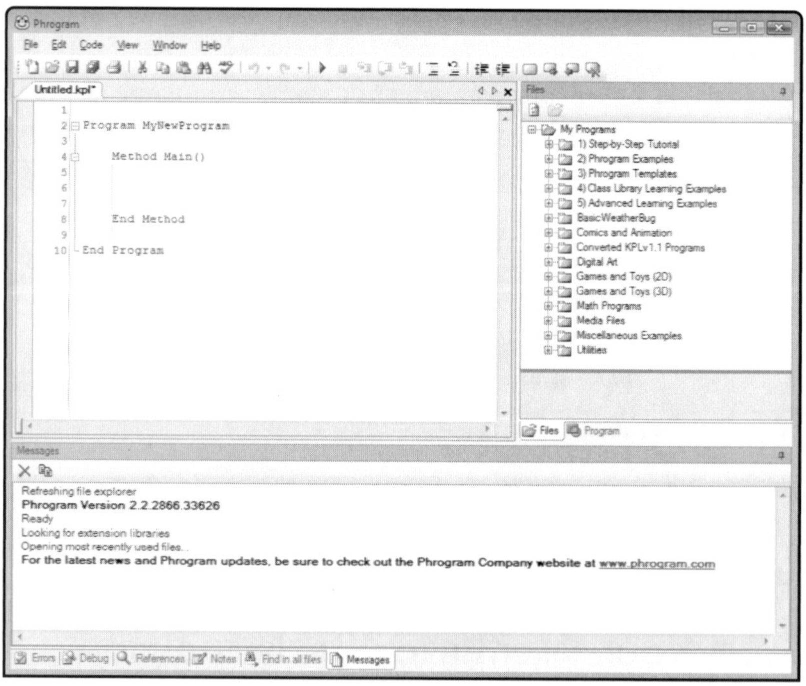


**FIGURE 1.14**

The Phrogram integrated development environment provides everything needed to develop and run Phrogram applications.

## Creating a New Phrogram Project

If this is the first time you have started Phrogram, it will start and automatically create a new program file. If you have tinkered around with Phrogram, it may start up by displaying a new program or it may load and display the last program or set of programs that you were working on when you last closed it. You can create a new Phrogram application at any time by clicking on the New Program command located on the File menu. In response, Phrogram will create a new Phrogram file, as shown in Figure 1.15.

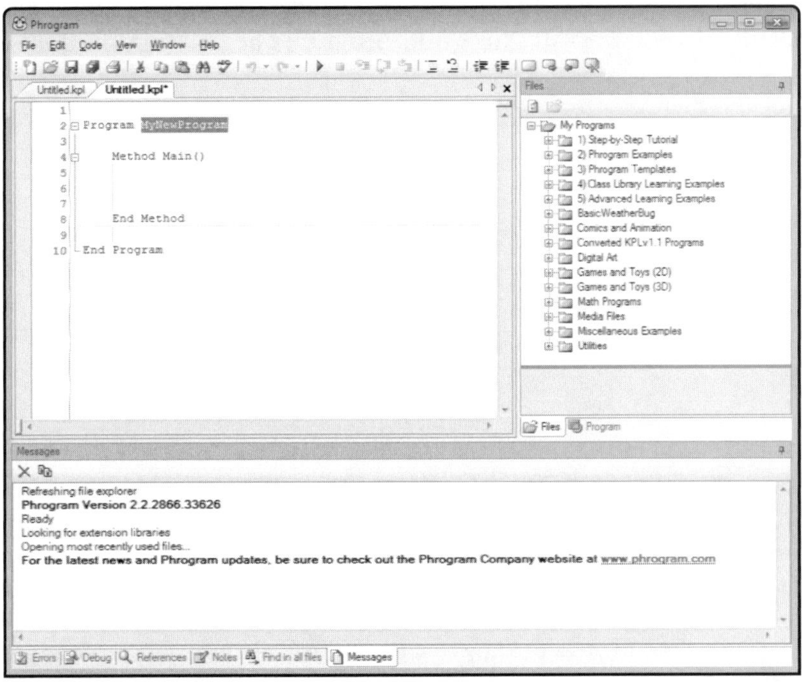

**FIGURE 1.15**

Creating a new Phrogram program.

As you can see in Figure 1.15, a second tabbed program file has been displayed, inside which four code statements have automatically been added. These statements provide a framework within which you will add the program code statements that make up your new application.

## Adding Program Code

When it comes right down to it, computer programming pretty much boils down to executing files containing lists of instructions that tell a computer what to do. Phrogram, like every other programming language, has specific rules that must be followed when formulating the program code statements that make up computer programs. These syntax rules specify how

Phrogram programs must be structured and how individual program code statements must be formatted for Phrogram to be able to recognize and understand your instructions.

HINT The terms *program* and *application* are used interchangeably within this book and are used to refer to executable software files.

Phrogram requires that every code statement be written on a separate line. Phrogram statements are made of different language keywords, each of which has its own syntax that must be exactly followed in order for the statement to execute correctly. Failure to follow proper statement syntax will result in an error. All Phrogram programs begin with the following four statements.

```
Program MyNewProgram

   Method Main()



   End Method

End Program
```

HINT Take note of the use of *white space* or blank lines in the code statements shown above. Adding white space helps to space out program statements and make them easier to read. You can add blank lines by pressing the Enter key. Also take note of the use of indentation, which helps to further visually organize program code statements. You can manually indent code statements by pressing the Tab key. By default, pressing the Tab key results in the insertion of four blank spaces. The addition of blank lines and indented program statements is purely cosmetic and has no effect on the execution of your Phrogram applications.

All Phrogram programs begin with the `Program` statement and end with an `End Program` statement. MyNewProgram is the default name that Phrogram assigns to a new program. You can change the name of the program to anything you want by simply overtyping the existing program name. Phrogram program names must, however, consist of a single word with no spaces. Go ahead and change the name of this program from MyNewProgram to HelloWorld.

All Program programs begin with a method named `Main()`. A *method* is a named collection of programming statements that are executed as a unit. For now, all you need to know is two things about methods. First, every Phrogram program starts out with a default method named

Main() and that program execution begins by executing the statements stored inside this method. Second, the end of any method is marked by an End Method statement. Any statements placed in between the opening and closing method statements are of that method and will be executed when that method is called upon to run.

The objective of this application is to display a text message of HelloWorld! in a window on the computer screen. This is accomplished by adding the statements shown in bold to the program's code file, as shown here:

```
Program HelloWorld

    Method Main()

        //Display a text message
        Print("Hello World!")

    End Method

End Program
```

You should also take note of how Phrogram has automatically indented the opening and closing method declaration statements. Doing so helps visually organize program code and makes your program files easier to read and maintain.

Any code statements placed inside the program's Main() method will automatically be executed when the program is run. The first statement that you added to the Main() method is a comment statement. *Comments* are statements that you add to an application's source code for the purpose of documenting what's going on in the program. Comments begin with the // characters. Phrogram regards any text that follows the // characters as a comment. Phrogram ignores comments when creating an executable version of your application. As such, comments have no effect on how your program runs.

The second statement that you added to the Main() method is responsible for displaying the text that appears in the application window when the program is run. Note that the text being displayed is wrapped inside double quotation marks which are also embedded inside a pair of parentheses. Once you have keyed in everything, your program's code file should look like the example shown in Figure 1.16.

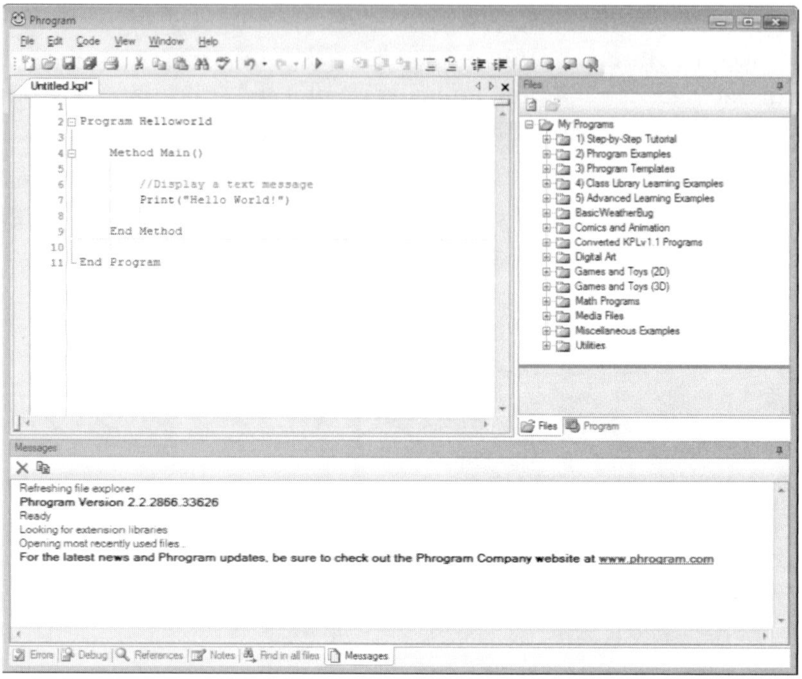

**FIGURE 1.16**

Adding code statements to your program's code file.

HINT

The second statement uses the `Print` method to display text on the screen. To use the `Print` method, the following syntax must be used.

```
Drawing.Print("Text")
```

Phrogram provides pre-built collections of program code call *methods*. These methods are organized into a hierarchy composed of libraries and classes. The `Print` method is located in the `Drawing` library. Using what is referred to as `.dot` notation, you specify a method by first referencing the library or class to which it belongs followed by a dot and then the name of the method. You can pass data to methods for processing by enclosing the data inside parentheses that follow the method's name. In the case of the `Print` method, the data being passed is syntactically represented by the word *Text*.

If this whole explanation of libraries, classes, and methods is difficult to understand right now, do not worry about it. By the time you have made your way to the end of this book, you'll be completely comfortable working with Phrogram language syntax. For now, all you need to know is that Phrogram allows you to execute this `Print` method without specifying the library to which it belongs and that it allows you to display any text characters you want as long as you enclose them inside a matching pair of double quotation marks.

## Saving Your Work

Once you have finished keying the code statements that make up your new application, you will need to save your work. To do this, all you have to do is click on the Save All command located on the File menu. In response, Phrogram will display the Save your new program window. Note that the name you assigned to your program when you retyped it on the first line of program code is the same name that Phrogram uses by default as your program name. You may change this if you want.

> **HINT** Phrogram lets you open and work on any number of program files at once. When you execute the Save All command, any changes made to open program files are saved. Alternatively, you can just save the currently selected program file by clicking on the Save command.

Once you have saved your program, you will find a file named HelloWorld.kpl located in the folder that you specified. .kpl is the three character file extension assigned to all Phrogram program files. By default, you will find a copy of your new program listed in the Files view of the Files Explorer window located on the right-hand side of the IDE, as shown in Figure 1.17.

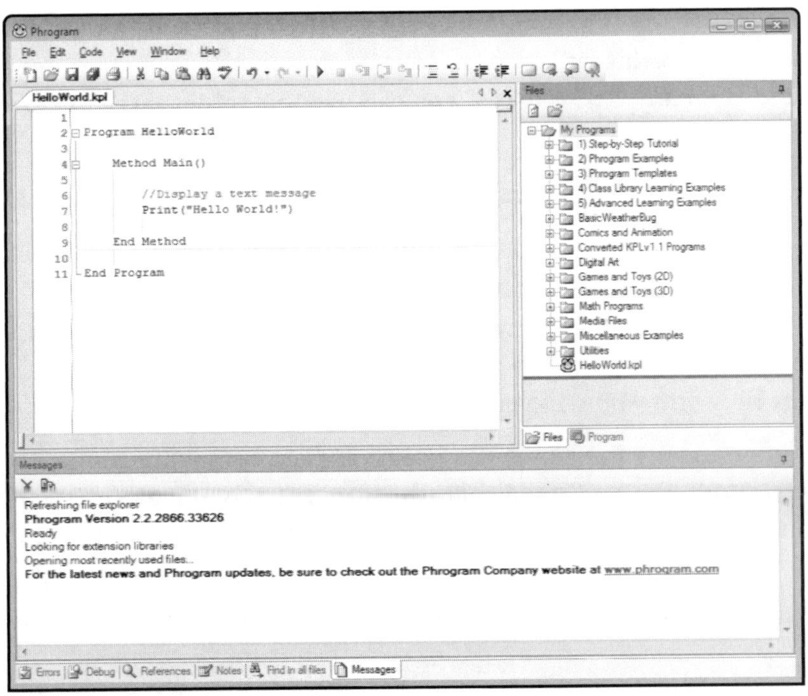


**FIGURE 1.17**

The Program IDE provides easy access to your new Phrogram application's code file.

HINT

All of the files and folders shown in the Files view of the Files Explorer window are shown as residing under the My Programs folder. This is a bit of trickery because if you check, you will find that these files are actually stored in a file named My Phrogram Files located in your Documents folder. You might want to create a folder named something like My Applications as a subfolder in My Phrogram Files folder and use it to store all of your Phrogram files. Once created, you can organize and store your applications in additional subfolders to help you stay organized.

### EXERCISES

**Before continuing, take a few minutes to get organized by completing the following exercises.**

1. **Close the HelloWorld program by clicking on the Close Program command located on the File menu.**
2. **Create a folder named MyGames in your \Documents\My Phrogram Files\ folder in which to store all of the Phrogram programs that you will be creating in this book.**
3. **Create a subfolder inside MyGames named HelloWorld and move the HelloWorld.kpl application into it.**
4. **Create a second folder named KidsJokes. You can use this folder later to store this chapter's game program.**

## Compiling and Testing Program Execution

If it is not currently open, re-open the HelloWorld program by locating it in the Files Explorer window and then double-clicking on it. When the Phrogram IDE opens your application, it will look a little different than you would expect it to, as shown in Figure 1.18.

By default, Phrogram automatically folds or hides program code belonging to methods to help reduce clutter in your program files. To redisplay the statements that make up the `Main()` method, click on the plus character located just to the left of the `Method Main()` statement.

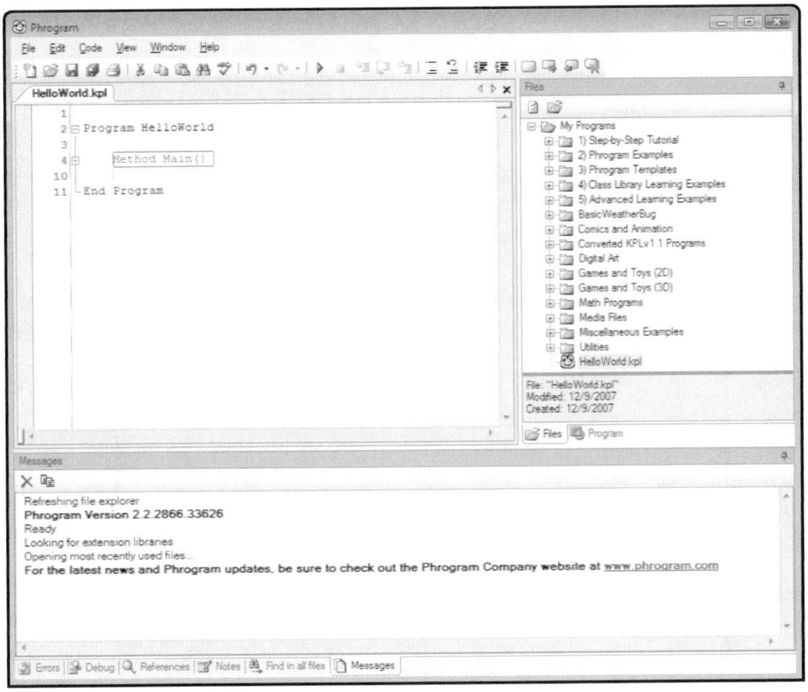

**Figure 1.18**

Phrogram has collapsed or *folded* the code statements located in the `Main()` method.

Now that you have saved your program, it is time to compile it. *Compiling* is the process that Phrogram goes through to generate an executable version of your program. You can do this by clicking on the Run Program command located on the Code menu. In response, Phrogram checks every statement in your program's code file for syntax errors. If none are found, Phrogram creates an executable file representing your application and then runs it as shown in Figure 1.19.

Note that the window opened by your Phrogram application has some unusual characteristics compared to the application windows that you are used to seeing as a Windows user. For starters, there is a toolbar located at the top of the window that contains two buttons. The first button is a pause button, which can be used to pause the execution of your application when it is running. The second button is an eject button, which you can click on to close the window when you are done working with your application.

Another interesting feature of this window is the placement of a ruler horizontally across the top of the window as well as vertically down the right side of the window. This visual marker can come in handy when you are developing graphical applications and need to execute precise control over the location of objects on the screen. One last feature to take note of is the display of the word Stopped in the window's titlebar. This word is automatically displayed in the titlebar at the end of a program's execution.

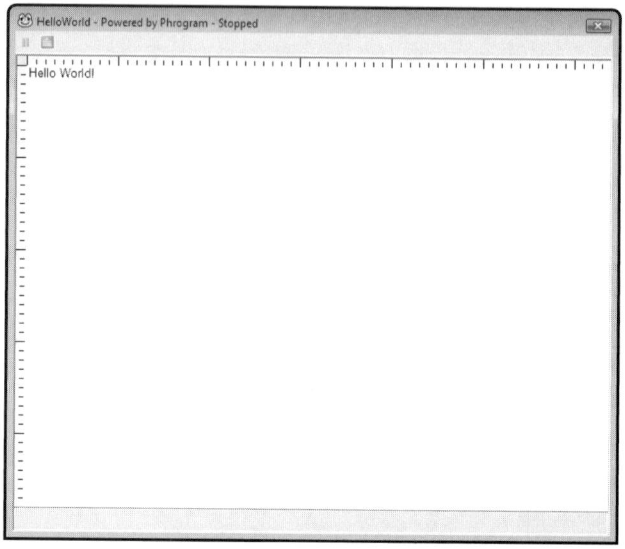


**FIGURE 1.19**

The output display when the HelloWorld application is executed.

## Creating a Distribution Package for Your New Application

Once you have created, compiled, and executed your Phrogram application and have it working exactly the way you want it to, the next and final step is to package your new application so that you can share it with other people. This means creating an installation package that when executed on someone else's computer will install a stand-alone copy of your application that does not need Phrogram to be installed for the application to execute. In addition, you can configure the installation package to create a new program group and icon on the user's Start menu.

**TRAP**

Your Phrogram application will still need .NET 2.0 and DirectX 9.0c to be able to run on the user's computer. Therefore, you should consider notifying your users of these requirements to eliminate any problems or confusion that would otherwise occur.

In order to execute on a computer where Phrogram is not installed, your Phrogram applications need access to the Phrogram run-time library files, which provide a library of files needed to run your application. To keep things as simple as possible, Phrogram automatically stores a copy of its run-time library files inside every distribution package. This way, when users install your distribution package, the Phrogram run-time library files are installed in a folder named bin alongside your application.

## Creating a Distribution Package

To create a new package, click on the Create Package command on Phrogram's File menu. In response, Phrogram displays the window shown in Figure 1.20.

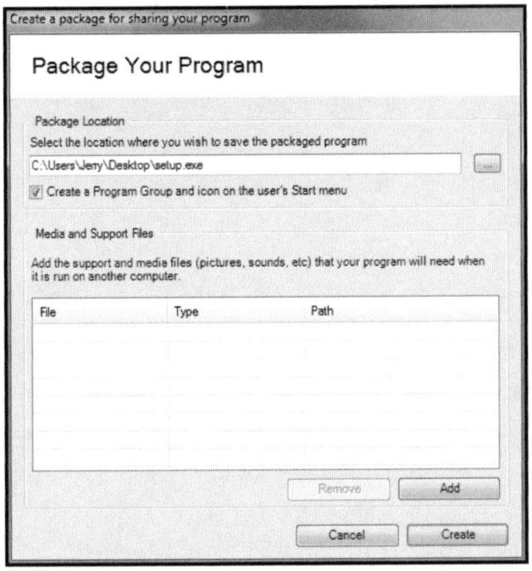


**FIGURE 1.20**

Creating a self-extracting installer that you can use to distribute and install a stand-alone copy of your Phrogram application.

By default, the installation package that you are creating will be saved in the same folder where your application file has been saved. You can modify this location by clicking on the ellipses button just to the right of the Package Location field. This opens a window allowing you to browse and specify a different location. By default, the Create a Phrogram group and icon on the user's Start menu option is automatically selected. However, you can clear this option if you want.

**HINT** The Create Package command only works on the Standard and Academic versions of Phrogram. If you are using the Express version, you will not be able to create distribution packages for your applications. If you want to be able to share your creations with others, for example as shareware over the Internet, you will need to upgrade to the Standard or Academic version of Phrogram.

If your application requires any audio or graphics files to execute, you need to include them as part of the distribution package. This is accomplished by clicking on the Add button location under the Media and Support Files area and then specifying the location and name of the file(s) to be included. You may include as many files as your application requires.

> **HINT** If your application makes use of any of the media files shipped as part of Phrogram, you will find them located in \My Documents\My Phrogram Files\Media files.

The last step in creating a distribution package is to click on the Create button, which instructs Phrogram to create and save your new distribution package. Figure 1.21 shows the icon that Phrogram creates for your application.

**FIGURE 1.21** The icon representing your application's distribution package.

At this point, your distribution package is ready to go. If you want, you can change its name prior to distributing it.

## Installing a Phrogram Application

Once it has been distributed, to install your new application, the users double-click on the package to start the installation process. Depending on the version of Microsoft Windows being used, a security window may be displayed. This window prompts the user for permission to run the application's installation program. To continue, the user must click on Allow, after which a window similar to the one shown in Figure 1.22 appears.

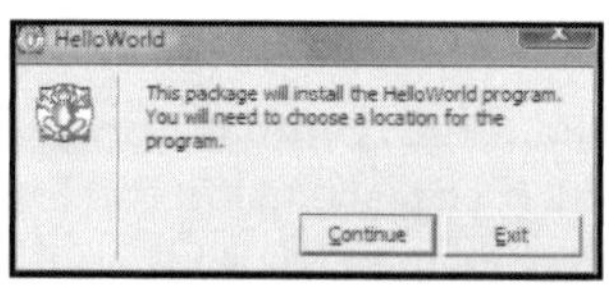


**FIGURE 1.22** Installing your new application.

To continue, the user must click on the Continue button. Next, a window similar to the one shown in Figure 1.23 displays, asking the user where to install the new application.

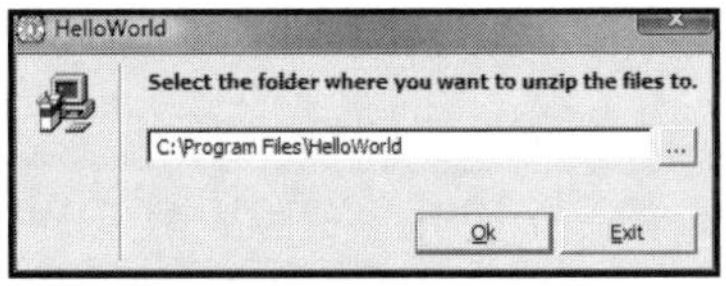


**FIGURE 1.23**
Users may install the application wherever they want.

Clicking on OK accepts the default location. Next, the user is prompted for permission to create a new folder for the application, as demonstrated in Figure 1.24.

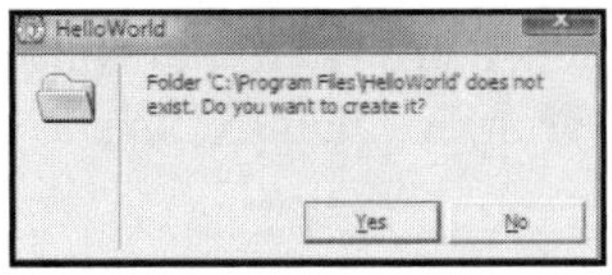


**FIGURE 1.24**
A new folder must be created to store the application.

To precede the user must click on Yes. The application is then installed on the user's computer after which a window similar to the one shown in Figure 1.25 displays.

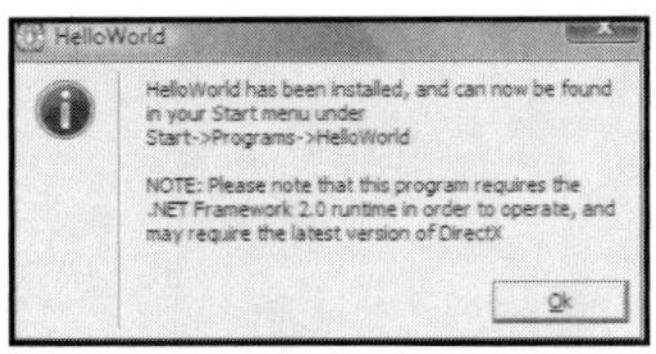


**FIGURE 1.25**
The user is given directions for running the application and is informed of application pre-requisites.

Once the user clicks on the OK button, the installation process ends and the application is ready to be used. To do so, all the user has to do is to click on Start and then locate the application program group in which the application resides. Clicking on the application starts it just like any other Windows application.

## EXTENDING PHROGRAM'S CAPABILITIES

Phrogram is an extensible programming language. Its capabilities can be extended through the purchase and installation of add-in libraries. These add-in libraries provide Phrogram with access to collections of pre-written program code that you can call upon from inside your program applications. Currently, a number of add-in modules are available for purchase from the Phrogram Company website. These modules include:

- **PhrogramTalk.** Provides the ability to create Phrogram applications that support chat, multi-player network games, and other types of online applications.

- **WeatherPro.** Provides access to real-time weather data that can be integrated into Phrogram applications.
- **PrecisionMath.** Eliminates rounding errors that occur in complex mathematical calculations and is designed to support the development of scientific and financial applications where precise calculations are required.
- **Extended I/O.** A free add-in that provides Phrogram with the ability to start and interact with external third-party applications.

Although these Phrogram add-in libraries are useful time savers, further discussion of them is outside the scope of this book. You can learn more about these four add-in libraries by visiting http://phrogram.com/content/drivertransition.aspx, as shown in Figure 1.26.

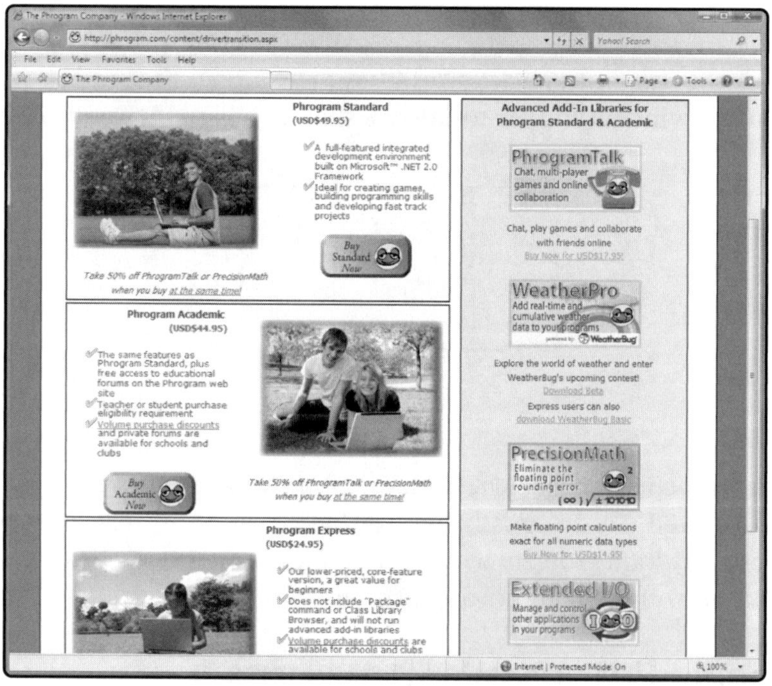


**FIGURE 1.26**

When this book was written, four add-in libraries were available at the Phrogram Company website.

**HINT** Add-in libraries are only applicable to the Standard and Academic version of Phrogram. You cannot use add-in libraries with Phrogram Express.

## Phrogram's Architecture

Phrogram makes use of a number of different tools and technologies to provide an outstanding learning and development environment. Specifically, development of most Phrogram applications depends on the following components.

- The Phrogram programming language
- Phrogram's integrated development environment or IDE
- The Microsoft .NET Framework
- DirectX

### The Phrogram Programming Language

The Phrogram programming language is similar in style and simplicity to BASIC. Phrogram is designed to be as simple to use as possible. It sports a concise, straightforward syntax, and a collection of language statements that make it easy for anyone just starting out to learn how to program.

HINT

*BASIC* is an acronym for *Beginners All-Purpose Symbolic Instruction Code*. BASIC was originally created in 1963 at Dartmouth College as an instructional programming language to be used to teach beginners how to program. However, over the decades, programming languages based on BASIC have grown in terms of size and complexity, making them not so *basic* anymore.

Despite its simplicity, the Phrogram programming language is amazingly robust and powerful, supporting both 2D and 3D graphics programming. Although there is an emphasis on game and graphics development, Phrogram can be used to develop any type of application you can think of.

As you will learn, Phrogram also supports object-oriented programming. As such, Phrogram programs view resources as objects. This includes resources like files and folders as well as custom objects defined by programmers that represent real-world concepts like space ships, balls, people, cars, and so on. You will learn about object-oriented programming in Chapter 7.

HINT

By introducing you to the fundamentals of object-oriented programming, Phrogram makes it easy for you to later make the jump to other business-oriented applications like Microsoft Visual Basic, C#, or C++, all of which are object-oriented programming languages.

## The Phrogram IDE

The Phrogram IDE is a powerful graphical program development environment that provides you with everything needed to create computer games and applications that run on Microsoft Windows. It includes a code editor filled with helpful features like statement color coding and automatic syntax checking. It can even assist you in the formulation of code statements.

The Phrogram IDE is very similar in its overall design and presentation to Microsoft Visual Studio, which is the IDE used by professional programmers to develop Visual Basic, C#, and C++ applications. However, Phrogram's IDE is a lot simpler and easier to learn.

> **HINT** Once you have learned how to work with the Phrogram IDE, you will have a big lead should you decide to make the jump to Microsoft Visual Basic, C#, or C++.

The Phrogram IDE includes a host of features, including an integrated debugger that you can use to track down and identify pesky bugs that prevent your applications and games from working the way you want them to. The Phrogram IDE also includes a built-in class browser that you will learn how to use to explore the different types of objects provided by the Phrogram programming language. Other IDE windows include a message window that displays messages and errors that occur while you are working and a picture browser.

The Phrogram IDE is packed with all kinds of helpful little goodies, providing you with everything needed to create, test, save, and execute Program games and applications. You will learn the ins and outs of working with the Phrogram IDE in Chapter 2.

## The .NET Framework

The *.NET Framework*, often referred to as *.NET*, is a software development and execution environment developed by Microsoft that is designed to support the execution of applications running on Microsoft Windows. .NET is used by software development companies and IT departments all over the world to create business applications. .NET supports the development and execution of desktop, network, and Internet-based applications using any .NET-compliant programming language. Microsoft has developed an entire suite of .NET compatible programming languages that include Visual Basic, C++, C#, and J#. In addition, many third-party developers, including the Phrogram Company, have developed their own .NET-compatible programming languages.

> **HINT** Phrogram requires .NET 2.0 be installed on the computer where you develop your applications as well as on any computer where the programs will run. Fortunately, .NET is in widespread use and most users now have it. However, you cannot count on its installation on everybody's computer, so you should

definitely consider listing .NET 2.0 as a pre-requisite for any computer game or applications you distribute or sell.

.NET acts as an interface between a programming language and the operating system and is responsible for compiling and managing the execution of programming applications. The .NET Framework provides .NET applications with access to system and network resources and when called upon automatically handles many tasks on behalf of the applications. One key component of .NET is the *CLR* (*common language runtime*), which is responsible for compiling applications into an executable format that the computer can understand and run.

Thanks to Phrogram, you do not need to become a .NET expert to develop Phrogram applications that run on Microsoft Windows. Instead, Phrogram manages all interaction with .NET for you behind the scenes, freeing you up to focus on the core logic required to create your Phrogram games and applications.

## DirectX

DirectX is a Microsoft Windows technology designed to support the development of high-end graphics applications and games. DirectX manages an application's interaction with graphics and audio hardware and game control devices allowing for the exchange of information. DirectX is made up of different components that have names like Direct3D and DirectMusic, which manage things like the display of graphics and sound playback. Collectively, these components are referred to as DirectX.

**HINT** Direct3D is used by Microsoft Windows, Microsoft Xbox, and Microsoft Xbox 360. You will sometimes see the terms Direct3D and DirectX used interchangeably to refer to DirectX.

DirectX is responsible for controlling interaction with input devices like the mouse, keyboard, and joysticks. Hardware manufacturers design and create DirectX-compatible software drivers to allow their video and audio cards and other hardware products to run on Microsoft Windows. Microsoft first introduced DirectX back in 1995 and has since updated it many times. As of the writing of this book, DirectX 10 was the current version.

DirectX 10 comes installed as part of Microsoft Vista. It replaces DirectX 9.0C. Prior to DirectX 10, all versions of DirectX were backward compatible. However, because of changes in its design, DirectX 10 is not backward compatible.

When this book was written, DirectX 10 was only available for Microsoft Vista and Microsoft did not appear to have plans to make it available on any other Microsoft operating system.

Therefore, DirectX 9.0C is the current version for computers running Windows 98, Me, 2000, and XP.

> **TRICK** Regardless of which Microsoft operating system you are using, you need to ensure DirectX 9.0C is installed if you plan on doing any 3D programming or if you want your application to be able to support joysticks. Even if your computer is running Microsoft Vista, you still need to install DirectX 9.0C. DirectX 9.0C installs separately from DirectX 10, so you won't have to worry about messing anything up when you install it.

## Looking at the Big Picture

Traditionally, game development was the lone privilege of a small group of highly paid and specialized programmers with expertise in the C and C++ programming languages, both of which took many years of time and effort to master. With the advent of languages like Phrogram, things are changing on this front. Phrogram helps to significantly simplify game and application development by automatically taking care of many of complex and mundane tasks involved in programming for you, freeing you up to focus on the high-level steps involved in application development.

Phrogram partly accomplishes this by leveraging the power of DirectX and .NET. In addition, Phrogram automatically manages all interaction with these two resources. You do not have to spend countless hours learning how DirectX and .NET work. As a result, game programming is no longer the exclusive realm of professional programmers. Expertise in DirectX and .NET is not a requirement for the development of powerful, modern Windows applications. Figure 1.27 depicts how Phrogram manages interaction with DirectX and .NET on behalf of your Phrogram applications.

As depicted in Figure 1.27, Phrogram acts as a wrapper or *interface* between your application and DirectX and .NET, providing your applications with everything required to create, compile, and execute. This includes support for 3D programming as well as joysticks and other types of game controllers.

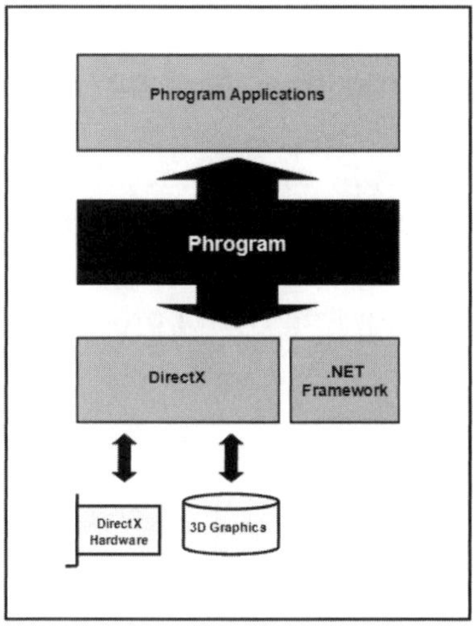


**Figure 1.27**
A depiction of the major technologies that come together to support Phrogram application development.

## Review Questions

1. How many versions of Phrogram are their? Which is most appropriate for students and teachers? Which is best for hobbyists and computer enthusiasts interested in exploring all of Phrogram's capabilities?
2. What is the .NET Framework? What version of .NET does Phrogram require?
3. What is DirectX? What programming capabilities does DirectX provide Phrogram with?
4. What are the four basic steps involved in creating and testing a Phrogram application?
5. What is an IDE? What are two features provided by the Phrogram IDE?
6. What is the purpose of a distribution package? What is the menu command that must be executed to begin the distribution package creation process?
7. What are comments? Why is adding comments to program source code a good programming principle?
8. What is an add-in library? Identify at least three add-in libraries currently available for Phrogram.
9. What are the differences between DirectX, Direct3D, and DirectMusic?
10. What does it mean to compile a program? What is the menu command that must be executed to compile and execute a Phrogram program?

## Back to the Kids Jokes Game

It's time to turn your attention back to the development of this chapter's main project, the Kids Jokes game. While developing this game you will help to reinforce your understanding of the steps involved in creating Phrogram applications. Since this book has yet to introduce you to all of the intricacies of the Phrogram programming language, don't worry too much about what each individual programming statement is doing. Rather than getting caught up in the details, for now focus on understanding the overall process involved in creating and executing Phrogram applications.

### Designing the Game

To help keep things as simple as possible, this game will be created by following a series of steps, as outlined here:

1. Create a new program project.
2. Document your application.
3. Configure the game's window.
4. Display the game's welcome message.
5. Display the game's first joke.
6. Display the game's second joke.
7. Display the game's third joke.
8. Display the game's closing screen.
9. Save and compile your new application.

As long as you take your time and do not make any typos or skip any of the steps outlined above, you'll have a fully functional Phrogram application up and running in no time.

#### Step 1: Creating a New Phrogram Project

The first step in creating a new Phrogram application is to create a new program. To do so, start Phrogram and click on the New Program command located on the File menu. In response, a new tab will be added to the Phrogram IDE's code editor representing a new program file. The following code statements are automatically added to the file and should be visible.

```
Program MyNewProgram

	Method Main()



	End Method

End Program
```

These statements provide an overall structure for your new application. Let's begin by assigning a more meaningful name to the application, which is done by replacing `MyNewProgram` with `KidsJokes` as the application's name on the first code statement. The rest of the program statements that will make up the KidsJokes application are explained in the sections that follow and will be inserted between the `Method Main()` and `End Method` statements.

### Step 2: Documenting Your New Program

Now that you have started a new program, it is time to begin adding the code statements needed to bring your new creation to life. Let's begin by adding the following comment statements to your program's code file.

```
//Program: KidsJokes.kpl
//Created: 11/24/2007
//Version: 1.0
//Author: Jerry Lee Ford, Jr.
//Description: This Phrogram game displays a series of jokes, demonstrating
//             the steps involved in controlling the display and appearance
//             of text.
```

As you can see, these statements provide some high-level documentation about the program and its purpose.

### Step 3: Configuring the Game's Window

The next set of code statements that you need to add to the program file is responsible for specifying configuration settings that will control the appearance of the window in which the Kids Jokes game is played. These statements, shown next, hide the window's toolbar, configure the window's size, and then display a text string of Kids Jokes in the toolbar. Next, a background color of light gray is set and the foreground color, used to display font text, is set to Firebrick (red). Next, the display of all text is set to bold and the window is displayed.

```
HideToolbar()
SetScreenSize (800, 600)
SetWindowTitle ("Kids Jokes")

SetConsoleBackgroundColor(LightGray)
SetConsoleFontColor(Firebrick)

SetConsoleFontStyle(True, False, False)

ShowConsole()
```

Each of these statements should be added to the `Main()` method, just after the comment statements that you added in the previous step. Do not worry about what each of these code statements does. You will learn about this in later chapters. For now, just key them in as shown.

## Step 4: Displaying a Welcome Message

The next set of code statements that you need to add to the Kids Jokes game displays a message welcoming the player and then pauses the game and waits for the player to press a key on the keyboard before continuing.

```
SetConsoleTextAlignment ("Center")
SetConsoleFont("Arial", 36)

ConsoleWriteLine("")
ConsoleWriteLine("")
ConsoleWriteLine("")
ConsoleWriteLine("")
ConsoleWriteLine("Welcome to the Kids Jokes Game!")

ConsoleWriteLine("")
ConsoleWriteLine("")
ConsoleWriteLine("")
ConsoleWriteLine("")

SetConsoleFont("Arial", 12)

ConsoleWriteLine("Press any key to continue.")
```

```
ConsoleReadKey()
ClearConsole()
```

These statements should be added to the `Main()` method, immediately after the last set of statements that you just added.

### Step 5: Displaying the Opening Joke

The next set of code statements that you need to add to the Kids Jokes game changes the font size and alignment settings and then displays the opening line of the game's first joke, after which the game is paused for three seconds. The joke's punch line is then displayed and the game pauses again, waiting for the player to press a key.

```
SetConsoleTextAlignment ("Left")
SetConsoleFont("Arial", 36)

ConsoleWriteLine("")
ConsoleWriteLine("Why did the math book visit the psychiatrist?")

Delay(3000)

ConsoleWriteLine("")
ConsoleWriteLine("Because it had problems.")

SetConsoleTextAlignment ("Center")

ConsoleWriteLine("")
ConsoleWriteLine("")
ConsoleWriteLine("")
ConsoleWriteLine("")

SetConsoleFont("Arial", 12)

ConsoleWriteLine("Press any key to continue.")

ConsoleReadKey()

ClearConsole()
```

These statements should be added to the `Main()` method, immediately after the last set of statements that you just added.

## Step 6: Displaying the Second Joke

The next set of code statements that you need to add to the Kids Jokes game is pretty much nothing more than a duplicate of the previous set of statements, except for the modification of the text representing the second joke.

```
SetConsoleTextAlignment ("Left")
SetConsoleFont("Arial", 36)

ConsoleWriteLine("")
ConsoleWriteLine("What is black and white and red all over?")

Delay(3000)

ConsoleWriteLine("")
ConsoleWriteLine("A sunburned penguin.")

SetConsoleTextAlignment ("Center")

ConsoleWriteLine("")
ConsoleWriteLine("")
ConsoleWriteLine("")
ConsoleWriteLine("")

SetConsoleFont("Arial", 12)

ConsoleWriteLine("Press any key to continue.")

ConsoleReadKey()
ClearConsole()
```

These statements should be added to the `Main()` method, immediately after the last set of statements that you just added.

## Step 7: Displaying the Third Joke

The code statements responsible for displaying the game's third joke are shown next and should be added to the `Main()` method, immediately after the last set of statements that you just added. Except for the text representing the third joke, this set of statements is identical to the two previous sets of statements.

```
SetConsoleTextAlignment ("Left")
SetConsoleFont("Arial", 36)

ConsoleWriteLine("")
ConsoleWriteLine("Why was the elephant kicked off of the beach?")

Delay(3000)

ConsoleWriteLine("")
ConsoleWriteLine("Because his trunk was down.")

SetConsoleTextAlignment ("Center")

ConsoleWriteLine("")
ConsoleWriteLine("")
ConsoleWriteLine("")
ConsoleWriteLine("")

SetConsoleFont("Arial", 12)

ConsoleWriteLine("Press any key to continue.")

ConsoleReadKey()
ClearConsole()
```

### Step 8: Displaying a Closing Screen

The last set of statements that need to be added to the Kids Jokes game are shown next. These statements display a message thanking the player for playing the game and then pause the application for five seconds, after which the game's window closes, ending the game.

```
SetConsoleFont("Arial", 36)

ConsoleWriteLine("")
ConsoleWriteLine("")
ConsoleWriteLine("")
ConsoleWriteLine("")
ConsoleWriteLine("Thanks for playing!")

Delay(5000)
```

These statements should be added to the `Main()` method, immediately after the last set of statements that you just added.

### Step 9: Saving and Compiling Your Application

Okay, that's all there is to the Kids Jokes game. If you have not already done so, save your new program file by clicking on the Save All command located on the File menu. Once you have saved your file, compile it by clicking on the Run the program button located on the Phrogram toolbar. Assuming that you have not made any typos, Phrogram will compile your new application and then run it. Once started, the Kids Jokes game should run as previously described at the beginning of the chapter.

## The Final Result

At this point, you should have everything you need to create and run the Kids Jokes game. As will be the case for every game project covered in this book, you completed the Kids Jokes game by following a specific series of steps. It is very easy to make one or more typos or to accidentally skip a step when developing computer programs. To help make sure that things are as clear as possible, a complete copy of the Kids Jokes game is provided next. This copy of the Kids Jokes game has been further enhanced through the liberal addition of comment statements. These comments provide a detailed explanation of what is going on throughout the code file.

```
//Program: KidsJokes.kpl
//Created: 11/24/2007
//Version: 1.0
//Author: Jerry Lee Ford, Jr.
//Description: This Phrogram game displays a series of jokes, demonstrating
//             the steps involved in controlling the display and appearance
//             of text.

Program KidsJokes

    Method Main()

    HideToolbar()   //Prevent the window's toolbar from being displayed
    SetScreenSize (800, 600)    //Set the screen size to 800x600 pixels
    SetWindowTitle ("Kids Jokes")    //Display the name of the game in
                                     //the Window's titlebar
```

```
SetConsoleBackgroundColor(LightGray)   //Set background color
SetConsoleFontColor(Firebrick)         //Set font color

// Set console font style to Bold, non-italic and non-underline
SetConsoleFontStyle(True, False, False)

ShowConsole()                      //Display the application window

//---------------------------------------------------
//Now it is time to display the game's opening screen
//---------------------------------------------------

SetConsoleTextAlignment ("Center")   //Set text alignment to center
SetConsoleFont("Arial", 36)          // Set font to Arial, point 36

//Display 4 blank lines followed by the joke's opening line
ConsoleWriteLine("")
ConsoleWriteLine("")
ConsoleWriteLine("")
ConsoleWriteLine("")
ConsoleWriteLine("Welcome to the Kids Jokes Game!")

//Display 4 blank lines
ConsoleWriteLine("")
ConsoleWriteLine("")
ConsoleWriteLine("")
ConsoleWriteLine("")

SetConsoleFont("Arial", 12)          // Set font to Arial, point 12

//Display instructions
ConsoleWriteLine("Press any key to continue.")

ConsoleReadKey()                 //Wait for the player to press a key
ClearConsole()                   //Clear the console
```

```
//---------------------------------------------------
//Now it is time to display the game's first joke
//---------------------------------------------------

SetConsoleTextAlignment ("Left")     //Set text alignment to left
SetConsoleFont("Arial", 36)          // Set font to Arial, point 36

//Display a blank line followed by the joke's opening line
ConsoleWriteLine("")
ConsoleWriteLine("Why did the math book visit the psychiatrist?")
Delay(3000)                //Pause three seconds before continuing

//Display a blank line followed by the joke's punch line
ConsoleWriteLine("")
ConsoleWriteLine("Because it had problems.")

SetConsoleTextAlignment ("Center")  //Set text alignment to center

//Display 4 blank lines
ConsoleWriteLine("")
ConsoleWriteLine("")
ConsoleWriteLine("")
ConsoleWriteLine("")

SetConsoleFont("Arial", 12)          // Set font to Arial, point 12

//Display instructions
ConsoleWriteLine("Press any key to continue.")

ConsoleReadKey()                //Wait for the player to press a key
ClearConsole()                  //Clear the console

//---------------------------------------------------
//Now it is time to display the game's second joke
//---------------------------------------------------

SetConsoleTextAlignment ("Left")     //Set text alignment to left
SetConsoleFont("Arial", 36)          // Set font to Arial, point 36
```

```
//Display a blank line followed by the joke's opening line
ConsoleWriteLine("")
ConsoleWriteLine("What is black and white and red all over?")

Delay(3000)                  //Pause three seconds before continuing

//Display a blank line followed by the joke's punch line
ConsoleWriteLine("")
ConsoleWriteLine("A sunburned penguin.")

SetConsoleTextAlignment ("Center")  //Set text alignment to center

//Display 4 blank lines
ConsoleWriteLine("")
ConsoleWriteLine("")
ConsoleWriteLine("")
ConsoleWriteLine("")

SetConsoleFont("Arial", 12)         // Set font to Arial, point 12

//Display instructions
ConsoleWriteLine("Press any key to continue.")

ConsoleReadKey()                //Wait for the player to press a key
ClearConsole()                  //Clear the console

//--------------------------------------------------
//Now it is time to display the game's third joke
//--------------------------------------------------

SetConsoleTextAlignment ("Left")    //Set text alignment to left
SetConsoleFont("Arial", 36)         // Set font to Arial, point 36

//Display a blank line followed by the joke's opening line
ConsoleWriteLine("")
ConsoleWriteLine("Why was the elephant kicked off of the beach?")
```

```
Delay(3000)                //Pause three seconds before continuing

//Display a blank line followed by the joke's punch line
ConsoleWriteLine("")
ConsoleWriteLine("Because his trunk was down.")

SetConsoleTextAlignment ("Center") //Set text alignment to center

//Display 4 blank lines
ConsoleWriteLine("")
ConsoleWriteLine("")
ConsoleWriteLine("")
ConsoleWriteLine("")

SetConsoleFont("Arial", 12)         // Set font to Arial, point 12

//Display instructions
ConsoleWriteLine("Press any key to continue.")

ConsoleReadKey()               //Wait for the player to press a key
ClearConsole()                 //Clear the console

//-----------------------------------------------------
//Now it is time to display the game's closing screen
//-----------------------------------------------------

SetConsoleFont("Arial", 36)   // Set font to Arial, point 36

//Display 4 blank lines followed by the game's closing message
ConsoleWriteLine("")
ConsoleWriteLine("")
ConsoleWriteLine("")
ConsoleWriteLine("")
ConsoleWriteLine("Thanks for playing!")

Delay(5000)          //Wait five seconds after which the game ends
```

```
    End Method

End Program
```

If you run into errors when you run your copy of this game, use this fully assembled copy of the game's source code file to compare against your application's source code to track down and find your errors.

HINT You will also find a copy of this application's source code file on the book's accompanying CD.

## Summary

This chapter provided an introduction to Phrogram. You learned how to install and activate Phrogram. You learned about the different versions of Phrogram and the features that they support. This chapter showed you how to create your first Phrogram application and guided you step by step through its creation and through the process of creating a distribution package. This chapter also provided you with an overview of the major components that support Phrogram application development. On top of all this, you learned how to create your first computer game.

Before you move on to Chapter 2, where you will learn all about Phrogram's IDE, consider spending a little time improving the Kids Jokes game by addressing the following list of challenges.

## Challenges

1. The jokes that make up the Kids Jokes game are not the funniest jokes to ever be told. Take a few extra minutes to replace them with jokes that better suit your personal sense of humor.
2. With only three jokes, it does not take very long for the player to complete the Kids Jokes game. Consider enhancing the game by adding a number of additional jokes. To add a new joke, copy and paste the statements required to tell a joke and then modify them as necessary to tell a new joke. Repeat this process for each new joke you want to add.
3. Consider adding additional `Print` statements to the end of the program file to display additional information on the game's final screen. In addition to thanking the player for playing the game, consider displaying the URL for your website as well as any other information that will help to associate you with your application.
4. Create a distribution package for the Kids Jokes game and then share it with a number of your friends and ask them for their feedback.

CHAPTER 2

# Getting Comfortable with the Phrogram Integrated Development Environment

Phrogram provides you with a simple yet powerful integrated development environment with which to create and execute Phrogram applications. In this chapter, you will learn all about the IDE and its major features. This includes how to customize the layout of the IDE and how to dock and pin IDE windows. You will learn how to work with Phrogram's Code Editor and to take advantage of many of its features, and you will learn about the different windows that can be displayed in the IDE's Explorer and Message panes. On top of all this, you will discover how to create your next Phrogram application, the Story Time game.

Specifically, you will learn:

- How to resize, dock, pin, and un-pin IDE windows
- About Phrogram's menu and toolbar commands
- How to work with the Code Editor and to leverage its features and capabilities
- How to add and remove different types of IDE windows
- How to work with the Explorer and Message panes

## Project Preview: The Story Time Game

In this chapter you will learn how to create the Story Time game. In this game, the player is prompted to answer a series of questions, without knowing the context in which the answers that are provided will be used. Once collected, the player's input is used to tell a mad-lib-styled story. The game starts by displaying a small popup dialog window, prompting the player for permission to begin game play, as shown in Figure 2.1.

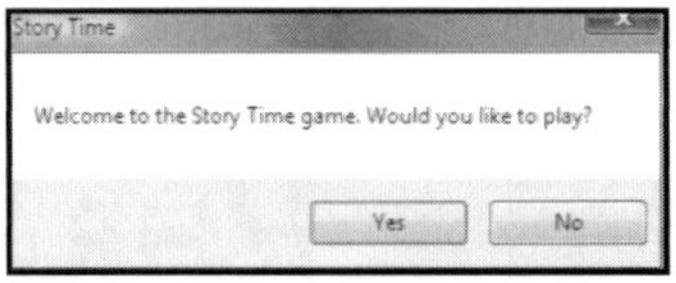


**Figure 2.1**
Player input is collected using buttons displayed on a popup dialog window.

If the player clicks on the No button, another popup dialog window displays, suggesting that the player consider returning to play another time. The game ends as soon as the player clicks on the OK button.

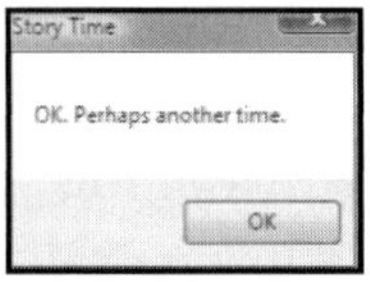


**Figure 2.2**
The game encourages the player to return and play again.

On the other hand, if the player elected to play the game when initially prompted, the popup dialog window shown in Figure 2.3 displays.

The window shown in Figure 2.3 displays the first of four questions. The player is supposed to respond to the question by typing an answer in the text box field that is provided and then clicking on the Submit button. Once the player has answered all four of the game's questions, the window shown in Figure 2.4 displays.

To allow the game to begin telling the story, the player is instructed to press a keyboard key. Next, the game displays the first of three paragraphs that make up the story, as shown in Figure 2.5.

Once the player reads the game's last paragraph and presses a keyboard key, the screen shown in Figure 2.6 displays.

After three seconds, the window shown in Figure 2.6 closes and the game terminates its execution.

**FIGURE 2.3**

A question displays at the bottom of the window.

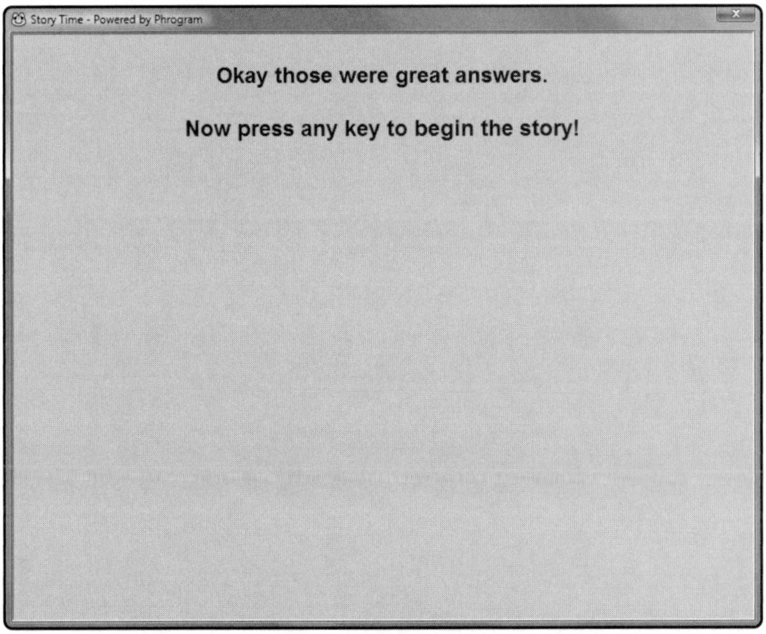


**FIGURE 2.4**

The game notifies the player that it is ready to begin telling its story.

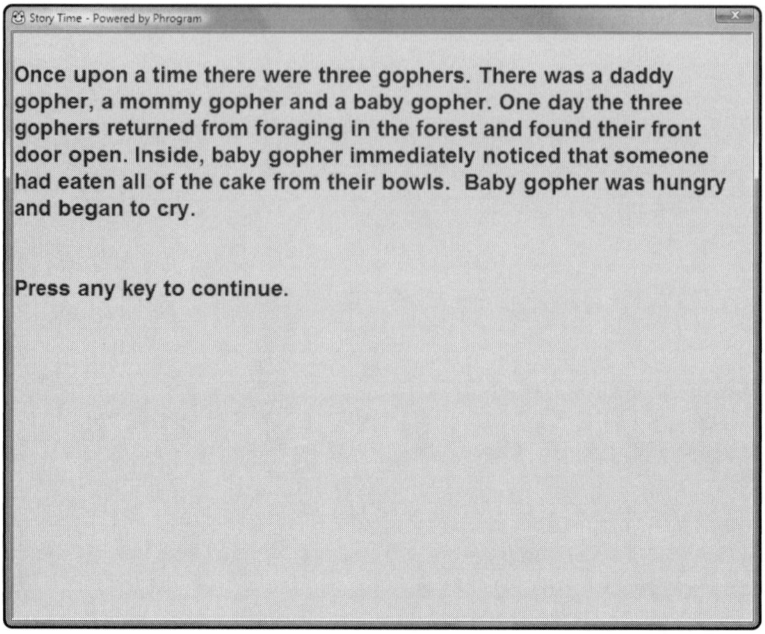


**FIGURE 2.5**

The player advances from paragraph to paragraph by pressing a keyboard key.

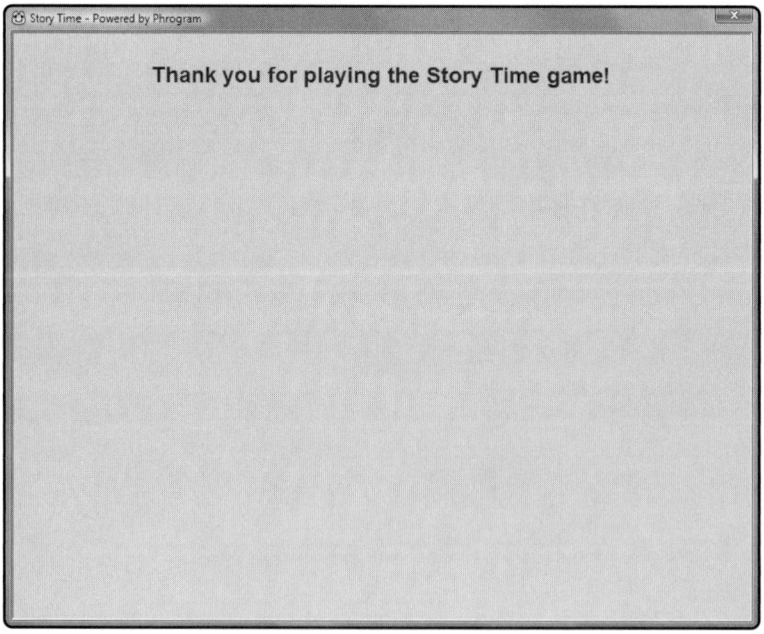


**FIGURE 2.6**

The game thanks the player for playing.

## Getting to Know the Phrogram IDE

Phrogram applications are built using Phrogram's IDE. The IDE provides you with tools that include a *compiler*, which translates your programs into executable applications, a *debugger*, which allows you to monitor program execution and assists in tracking down errors, and a wide assortment of commands and windows for managing your program projects. Figure 2.7 shows how the Phrogram IDE looks when first started.

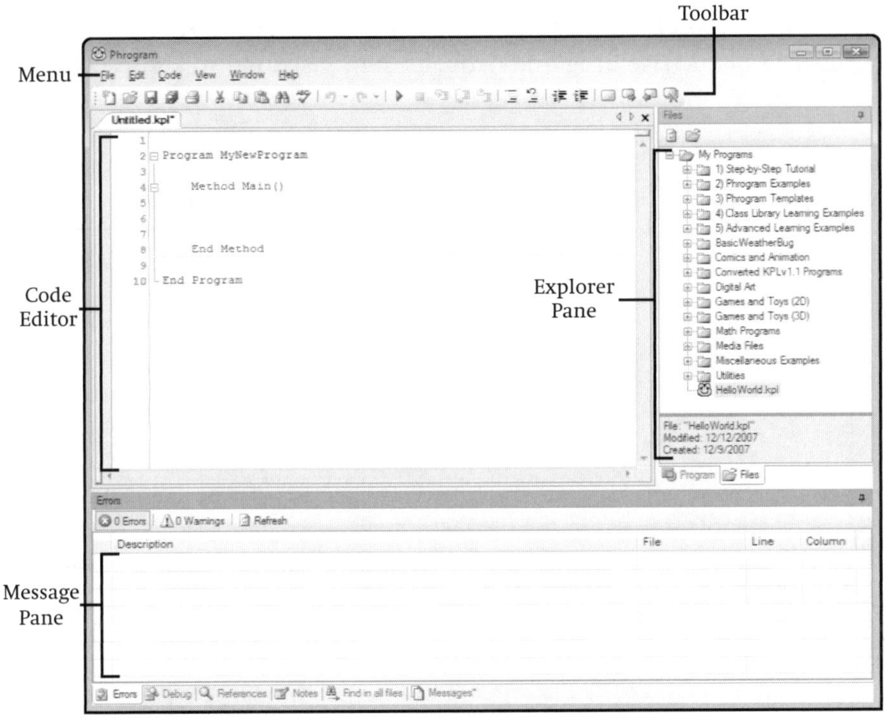


**Figure 2.7**

The Phrogram IDE is organized into a series of panes in which different windows are displayed.

The Phrogram IDE consists of a standard menu, toolbar, and a collection of different windows that are displayed in one of three panes. Although compact and streamlined compared to many other programming languages' IDEs, Phrogram's IDE consists of more windows than can be displayed at one time. Using the same presentation and organization tools as those used by Microsoft Visual Studio, Phrogram provides you with a number of clever ways of managing shared space within the IDE.

As shown in Figure 2.7, the IDE's default layout displays a number of different components. You will learn more about each of these components as you work your way through this chapter.

## Undocking IDE Windows

As Figure 2.7 shows, the Phrogram IDE's default layout places the Code Editor on the top-left side of the IDE, the Explorer pane at the top-right side of the IDE, and the Message pane at the bottom of the IDE. As you are about to learn, you are free to change the location of these panes in a variety of different ways.

One way to make additional space available within the IDE is to undock or move one or more of the panes from the IDE. When you do so, the pane disconnects from the IDE, allowing you to move it to any location on the screen. To undock a pane and move it somewhere else, simply click on the pane's titlebar area and use drag and drop, as demonstrated in Figure 2.8.

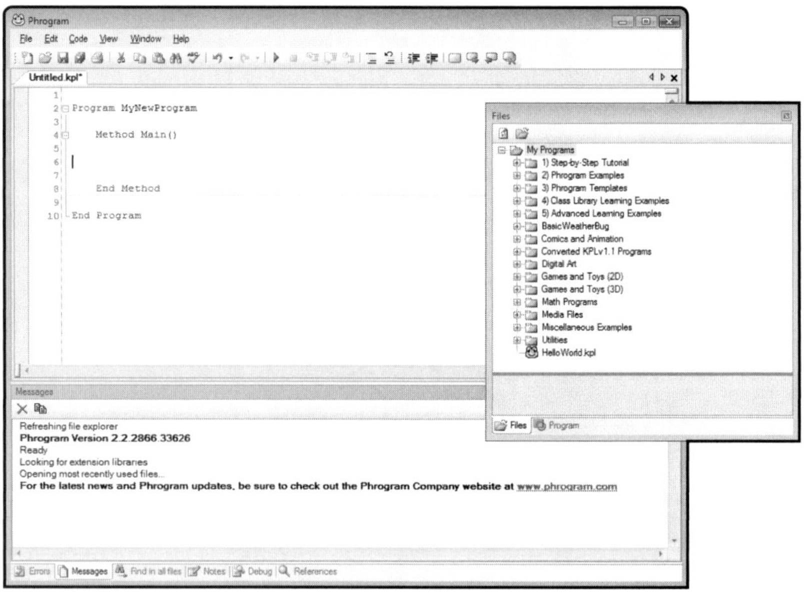


**FIGURE 2.8**

By undocking a pane, you can move it to any location on the screen and free up additional workspace within the IDE.

**HINT** Undocking only works with the Explorer pane and the Message pane. You cannot undock the Code Editor pane.

When you use drag and drop to move the pane around within the IDE, a series of graphic indicators appear as shown in Figure 2.9. By moving the pane over one of the graphic indicators and then releasing the left mouse button, you instruct the IDE to re-dock the pane at the indicated location within the IDE.

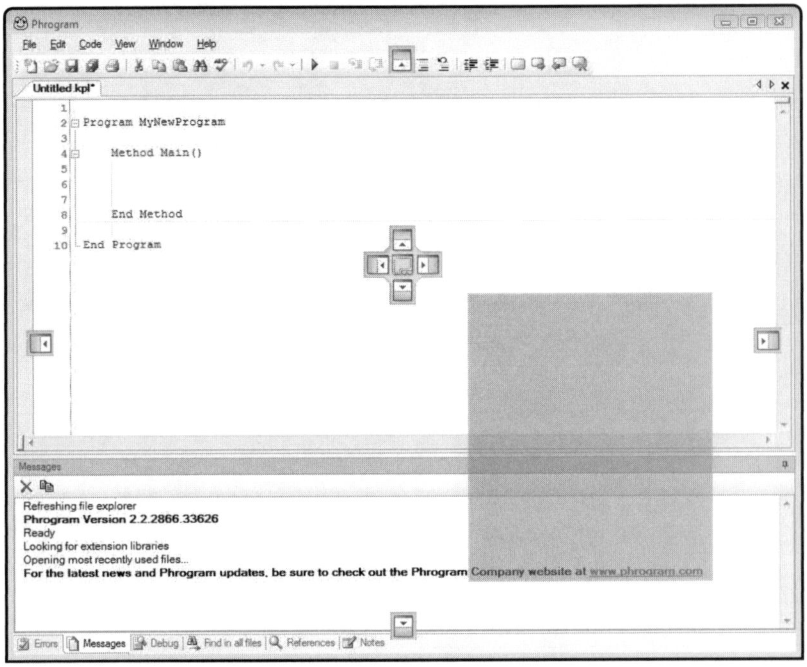

FIGURE 2.9

As you drag a pane around in the IDE, graphical indicators appear to help you tell the IDE where you want to re-dock the pane.

Using this feature, you can easily reorganize the layout of the IDE to suit your own preferences. As you will see when you experiment with this feature, you can dock a pane with the same space used by another pane or you may dock a pane to any of the outside edges of the IDE and the IDE will automatically re-adjust the organization of the IDE to accommodate your changes. Figure 2.10 shows an example of an IDE in which the Message pane and the Explorer pane have been moved and docked to different locations.

## Resizing IDE Windows

Another feature supported by Phrogram is the ability to resize each of the panes displayed within the IDE. This allows you to, for example, increase or decrease the amount of space allocated to the Code Editor, without having to close another pane to make additional space available.

Resizing a pane is easy. All you have to do is move the pointer over the inner edge of the pane and then, using drag and drop, move the edge of the pane to a new location. Figure 2.11 shows an example in which the size of the Message pane has been increased to take up half of the available space in the IDE. You can compare this to Figure 2.10 to see the overall effect that this has had on the IDE.

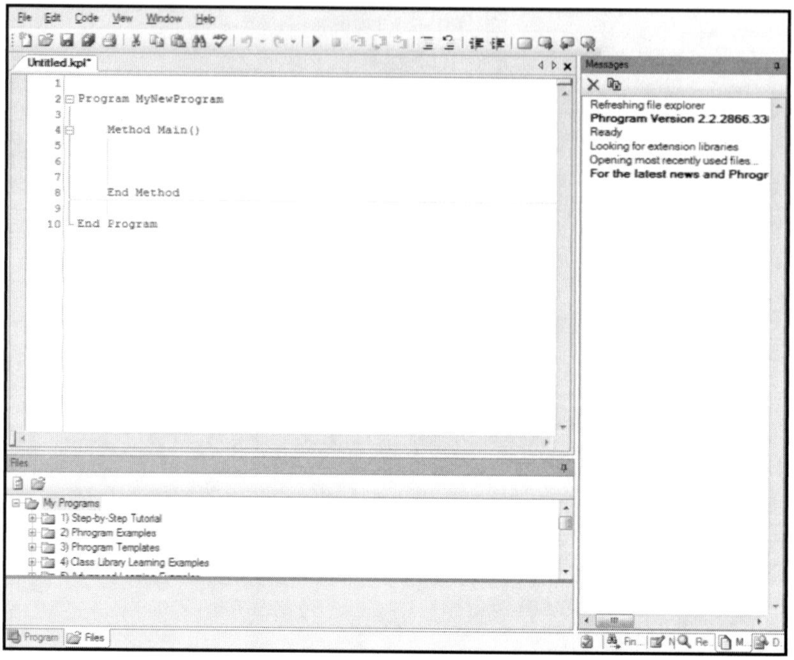


**FIGURE 2.10**

Reconfiguring the location of panes in the IDE to suit your personal preferences.

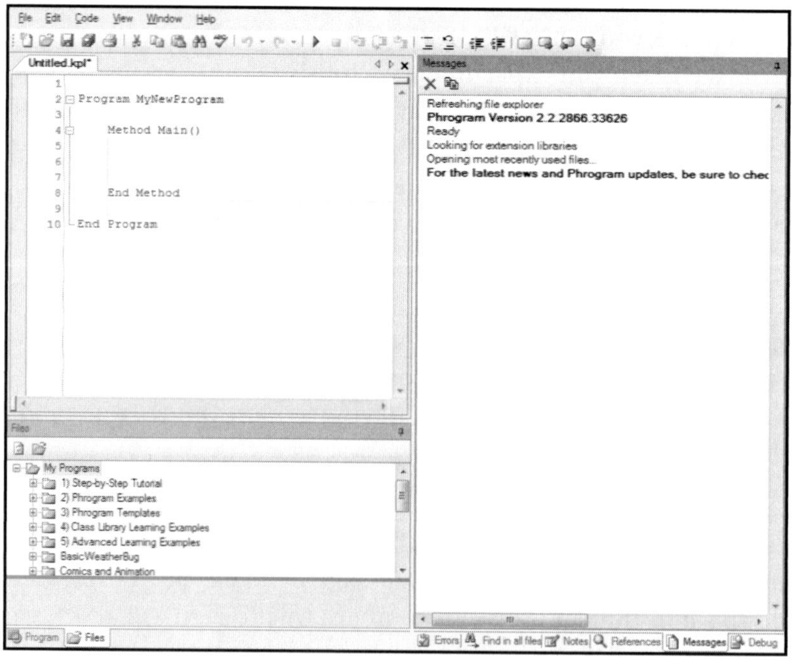


**FIGURE 2.11**

Change the size of IDE panes.

## Creating Workspace by Unpinning Windows

Another space-saving feature that you will find extremely useful is the ability to pin and unpin IDE windows. If you look closely at the Explorer pane and the Message pane, you will see that both of them display an image of a small pin or thumbtack in the upper-right corner of their toolbars. Clicking on the pin activates an auto hide feature that shrinks the pane to one or more tabs, which are then displayed along the edge of the IDE where the pane is docked. The result is more space in the Code Editor, as demonstrated in Figure 2.12.

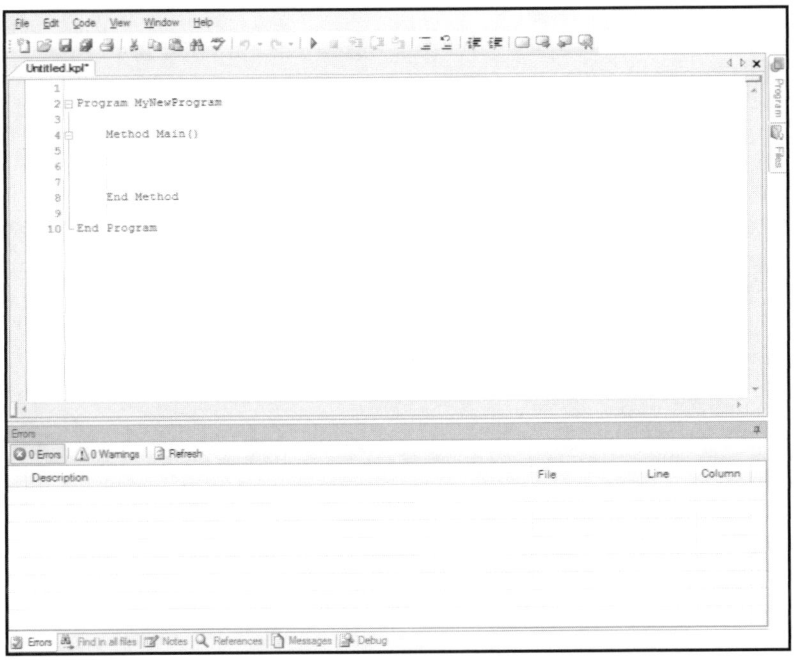


**FIGURE 2.12**

Unpinning the Explorer pane minimizes it to a collection of tabs within the IDE.

The advantage of pinning is that it lets you free up additional space in the IDE without making you close any windows. Later, when you need to work with a pinned pane, you can unpin it by clicking on one of its tabs. When you do so, the pane is restored to its previous size. This opens the pane so that you can work with it. When you click on another part of the IDE, the pane shrinks back down to its pinned tab view again. However, you can permanently restore a pane back to its former size and location by pinning it. To do so, click on one of its tabs and when the pane reopens, click on the image of the pin in the pane titlebar.

## Working with Tabbed Windows

Because the IDE consists of multiple panes, the Phrogram IDE employs a number of organizational tricks that let you manage its limited amount of space. One way that space is shared is through the display of one or more windows in the same pane. To ensure that each window is easily accessible, it is assigned a tab that when selected displays the window. You can view any window opened in the same pane by clicking on its tab, as demonstrated in Figure 2.13.

**FIGURE 2.13**

Tabs at the bottom of the Message pane provide single-click access to different windows that share space within the pane.

# GETTING COMFORTABLE WITH PHROGRAM MENUS

The Phrogram IDE includes a menu system packed with commands that give you total control over the IDE and your programs. Phrogram's menus are dynamic, automatically graying out features when they do not apply to the current situation. The following list identifies each of the high-level menus found in the IDE.

- File
- Edit
- Code
- View
- Window
- Help

Depending on whether you have enabled its advanced options, which you can do by clicking on the View menu and selecting or clearing the View Advanced Options option, the Program IDE displays different sets of commands on many of its menus. As you will see, when advanced options are enabled, you get access to commands that allow you to create distribution packages, manipulate comments, indentation and bookmarks, and access additional IDE windows.

## Working with the File Menu

Depending on whether the View Advanced Options option has been enabled, the Phrogram File menu displays one of the collections of commands as shown in Figure 2.14. The File menu provides access to commands that create new program files and open existing program files.

This menu also contains commands for saving and closing program files. From here, you can also print file contents and exit the Program IDE.

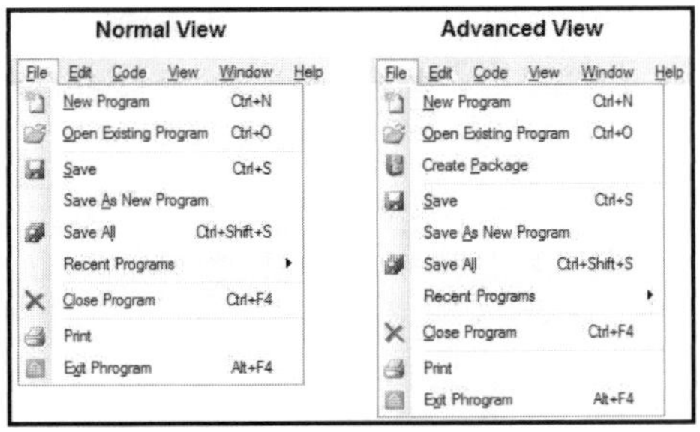


**FIGURE 2.14**

The File menu provides access to commands that create, open, and save Phrogram programs.

In its advanced view, the File menu also provides you with access to the Create Package command, which as you learned in Chapter 1, "Introduction to Phrogram," lets you create a distribution package for your Phrogram applications so that they can be installed and run on other computers.

**HINT**

Just to the left of each menu command you will see a graphic icon representing the command's purpose. A number of the commands found on Phrogram menus are also included on the IDE toolbar using these same icons. Just to the right of some commands, you will find shortcuts that identify how to access the command directly from the keyboard.

## Working with the Edit Menu

The Phrogram IDE's Edit menu, shown in Figure 2.15, provides access to commands that you will need to use when working with the Phrogram IDE's Code Editor. Enabling View Advanced Options does not add additional commands to this menu.

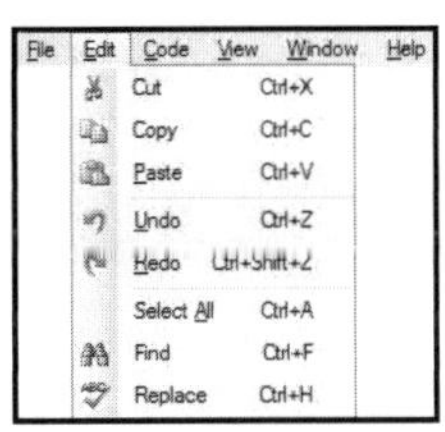


**FIGURE 2.15**

The Edit menu provides access to commands that are designed to work with the Code Editor.

The commands located on the Edit menu include all of the standard editing commands that are included with most Windows applications, including Cut, Copy, and Paste. Also included on this menu are the Find and Replace commands.

## Working with the Code Menu

The Phrogram IDE's `Code` menu, shown in Figure 2.16, varies significantly depending on whether you have enabled View Advanced Options. This menu provides access to the Run Program command, which lets you compile and execute Phrogram programs from within the IDE. The Code menu provides access to three additional commands that are used to control program execution when you execute your program in debug mode.

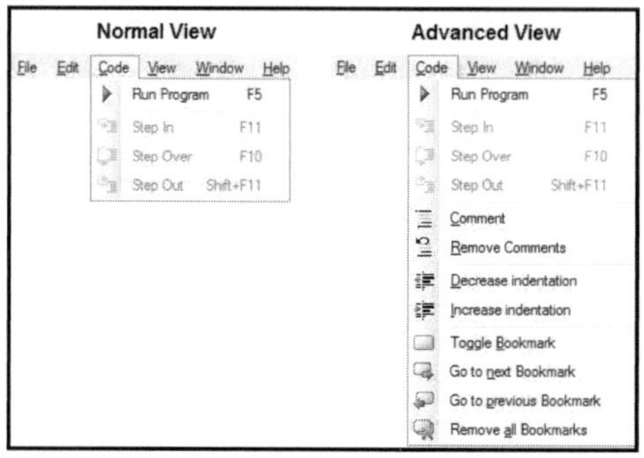


**FIGURE 2.16**

The Code menu provides access to commands that compile and execute Phrogram programs and control program execution in debug mode.

**TRAP** If you find that the Code menu's Run Program command (and its corresponding toolbar button) is grayed out when you go to run your program, this indicates that you already have another instance of the program running, which you have forgotten to close. To get out of this situation, minimize Phrogram, locate the other instance of your program, and close it. When you redisplay Phrogram, the Run Program command should be available again.

**HINT** You will learn how to work with the Step In, Step Over, and Step Out debug commands in Chapter 10, "Debugging Your Applications."

When View Advanced Options are enabled, the Code menu also provides you with access to the following commands.

- **Comment.** Instructs Phrogram to comment out any currently selected code statements.
- **Remove Comments.** Instructs Phrogram to uncomment any currently selected code statements.
- **Decrease Indentation.** Instructs Phrogram to decrease the indentation of all currently selected code statements.
- **Increase Indentation.** Instructs Phrogram to increase the indentation of all currently selected code statements.

- **Toggle Bookmark.** Instructs Phrogram to toggle the bookmark status of all currently selected code statements.
- **Go to Next Bookmark.** Instructs Phrogram to move to the next bookmark in the current code file.
- **Go to Previous Bookmark.** Instructs Phrogram to move to the previous bookmark in the current code file.
- **Remove All Bookmarks.** Instructs Phrogram to remove all bookmarks from the current code file.

HINT

You will learn more about indentation and bookmarks a little later in this chapter.

## Working with the View Menu

Depending on whether the View Advanced Options option has been enabled, the Phrogram View menu displays one of the collections of commands, as shown in Figure 2.17. The View menu provides access to commands that display different IDE windows.

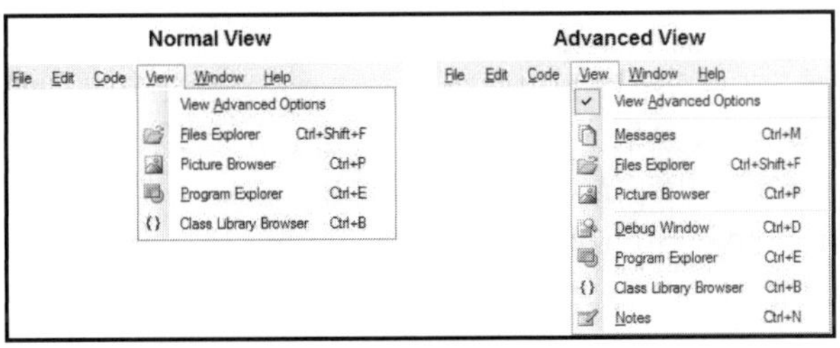


**FIGURE 2.17**

The View menu provides access to all of the windows supported by the Phrogram IDE.

As you can see in Figure 2.17, View Advanced Options provides you with access to several additional windows. Each of these windows is discussed in detail later in this chapter.

## Working with the Window Menu

The Phrogram IDE's Window menu, shown in Figure 2.18, provides access to all of the files that you have opened in the Phrogram IDE, offering an alternative means of selecting and working with windows. Enabling View Advanced Options does not add additional commands to this menu.

**FIGURE 2.18**

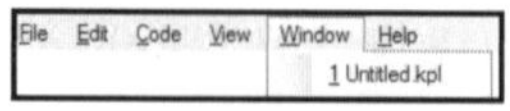


The Window menu provides access to any files currently opened in the IDE.

### Working with the Help Menu

The Phrogram IDE's `Help` menu, shown in Figure 2.19, provides access to copies of Phrogram's beginner tutorial and user guide PDF documents. It also offers links to the Phrogram Company website and to its online technical support page. Enabling View Advanced Options does not add additional commands to this menu.

**FIGURE 2.19**

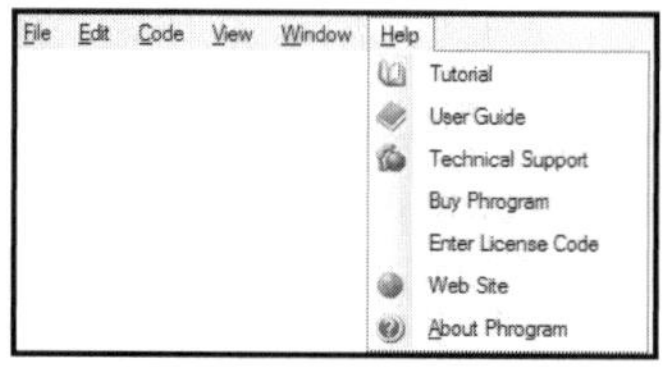


The Help menu provides easy access to Phrogram documentation and online resources.

The Help menu also provides access to the Enter License Code command, allowing you to register your copy of Phrogram once you have purchased it, and to the About Phrogram command. The About Phrogram command displays the About Phrogram window where you can view detailed information about Phrogram, including the version you are currently running as well as version information about key Phrogram component files.

## Working with Phrogram IDE Toolbar

As with most Windows applications, Phrogram makes it easy to access commonly used commands by placing them on its toolbar. As with the Phrogram IDE's menus, the number of buttons displayed on the Phrogram IDE toolbar vary based on whether View Advanced Options has been enabled, as demonstrated in Figure 2.20. In addition, toolbar button availability is dynamic, with some buttons becoming grayed out and non-accessible depending upon what you are doing at the time.

**FIGURE 2.20**

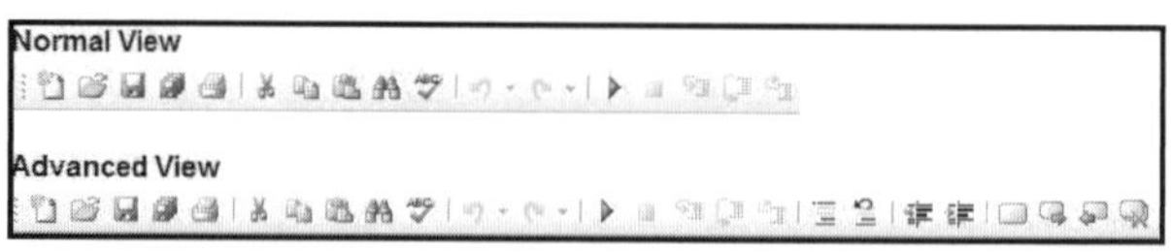


Phrogram's toolbar provides single-click access to commonly used IDE commands.

It takes time to learn everything there is to know about the Program IDE, including learning what all of the buttons on its toolbar do. As a shortcut, you can display a ToolTip that reminds you what each toolbar button does by moving your cursor over it. The following list shows the ToolTips associated with each of the Phrogram IDE's toolbar buttons, starting from left to right. The entries listed in italics represent toolbar buttons available only when View Advanced Options has been enabled.

- Create a new program
- Open an existing program
- Save the active program
- Save all programs
- Print the program code
- Cut the selected text to the clipboard
- Copy the selected text to the clipboard
- Paste from the clipboard to the cursor position
- Find text
- Replace
- Undo last change
- Redo
- Run the program
- Stop the running program
- Step Into
- Step Over
- *Step out of the current method*
- *Comment the selected lines of code*
- *Uncomment the selected lines of code*
- *Decrease indent for the selected lines of code*
- *Increase indent for the selected lines of code*
- *Set (or remove if set) a bookmark on the current line of code*
- *Go to the next bookmark*
- *Go to the previous bookmark*
- *Clear all bookmarks*

## Getting to Know the Code Editor

The Phrogram IDE Code Editor pane, shown in Figure 2.21, is the IDE feature you will use most when creating new Phrogram applications. It allows you to display, view, and edit the program statements that make up your programs. Unlike the Explorer and Message pages, you cannot pin or close the Code Editor pane, so it is always in plain site.

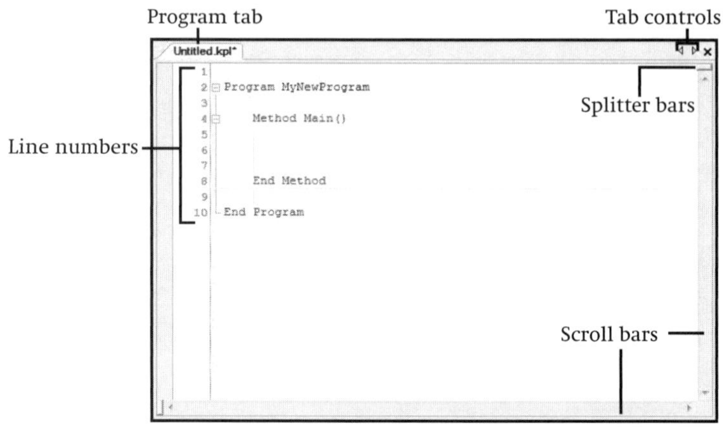


**Figure 2.21**

The Code Editor provides a wide range of advanced editing features.

The first time you start Phrogram, a new program is created. What happens upon subsequent startups of Phrogram depends on the state in which you leave it when you last closed it down. If you close all open program files prior to closing Phrogram, the next time you start Phrogram it will create a new empty program for you. However, if you had any open files when you closed Phrogram, Phrogram will reload those files the next time it starts.

**HINT** Take note of the line numbers displayed on the left-hand side of the Code Editor. These line numbers are for display purposes only and are not part of your code files. Their primary purpose is to provide you with an idea of the size of your programs and your location within your program files when you are working it. Line numbers are also helpful when used in conjunction with error messages, helping you to home in on the statements where errors are detected.

The Program Editor supports a wide range of advanced features, all of which are designed to help you work faster and more efficiently. These features include

- Color coding, indentation, and white space
- Support for editing multiple files at the same time
- The ability to split the Code Editor into two parts
- Context-sensitive menus

- The ability to view folded program code without unfolding it
- Automatic syntax checking and error reporting
- Context-sensitive code development assistance
- IntelliSense

Each of these features is covered in detail in the sections that follow.

## Color Coding, Indentation, and Spacing

You probably noticed when you were creating the Hello World and Kids Jokes applications back in Chapter 1 that the Phrogram IDE displayed different statements using different colors and that some statements have consisted of words displayed in two or more colors. Phrogram uses statement color coding to help make program code easier to read. Specifically, Phrogram applies the following color coding scheme to all program files.

- All comments display as green.
- Text strings display as brown.
- Language keywords display as blue.
- Data type specifications display as light blue.
- Everything else displays in black.

In addition to statement color coding, you may have noticed that certain statements were automatically indented when you keyed them in. Phrogram does this to make things easier to read and understand. Indentation helps to group related code statements together and helps to visually organize program code.

If you look closely at the program code statements that make up the Kids Jokes game, you will see that Phrogram is also displaying vertical gray lines that help to identify statements that share the same level of indentation, as demonstrated in Figure 2.22.

On top of all this, Phrogram also allows you to make liberal use of white space by inserting blank lines to make things easier to read and understand, as shown in Figure 2.22. As you can see, white space also helps to visually separate groups of statements and makes your overall program easier to manage.

## Working with More than One File at a Time

Phrogram lets you work with more than one program file at a time. This can be helpful when you need to copy and paste portions of code from one file to another. Each program file that you open is represented by a tab displayed at the top of the Code Editor. For example, Figure 2.23 shows an example of the Code Editor being used to edit four program files.

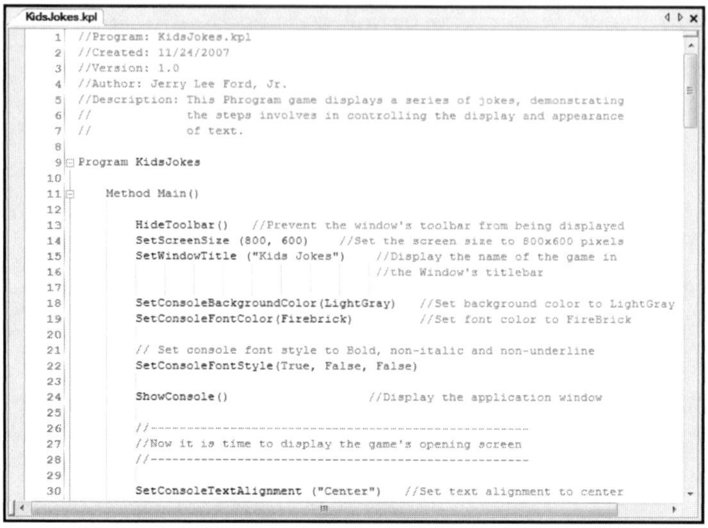


**FIGURE 2.22**

Indentation results in code that is easier to understand and manage.

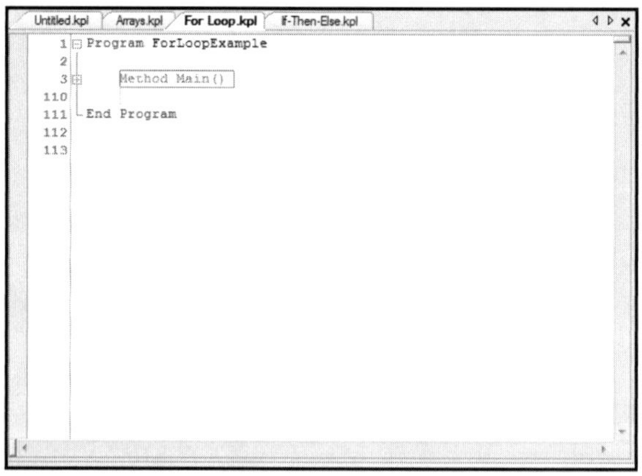


**FIGURE 2.23**

The Code Editor can be used to edit an unlimited number of program files at the same time.

You can jump from program file to program file by selecting their tabs. If the number of open files results in more tabs than can be displayed at once, the left and right arrow buttons located at the upper-right corner of the Code Editor change from clear to black and can then be used to navigate backwards and forwards through each open program file.

## Dividing the Code Editor's Display Area

Another way that Phrogram lets you better use the limited amount of space available in the Code Editor is by splitting the available space into two parts using the splitter bar handles located in the upper-right corner and the lower-left corner of the Code Editor. For example, by dragging the horizontal splitter bar halfway down the code area, as demonstrated in Figure 2.24, you can split the available space in half.

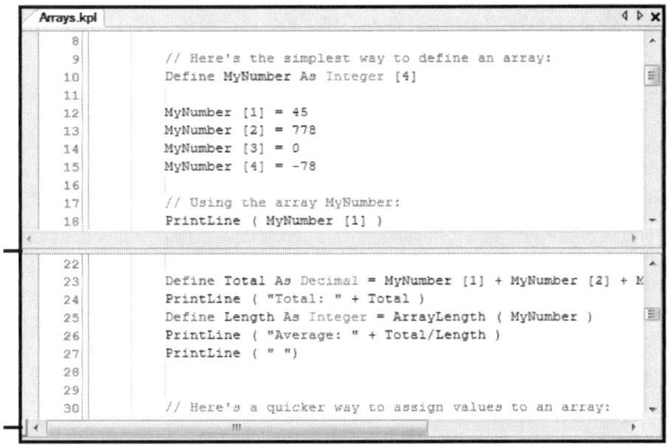


**FIGURE 2.24**

You can split the space available in the Code Editor into two logical views.

Once split, each portion of the Code Editor functions independently. This allows you to view and edit two separate parts of a program file at the same time, saving you the trouble of having to repeatedly scroll up and down from one location to another.

## Context-Sensitive Menus Commands

In addition to its menus and toolbar, Phrogram IDE also makes commands available to you via context-sensitive menus that you can access by clicking on different parts of the Code Editor. For example, you can right-click on any program tab in the Code Editor and access commands for saving and closing program files, as demonstrated in Figure 2.25.

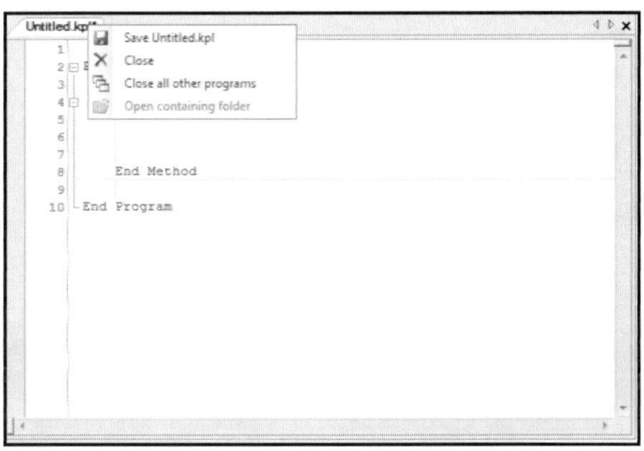

**FIGURE 2.25**

Accessing the Code Editor tab's context menu.

Another way of accessing context-sensitive commands in the Code Editor is to right-click on any free space inside the Code Editor. In response, the context menu shown in Figure 2.26 displays. As you can see, most of the commands that are displayed are also accessible from the Edit menu. However, two additional commands are made available here that you will not find elsewhere. These are the Toggle Bookmark and Delete commands.

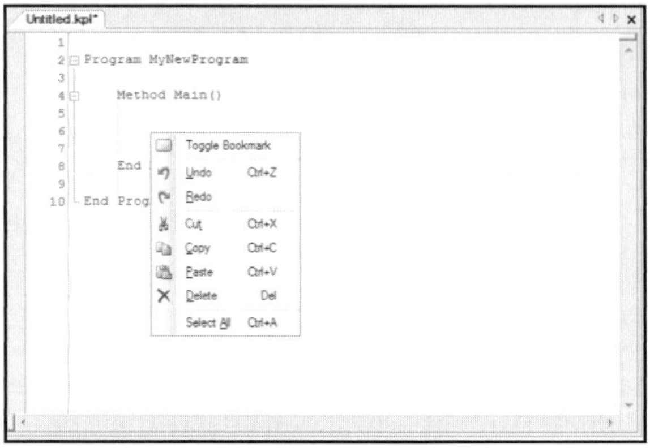

**FIGURE 2.26**

Accessing the Code Editor area's context menu.

The Toggle Bookmark commands let you place or remove a bookmark at the line upon which you right-clicked. Bookmarks are placeholders within a code file and can be quite useful in long code files. You can use this bookmark to quickly return to this point in the program file by later using the Go to Next Bookmark and Go to Previous Bookmark commands located on the Code menu. The Delete command deletes the character that immediately follows on the line where you right-click or, if there are no more characters on that line, deletes the rest of the line.

## Viewing Folded Program Code

To help conserve space within the Code Editor, the Phrogram IDE automatically folds program code belonging to all of the following types of collections of program statements. You will learn about each of these types of collections of statements in later chapters.

- Functions
- Methods
- Loops
- Structures
- If...Then blocks

As you have already seen, you can click on the plus sign indicator just to the left of a folded collection of code to unfold it and view its contents. Alternatively, the Phrogram IDE allows you to view folded statements without unfolding them. To do so, move the pointer over the statement representing the folded collection of statements for a few seconds. In response,

Phrogram will display the statements that have been folded in a ToolTip, as demonstrated in Figure 2.27.

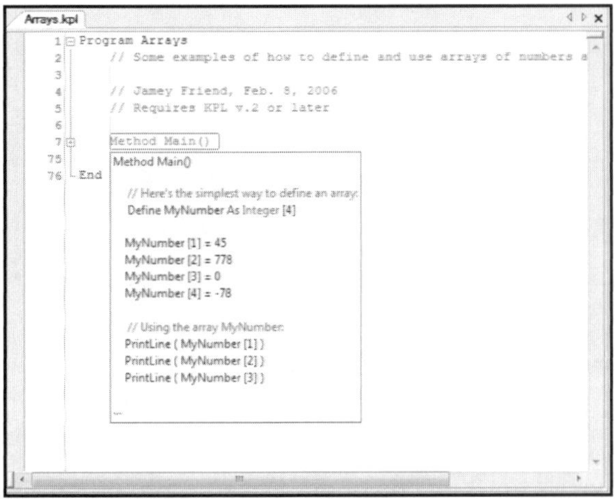


**FIGURE 2.27**

Viewing folded program code without unfolding it.

If the number of statements that have been folded are too numerous to display within the ToolTip, an ellipsis will be displayed in the lower-left corner of the ToolTip, as demonstrated in Figure 2.27. If this is the case, you will have to unfold the collection of statements to be able to view all of them.

## Automatic Syntax Checking and Error Reporting

Another way that the Phrogram IDE helps you when you are keying in program statements is through automatic syntax checking. It accomplishes this by monitoring you as you type, and if it finds that you have mistyped a language keyword or failed to follow the required syntax, it identifies the error by underlining it with a squiggly red line. In addition, a brief error message is displayed that explains the error that is being flagged. For an example of how this works, look at Figure 2.28.

Here, the `Print` command was accidentally mistyped as `Prant`. Since Phrogram was unable to recognize the command, it flagged it as an error. By pointing out syntax errors as soon as it discovers them, Phrogram helps keep you on the straight and narrow, allowing you to fix syntax errors right away.

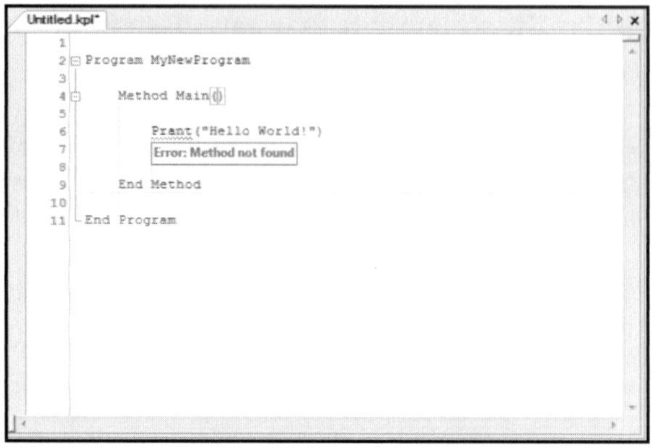


**FIGURE 2.28**

The Phrogram IDE automatically reports syntax errors as soon as it discovers them.

## Context-Sensitive Code Development Assistance

Phrogram was designed to be as programmer-friendly as possible. As such, it is constantly trying to help make things as easy as possible on you. One way that it does this is by automatically showing you the syntax required by commands as you type them in. For example, Figure 2.29 shows an example of a small Phrogram program in which the programmer is in the process of adding her first code statement. As soon as the programmer types the command `Print` followed by the required left parenthesis, Phrogram automatically displays a ToolTip that shows the command's syntax. In addition, a brief description of the command is provided and each of its parameters is explained.

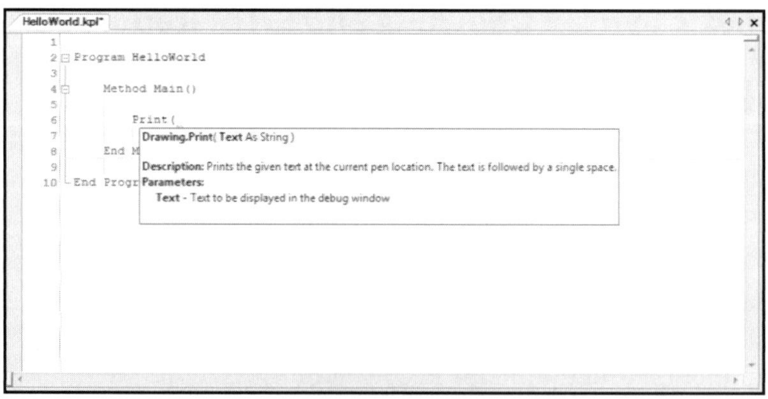


**FIGURE 2.29**

The Phrogram IDE keeps an eye on what you are doing and displays context-sensitive command information to help you properly formulate code statements.

As you can see from this example, Phrogram constantly keeps an eye on what you are doing and offers up assistance. Beginner programmers really benefit from this type of assistance. Advanced programmers do not usually require this level of assistance. As you will see as you spend more time working with Phrogram, it implements context-sensitive assisted code development in a very unobtrusive manner, which meets the needs of beginner programmers without becoming too intrusive for more advanced programmers.

**HINT** Some programming languages refer to context assisted code development as *Intellisense*. Intellisense is a feature supported by all of Microsoft's Visual Studio programming languages.

Rather than wait on Phrogram to offer up assistance when keying in your code statements, you can invoke its assistance at any time by pressing Ctrl+J or Ctrl+Space. For example, if you press Ctrl+J before typing in anything on a line, Phrogram will display a listing of all possible commands, as demonstrated in Figure 2.30.

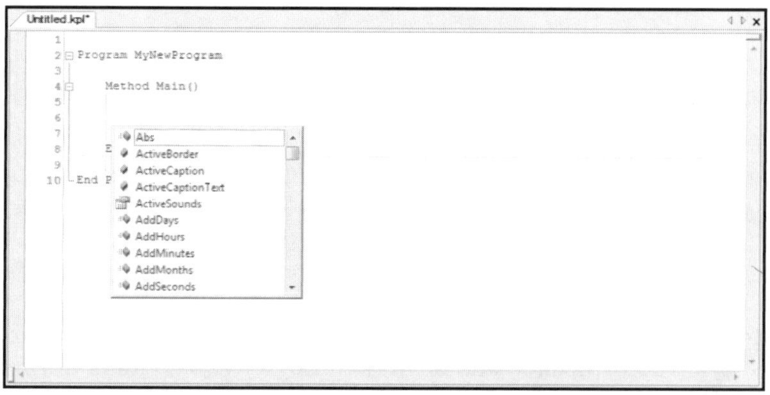


**FIGURE 2.30** You can press CTRL+J at any time to prompt Phrogram for assistance in formulating your code statements.

Once displayed, you can select any item from this resulting list in order to view a ToolTip showing its syntax, as demonstrated in Figure 2.31.

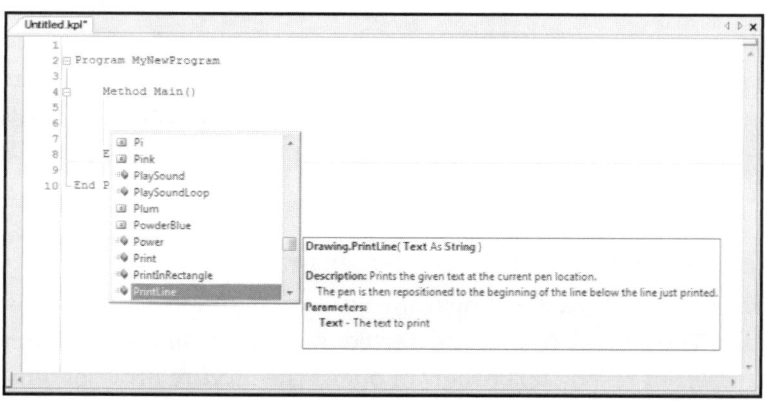


**FIGURE 2.31** Drilling down to view syntax specific to the selected item.

If you know the first few letters of the command you want to work with, you can significantly reduce the size of the list that is displayed when you invoke Phrogram assistance, as demonstrated in Figure 2.32.

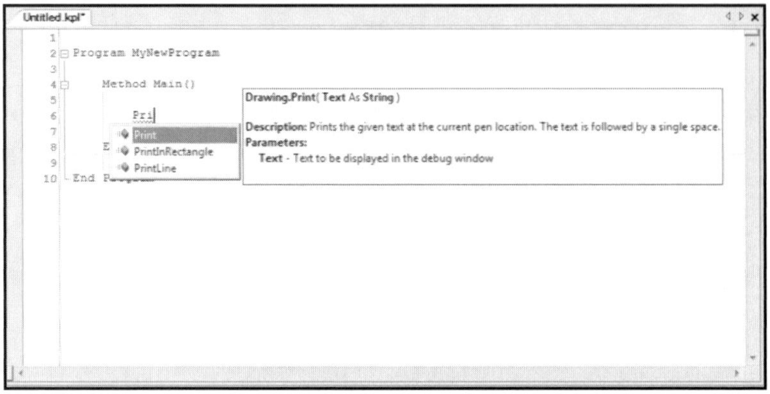


**FIGURE 2.32**

Phrogram is able to display a much more focused list of possible matching commands for you to choose from.

Here, the characters Pri were entered and then the CTRL+J command was executed. As a result, it was much easier to locate the Print command's syntax.

**FIND IT ONLINE**

This chapter has taught you a lot about the program development features provided by the Phrogram IDE. You can learn more by monitoring the posting in the Beginners Corner. Put this book down for a few minutes and visit www.phrogram.com/forums/ and browse through the Beginners Corner postings, looking for postings about the IDE. This will provide insight to the types of problems that other Phrogram programmers are running into and hopefully offer solutions for overcoming these problems.

## Working with Other Windows that Display in the Code Editor

Another trick employed by the Phrogram IDE to save space and make things easier to work with is the saving of workspace within the Code Editor, Explorer pane, and the Message pane. In addition to supporting the creation and editing of program code in the Code Editor, the Phrogram IDE also uses its space when displaying the Picture Browser window and the Class Library Browser window.

### Viewing Image Files with the Picture Browser

The Picture Browser window lets you preview the image files that you want to work with in your Phrogram applications. The Picture Browser is started by clicking on the View menu and then selecting Picture Browser. In response, Phrogram opens the Picture Browser window in the Code Editor pane, as demonstrated in Figure 2.33.

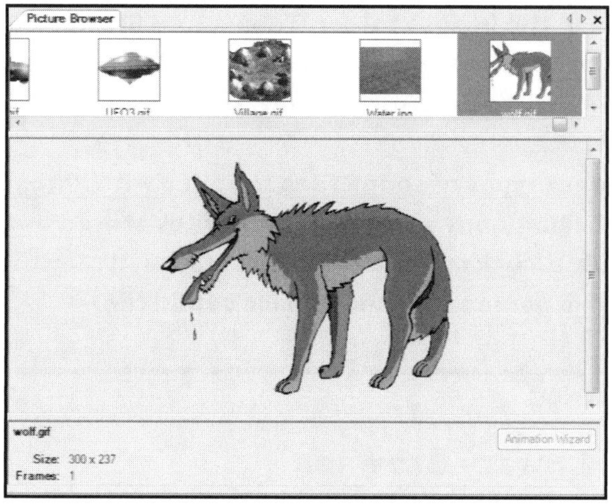


**FIGURE 2.33**

The Picture Browser lets you view all of the graphic files stored in Phrogram's Images folder.

The Picture Browser window is assigned a tab, allowing you to select it in the Code Editor. The Picture Browser window is divided into two sections. At the top of the window you will find a thumbnail view of all the image files. The bottom portion of the window is used to display the currently selected image. Use the scroll bar that separates these two portions of the window to control the view of all of the image files.

**HINT**

Phrogram can work with many different types of graphics files, including .png, gif, .jpg, and .bmp files. You can add your own graphic files to Phrogram by adding them to the Images folder, located in \My Phrogram Files\Media Files folders, which you will find inside your Documents folders.

## EXERCISES

**Phrogram comes jam-packed with tons of animation and graphic files. It also comes with many dozen audio files, all of which you can incorporate in your own Phrogram applications. You can access the media files using the Files window by drilling down in the Media files folder. Before continuing on with this chapter, spend a few minutes familiarizing yourself with the media files supplied with Phrogram by completing the following exercises.**

1. **Start Phrogram and click on the Files tab in the Explorer window. If it is not already expanded, expand the My Programs folder and then the Media Files folder. Expand both the Images and Sounds folders and briefly examine them to get a feel for the number of media files provided by Phrogram.**

2. **Double-click on an image in the Images folder. The Picture Browser window will open in the Code Editor pane and display the selected file. Using the scrollbar located at the top of the Picture Browser window, move around and randomly select a few more images.**
3. **To get a feel for the different types of sound files supplied with Phrogram, spend a few minutes double-clicking on the different .wav files stored in the Sounds folder. Each time you double-click on a .wav file, Phrogram will play the file. Also, take note of the descriptive names assigned to each sound file.**

## Working with the Class Library Browser

The Class Library Browser window provides access to a large collection of pre-written program code that you can incorporate into your Phrogram applications. The Class Library Browser is started by clicking on the View menu and then selecting Class Library Browser. In response, the Class Library Browser is displayed in the Code Editor pane, as demonstrated in Figure 2.34.

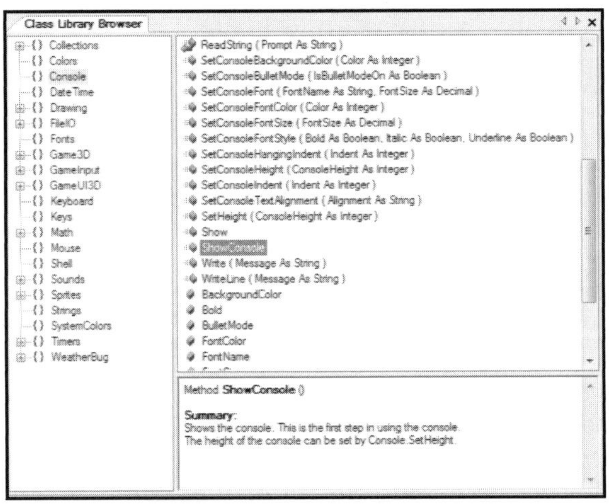


**FIGURE 2.34**

The Class Library Browser lets you browse all of Phrogram's libraries and classes.

You will find this window to be of invaluable assistance later when you learn more about object-oriented programming in Chapter 7, "Getting Comfortable with Object-Oriented Programming."

HINT

If you download and install any of the optional Phrogram add-in libraries, you will see objects provided in these libraries displayed in the Class Library Browser.

## WORKING WITH THE EXPLORER PANE

By default, the Explorer pane is displayed on the upper-right side of the Phrogram IDE. However, you can move it to another location within the IDE and pin and unpin it as you see fit. The Explorer pane's space is shared by two windows, the File and Programs windows. However, you can move windows located in the Message pane into the Explorer pane by left-clicking on the window's tab, dragging, and dropping it onto the center of the Explorer pane.

### Navigating the File Window

The File window, shown in Figure 2.35, is displayed by default in the Explorer window and shares this space with the Program window. You can switch between these two windows by clicking on their respective tabs.

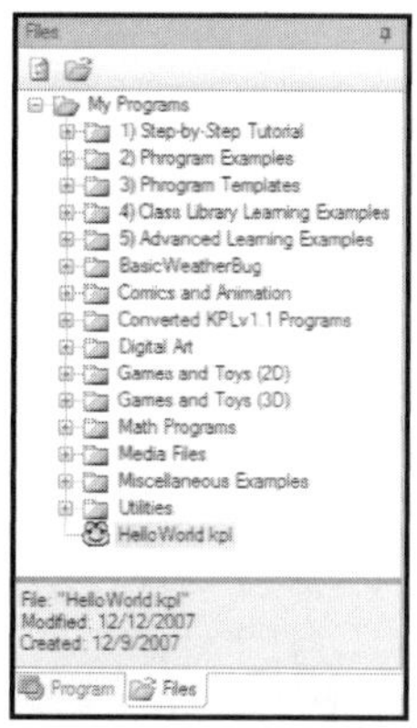


**FIGURE 2.35**

The Files view in the Explorer pane provides you with easy access to everything in My Programs.

The Files window displays a listing of all the files and folders stored in your My Phrogram Programs folder. Inside this folder, you will find a large collection of sample code, applications, graphics, and sound files and many other goodies like comics and animation programs. When you drill down into one of the subfolders shown in the files window and select a file, the file's name, modification date, and creation date are displayed at the bottom of the Explorer pane, just above the window tabs. You can open any file that you find by double-clicking on it. This gives you easy access to all of the sample code and media files shipped as part of Phrogram, as well as to any files that you have stored in the My Phrogram Programs folder.

**HINT** The My Phrogram Programs folder is stored in your My Documents folder. If you want, you can add subfolders to the My Phrogram Programs folder or any of its subfolders and use the new folder to store your own files.

## A Sneak Peak at the Program Window

The Program window, shown in Figure 2.36, provides a view of all the objects that are defined within your Phrogram application, including any object properties and methods that are in use.

**FIGURE 2.36**

The Program view in the Explorer pane displays a listing of all of the objects, methods, and properties used in your Phrogram application.

You have not learned about object-oriented programming yet. This topic is covered later in Chapter 7. So for now, you do not need to worry about the Program window or its use.

# TAKING ADVANTAGE OF THE MESSAGE PANE

The Message pane is located at the bottom of the Phrogram IDE. By default, the message pane displays the Errors window. However, if you enable the IDE's Advanced Views option, the Messages, Debug, Find in all files, References, and Notes windows will be displayed. Each of these windows is reviewed in the sections that follow.

## The Errors Window

The Errors window, shown in Figure 2.37, displays error and warning messages generated by Phrogram when you are working with the Code Editor or when you attempt to run your programs. An *error* is a problem that prevents your program from executing. A *warning* is a problem that may have a severe impact on the execution of your program.

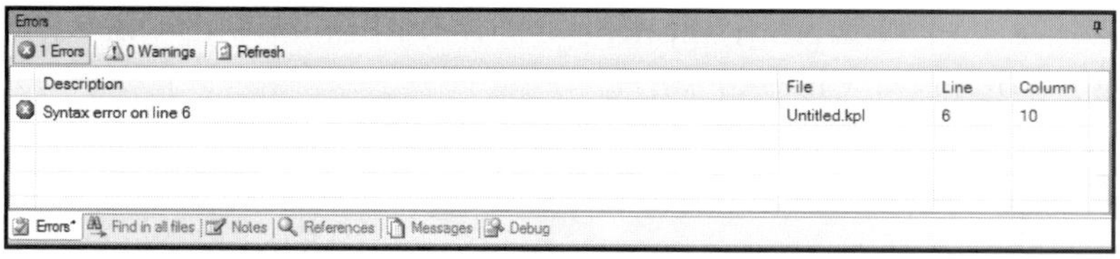


**FIGURE 2.37**

Syntax errors occur when you mistype a code statement or fail to follow Phrogram syntax rules when formulating your code statements.

When Phrogram displays an error or warning, as demonstrated in Figure 2.37, it displays a brief error message in the Errors window along with the line number of the statement where the error was detected. If you double-click on the error message, Phrogram will jump to the corresponding statement in the Code Editor, saving you the trouble of having to scroll up or down to find it in lengthy code files. Using the information provided in the error message, you can track down and fix most program errors quickly.

> **HINT** For problems that are not easily resolved, you will need to employ the debugging techniques covered in Chapter 7 to locate and fix the errors.

## The Debug Window

The Debug window, shown in Figure 2.38, is used in conjunction with Phrogram's built-in debugger. A *debugger* is a program or utility that is used to compile and execute a program within a special environment that allows the programmer to exercise detailed control over the program. Using Phrogram's debugger and the Debug window, you can visually monitor values assigned to the variables used in your applications and verify whether the values are being set properly.

> **HINT** A variable is a location in the computer's memory where your program can store data. You will learn all about variables and their usage in Chapter 3, "Learning How to Work with Data."

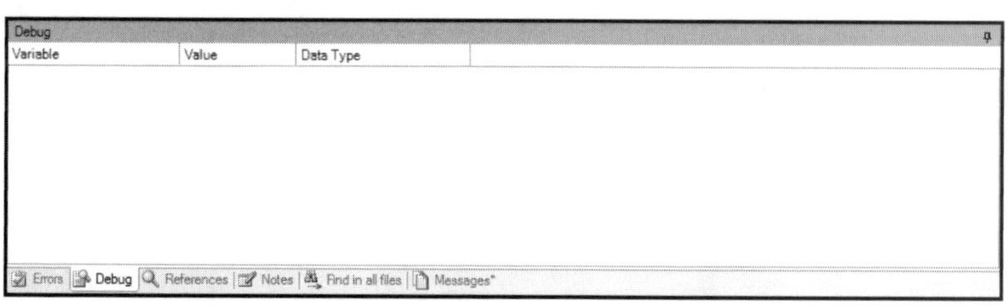


**FIGURE 2.38**

The Debug window lets you view and track the values assigned to variables when you are debugging your application.

You will learn how to debug your Phrogram applications, including how to work with the Debug window, later when you get to Chapter 10.

## The References Window

As your Phrogram applications grow in size and complexity, they will become more and more difficult to work with. As a result, working with variables spread all throughout your code files will become more challenging as well. To help make tracking down and locating all instances of a given variable easier, Phrogram provides access to the References window, which displays a list of all the variables found in all open files for a specified variable.

To take advantage of this window, right-click on a variable, select Find All References from the context menu that appears, and Phrogram will display a list showing the line number of every statement where that variable is referenced, as demonstrated in Figure 2.39.

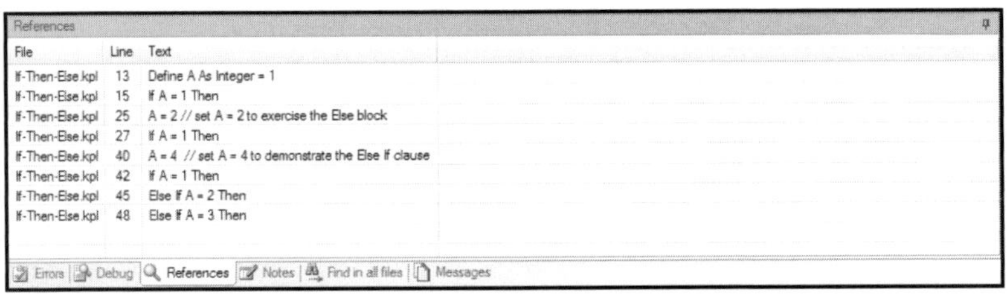


**FIGURE 2.39**

Using the References window to display a list of all the code statements containing a variable named A.

If you have more than one code file open, Phrogram will perform the reference search on every code file you are working with and will display the name of the program in which matches occur. Note that display results include the name of the code file in which matches are found as well as the line number and code statement of each match.

## The Notes Window

In addition to allowing you to embed any number of comments inside your application's code file, Phrogram also allows you to store notes about your applications or anything you wish using the Notes window. As demonstrated in Figure 2.40, you can type any amount of text in the Notes window, which acts as a simple text pad.

**FIGURE 2.40**

The Notes window provides a convenient means of storing notes within the Phrogram IDE.

You may write anything you want in the Notes window. The text that you type in the Notes window is available to you regardless of which application you may be working with and is not associated with a specific application.

## The Find in All Files Window

The Find in All Files window is designed to be used in conjunction with the Find command located on the Edit menu. When executed, the Find command displays the window shown in Figure 2.41.

**FIGURE 2.41**

Using the Find command to track down a file or folder.

To perform a normal search, enter a text string in the Find what: field and press the Find Next button. In response, Phrogram searches the current Phrogram file for the first match. If you want to perform a broader search that will include all of the .kpl source code files located in your My Phrogram Programs folder, you can select the Find in All Files option before performing your search and Phrogram will display a list of all matching instances, as demonstrated in Figure 2.42.

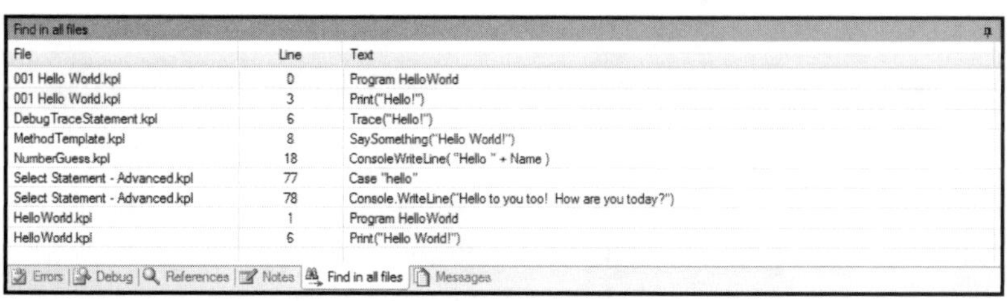


**FIGURE 2.42**

The file name, line number, and text of each code statement where a match is found is displayed when a Find operation is performed using the Find in All Files option.

## The Messages Window

The Messages window, shown in Figure 2.43, displays messages generated by Phrogram when first started as well as when you perform different actions like running your Phrogram applications. By keeping an eye on the information written to this window you can learn a lot about what Phrogram is doing behind the scenes while you are working with it.

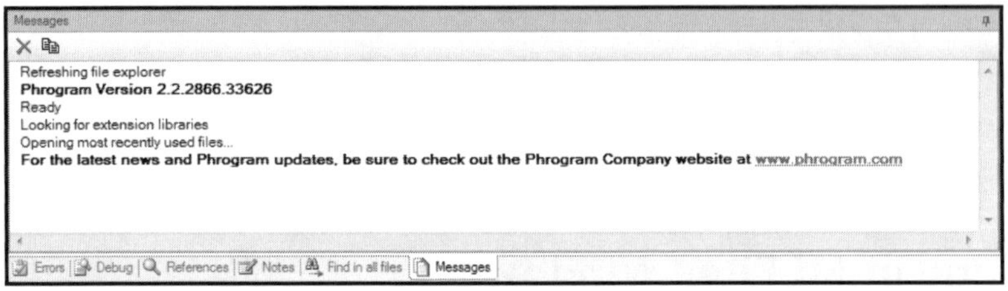


**FIGURE 2.43**

Phrogram displays messages on the Messages window whenever key events occur.

### REVIEW QUESTIONS

1. **How do you undock an IDE window? Once undocked, how to you redock a window?**
2. **What is the benefit provided by unpinning IDE panes? Which two panes can be pinned? Which pane cannot be pinned?**
3. **What types of commands are found on the IDE's `Code` menu? List each command and describe its purpose.**
4. **How are advance IDE options enabled? Once enabled, how are they disabled?**
5. **List at least five major Code Editor features.**
6. **A statement displayed in green in the Code Editor is what type of statement?**
7. **What color does the IDE use when displaying program keywords?**
8. **Identify three different ways of accessing and executing Phrogram commands.**
9. **When does the Phrogram IDE perform syntax checking?**
10. **What combination of keystrokes can be used to initiate Intellisense?**

## BACK TO THE STORY TIME GAME

Okay, now it is time to turn your attention back to the development of this chapter's main project, the Story Time game. Since this book has not provided you with a review of the statements that make up Phrogram's programming language, do not get caught up spending too much time trying to figure out what each individual statement in this program does. Instead, continue to keep your attention focused on the overall process involved in working with the Phrogram IDE.

## Designing the Game

To keep things as simple as possible, this game will be created by following a series of steps, as outlined here:

1. Create a new program.
2. Document your application.
3. Define application variables.
4. Configure the game's window.
5. Get permission to start the game.
6. Collect player input.
7. Get ready to tell the story.
8. Display the first part of the story.
9. Display the second part of the story.
10. Display the last part of the story.
11. Thank the player for playing.
12. Handle early termination of game play.
13. Save your new application.

### Step 1: Creating a New Phrogram Project

The first step in developing the Story Time application is to create a new Phrogram program. Do so by clicking on the New Program command located on the File menu. In response, a new program file will be added to the Code Editor and the following code statements will be automatically added to the file.

```
Program MyNewProgram

          Method Main()



          End Method

End Program
```

Next, assign a meaningful name to the application, by replacing `MyNewProgram` with `StoryTime` as the application's name on the first code statement. The rest of the program statements that will make up the `StoryTime` game are provided in the sections that follow. These statements should be inserted between the `Method Main()` and `End Method` statements shown above.

## Step 2: Documenting Your New Program

The next step in the development of the Story Time game is to add the following comment statements to your program's code file.

```
//Program: StoryTime.kpl
//Created: 11/24/2007
//Version: 1.0
//Author: Jerry Lee Ford, Jr.
//Description: This Phrogram game generates a mad-lib-styled story using
//             input provided by the player.
```

As you can see, these comment statements provide a little high-level documentation about the application and its purpose.

## Step 3: Defining Application Variables

The Story Time game uses information collected by the player to help tell its story. To store this information, as well as a few other pieces of data used during the execution of the game, you need to define a number of variables in which to store this data. This is accomplished by adding the following statements to the program file.

```
Define Dessert As String
Define Animal As String
Define Teacher As String
Define Toy As String
Define Reply As Boolean
Define Intro1 As String
Define Intro2 As String
```

HINT A *variable* is a pointer to a location in memory where data is stored. You will learn all about variables and how to work with them in Chapter 3, "Learning How to Work with Data."

Each of these statements should be added to the `Main()` method, just after the comment statements that you added in the previous step.

## Step 4: Configuring the Game's Window

The next set of code statements that you need to add to your new application are responsible for configuring the console settings that will control the appearance of the window in which the game is played. These statements, shown next, hide the window's toolbar, configure the window's height and width, and then display a text string of Story Time in its titlebar. The window's background color is then set to light gray and its foreground color, which will be used to display text, is set to dark blue. Next, the display of text is set to bold, the font type is set to Arial with a point size of 18, and the application window is displayed.

```
HideToolbar()
SetScreenSize (800, 600)
SetWindowTitle ("Story Time")

SetConsoleBackgroundColor(LightGray)
SetConsoleFontColor(DarkBlue)

SetConsoleFontStyle(True, False, False)
SetConsoleFont("Arial", 18)

ShowConsole()
```

Each of these statements should be added to the `Main()` method, just after the statements that you added in the previous step. Do not worry right now about what each of these code statements does. You will learn about that in later chapters. For now, just key them in as shown.

### Step 5: Inviting the Player to Play the Game

Before continuing, the game prompts the player for confirmation that she wishes to play. The player's input is then analyzed using an `If` statement code block to determine which of two possible courses of action to take. This is accomplished by adding the following statements to the `Main()` method, just after the statements that you added in the previous step.

```
Intro1 = "Welcome to the Story Time game."
Intro2 = "Would you like to play?"

Reply = Confirm(Intro1 + " " + Intro2, "Story Time")

If Reply = True Then

Else

End If
```

**HINT** The `If` statement code block shown above allows you to analyze data and then determine which of two sets of programming statements should be executed based upon that analysis. You will learn all about the `If` statement and its many variations in Chapter 4, "Making Decisions with Conditional Logic."

These statements should be added to the `Main()` method, immediately after the last set of statements that you just added.

### Step 6: Collecting Player Input

The next thing the Story Time game does is display a series of four questions, each of which prompts the player to type in a specific piece of information that the game will later use when telling its story. This is accomplished by adding the following statements to the `If` statement code block located inside the `Main()` method, immediately after the last set of statements that you just added. Specifically, these statements and all of the statements in steps 7 through 11, should be placed inside the `If` statement code block, immediately after the opening `If` statement and before the `Else` keyword.

```
Dessert = Console.ReadString("What is your favorite junk food?")
Animal = Console.ReadString("Type the name of a funny animal.")
Teacher = Console.ReadString("Who was your 3rd grade teacher?")
Toy = Console.ReadString("Type the name of your favorite toy.")
```

As you can see, the first question asked of the player is `"What is your favorite junk food?"` The player's input is stored in a variable named `Dessert`. The next three statements ask different questions and store the player's input in different variables.

### Step 7: Getting Ready to Tell the Story

Once all four questions have been answered, the window is cleared and a message is displayed informing the player that the game is ready to begin telling its story. This is accomplished by adding the following statement to the `Main()` method, just after the statements that you added in the previous step.

```
ClearConsole()

SetConsoleTextAlignment("Center")

ConsoleWriteLine("")

ConsoleWriteLine("Okay, those were great answers.")
ConsoleWriteLine("")
```

```
ConsoleWriteLine("Now press any key to begin the story!")

Console.ReadKey()
```

To continue on and begin reading the story, the player must press a key, after which the game begins to tell its story a paragraph at a time.

### Step 8: Displaying the First Part of the Story

The story's opening paragraph is displayed by the following set of programming statements, which clear the screen, left justify the display of all text, and then display the text that makes up the story. Take note that the variables used to store input previously collected from the player have been embedded within the story's text, allowing the player's input to be used as part of the story through a process known as concatenation.

HINT *Concatenation* is the process in which two text strings are added together to create a new larger string. You will learn more about concatenation in Chapter 3.

```
ClearConsole()

SetConsoleTextAlignment ("Left")

ConsoleWriteLine("")

ConsoleWrite("Once upon a time there were three " + Animal)
ConsoleWrite("s. There was a daddy " + Animal + ", a ")
ConsoleWrite("mommy " + Animal + " and a baby " + Animal)
ConsoleWrite(". One day the three " + Animal + "s returned ")
ConsoleWrite("from foraging in the forest and found their ")
ConsoleWrite("front door open. Inside, baby " + Animal)
ConsoleWrite(" immediately noticed that someone had eaten ")
ConsoleWrite("all of the " + Dessert + " from their bowls. ")
ConsoleWrite(" Baby " + Animal + " was hungry and began to ")
ConsoleWriteLine("cry.")

ConsoleWriteLine("")
ConsoleWriteLine("")
ConsoleWriteLine("Press any key to continue.")

Console.ReadKey()
```

The last text statement displayed provides instructions that tell the player to press a key on the keyboard to continue.

## Step 9: Displaying the Second Part of the Story

The next set of statements to be added to the program are nearly identical to the last set of statements. These statements display the game's second paragraph. These statements should be added to the `Main()` method, immediately after the last set of statements that you just added.

```
ClearConsole()
ConsoleWriteLine("")

ConsoleWrite("To try and make baby " + Animal + " feel ")
ConsoleWrite("better, daddy and mommy " + Animal + " took ")
ConsoleWrite("baby " + Animal + " to the family room to ")
ConsoleWrite("watch " + Teacher + " on the television. ")
ConsoleWrite("However, upon entering the room ")
ConsoleWrite("they found that someone had broken baby ")
ConsoleWrite(Animal + "'s " + toy + ". Baby ")
ConsoleWrite(Animal + " broke down into tears and could ")
ConsoleWriteLine("not stop sobbing.")

ConsoleWriteLine("")
ConsoleWriteLine("")
ConsoleWriteLine("Press any key to continue.")

Console.ReadKey()
```

## Step 10: Displaying the Final Part of the Story

The story's third and final paragraph is displayed by adding the following statements to the program file, immediately after the last set of statements that you just added.

```
ClearConsole()
ConsoleWriteLine("")

ConsoleWrite("After finally calming the young " + Animal)
ConsoleWrite(" down, daddy " + Animal + " and mommy ")
ConsoleWrite(Animal + " decided to put baby " + Animal)
ConsoleWrite(" to bed. However, upon ")
```

```
ConsoleWrite("reaching their bedroom, they found that ")
ConsoleWrite("someone was already sleeping in their bed. ")
ConsoleWrite("That night all three " + Animal + "s slept ")
ConsoleWrite("well. While baby " + Animal + "'s toy was ")
ConsoleWrite("still broken everyone's tummies were now full ")
ConsoleWrite("and no one in the forest ever dared enter ")
ConsoleWrite("the " + Animal + "'s house again.")

ConsoleWriteLine("")
ConsoleWriteLine("")
ConsoleWriteLine("THE END")

ConsoleWriteLine("")
ConsoleWriteLine("")
ConsoleWriteLine("Press any key to continue.")

Console.ReadKey()
```

As you can see, except for the text representing the story, these statements are identical to those that you added in the previous section.

### Step 11: Thanking the Player

Once the story's final paragraph has been displayed, and the player has read it and pressed a keyboard key, the screen is cleared and a message is displayed thanking the player for taking time to play the game. This is accomplished by adding the following statements to the program file, immediately after the last set of statements that you just added.

```
ClearConsole()
ConsoleWriteLine("")

SetConsoleTextAlignment ("Center")

ConsoleWriteLine("Thank you for playing the Story Time game!")

Delay(3000)
```

The last statement uses the `Delay` command to pause program execution for three seconds, after which the game's window closes and the game's execution terminates.

### Step 12: Handling Early Termination

The last statement to be added to the Story Time game is shown next. This statement is executed only in the event that the player decides not to play the game when prompted for confirmation back in step 5. Its purpose is to display a message in a popup dialog window that asks the player to consider returning to play the game another time.

```
Alert("OK. Perhaps another time.", "Story Time")
```

This statement should be placed inside the game's `If` statement code block. Specifically, this statement should be inserted after the `Else` keyword and before the closing `End If` statement.

### Step 13: Saving Your Application

At this point, your copy of the Story Time game should be complete. If you have not already done so, save your new program file by clicking on the Save All command located on the File menu. Take a moment to check the Errors window located on the Message pane to see if Phrogram has flagged any syntax errors. If it has, use the information provided in the error message(s) to track down and correct each error.

## The Final Result

Once you have finished keying in the application's program statements and eliminated any syntax errors that you may have accidentally made, compile and run the game by clicking on the Run the Program button on the IDE toolbar. In the event that you run into any errors when trying to run your program, you will need to track down and eliminate your mistakes. To help make sure that things are as clear as possible, a complete copy of the Story Time game is provided next. This copy of the game has been enhanced through the addition of comment statements that provide detailed information about what is going on throughout the code file.

```
//Program: StoryTime.kpl
//Created: 11/24/2007
//Version: 1.0
//Author: Jerry Lee Ford, Jr.
//Description: This Phrogram game generates a mad-lib-styled story using
//             input provided by the player.

Program StoryTime

    Method Main()

        //Define the variables used throughout the program to store data
```

```
Define Dessert As String
Define Animal As String
Define Teacher As String
Define Toy As String
Define Reply As Boolean
Define Intro1 As String
Define Intro2 As String

HideToolbar()   //Prevent the window's toolbar from being displayed
SetScreenSize (800, 600)    //Set the screen size to 800x600 pixels
SetWindowTitle ("Story Time")        //Display the name of the game
                                     //in the Window's titlebar

SetConsoleBackgroundColor(LightGray)        //Set background color
SetConsoleFontColor(DarkBlue)               //Set font color

// Set console font style to Bold, non-italic and non-underline
SetConsoleFontStyle(True, False, False)
SetConsoleFont("Arial", 18)          // Set font to Arial, point 18

ShowConsole()    //Display the console

//Outline the text of the game's welcome message
Intro1 = "Welcome to the Story Time game."
Intro2 = "Would you like to play?"

//Display the game's welcome message in a popup dialog window and
//prompt the player to click on Yes to play the game or No to quit
Reply = Confirm(Intro1 + " " + Intro2, "Story Time")

//Analyze the player's response
If Reply = True Then               //If Reply equals true then the
                                   //player clicked on the Yes button

    //Prompt the player to answer four questions and store each
    //answer in a separate variable
    Dessert = Console.ReadString("What is your favorite junk food?")
    Animal = Console.ReadString("Type the name of a funny animal.")
```

```
Teacher = Console.ReadString("Who was your 3rd grade teacher?")
Toy = Console.ReadString("Type the name of your favorite toy.")

ClearConsole()   //Clear the console

//Set text alignment to center
SetConsoleTextAlignment("Center")

ConsoleWriteLine("")  //Write a blank line on the console

//Let the player know that it is ready to tell the story
ConsoleWriteLine("Okay, those were great answers.")
ConsoleWriteLine("")
ConsoleWriteLine("Now press any key to begin the story!")

Console.ReadKey()    //Wait for the player to press a key

ClearConsole()       //Clear the console

SetConsoleTextAlignment ("Left")   //Set text alignment to left

ConsoleWriteLine("")  //Write a blank line on the console

//Display the game's first paragraph substituting the player's
//input throughout the story
ConsoleWrite("Once upon a time there were three " + Animal)
ConsoleWrite("s. There was a daddy " + Animal + ", a ")
ConsoleWrite("mommy " + Animal + " and a baby " + Animal)
ConsoleWrite(". One day the three " + Animal + "s returned ")
ConsoleWrite("from foraging in the forest and found their ")
ConsoleWrite("front door open. Inside, baby " + Animal)
ConsoleWrite(" immediately noticed that someone had eaten ")
ConsoleWrite("all of the " + Dessert + " from their bowls. ")
ConsoleWrite(" Baby " + Animal + " was hungry and began to ")
ConsoleWriteLine("cry.")

ConsoleWriteLine("")  //Write a blank line on the console
ConsoleWriteLine("")  //Write a blank line on the console
```

```
ConsoleWriteLine("Press any key to continue.")

Console.ReadKey()    //Wait for the player to press a key

ClearConsole()        //Clear the console
ConsoleWriteLine("")  //Write a blank line on the console

//Display the game's second paragraph substituting the
//player's input throughout the story
ConsoleWrite("To try and make baby " + Animal + " feel ")
ConsoleWrite("better, daddy and mommy " + Animal + " took ")
ConsoleWrite("baby " + Animal + " to the family room to ")
ConsoleWrite("watch " + Teacher + " on the television. ")
ConsoleWrite("However, upon entering the room ")
ConsoleWrite("they found that someone had broken baby ")
ConsoleWrite(Animal + "'s " + toy + ". Baby ")
ConsoleWrite(Animal + " broke down into tears and could ")
ConsoleWriteLine("not stop sobbing.")

ConsoleWriteLine("")  //Write a blank line on the console
ConsoleWriteLine("")  //Write a blank line on the console
ConsoleWriteLine("Press any key to continue.")

Console.ReadKey()    //Wait for the player to press a key

ClearConsole()        //Clear the console
ConsoleWriteLine("")  //Write a blank line on the console

//Display the game's final paragraph substituting the
//player's input throughout the story
ConsoleWrite("After finally calming the young " + Animal)
ConsoleWrite(" down, daddy " + Animal + " and mommy ")
ConsoleWrite(Animal + " decided to put baby " + Animal)
ConsoleWrite(" to bed. However, upon ")
ConsoleWrite("reaching their bedroom, they found that ")
ConsoleWrite("someone was already sleeping in their bed. ")
ConsoleWrite("That night all three " + Animal + "s slept ")
ConsoleWrite("well. While baby " + Animal + "'s toy was ")
```

```
        ConsoleWrite("still broken everyone's tummies were now full ")
        ConsoleWrite("and no one in the forest ever dared enter ")
        ConsoleWrite("the " + Animal + "'s house again.")

        ConsoleWriteLine("")  //Write a blank line on the console
        ConsoleWriteLine("")  //Write a blank line on the console
        ConsoleWriteLine("THE END")

        ConsoleWriteLine("")  //Write a blank line on the console
        ConsoleWriteLine("")  //Write a blank line on the console
        ConsoleWriteLine("Press any key to continue.")

        Console.ReadKey()    //Wait for the player to press a key

        ClearConsole()       //Clear the console
        ConsoleWriteLine("")  //Write a blank line on the console

        //Set text alignment to center
        SetConsoleTextAlignment ("Center")

        //Display a message thanking the player for playing the game
        ConsoleWriteLine("Thank you for playing the Story Time game!")

        Delay(3000)   //Wait 3 seconds before allowing the game to end

      Else    //Execute the following statements when the player clicks
              //on the No button

        //Display a message in a popup window inviting the player to
        //play again another time
        Alert("OK. Perhaps another time.", "Story Time")

      End If

   End Method

End Program
```

Assuming that you followed along carefully with the instructions presented in this chapter, your copy of the Story Time game should run exactly as described at the beginning of this chapter. However, if you run into any errors when you try to execute your new game, you can use this fully assembled copy of the game's source code file to compare against in order to track down and eliminate your errors.

HINT You will also find a copy of this application's source code file on the book's companion CD.

## Summary

In this chapter, you learned the ins and outs of working with the Phrogram IDE. You learned how to reconfigure the layout of the IDE to suit your personal preferences and to work more efficiently with the IDE's Code Editor. This included learning how to split the editor's work space into two parts, how to access different contextual menus, and how to use the Code Editor to display other IDE windows. You learned all about each of the Phrogram IDE menu and toolbar commands. You also learned how to work with many of the windows that are displayed in the Explorer and Message panes.

Before you move on to Chapter 3, consider spending a little time improving the Story Time game by addressing the following list of challenges.

### Challenges

1. **As currently written, the Story Time game's story is only a few paragraphs long. Consider expanding the story's dialogue to make it longer and more interesting.**
2. **Currently, the Story Time game collects four pieces of information from the user. Consider reviewing the game once you have expanded it and look for other opportunities to collect and include player input.**
3. **Consider expanding on the information displayed on the game's final screen by including your URL or any other information that will help to associate you with your new application.**
4. **Create a distribution package for your new game and share with a few friends, asking them to provide you with feedback.**

# Part II

## Learning How to Write Phrogram Programs

CHAPTER 3

# Learning How to Work with Data

The Phrogram programming language is designed to be easy to learn. It consists of a small collection of descriptive keywords whose syntax has been kept as simple and straightforward as possible to ensure that Phrogram meets the needs of first-time programmers. This is the first of four chapters whose purpose is to teach you the basics of Phrogram programming and language syntax. In this chapter, you will learn how to create and store data during application execution as well as how to later retrieve and process that data. This chapter also reviews a number of key programming statements that you have worked with in previous chapters when interacting with the application window and controlling its appearance and functionality. On top of all this, you will learn how to create your next Phrogram application, the Number Guessing game.

Specifically, you will learn:

- How to create and store individual pieces of data using variables
- How to use constants to store data that does not change during program execution
- How to store groups of related data in arrays and structures
- How to work with methods that facilitate string and numeric operations
- More about the program statements you have been using to control and interact with application windows

## Project Preview: The Number Guessing Game

This chapter's game project is the Number Guessing game, which challenges the player to guess a randomly generated number from 1 to 100 in as few guesses as possible. This game will further reinforce your understanding of how to work with variables. Variables are used to store the player's response when prompted to play the game, store player guesses, keep track of the number of guesses that have been made, and to keep track of the game's randomly generated number. This Phrogram game also demonstrates how to generate random numbers, which is an important feature used in many computer games as a means of introducing random events to which the player must react.

The Number Guessing game begins by displaying a welcome message and prompting the player for permission to begin a new game, as shown in Figure 3.1.

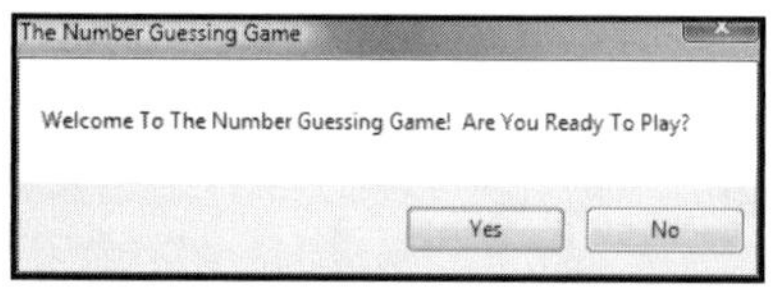


**Figure 3.1**

The Number Guessing game welcomes the player and waits for the player's response.

Figure 3.2 shows the popup dialog window that is displayed in the event the player decides not to play the game.

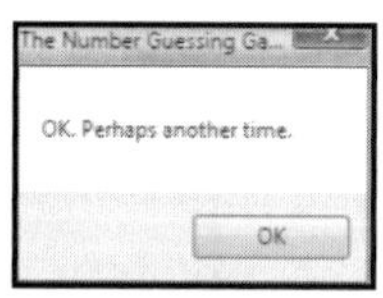


**Figure 3.2**

The player is encouraged to return and play another time.

If, on the other hand, the player elects to play the game, the window shown in Figure 3.3 is displayed, prompting the player to make an initial guess.

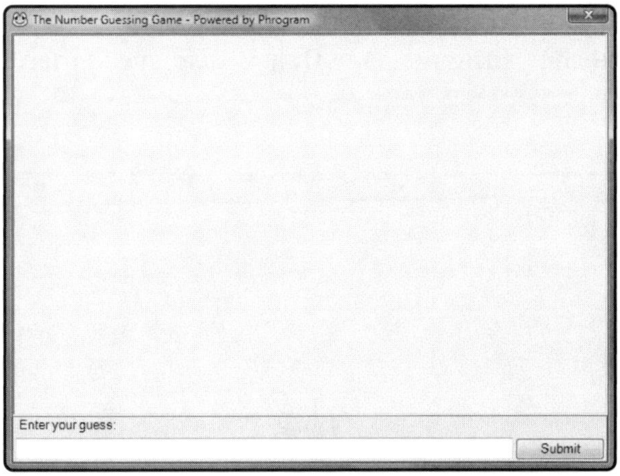


**FIGURE 3.3**
The player is prompted to enter a guess.

The game is designed to only accept numeric input. If the player attempts to press any non-numeric data, it is ignored by the game. The game also prevents the player from pressing the Enter key without first typing in a numeric guess. Any attempt to do so results in the display of the popup dialog window shown in Figure 3.4.

**FIGURE 3.4**
The game prevents the player from pressing the Enter key without first entering a guess.

The Number Guessing game also checks the value of the numeric input provided by the player to ensure that it is valid. Specifically, the game checks to make sure that the player's guess is in the range of 1 to 100. If the player attempts to enter a value that falls outside of this range, the popup dialog window shown in Figure 3.5 displays.

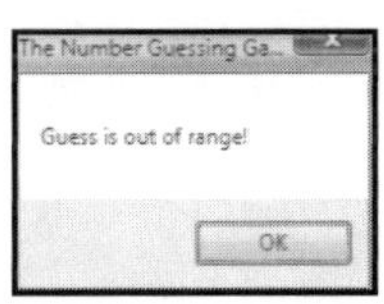


**FIGURE 3.5**
The game validates the player's input to ensure that it falls within the range of 1 to 100.

Valid guesses are analyzed and the result of the player's guess is displayed on the game's main window. For example, Figure 3.6 shows the message that is displayed when the player has submitted a guess that is too low.

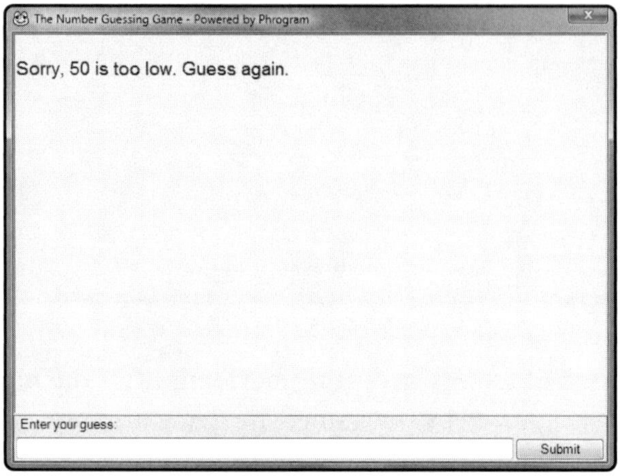


**FIGURE 3.6**
The player's guess is too low.

Figure 3.7 shows another example of a missed guess. This time the player has submitted a guess that was too high.

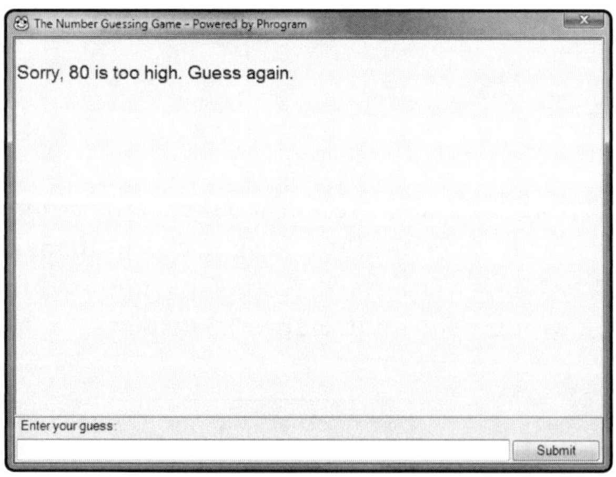


**FIGURE 3.7**
The player's guess is too high.

There is no limit to the number of guesses that the player can make. Using the information provided by the game, the player can gradually home in on the game's secret number. Figure 3.8 shows an example of the message that is displayed once the player finally guesses the game's secret number.

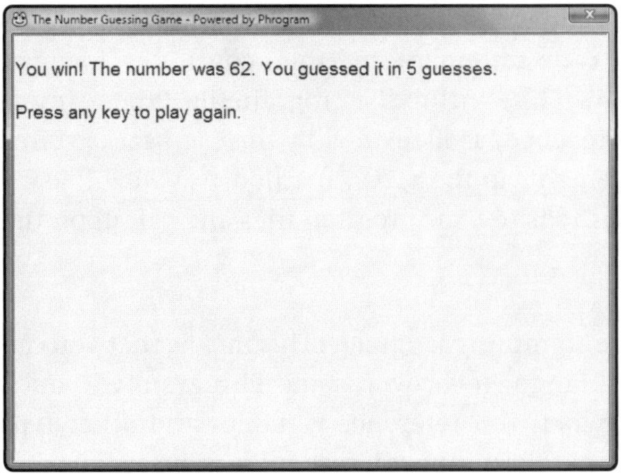


**FIGURE 3.8**

The player guessed the secret number in five guesses.

As you can see, the game displays the secret number and the total number of guesses that it took for the player to guess it. The player is then prompted to play another game by pressing any key. The player may play as many games as desired and may terminate game play at any time by clicking on the close button located in the upper-right corner of the game window.

## More Phrogram Programming Language Basics

As you already know, all new Phrogram programs begin with the four statements shown next. The first and last statements identify the beginning of the code file and the program's name. The last statement identifies the end of the program. The code statements that make up the program file reside within these two statements.

```
Program MyNewProgram

    Method Main()



    End Method

End Program
```

As you will learn in Chapter 7, "Getting Comfortable with Object-Oriented Programming," Phrogram is an object-oriented programming language. Phrogram programs interact with objects and execute methods associated with those objects. Every Phrogram program contains at least one method named `Main()`. When executed, Phrogram begins program execution starting with the first code statement in the `Main()` method. Within the `Main()` method, processing begins with the first code statement and then continues downward. Each code statement must be placed on its own line within the program file. Processing continues until the end of the `Main()` method is reached, as identified by the `End Method` statement. You can include any number of code statements in the `Main()` method. As you will learn in Chapter 7, you can create and add other methods to your program files and call upon them to execute.

## Case Sensitivity

Phrogram is a case-insensitive programming language. This means that you can use any form of capitalization when keying in language keywords and Phrogram will automatically recognize it. This also means that when you reference variables and other types of program identifiers within your applications, Phrogram will recognize them as long as you spell them correctly. Any identifier is a named resource within a program file. Examples of identifiers include variable, array, structure, and method names.

## Understanding Statement Syntax

Like all programming languages, Phrogram's programming languages require that you follow a very strict set of rules, referred to as syntax, when formulating code statements. Any deviation from its syntax will result in an error. As you work your way through the rest of this book, you will be introduced to many Phrogram keywords that make up the programming language. Phrogram provides a specific syntax for each of these keywords. In addition, Phrogram enforces a strict object-oriented syntax that you will have to follow. As you make your way through this book, you will receive specific instruction on the proper application of Phrogram programming language syntax.

## Multi-line Comments

One of the most important habits to get into when just starting out as a new programmer is to remember to document your new programs by embedding comment statements in them. Back in Chapter 1 you learned that you can add comments to your Phrogram applications by preceding them with // characters. Comments can be appended to the end of other code statements or can be placed on lines by themselves, as demonstrated here:

```
//Program: StoryTime.kpl
//Created: 11/24/2007
//Version: 1.0
//Author: Jerry Lee Ford, Jr.
//Description: This Phrogram game generates a mad-lib style story using
//             input provided by the player.
```

Phrogram supports a second type of comment known as a block comment. Using block comments, you can easily create multi-line comments. Block comments begin with the /* characters and end with the */ characters. Anything in between these characters is treated by Phrogram as a comment, as demonstrated here:

```
/*
Program: StoryTime.kpl
Created: 11/24/2007
Version: 1.0
Author: Jerry Lee Ford, Jr.
Description: This Phrogram game generates a mad-lib style story using
             input provided by the player.
*/
```

> **TRICK** You can use the Comment command to comment any selected code statements and the Remove Comments command to uncomment any selected code statements. Both of these commands are located on the Code menu.

## Storing and Processing Program Data

All computer applications require data in order to run. *Data* represents a piece of information that your Phrogram applications collect, store, modify, and process when executing. Applications get access to data in a variety of different ways. For starters, the data may be embedded directly within program code. Take for example, the HelloWorld.kpl application that you created in Chapter 1. When executed, this application displays a string containing embedded text (e.g., the data with which the application worked).

Applications can also retrieve data from files stored on the computer or on network drives. They may also access databases where data is stored. Financial applications may retrieve data and time data from the system clock in order to create date/time stamped records. Data can also be collected interactively from users. For example, interactive computer games collect moves and input from the player when executing. An arcade-style game might depend on data supplied to the application through a joystick, for example.

Once a computer program has retrieved data, it needs a place to store it while working with it, which it does by storing it in computer memory. The memory location where individual pieces of data are stored is referred to as an address. To retrieve data, applications must refer to the memory address where the data is stored. Like other modern programming languages, Phrogram simplifies the process of storing and retrieving data from memory by allowing you to create and associate data with constants, variables, arrays, and structures. For example, to store an individual piece of data in a Phrogram program, all you have to do is create a variable and assign the data to it, and Phrogram will handle its storage in memory for you. Later, when you need to access the data and work with it again, all you have to do is reference the name of the variable in which it is stored and Phrogram will automatically retrieve the data from memory for you.

## Working with Different Types of Data

Like many programming languages, Phrogram supports the use of many different types of data. This is important because different types of data must be treated differently. For example, with numeric data, you can perform addition, subtraction, multiplication, and division. However, the operations do not apply to other types of data. These types of operations cannot be applied to text data. Text is a type of string data. Strings can be merged or concatenated together to create a new, larger string. You cannot do this with numeric data.

Data type specification also influences how efficiently data is stored in computer memory. While Phrogram supports different numeric data types, each data type is designed to handle different ranges and types of numbers, each of which requires a different amount of memory. By properly specifying numeric data type, you help ensure that your applications don't waste computer memory.

Since different types of data are subject to different types of processing, specification of data type also places limits on the types of things that your applications can do with the data that it processes. Phrogram will allow you to subtract one number from another number. However, if you attempt to subtract one string from another string, you will get an error.

The following list outlines the different data types supported by Phrogram.

- **String.** A set of characters enclosed in double quotation marks.
- **Boolean.** A Boolean value of either `True` or `False`.
- **Decimal.** A floating point or real number in the range of −79,228,162,514,264,337,593, 543,950,335 to 79,228,162,514,264,337,593,543,950,335.
- **Integer.** An absolute or whole number in the range of −2,147,483,648 to 2,147,483,647.

HINT Phrogram supports the use of decimal numbers with a decimal precision of up to 28 digits. For example, Phrogram is capable of recognizing a positive non-zero value as small as .0000000000000000000000000001.

Phrogram requires that you specify the data type whenever you need to define and work with data collected by your programs. As such, you will see numerous examples of different data type declarations throughout this chapter as you learn how to store data in your Phrogram applications.

HINT Many programming languages, like Microsoft Visual Basic, support a larger range of data types.

## Options for Storing Data

Like all other programming languages, Phrogram provides a number of different ways of storing data in memory when your applications execute. In addition to providing you with different ways of storing individual pieces of data, Phrogram recognizes that certain types of data are related and offers different ways of storing collections of related data as a single unit. A list of the different ways to store individual and collections of data is provided here:

- Constants
- Variables
- Arrays
- Structures
- Classes

Each of the above storage options has its own unique characteristics and is best suited to specific types of situations. *Constants* represent data whose value is known at development and whose value never changes. *Variables* represent data whose value may change during the execution of an application. *Arrays* are collections of related data, such as a list of customer names, which are stored and processed as a unit. *Structures* are custom-defined collections of variables, such as individual's names, addresses, and phone numbers, which can be managed together as a unit. *Classes* represent an object-oriented programming construct that you will learn about in Chapter 7.

# Storing Data That Never Changes in Constants

A *constant* is the name assigned to a value that does not change during the execution of an application. Constants are used in situations where you need to work with a value that you know will never change. For example, pi is a commonly used mathematical constant used in scientific and mathematical applications. Since the value of pi is unvarying, it is a good candidate for assignment to a constant. Once defined, you can reference the value of a constant from anywhere within an application where it has been defined.

## Predefined Phrogram Constants

To help make things easier on you, Phrogram comes with a number of predefined constants that you can reference from within your applications without having to formally define them.

For example, Table 3.1 provides a listing of mathematical constants that are provided by Phrogram's `Math` library.

**Table 3.1 Mathematical Constants Provided by the Math Library**

| Key | Description |
|---|---|
| Degrees | An integer value of 1, representing an angle measurement unit in degrees. |
| E | A decimal value of the number e (2.71828). |
| Epsilon | A decimal value of 4.94066e-324. |
| Pi | A decimal value of Pi (3.14159...). |
| Radians | An integer value of 1, representing an angle of measurement in radians. |

Phrogram supplies many different collections of constants that you can reference when needed. For example, later in this chapter you will learn about collections of color and font constants that you can use when working with application console windows.

## Creating Custom-Defined Constants

In addition to referencing Phrogram's internal collections of constants, you can define your own custom constants using the `Constant` keyword, which has the following syntax.

```
Constant ConstantName As DataType = Value
```

*ConstantName* represents the name that you are defining. *DataType* specifies the type of data that the constant will store, and *Value* represents the data being stored. To better understand how to define a constant, look at the following example.

```
Constant cWinningScore As Integer = 1000000
```

Here, a constant named `cWinningScore` has been defined as an integer and assigned a value of 1000000. This value might be added to a computer game to indicate the score required for the player to win and could be referenced during game play to determine if the player has won. Following along with this line of thought, you might also define additional constants that are referenced throughout game play to determine when the player has earned an extra life or space ship (in a first-person shooter game), as demonstrated here:

```
Constant cFirstExtraShip As Integer = 10000
Constant cSecondExtraShip As Integer = 100000
```

**HINT** Take note of the names assigned to the constants shown above. Each constant name consists of descriptive words and each word begins with a capital letter followed by all lowercase letters. This naming convention is referred to as *camel case*, and as you can see, applying this naming convention to constant names helps to make them more descriptive and easier to identify. Further, note that each constant name begins with a lowercase letter c, which is added to make it obvious that they are constants.

By assigning a value to a constant instead of to a variable, as described a little later in this chapter, you eliminate any possibility that the data might be accidentally modified during application execution. You also end up with more efficient program code because constants generally require less memory than variables. Constants also make your program code easier to read and understand. For example, instead of having to embed the number 3.14159 over and over again throughout a mathematical program, you could instead refer to pi, which is a far more intuitive indicator of the value being used.

## Placement of Constants

In Phrogram, constants are global, meaning that they can be accessed from any location within the application. As such, constants must be defined at the top of the code file, after the opening Program statement and before the `Main()` method, as demonstrated here:

```
Program SpaceBattle

    Constant cWinningScore As Integer = 1000000
    Constant cExtraShip As Integer = 10000
    Constant cExtraShip As Integer = 100000

        Method Main()

            //Program code statements go here

        End Method

End Program
```

**TRAP** If you attempt to change a constant's value, you will receive an error message stating that the constant is read-only.

You will get the chance to work with constants again later in this chapter when you work on the Number Guessing game.

## Saving Individual Pieces of Data in Variables

Any time you have data to work with and modify, you need a way of storing and keeping track of it. In Phrogram as in other programming languages, this is accomplished by storing the data in variables. A *variable* is a pointer to a location in memory where a value is stored. Some programming languages make variable declaration optional. However, in Phrogram, all variables must be explicitly declared. This is done using the `Define` keyword and the following syntax.

```
Define VariableName As DataType [= Value]
```

*`VariableName`* is a placeholder representing the name of the variable that is being declared. *`DataType`* specifies the type of data that will be stored in the variable. As previously stated, Phrogram supports four different data types, including string, Boolean, decimal, and integer. *`Value`* is optional; when specified, it represents the value assigned to the variable. Note that the equals (=) assignment operator is required when assigned a value to a variable that is being defined.

HINT Variables are sometimes referred to as identifiers in Phrogram's official documentation.

## Defining and Assigning Data to Variables

To better understand how to work with variables, let's look at a few examples.

```
Define StoryIntro As String
StoryIntro = "Once upon a time there was a big bad wolf…"
```

Here, a variable name `StoryIntro` has been defined and assigned a data type of string. Next, a text string value (enclosed in matching double quotation marks) is assigned to `StoryIntro`. Because a variable's value can be modified, you could change the text string assigned to `StoryIntro`, as demonstrated here:

```
Define StoryIntro As String = "Once upon a time there was a big bad wolf…"
```

The following example demonstrates how to define and assign values at the same time.

```
Define x As Integer = 100
Define y As Integer = 0
Define z As Integer = -100
```

Here, three integer variables have been defined and assigned initial values. Integer variables are great for situations in which you need to work with whole numbers. However, if you need to work with real numbers, then you will need to define the variables with a data type of decimal, as demonstrated here:

```
Define x As Decimal = 100.1
Define y As Decimal = 79228162514264337593543950335.0
Define z As Decimal = -79228162514264337593543950335.0
```

In this final example, a Boolean variable is defined and assigned a default value of True.

```
Define PlayerReply As Boolean = True
```

HINT Variables are also used when working with objects (as object variables), which you will learn about in Chapter 7.

## Rules for Naming Variables

Phrogram variable names can be of any length. However, you will find that short, descriptive variables names work best. Like all programming languages, Phrogram has a few rules that must be followed when creating variable names in order to prevent errors from occurring. These rules are outlined here:

- Variable names must begin with a letter or the underscore character.
- Variable names can only consist of letters, numbers, and the underscore characters.
- Variable names cannot include blank spaces.
- Variable names cannot be Phrogram language keywords.

The following list provides examples of valid variable names.

- TotalScore
- Total_Score
- _Total_Scrore

In contrast, the following list provides examples of invalid variable names.

- Total Score
- Total-Score
- 123_And_Counting

The first variable name listed above is invalid because it includes a blank space. The second variable name is invalid because it includes an invalid (-) character. The third variable is invalid because it begins with a number.

Unlike many programming languages, Phrogram is case-insensitive. As a result, differences in capitalization do not bother it. As a result, from Phrogram's point of view, all of the following variable names are equivalent.

- totalscore
- TotalScore
- TOTALSCORE
- ToTaLScOrE

HINT As with constants, make sure you assign descriptive names to your variables to make them easier to identify and to help make your program code self-documenting.

## Understanding Variable Scope

An important concept for you to understand when working with variables is that of scope. The term *scope* refers to the area within an application where a variable can be accessed. Phrogram supports three different types of variable scope, as outlined here:

- **Global.** Variables defined within the Program code block. These variables are accessible from any location within a program file.
- **Method.** Variables that are defined within a method or its parameter lists. These variables are accessible only within the methods where they are defined.
- **Class.** Variables defined within a class block. These variables are accessible only within the class where they are defined.

You will learn more about class scope in Chapter 7.

### Defining Global Variables

Variables with a global scope can be accessed from any location within the program file where they are defined. To set up global variables, place the definition statement for the variable at the top of the program file, immediately after the opening program statement, before the `Main()` methods, as demonstrated here:

```
Program SpaceBattle

    Define ApplicationName As String = "Space Battle"
```

```
    Method Main()

        //Program code statements go here

    End Method

End Program
```

Here a variable named `ApplicationName` has been defined and made global in scope, allowing it to be accessed from anywhere within the program file.

## Defining Method Variables

Access to variables with a method scope is limited to the methods in which they are defined. As such, variables defined within the Main() method can only be accessed within that method, as demonstrated here:

```
Program SpaceBattle

    Method Main()

        Define ApplicationName As String = "Space Battle"

        //Program code statements go here

    End Method

End Program
```

Because a method variable is only accessible within the method in which it is defined, it cannot be referenced from other methods. As such, you can define variables with the same name in different methods and Phrogram will treat them as different variables.

HINT

It is considered a good programming practice to limit the scope of variables as much as possible. As such, you should use method variables in place of global variables whenever possible. This conserves memory by shortening the variable's life span and eliminates any chance of accidentally modifying a variable's value from somewhere outside the method (which can happen with global variables).

## Working with String Data and Variables

Phrogram provides many different ways of manipulating and processing the contents of string variables. This includes concatenating them to create larger strings as well as a host of built-in string manipulation methods provided by the Phrogram `Strings` library.

### Concatenating Strings

*Concatenation* is the process of joining together two or more strings to create a new larger string. In Phrogram, concatenation is performed using the + operator as demonstrated here:

```
Intro1 = "Welcome to the Story Time game."
Intro2 = "Would you like to play?"

Print(Intro1 + " " + Intro2)
```

Here, two string variables have been defined. These two string variables are then concatenated, along with a third empty string, and displayed using the `Print method`.

### Taking Advantage of String Methods

Like most programming languages, Phrogram provides programmers with access to a prebuilt collection of methods, each of which is designed to perform a specific type of operation on a string. For example, Program provides methods that you can use to search strings, extract portions of string, and convert string characters from lowercase to uppercase and vice versa. A list of these string manipulation methods is provided next.

HINT Program's string methods are provided by its `Strings` library. You will learn more about Phrogram libraries and classes in Chapter 7.

- `Compare()`. Performs a comparison of two strings.
- `EndsWith()`. Determines if the end of a string matches a specified pattern.
- `Equals()`. Determines if two strings are equal.
- `FormatString()`. Replaces specified matching text within a string.
- `IndexOf()`. Finds a pattern within a specified string.
- `Insert()`. Inserts a text inside a string.
- `LastIndexOf()`. Finds the last occurrence of one string within another string.
- `Length()`. Returns a string's length.
- `PadLeft()`. Appends specified characters to the beginning of a string.

- `PadRight()`. Appends specified characters to the end of a string.
- `Remove()`. Deletes specified characters from a string.
- `Repeat()`. Creates a new string made up of a repeated set of characters.
- `Replace()`. Replaces a specified part of a string.
- `Split()`. Converts a string into a string array.
- `StartsWith()`. Determines if a string begins with a specified pattern.
- `SubString()`. Retrieves a portion of a string.
- `ToLowerCase()`. Converts and returns a string in all lowercase characters.
- `ToUpperCase()`.Converts and returns a string in all uppercase characters.
- `Trim()`. Removes blank spaces from the beginning and ending of a string.

The following example demonstrates how to work with several of the methods listed above.

```
Define Message As String = "   In the end there can be only one.   "

ConsoleWriteLine(Length(Message))
ConsoleWriteLine(ToLowerCase(Message))
ConsoleWriteLine(ToUpperCase(Message))
ConsoleWriteLine(Trim(Message))
```

Here, a string variable named `Message` is defined and assigned a text string. The text string begins and ends with three blank spaces. Next, the `Length` of the string stored in `Message` is displayed using the `Length()` method. The third statement uses the `ToLowerCase()` method to convert the string to all lowercase characters. The fourth statement uses the `ToUpperCase()` method to convert the string to all uppercase characters. Finally, the `Trim()` method is used to remove the blank spaces from the beginning and ending of the string.

**HINT** You will see another example of the `ToUpperCase()` method in action when you work on this chapter's game project. To see additional examples of most of Phrogram's `String` methods, open the Strings.kpl program located under My Programs\5) Advanced Learning Examples\Strings in the Files window.

## Working with Numeric Data and Variables

As is the case with strings, Phrogram provides many different ways of manipulating and processing the values assigned to numeric variables. This includes a number of shortcut operators that you can use when performing basic addition, subtraction, multiplication, and division as well as a large collection of numeric methods provided by the Phrogram `Math` library.

## Numeric Variable Assignment Shortcuts

Addition, subtraction, multiplication, and division in Phrogram are performed exactly as is done in everyday life. Specifically, the + character is used to perform addition, the - character is used to perform subtraction, the * character is used to perform multiplication, and the / character is used to perform division, as demonstrated here:

```
Print(1 + 5)      //Displays a value of 6
Print(6 - 1)      //Displays a value of 5
Print(3 * 3)      //Displays a value of 9
Print(6 / 2)      //Displays a value of 3
```

In addition to supporting these traditional mathematical operations, Phrogram also supplies you with access to a number of shortcut operators that allow you to add, subtract, multiply, and divide using an abridged syntax that is less prone to errors. For example, the following statements define a variable used to keep track of the depth of a fictional submarine. The submarine's depth is then decremented by decreasing the value of `SubDepth` by 1. This is accomplished by setting `SubDepth` equal to `SubDepth -1`.

```
Define SubDepth As Integer = 0
SubDepth = SubDepth - 1
```

Rather than calculating the submarine's depth in this manner, you could use the following shortcut approach.

```
Define SubDepth As Integer = 0
SubDepth -= 1
```

Here, -= operator is used to automatically decrement the value of the variable that precedes it by a specified value, which in the above example is 1. Similarly, you could raise the depth of the submarine by adding to the value of `SubDepth` as demonstrated here:

```
Define SubDepth As Integer = 0
SubDepth = SubDepth + 1
```

Or, using the += operators, you should perform the same calculation as shown here:

```
Define SubDepth As Integer = 0
SubDepth += 1
```

Phrogram also supports shortcuts for multiplication and division. For example, you might manipulate the speed at which the submarine is traveling by changing the value assigned to a variable named `SubSpeed`, as demonstrated here:

```
Define SubSpeed As Integer = 5
SubSpeed = SubSpeed * 4
```

Using the *= operator, you could rewrite this example as shown here:

```
Define SubSpeed As Integer = 5
SubSpeed *= 4
```

You might also control the degree of the angle at which the submarine dives when submerging by modifying the value assigned to a variable named `SubDiveAngle` as demonstrated here:

```
Define SubDiveAngle As Integer = 50
SubDiveAngle = SubDiveAngle / 5
```

Alternatively, using the /= operator, you could rewrite this example as shown here:

```
Define SubDiveAngle As Integer = 50
SubDiveAngle /= 5
```

**FIND IT ONLINE**

The Precision Math Advanced Add-in Library, available on the Phrogram Company website (www.phrogram.com), extends Phrogram's default decimal precision from 28 to 38 digits. In addition, it eliminates rounding errors that can occur when working with floating point numbers. At the time that this book was published, the Precision Math Add-in Library was selling for $14.95. If you plan on developing applications that involve complex mathematical calculations that require a high level of precision, you may well find this add-in worth the extra money.

**HINT**

You will learn a lot more about Phrogram's support for mathematics in Chapter 4, "Making Decisions with Conditional Logic."

## Taking Advantage of Numeric Methods

Phrogram supports both integer and decimal numbers, as demonstrated here:

```
TotalScore = 50           //Integer
CashBalanace  = 100.99    //Floating point number
```

Like other programming languages, Phrogram provides access to a host of built-in methods, which can be used in conjunction with both integer and decimal values. The following list highlights many of the numeric methods provided by Phrogram's `Math` library.

- `Abs()`. Returns the absolute value of a number.
- `Exp()`. Returns the exponent of a number.
- `Log()`. Returns the natural log of a number.
- `Max()`. Returns the larger of two numbers.
- `Min()`. Returns the lesser of two numbers.
- `Power()`. Returns the value of a number raised to a specified power.
- `Random()`. Returns a random number between two specified values.
- `Round()`. Returns the rounded value of a specified number.
- `Sign`. Returns the sign of a specified number.
- `Sin`. Returns the sin of a specified angle.
- `Sqrt()`. Returns the square root of a number.
- `Tan`. Returns the tangent of an angle.

HINT To learn more about the syntax of each of the numeric methods listed above, open the Class Library Browser window and select the `Math` library. This will display a listing of all the numeric methods supported by Phrogram, including those listed above. You can view detailed information about any of these methods by selecting it.

By taking advantage of these and the many other methods provided by Phrogram, you can save yourself the trouble of having to reinvent the wheel when you need to perform complex mathematical calculations. This helps keep your program code simple and easier to maintain.

For example, the `Random()` method, which has the following syntax, is used to generate random numbers.

```
Random(MinValue As Integer, MaxValue As integer)
```

*MinValue* specifies the low end of the range from which a random number is to be generated, and *MaxValue* specifies the high end of that range. Therefore, using the `Random()` method, you can generate random numbers within your Phrogram applications and games, as demonstrated here:

```
Print(Random(1, 10))    //Display a random number from 1 to 10
```

Here, a random number from 1 to 10 is generated every time this statement is executed.

HINT The `RandomDecimal()` method works exactly like the `Random()` function, except that it returns a randomly selected decimal number.

This next example demonstrates how to use the `Round()` method to round decimal numbers to an integer value. This method has the following syntax.

```
Round(Value As Decimal)
```

Here, *`Value`* represents the decimal number that is to be rounded. For example, in the following statement, the `Round()` method is used to round a decimal value set at 99.99 upwards to the nearest whole number (e.g., 100).

```
Define TotalScore As Decimal
TotalScore = 99.9
Print(Round(TotalScore))    //100 is displayed
```

In this final example, the `Sqrt()` method, whose syntax is outlined below, is used to retrieve the square root of the number 9.

```
Sqrt(Value As Decimal) As Decimal
```

Here, *`Value`* represents the decimal number that is to be rounded. When used as shown below, the value returned by the `Sqrt()` method is displayed in the console window.

```
Print(Sqrt(9))    //3 is displayed
```

**HINT** When viewing information about the methods provided by the `Math` library in the Class Library Browser window, take note of the small icon displayed just to the left of each method that is listed. These icons, shown in Table 3.2, identify whether you are looking at a constant, property, or a method. For methods, either of two possible icons may be displayed that indicate whether the method returns a value when called.

**Table 3.2 Mathematical Constants Provided by the Math Library**

| Icon | Type | Description |
|---|---|---|
|  | Constant | A value that never changes. |
|  | Property | A variable used to control or describe some aspect of an object with which it is associated. |
|  | Method | A method that performs a specified action but does not return a result. |
|  | Method | A method that performs a specified action and returns a result. |

Since the `Sqrt()` method returns a result, it can be used to return the square root of 9, which is then stored in a variable named `x`.

```
Define x As Decimal
x = (Sqrt(9))
```

If you look back at the syntax of the `Sqrt()` method, you will see that the value that it returns will always be a decimal.

## Storing and Managing Related Collections of Data in Arrays

In many cases, variables will be all that you need to store and work with the data that is collected and processed by your applications. However, there may be times when you find yourself working on the development of games and applications that involves the use of large amounts of information. As useful as variables can be, they tend to lose value as the amount of data that you need to work with at any point in time increases. Fortunately, in most situations, the data processed by an application is closely related. For example, suppose you wanted to create an application that maintained a list of all your friends' email addresses. In this type of application, you will need to work with text strings representing email addresses. Managing one hundred friends would require the use of one hundred variables. In these situations, you can usually turn to arrays as your solution.

An array is an index list of data stored and managed as a unit. In Phrogram applications, all the data stored in an array must be of the same data type. Data stored in an array is assigned an index position, beginning with index position 1. The second item stored in an array would be assigned to index position 2, the third item to index position 3, and so on. Once stored, you access the data, or items, stored in an array based on their index position within the array.

**HINT** In most programming languages, arrays begin at index position 0. As a result, an array of 10 items would begin at index position 0 and end at index position 9. By starting array index positions at position 1, Phrogram makes things more intuitive.

Phrogram includes support for single-dimensional, double-dimensional, three-dimensional, and larger arrays. A single-dimensional array can be likened to a simple list. You can think of a two-dimensional array as being similar to a table stored in an Excel spreadsheet made up of rows and columns. With each additional dimension, arrays grow larger and more complex in size.

### Defining and Populating an Array with Data

Like variables, arrays are defined using the `Define` keyword and the following syntax.

```
Define ArrayName As DataType[Expression]
```

*ArrayName* represents the name of the array being defined. *DataType* is a placeholder that specifies the type of data to be stored in the array. Arrays can be used to store any of the data types supported by Phrogram. *Expression* is a comma-separated list of numbers representing the number of dimensions in an array (as well as the length of each dimension).

The following statement demonstrates how to define a small single-dimensional array named `aFriends` that is capable of storing 5 items.

```
Define aFriends As String[5]
```

> **HINT** Array names are subject to the same naming rules as variable names. Note that in the above example, a small lowercase letter `a` was added to the beginning of the array name to help visually distinguish it from variable names.

Once created, you can assign data to the array, as demonstrated here:

```
aFriends[1] = "Alexander"
aFriends[2] = "William"
aFriends[3] = "Molly"
aFriends[4] = "Jerry"
aFriends[5] = "Mary"
```

Here an array containing five elements has been created. As you can see, in order to assign a value to the array, you must specify the name of the array followed by an array index position, enclosed in a matching pair of brackets.

> **TRAP** When assigning data to an array, do not assign data to an index position outside the scope that has been defined for the array. For example, if you were to attempt to add an item at index position 6 or higher in the previous example, a runtime error would occur, as demonstrated in Figure 3.9.

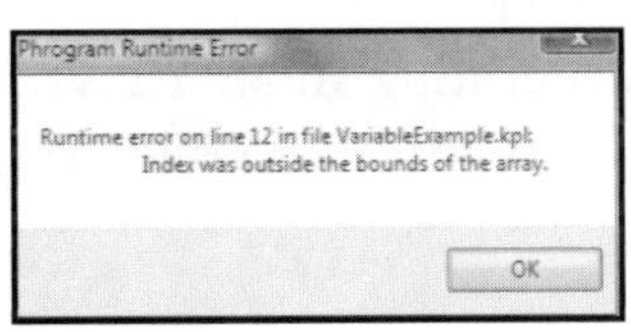


**FIGURE 3.9**

An error occurs if you attempt to reference an index position that is outside of the range defined for the array.

## Retrieving Data from an Array

Once created and populated with data, you can retrieve array items by specifying the name of the array followed by the index number of the element to be retrieved, as demonstrated here:

```
Define aFriends As String[5]

aFriends[1] = "Alexander"
aFriends[2] = "William"
aFriends[3] = "Molly"
aFriends[4] = "Jerry"
aFriends[5] = "Mary"

Print("My first friend is " + aFriends[1] + ".")
```

Here, the first element stored in an array named `aFriends` is retrieved and displayed in a console window, as shown in Figure 3.10.

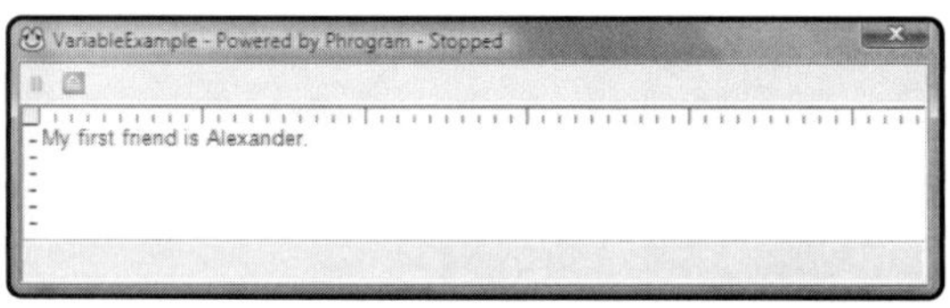


**FIGURE 3.10**
Retrieving and displaying the first item stored in an array.

**HINT** Referencing data stored in an array an item at a time is okay when working with small arrays. However, this is not a practical way to process the contents of arrays that may contain hundreds or thousands of items. For arrays of this size, you will need to set up a loop to process all of the items stored in the array. You will learn all about loops in Chapter 5, "Using Loops to Process Data."

## Shortcuts for Creating Small Arrays

Phrogram provides you with a shortcut for defining small arrays in which you define and populate an array in a single statement using the following syntax.

```
Define ArrayName As DataType = Expression
```

*`Arrayname`* represents the name of the array being defined. *`DataType`* is a placeholder that specifies the type of data to be stored in the array. *`Expression`* is a comma-separated list of items enclosed within a matching pair of squiggly brackets.

For example, instead of defining a small array using the six statements shown here:

```
Define aToys As String[5]

aToys[1] = "Legos"
aToys[2] = "Blocks"
aToys[3] = "Balls"
aToys[4] = "Dolls"
aToys[5] = "Marbles"
```

You should could define and populate the array in a single statement, as shown here:

```
Define aToys As String[] = {"Legos", "Blocks", "Balls", "Dolls", "Marbles"}
```

### Splitting Up a String Into an Array

Another shortcut that you can use for creating arrays involves the use of the `Strings` library's `Split()` method, which splits up the contents of a string into an array using the following syntax.

```
Split(Value As String, Delimiter As String [, IgnoreCase As Boolean])
```

*`Value`* represents the string that is to be split. *`Delimiter`* specifies character(s) to be used when determining where to split the string. `IgnoreCase` is optional. When used it instructs Phrogram to ignore case when identifying delimiters.

To better understand how to work with the `Split()` function, take a look at the following example.

```
Define aToys As String [] = Split("Legos Blocks Balls Dolls Marbles", " ")
```

Here, an array named `aToys` is created. Using a blank space as the delimiter, the array is then populated with five items, extracted from a string.

## Determining an Array Size

Another useful `Strings` library method that you should be familiar with when working with arrays is the `Length()` method. This method returns an integer value specifying the length of an array. This method has the following syntax.

```
Length(Value as String) As Integer
```

When used with an array, *`Value`* represents the name of the array whose length is to be determined. To better understand how this method works, take a look at the following example.

```
Define aToys As String[10]

aToys[1] = "Legos"
aToys[2] = "Blocks"
aToys[3] = "Balls"
aToys[4] = "Dolls"
aToys[5] = "Marbles"

Print("The length of aToys is " + ArrayLength(aToys) + ".")
```

Here, an array named aToys is defined and then populated with five items, after which the length of the array is displayed in a text message on the application window, as demonstrated in Figure 3.11.

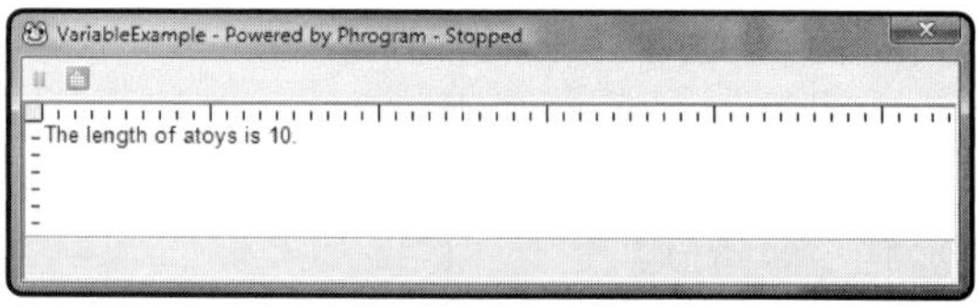


**FIGURE 3.11**

Determining the length of an array.

## Working with Multi-Dimensional Arrays

As has already been stated, Phrogram allows programmers to define arrays consisting of more than one dimension. For example, the following statements define a 32-dimensional array capable of storing 10 elements (which you can think of as being similar to a spread sheet made up of five rows and two columns).

```
Define Family As String[5, 2]

Family[1, 1] = "Alexander"
Family[1, 2] = "son"

Family[2, 1] = "William"
Family[2, 2] = "son"

Family[3, 1] = "Molly"
Family[3, 2] = "daughter"
```

```
Family[4, 1] = "Jerry"
Family[4, 2] = "father"

Family[5, 1] = "Mary"
Family[5, 2] = "mother"

Print("My second oldest child is my " + Family[2, 2] + ".")
Print("His name is " + Family[2, 1] + ".")
```

Note that in order to define a multi-dimensional array, you must specify a list of two or more numeric values within square brackets as part of its definition statements. Once defined, you may populate the array with data as shown in the above example and then retrieve and process the data as necessary during program execution. Figure 3.12 shows the output that is generated when the above example is executed.

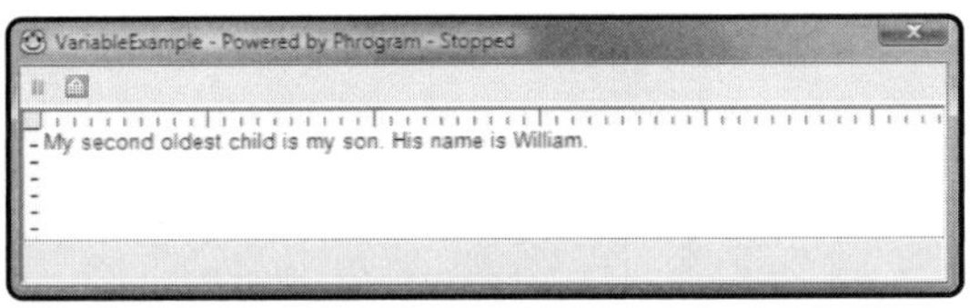


**FIGURE 3.12**

Retrieving data from a two-dimensional array.

Although Phrogram provides support for arrays greater than one or two dimensions, things begin getting complicated. As such, working with arrays greater than two dimensions is outside the scope of this book.

## Storing Related Variables in a Structure

Phrogram offers an additional means of storing and managing data known as a structure. A *structure* lets you define a collection of loosely related variables that can be referenced as a unit. Structures let you store and process multiple pieces of information as variables as if they were a single entity. The syntax used to define a structure is outlined here:

```
Structure StructureName
  Identifier AS DataType
  .
  .
  .
End Structure
```

*StructureName* represents the name of the structure, and *Identifier* represents the name of a variable belonging to the structure. You can include any number of identifiers in the structure definition. *DataType* is used to identify the type of data associated with each variable within the structure. Structures must be placed at the beginning of program files, immediately after the opening program statement and before the `Main()` method.

To better understand how to use a structure within a Phrogram application, look at the following example.

```
Program StructureDemo

    Structure BowlingPin

        Color As String
        Type As String

    End Structure

    Method Main()

        Define Pin1 As BowlingPin
        Define Pin2 As BowlingPin
        Define Pin3 As BowlingPin

        Pin1.Color = "White"
        Pin1.Type = "Regular"

        Pin2.Color = "White"
        Pin2.Type = "Regular"

        Pin3.Color = "Red"
        Pin3.Type = "Special"

        Print("Pin1 is a " + Pin1.Type + " " + Pin1.Color + " pin.")
        Print("Pin2 is a " + Pin2.Type + " " + Pin2.Color + " pin.")
        Print("Pin3 is a " + Pin3.Type + " " + Pin3.Color + " pin.")
```

```
    End Method

End Program
```

Here, a structure named `BowlingPin` has been defined. The structure has two variables defined within it, representing different qualities of a bowling pin. Once defined, you can use a structure as a template for defining new variables. This is done using dot notation in which the . character is appended to the end of the variable name followed by one of the variable names defined in the structure. Once data has been assigned, you can work with it as necessary.

In the above example, the `BowlingPin` structure is used as the basis for defining three sets of variables. Each set consists of two variables. Note that when defined within a structure, you do not include the `Define` keyword when defining a variable, nor can you assign a value to the variables. Instead, data is assigned later, using the dot notation previously described. When executed, this example displays the output shown in Figure 3.13.

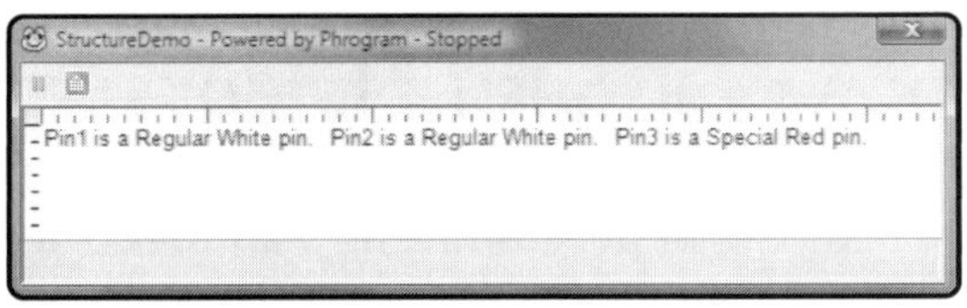


**FIGURE 3.13**

Using structures to keep track of related pieces of data.

HINT: Structures are often used to keep track of objects (characters, cars, tanks, etc.) and their statuses (names, colors, energy level, etc.) in computer games.

## PHROGRAM LANGUAGE KEYWORDS

Like every programming language, Phrogram is made up of a number of keywords, each of which has a specific meaning and purpose. These *keywords*, sometimes referred to as *reserved* words, must be used in accordance with syntax rules outlined by Phrogram for each keyword.

Reserved words cannot be used as identifier names. Therefore, you cannot, for example, assign a variable a name of `If` or `Define`. Table 3.3 provides a listing of Phrogram's keywords. Note that not all of the reserved words listed in Table 3.3 are currently supported by Phrogram but are reserved for future use.

**Table 3.3 Phrogram Language Keywords**

| | | | |
|---|---|---|---|
| And | Else | Inherits | Public |
| As | ElseIf | Integer | Return |
| Boolean | End | Interface | Select |
| Break | Enum | Loop | Set |
| Case | Exit | Method | Step |
| Class | False | Mod | String |
| Constant | For | Module | Structure |
| Constructor | Function | Next | Then |
| Continue | Get | Not | To |
| Decimal | Global | Operator | True |
| Define | Goto | Or | Var |
| Do | Handles | Private | While |
| DownTo | If | Program | |
| Each | Implements | Property | |

# Essential Console Windows and Shell Methods

In Chapters 1 and 2 you created the Kids Jokes and Story Time games by following a very specific set of directions that involved keying in programming statements to which you have not yet been introduced with the promise that you would soon be taught about the purpose and usage of these statements. Now it is time for this book to begin making good on this promise. In the next three sections, a series of methods and constants provided by the `Drawing`, `Console`, and `Shell` libraries will be reviewed. Each of these methods and constants was used in Chapters 1 and 2 or will be used later in this chapter's game project.

## Drawing Text on the Screen

You have observed the use of the `Print()` method on numerous occasions in this book. This method is provided by Phrogram's `Drawing` library. When used, the `Print()` method draws (displays) text passed to it as an argument on the console window using the following syntax.

```
Print(Text As String)
```

Here, *`Text`* represents one or more characters enclosed inside a matching pair of double quotations marks. This text may be hard coded within the statement or passed to it as an argument in the form of a variable.

The `Print()` method can be used to display both string and numeric data, as demonstrated here:

```
Print("Hello World!")
Print(1000)
```

Note that text must be placed within a matching set of double quotation marks and that numeric data does not. Back-to-back use of `Print()` methods results in text output that is separated and followed by a single blank space, as demonstrated here:

```
PRINT "In the end"
PRINT "there can be only one."
```

When executed, this statement displays the output shown here:

```
In the end there can be only one.
```

## Working with the Window's Console

Phrogram's `Console` library provides access to dozens of methods that give you control over the application windows, also referred to as consoles or console windows. Using these methods, you can read from and write to the console. You can also control color and font specifications as well as display and clear the console window.

### Specifying a Background Color for the Console Window

The `Console` library's `SetConsoleBackgroundColor()` method provides the ability to set the background color for the console window using the following syntax.

```
SetConsoleBackgroundColor(Color As Integer)
```

Here, *`Color`* is a placeholder representing one of 140 color constant values provided by Phrogram's Colors library. These color constants, listed in Table 3.4, can be specified by either their name or their number.

**Table 3.4 Color Constants Provided by the Colors Library**

| Color | No. | Color | No. | Color | No. |
|---|---|---|---|---|---|
| AliceBlue | 1 | GhostWhite | 48 | NavajoWhite | 95 |
| AntiqueWhite | 2 | Gold | 49 | Navy | 96 |
| Aqua | 3 | Goldenrod | 50 | OldLace | 97 |
| Aquamarine | 4 | Gray | 51 | Olive | 98 |
| Azure | 5 | Green | 52 | OliveDrab | 99 |
| Beige | 6 | GreenYellow | 53 | Orange | 100 |
| Bisque | 7 | Honeydew | 54 | OrangeRed | 101 |

| Color | Value |
|---|---|
| Black | 8 |
| BlanchedAlmond | 9 |
| Blue | 10 |
| BlueViolet | 11 |
| Brown | 12 |
| BurlyWood | 13 |
| CadetBlue | 14 |
| Chartreuse | 15 |
| Chocolate | 16 |
| Coral | 17 |
| CornflowerBlue | 18 |
| Cornsilk | 19 |
| Crimson | 20 |
| Cyan | 21 |
| DarkBlue | 22 |
| DarkCyan | 23 |
| DarkGoldenrod | 24 |
| DarkGray | 25 |
| DarkGreen | 26 |
| DarkKhaki | 27 |
| DarkMagenta | 28 |
| DarkOliveGreen | 29 |
| DarkOrange | 30 |
| DarkOrchid | 31 |
| DarkRed | 32 |
| DarkSalmon | 33 |
| DarkSeaGreen | 34 |
| DarkSlateBlue | 35 |
| DarkSlateGray | 36 |
| DarkTurquoise | 37 |
| DarkViolet | 38 |
| DeepPink | 39 |
| DeepSkyBlue | 40 |
| DimGray | 41 |
| DodgerBlue | 42 |
| Firebrick | 43 |
| FloralWhite | 44 |
| ForestGreen | 45 |
| Fuchsia | 46 |
| Gainsboro | 47 |
| HotPink | 55 |
| IndianRed | 56 |
| Indigo | 57 |
| Ivory | 58 |
| Khaki | 59 |
| Lavender | 60 |
| LavenderBlush | 61 |
| LawnGreen | 62 |
| LemonChiffon | 63 |
| LightBlue | 64 |
| LightCoral | 65 |
| LightCyan | 66 |
| LightGoldenrodYellow | 67 |
| LightGray | 68 |
| LightGreen | 69 |
| LightPink | 70 |
| LightSalmon | 71 |
| LightSeaGreen | 72 |
| LightSkyBlue | 73 |
| LightSlateGray | 74 |
| LightSteelBlue | 75 |
| LightYellow | 76 |
| Lime | 77 |
| LimeGreen | 78 |
| Linen | 79 |
| Magenta | 80 |
| Maroon | 81 |
| MediumAquamarine | 82 |
| MediumBlue | 83 |
| MediumOrchid | 84 |
| MediumPurple | 85 |
| MediumSeaGreen | 86 |
| MediumSlateBlue | 87 |
| MediumSpringGreen | 88 |
| MediumTurquoise | 89 |
| MediumVioletRed | 90 |
| MidnightBlue | 91 |
| MintCream | 92 |
| MistyRose | 93 |
| Moccasin | 94 |
| Orchid | 102 |
| PaleGoldenrod | 103 |
| PaleGreen | 104 |
| PaleTurquoise | 105 |
| PaleVioletRed | 106 |
| PapayaWhip | 107 |
| PeachPuff | 108 |
| Peru | 109 |
| Pink | 110 |
| Plum | 111 |
| PowderBlue | 112 |
| Purple | 113 |
| Red | 114 |
| RosyBrown | 115 |
| RoyalBlue | 116 |
| SaddleBrown | 117 |
| Salmon | 118 |
| SandyBrown | 119 |
| SeaGreen | 120 |
| SeaShell | 121 |
| Sienna | 122 |
| Silver | 123 |
| SkyBlue | 124 |
| SlateBlue | 125 |
| SlateGray | 126 |
| Snow | 127 |
| SpringGreen | 128 |
| SteelBlue | 129 |
| Tan | 130 |
| Teal | 131 |
| Thistle | 132 |
| Tomato | 133 |
| Turquoise | 134 |
| Violet | 135 |
| Wheat | 136 |
| White | 137 |
| WhiteSmoke | 138 |
| Yellow | 139 |
| YellowGreen | 140 |

For example, when executed, the following statement will set the console window's background color to `DarkGreen`.

```
SetConsoleBackgroundColor(Darkgreen)
```

## Specifying the Color to be Used to Display Font Text

The `Console` library's `SetConsoleFontColor()` method provides the ability to specify the color to be used when displaying font text in the console window using the following syntax.

```
SetConsoleFontColor(Color As Integer)
```

`Color` is a placeholder representing one of the color constant values provided by the `Colors` library.

For example, when executed, the following statement will set `Yellow` as the color to use to display font text in the console window.

```
SetConsoleFontColor(Yellow)
```

## Specifying Font Style Attributes

The `Console` library's `SetConsoleFontStyle()` method specifies whether font text should be displayed in bold, italic, or underlined, using the following syntax.

```
SetConsoleFontStyle(Bold As Boolean, Italic As Boolean, Underline As Boolean)
```

For example, when executed, the following statement will instruct Phrogram to display any text that follows in bold font (with no italics and no underline).

```
SetConsoleFontStyle(True, False, False)
```

## Specifying the Font Type and Size

The `Console` library's `SetConsoleFont()` method specifies the font type and point size for text displayed in the console window, using the following syntax.

```
SetConsoleFont(FontName As String, FontSize As Decimal)
```

Here, *`FontName`* is a placeholder representing one of dozens of font constant values provided by Phrogram's `Fonts` library. These font constants are listed in Table 3.5. *`FontSize`* is a placeholder representing the point size to be used when displaying font text, where each point equals 1/72 of an inch.

For example, when executed, the following statement sets the font type to Arial with a point size of 14.

```
SetConsoleFont("Arial", 14)
```

**Table 3.5 Named Fonts Provided by the Fonts Library**

| Font | String |
|---|---|
| Arial | "Arial" |
| ArialBlack | "Arial Black" |
| ArialNarrow | "Arial Narrow" |
| ArialUnicodeMS | "Arial Unicode MS" |
| BookAntiqua | "Book Antiqua" |
| BookmanOldStyle | "Bookman Old Style" |
| Century | "Century" |
| CenturyGothic | "Century Gothic" |
| ComicSansMS | "Comic Sans MS" |
| Garamond | "Garamond" |
| Georgia | "Georgia" |
| Impact | "Impact" |
| LucidaConsole | "Lucida Console" |
| LucidaSans | "Lucida Sans" |
| LucidaSansUnicode | "Lucida Sans Unicode" |
| MicrosoftSansSerif | "Microsoft Sans Serif" |
| Symbol | "Symbol" |
| Tahoma | "Tahoma" |
| TimesNewRoman | "Times New Roman" |
| TraditionalArabic | "Traditional Arabic" |
| TrebuchetMS | "TrebuchetMS" |
| Verdana | "Verdana" |
| Webdings | "Webdings" |
| Wingdings | "Wingdings" |

## Controlling Text Alignment

The `Console` library's `SetConsoleTextAlignment()` method specifies the alignment for text displayed in the console window using the following syntax.

```
SetConsoleTextAlignment(Alignment As String)
```

Here, valid options for *Alignment* include "left", "center", and "right".

For example, the following statement sets the alignment of any font text that follows to center, ensuring that the text is centered relative to its vertical location on the screen.

```
SetConsoleTextAlignment("Center")
```

### Displaying the Console Window

The `Console` library's `SetConsole()` method displays the console window, using the following syntax.

```
ShowConsole()
```

As you can see, this method takes no arguments and thus is used by simply typing in its name, as demonstrated here:

```
ShowConsole()
```

### Clearing the Console Window

The `Console` library's `ClearConsole()` method clears the console window when called using the following syntax.

```
ClearConsole()
```

Like the `ShowConsole()` method, the `ClearConsole()` method accepts no arguments and is used by simply typing in its name, as demonstrated here:

```
ClearConsole()
```

### Retrieving User Keystrokes

The `Console` library's `ConsoleReadKey()` method retrieves a single keystroke entered by the user at the console window, using the following syntax.

```
ConsoleReadKey() As String
```

For example, you have seen this method used many times already in this book to pause application execution until the player presses a keyboard key, as demonstrated here:

```
ConsoleReadKey()
```

However, this method can also be used to retrieve the keystroke that the user pressed, as demonstrated here:

```
Define UserInput As String
UserInput = ConsoleReadKey()
```

Here, the key pressed by the user is stored in a variable named `UserInput`.

### Retrieving Text Strings from the Console Window

The `Console` library's `ReadString()` method retrieves a text string entered by the user in the console window using the following syntax.

```
ReadString(Prompt As String) As String
```

Here, *Prompt* is a text string used to display a message prompt that instructs the user to enter text. For example, the following statements use the `ReadString()` method to prompt the player to enter her name.

```
Define PlayerName As String
PlayerName = Console.ReadString("What is your name?")
```

When executed, this example displays the prompt at the bottom of the console window in which the user must provide the required input, as demonstrated in Figure 3.14.

**FIGURE 3.14**

Collecting text input from the user.

Once provided, the player's input is assigned to the `PlayerName` string variable.

### Retrieving Number Input from the Console Window

The `Console` library's `ReadInt()` method retrieves an integer value entered by the user in the console window, using the following syntax.

```
ReadInt(Prompt As String) As Integer
```

*Prompt* is a text string used to display a message prompt. If the user attempts to enter anything other than a numeric value, the input is blocked, forcing the user to enter an integer value. For example, the following statements use the `ReadString()` method to prompt the player to enter her age.

```
Define PlayerAge As Integer
PlayerAge = Console.ReadInt("How old are you?")
```

## Working with Shell Library Methods

Phrogram's `Shell` library provides access to dozens of methods that let you display popup dialog windows, pause application execution, hide the console window's toolbar, set screen height and width, and display messages in the console window's titlebar. The following sections highlight the `Shell` library methods that you have worked with so far in this book.

### Hiding the Console Window's Toolbar

The `Shell` library's `HideToolbar()` method suppresses the display of the console window toolbar, using the following syntax.

```
HideToolbar()
```

As you can see, this method takes no arguments and thus is used by simply typing in its name, as demonstrated here:

```
HideToolbar()
```

### Specifying the Size of the Screen Display in the Console Window

The `Shell` library's `SetScreenSize()` method sets the width and height of the program screen in the console window, using the following syntax.

```
SetScreenSize(Width As Integer, Height As Integer)
```

Here, *`Width`* is an integer value representing the width of the screen in pixels, and *`Height`* is an integer value representing the height of the screen in pixels. A *pixel* (picture element) is the smallest addressable area that can be written to or drawn on the screen or window.

The following statement demonstrates how to use the `SetScreenSize()` method to tell Phrogram to set the size of the console window to accommodate a screen size that is 600 pixels wide by 400 pixels high.

```
SetScreenSize (600, 400)
```

### Displaying a Message on the Console Window's Titlebar

The `Shell` library's `SetWindowTitle()` method specifies a text string that will be displayed in the console window's titlebar, using the following syntax.

```
SetWindowTitle(Title As String)
```

*`Title`* is a text string that you want to display in the console window titlebar. For example, the following statement displays a text string of `"Space Battle"` in the console window's titlebar.

```
SetWindowTitle("Space Battle")
```

### Pausing Application Execution

The `Shell` library's `Delay()` method pauses application execution a specified number of milliseconds using the following syntax.

```
Delay(Milliseconds As Integer)
```

As shown here, the `Delay` method requires that you pass it a single argument, an integer value representing the number of milliseconds to pause. One millisecond is 1/1000 of a second.

For example, to pause for a complete second, you would pass a value of 1000 as an argument to the Delay method, as demonstrated here:

```
Delay(1000)
```

## Displaying Popup Dialog Windows That Collect User Input

The Shell library's Confirm() method displays a popup dialog window that displays a text string and two buttons labeled Yes and No. Application execution is paused until the user clicks on one of the window's buttons. This method has the following syntax.

```
Confirm(Message As String, Title As String)
```

*Message* represents a text string that will be displayed in the popup dialog window. *Title* represents a text string that will be displayed in the popup dialog window's titlebar. For example, the following statements display a popup dialog window that prompts the player for permission to begin the game.

```
Define PlayerReply As Boolean = True

PlayerReply = Confirm("Would you like to play? ", "Story Time")
If PlayerReply = True Then
    Print("OK, Let's Play!")
Else
    Print("OK, maybe next time.")
End If
```

The player responds to the popup dialog window by clicking on either its Yes or No button or by clicking on the Close button located in the upper-right corner of the window. A Boolean value of True is assigned to a variable named PlayerReply if the player clicks on the Yes button. Otherwise a value of False is assigned to PlayerReply. The Close button located in the upper-right corner of the popup dialog window does not respond when clicked, forcing the player to click on either the Yes or No button. In the above example, the player's response is analyzed to determine which course of action should be taken next. Figure 3.15 shows an example of the popup dialog window that is produced when the example is executed.

**FIGURE 3.15**

Collecting player input using a popup dialog window.

## Displaying Popup Dialog Windows That Display Text Messages

The `Shell` library's `Alert()` method displays a popup dialog window that displays a text string and a button labeled OK. Application execution is paused until the user clicks on the window's OK button or presses the Enter key. This method has the following syntax.

```
Alert(Message As String, Title As String)
```

*Message* represents a text string that will be displayed in the popup dialog window. *Title* represents a text string that will be displayed in the popup dialog window's titlebar. For example, the following statement displays a popup dialog window that informs the player when the game's battleship has been sunk.

```
Alert("You sank my battleship", "Battleship")
```

Figure 3.16 shows how the popup dialog window looks when displayed.

**FIGURE 3.16**

Display a text message in a popup dialog window.

### EXERCISES

**So far, this chapter has covered a lot of ground in its discussion of arrays and structures. It also reviewed a number of `Console` library methods. To further reinforce your understanding of these important concepts and language features, complete the following hands-on exercises.**

**1. Using the Explorer window, open, review, and execute the following Phrogram programs (found on the CD accompanying this book), each of which provides further instructions and examples of how to work with arrays.**

- **Arrays.kpl located in the Phrogram examples folder.**
- **ArrayResize.kpl located in the Arrays subfolder found in the Advanced Learning Examples folder.**
- **MultiDimensionalArray.kpl located in the Arrays subfolder found in the Advanced Learning Examples folder.**

2. Using the Explorer window, open, review, and execute the following Phrogram program, which provides additional instruction and an example of how to work with structures.
   - Structure Template.kpl located in the Phrogram Templates folder.
3. Using the Explorer window, open, review, and execute the following Phrogram programs, each of which provides further instructions and examples of how to work with `Console` library methods.
   - Console.kpl located in the Console subfolder found in the Class Library Learn Examples folder.
   - ConsoleFonts.kpl located in the Console subfolder found in the Class Library Learn Examples folder.
   - Consort.sort.kpl located in the Console subfolder found in the Class Library Learn Examples folder.

## Review Questions

1. Explain how case sensitivity affects Phrogram keywords. Does it have any impact on the naming of identifiers?
2. Describe two ways in which comments can be added to Phrogram program files.
3. List and define the four types of data that Phrogram supports.
4. Explain the differences between a variable and a constant.
5. List three rules that apply to the naming of variables.
6. Explain the difference between method and global variables.
7. What is concatenation?
8. What is a reserved word? Provide an example of three reserved words that you have worked with in this chapter.
9. Demonstrate how to create an array named `aBestFriends` and then show how to populate that array with at least five items.
10. Define the term structure. Can you provide an example of a situation in which structures might prove useful?

## Back to the Number Guessing Game

Now it is time to turn your attention back to the development of the Number Guessing game. The development of this game will help to reinforce your understanding of the use of variables as a mechanism for storing Boolean, string, and numeric program data. In addition, you will get the opportunity to work further with the `Math` library's `Random()` method and to perform string concatenation, as well as to gain a further appreciation of how to work with various `Console` and `Shell` library methods.

### Designing the Game

To help keep things as simple as possible, the Number Guessing game will be created in a series of 10 steps, as outlined here:

1. Create a new program project.
2. Document your application.
3. Define a global constant.
4. Define method variables.
5. Configure the game's window.
6. Prompt the player for permission to begin.
7. Analyze the player's response.
8. Control game play.
9. Suggest the player play again another time.
10. Save and compile your new application.

As long as you take your time and do not make any typos or skip any of the steps outlined above, you'll have a fully functional Phrogram application up and running in no time at all.

#### Step 1: Creating a New Phrogram Project

The first step in creating a new Phrogram application is to create a new program. To do so, start Phrogram and click on the New Program command located on the File menu. In response, a new program file is created and displayed in the IDE. These statements provide an overall structure for your new application. Next, assign a more meaningful name to the application, which is done by replacing MyNewProgram with NumberGuess as the application's name on the first code statement.

The rest of the program code statements that will make up the NumberGuess application are explained in the sections that follow and will be inserted between the program file's `Method Main()` and `End Method` statements.

### Step 2: Documenting Your New Program

With your new program file now created, it is time to begin adding the code statements needed to make your new game do what it is supposed to do. Begin by adding the following comment statements to the program's code file, immediately following the opening `Main()` method statement.

```
//Program: NumberGuess.kpl
//Created: 12/26/2007
//Version: 1.0
//Author: Jerry Lee Ford, Jr.
//Description: This Phrogram game demonstrates how to generate random
//             numbers and to use variables as a means of storing and
//             processing data collected during game play using input
//             provided by the player.
```

As you can see, these statements provide a little high-level documentation about the program and its purpose.

### Step 3: Defining a Global Constant

The name of the Number Guessing game is displayed in the titlebar at the top of the game's console window as well as in the titlebar of all the game's popup dialog windows. Rather than hard coding the name of the game over and over again throughout different parts of the program file, let's define a constant and assign it the name of the game as its value. This way, you can refer to the game's name whenever necessary using the constant. This is accomplished by adding the following statements to the beginning of the program file, immediately after the program statement and before the `Main()` method.

```
//Global constant used to store the name of the game
Constant cGameTitle As String = "The Number Guessing Game"
```

Once added, you can specify `cGameTitle` in place of the game's name whenever you need to refer to it and if sometime down the road you decide to return and change the game's name, you will not have to hunt down and change it over and over again.

### Step 4: Defining Method Variables

The next step in the development of the Number Guessing game is to define a number of variables that will be used throughout the `Main()` method to keep track of different data, including player input, the number of guesses made by the player, and the game's randomly generated number. This is accomplished by adding the following statements to the `Main()` method.

```
//Define the variables used throughout the program to store data
Define Reply As Boolean = False     //Used to store player input
Define GameOver As Boolean          //Identifies end of game
Define Guess As Integer             //Stores player guesses
Define NoOfGuesses As Integer = 0   //Keeps count of player guesses
Define RandomNumber As Integer      //Stores the game's random #
Define Msg As String                //Stores a display string
```

As you can see, comments have been added to the right of each variable definition that explain each variable's purpose.

### Step 5: Configuring the Game's Window

The next set of code statements that you need to add to the Number Guessing game is responsible for configuring the appearance of the window in which the game is played. These statements, shown next, hide the window's toolbar, specify the screen's size, and then display the game's name (by referencing the `cGameTitle` constant) as a text string on the window's toolbar. The background color is then set to `WhiteSmoke` and the foreground color, used to display font text, is set to `DarkBlue`. Lastly, a font type of Arial is specified with a point size of 14.

```
HideToolbar()   //Prevent the window's toolbar from being displayed
SetScreenSize (600, 400)    //Set the screen size to 600x400 pixels
SetWindowTitle (cGameTitle)  //Display the name of the game in the
                            //Window's titlebar


SetConsoleBackgroundColor(WhiteSmoke)        //Set background color
SetConsoleFontColor(DarkBlue)                //Set font color


SetConsoleFont("Arial", 14)         // Set font to Arial, point 14
```

Each of these statements should be added to the `Main()` method, just after the variable definitions that you just added in the previous step.

### Step 6: Prompting the Player for Permission to Begin

Next, add the following statements to the `Main()` method, immediately following the statements that you added in the previous step.

```
//Outline the text of the game's welcome message
Msg = "Welcome To " + cGameTitle + "!  Are You Ready To Play?"

//Display the game's welcome message in a popup dialog window and
```

```
//prompt the player to click on Yes to play the game or No to quit
Reply = Confirm(Msg, cGameTitle)
```

These statements use the `Shell` library's `Confirm()` method to format and display a popup dialog window that contains a welcome message that prompts the player to either press the Yes button to begin game play or the No button to terminate program execution.

### Step 7: Analyzing the Player's Response

Once collected, the player's response to the popup dialog window produced in the previous step must be analyzed to determine which button the player clicked on. This is accomplished by adding the following statements to the `Main()` method, immediately following the statements that you added in the previous step.

```
//Analyze the player's response
If Reply = True Then                //If Reply equals True then the
                                    //player clicked on the Yes button


Else    //Execute the following statements when the player clicks
        //on the No button


End If
```

These statements create the logical framework that will control the execution of the rest of the game. Specifically, if the player clicks on the popup dialog window's Yes button, then the value assigned to the `Reply` variable will be set equal to `True`, in which case all of the program statements that you are going to insert between the `If` and `Else` statements in Step 8 will be executed. If, however, the player clicks on the No button, the statements that you will place between the `Else` and the `End If` statements (in Step 9) will be executed.

### Step 8: Controlling Overall Game Play

The next set of program code statements to be added to the Number Guessing game is shown below and should be inserted into the code statements that you just added to the `Main()` method. Specifically, you should insert these statements just after the `If` statement and just before the `Else` statement.

```
While True                       //Create a loop that runs forever


    //Generate a number from 1 to 100
    RandomNumber = Random(1, 100)


    //Reset value of variable used to keep track of
```

```
//the number of guesses made by the player
NoOfGuesses = 0

ClearConsole()       //Clear the console

GameOver = False  //Variable used to control loop execution

While GameOver = False  //Loop until the game is over

    //Prompt the player to enter a guess
    Guess = ConsoleReadInt("Enter your guess:", False)

    ClearConsole()       //Clear the console

    //Discard guesses less than 1 and greater than 100
    If Guess < 1 Or Guess > 100 Then

        Alert("Guess is out of range!", cGameTitle)

    Else

        //Keep count of valid guesses
        NoOfGuesses = NoOfGuesses + 1

        //Determine if the player's guess was correct
        If Guess = RandomNumber Then

            ConsoleWriteLine("")

            ConsoleWrite("You win! The number was ")
            ConsoleWrite(RandomNumber + ". ")
            ConsoleWrite("You guessed it in ")
            ConsoleWrite(NoOfGuesses + " guesses.")
            ConsoleWriteLine("")
            ConsoleWriteLine("")
            ConsoleWriteLine("Press any key to play again.")

            //Wait for the player to press a key
```

```
                ConsoleReadKey()

                GameOver = True  //Change variable value to
                                 //indicate the game is over

            End If

            //Determine if the player's guess was too high
            If Guess > RandomNumber Then

                ConsoleWriteLine("")
                ConsoleWrite("Sorry, " + Guess + " is too ")
                ConsoleWrite("high. Guess again.")

            End If

            //Determine if the player's guess was too low
            If Guess < RandomNumber Then

                ConsoleWriteLine("")
                ConsoleWrite("Sorry, " + Guess + " is too ")
                ConsoleWrite("low. Guess again.")

            End If

        End If

    End While

End While
```

These statements are responsible for controlling the overall play of the game. These statements include a number of programming language features that you have not learned about yet, including conditional programming logic and loops. Rather than putting the cart before the horse and attempting to explain what each of these statements does, I am going to refer you to the comments embedded within the program code that explain in detail what is going on and instead focus on what is going on at a high level.

For starters, a random number from 1 to 100 is generated. Then the player is prompted to guess the number. The player can make as many guesses as needed to figure out the number. After each incorrect guess, a message is displayed that tells the player whether the guess was too high or too low. Game play continues until the player finally guesses the number, at which time the player is congratulated and told how many guesses it took to guess the number. As soon as one game ends, a new game, along with a new random number begins. Game play continues until the player eventually decides to stop playing and closes the game window.

### Step 9: Prompting the Player to Play Another Time

The final set of program statements that you need to add to the Number Guessing game program file are shown next and need to be added to the end of the `Main()` method, just after the `Else` statement and before the `End If` statement that you added in Step 7.

```
//Display a message in a popup window inviting the player to
//play again another time
Alert("OK. Perhaps another time.", cGameTitle)
```

These statements are executed only if the player elects not to play the game by clicking on the No button when initially prompted for permission to begin game play. When executed, these statements display a message that prompts the player to consider returning to play another time.

### Step 10: Saving and Compiling Your Application

All right, you now have everything you need to complete the development of the Number Guessing game. If you have not already done so, save your new program file. Next, try compiling your new application. Assuming that you did not make any typos along the way, Phrogram should not have any problems compiling and running your new application. Once started, the Number Guessing game should execute as was described at the beginning of the chapter.

## The Final Result

If you run into any problems when compiling the Number Guessing game, then you have most likely skipped a step or mistyped one or more program code statements somewhere along the way. You should be able to use the error messages that are generated to track down any errors.

**HINT** You will also find a copy of this application's source code file on the book's accompanying CD.

## Summary

This chapter has shown you the basic steps involved in working with constants, variables, arrays, and structures and explained the different types of data that are supported by Phrogram. You learned about a host of different constants that Phrogram puts at your fingertips. You also learned about different string and numeric methods that you can leverage in your program applications to simplify the development of your own program code. On top of all this, this chapter made good on the promises made in Chapters 1 and 2 to explain how a number of the programming statements work, specifically those related to controlling and interacting with the console window and those involved in displaying popup dialog windows.

Before you move on to Chapter 4, consider spending a little time improving the Number Guessing game by addressing the following list of challenges.

### Challenges

1. **As currently written, the Number Guessing game is hard coded to retrieve random numbers from 1 to 100. Consider modifying the game to allow the player to specify a different upper range.**
2. **Consider modifying the game so that it keeps track of the total number of games played and the average number of moves per game and displays this information at the end of each game.**
3. **Create a distribution package for your new game and share with a few friends, asking them to provide you with feedback.**

CHAPTER 4

# Making Decisions with Conditional Logic

To create applications and games of any level of complexity or sophistication, you need to learn how to apply conditional logic in order to analyze application data. Conditional logic allows your applications to choose between different sets of actions based on the data that is presented. In Phrogram, conditional logic is implemented using the `If...Then` and `Select...Case` code blocks along with comparison and logical operators. In addition to learning the basics of conditional logic, this chapter will also guide you through the creation of your next computer application, the Rock, Paper, Scissors game.

Specifically, you will learn:

- How to set up `If...Then` code blocks in order to perform different types of logical comparisons
- How to embed `If...Then` code blocks within each other to develop more complex logical tests
- How to set up `Select...Case` code blocks to compare a single condition against a range of different values
- How to work with Phrogram's comparison operators to perform different types of comparisons

## Project Preview: The Rock, Paper, Scissors Game

This chapter's application project is the Rock, Paper, Scissors game. This game pits the player against the computer in a computerized implementation of the children's Rock, Paper, Scissors game. The player submits moves by typing them in a text field located at the bottom of the application window. Valid moves are Rock, Paper, and Scissors. Once the player has submitted a valid move, the game generates a random move on behalf of the computer. The winner of the game is then determined based on the following set of rules.

- Rock crushes scissors
- Paper covers rock
- Scissors cut paper
- Matching moves result in a tie

As Figure 4.1 shows, the game begins by displaying a message, prompting the player for permission to begin game play.

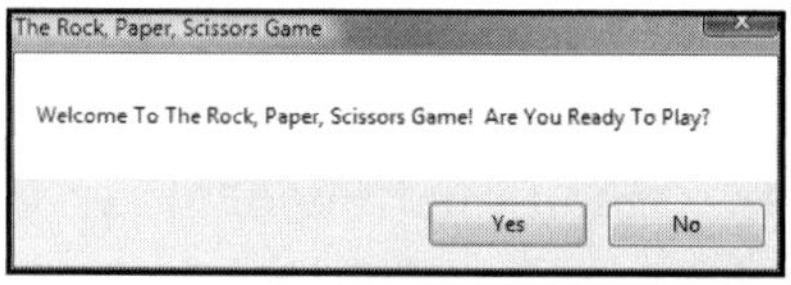


**Figure 4.1**

The welcome screen for the Rock, Paper, Scissors game.

If the player clicks on the No button, the game ends. If the player clicks on the Yes button, a new game is started and the window shown in Figure 4.2 is displayed.

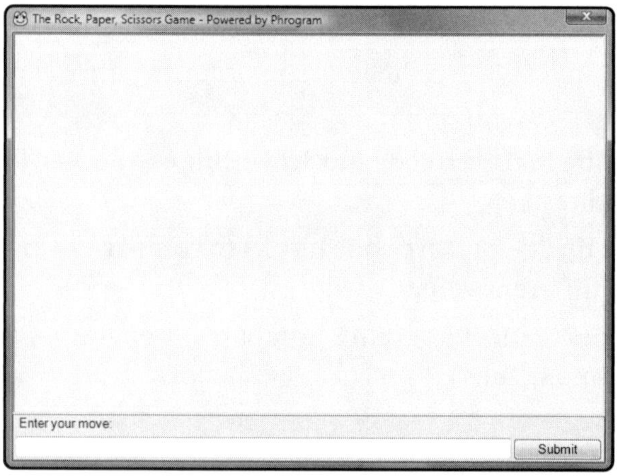


**Figure 4.2**

The player submits moves by typing them in at the bottom of the window.

To play, the player must key in a move (Rock, Paper, or Scissors) in the text field provided at the bottom of the window. The game then validates the player's input. If the player submits an invalid move, the move is rejected and the popup dialog window shown in Figure 4.3 displays.

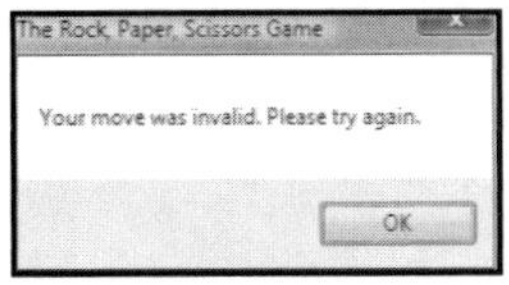


**FIGURE 4.3**

The game automatically validates player input.

Once the player's move has been validated, the game generates a random move on behalf of the computer. Figure 4.4 shows an example of a game in which the computer has won.

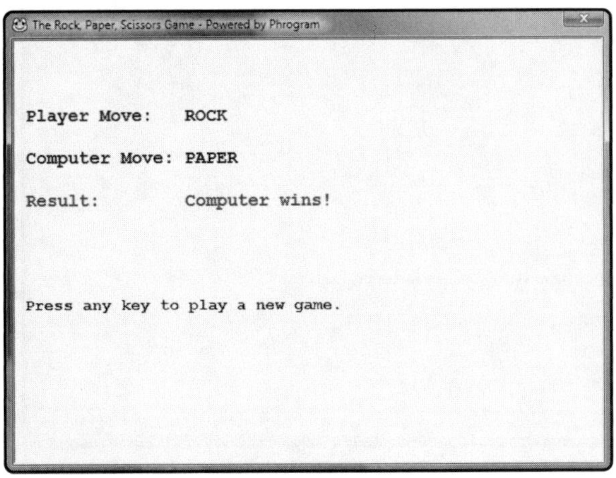


**FIGURE 4.4**

Paper covers rock so the computer wins.

Figure 4.5 shows an example of a game where the player and the computer have tied.

Figure 4.6 shows an example of a game where the player has won.

At the end of each round of play the player is prompted to press any key to start a new game. Game play continues until the player clicks on the Close button located in the upper-right corner of the game window.

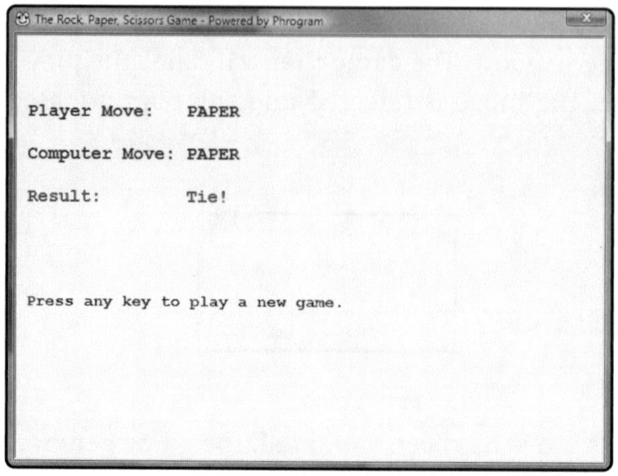


**FIGURE 4.5**

Matching moves result in a tie game.

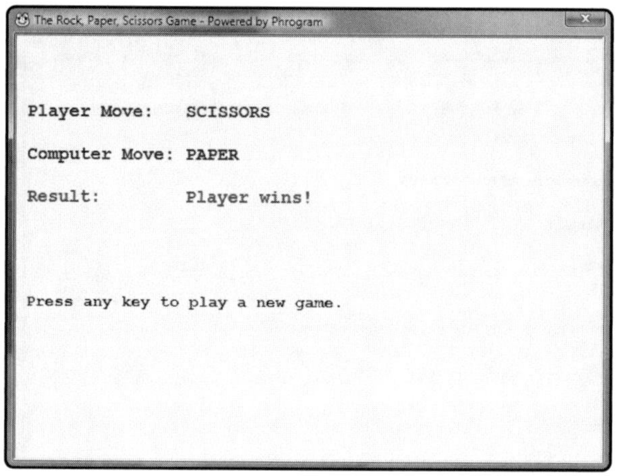


**FIGURE 4.6**

Scissors cut paper so the player wins.

## ANALYZING DATA USING CONDITIONAL LOGIC

In the Kids Jokes game, which you developed in Chapter 1, each programming statement in the program file was executed sequentially, beginning with the first statement in the `Main()` method and ending with the last statement in the method. This worked because the Kids Jokes application did not involve any complex logic. The game simply displayed successive series of text strings in a predefined order. However, sequential processing only works for the simplest of programs.

In order to develop a computer game or application of any level of complexity, you must apply conditional logic. For example, computer games require interaction with the user that involves the collection and analysis of data supplied by the user. This data may be provided by the keyboard, mouse, or through a controller like a joystick. By analyzing player input, your game is able to adjust its execution accordingly.

Conditional logic is an easy concept to understand because we are taught its basic principles as children and apply it constantly in our everyday lives. For example, anytime you go to the video store, you must decide what type of movie you want to rent. Do you want to be scared silly or made to laugh until your stomach hurts? Based on the result of this decision, you know what sections of the store you want to browse. This same type of logic is applicable to computer applications. For example, take a look at Figure 4.7.

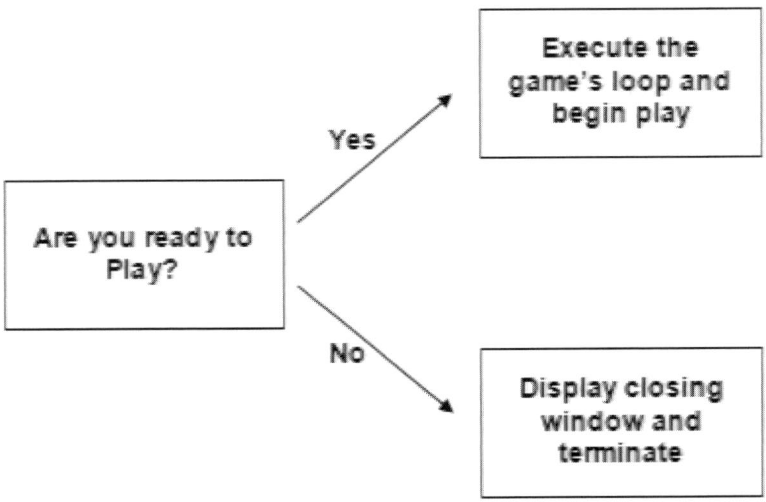


**FIGURE 4.7**
A depiction of the programming logic used to determine if an application should terminate.

In Figure 4.7, a simple flowchart is used to depict the basic logic used to govern an application's execution, based on input provided by the user when prompted for permission to begin game play. As you can see, two separate courses of action are outlined. Which one is executed depends on the analysis of the input provided by the user. If the user decides to play the game and provides input of Yes, then game play begins. However, if the user provides input of No, then the application's window is closed and the game's execution is terminated. This logical outline can easily be translated into program code as demonstrated here:

> **HINT** A *flowchart* is a graphical depiction of some or all of an application's logical flow. Programmers develop flowcharts in order to outline the overall logic involved in developing a computer application. Once completed, a flowchart can be used to verify that the programmer's logical approach is sound. This gives programmers a chance to identify any flaws in the logical design of the program before investing the time and effort required to develop the application.

```
Reply = Confirm("Welcome to My Game. Are you ready to play?", "My Game")
If Reply = True Then    //The player clicked on Yes
    While True
        Statements
    End While
Else                    //The player clicked on No
    Alert("OK. Perhaps another time.", "My Game")
End If
```

As you can see, this example begins by using the `Confirm()` method to display a popup dialog window that prompts the player to click on either of two buttons, Yes or No. If the player clicks on the Yes button, the program code statements located between the `If` statement and the `Else` keyword are executed. On the other hand, if the player clicked on the No button, the program code statements located between the `Else` keyword and the closing `End If` statement are executed.

When it comes down to it, conditional logic is an evaluation as to whether a condition is true or false followed by the execution of different program code statements based on the results of that analysis. Phrogram provides you with two different ways of implementing conditional logic within your applications, as listed here:

- `If…Then`. A code block designed to test a condition and then selectively execute program code statements based on the result of that analysis.
- `Select…Case`. A code block designed to test a condition to a range of possible matching values and then to execute the program code statements associated with the matching value.

> HINT: A *code block* is a collection of statements executed as a unit. Code blocks have an opening and closing statement within which other program code statements are embedded.

## Working with If...Then Code Blocks

The `If…Then` code block is so fundamental to the development of computer applications that it is almost impossible to write an application without using it. If you go back and check, you will see that that `If…Then` code blocks were used in Chapters 2 and 3 when developing the Story Time and Number Guessing games. To develop a better appreciation of the mechanics involved in working with the `If…Then` statement, look at the following example.

```
If I win the lottery Then
  I will quit my job
```

```
  Buy a boat
  Go on a long vacation
Else
  I will show up at work on Monday
  Work overtime
  Take a weekend trip
End If
```

This pseudo code provides a rough example of how to use an `If…Then` code block to test a condition and determine an appropriate course of action. The opening statement begins with the keyword `If` and specifies the condition that is being tested followed by the `Then` keyword. Next, a set of three program code statements are specified, each of which will be executed if the condition that is tested evaluates as being `True`. If, however, the tested conditional evaluates as being `False`, then the three program code statements that follow the `Else` keyword and precede the `End If` keywords are executed. An important point to take note of here is that in this example, two sets of statements have been outlined of which only one set is ultimately executed.

**HINT** The term *pseudo code* refers to an English-like outline of some or all of the logic involved in the development of a computer application. When outlining an application using pseudo code, your focus is on developing the high-level logic required to accomplish a particular task. By focusing only on the high-level logic involved, you remove any consideration about the specific programming statements required to implement your solution. By taking the time to outline the high-level logic required to create an application in pseudo code, you provide yourself with an outline that you can then follow when writing your actual application.

## If...Then Syntax

Phrogram supports many different variations of `If…Then` code blocks. This allows you to adapt them to handle many different types of situations, using the syntax outlined here:

```
If Condition Then
    Statements
Else If Condition Then
    Statements
Else If Condition Then
.
.
.
```

```
Else
   Statements
End If
```

*Condition* represents an expression that results in a value of True or False. *Statements* is a placeholder representing one or more code statements that are conditionally executed based on the value of the tested condition. Else If is an optional keyword that when used allows you to specify additional conditions that are to be evaluated. You may include as many Else If statements as are required. *Else* is an optional keyword that executes an alternate set of program code statements in the event that none of the preceding conditional tests evaluate as being True. The closing End If statement is required in order to mark the end of the If...Then code block.

As the next several sections will demonstrate, the If...Then code block is quite flexible and can be used in a number of different ways.

## Testing in a Single Condition

In its simplest form, the If...Then code block can be used to test for a single condition and will either execute or not execute a set of statements based on its evaluation, as demonstrated here:

```
Define PlayerAge As Integer = 21

If PlayerAge >= 18 Then
    Print("OK, you can play.")
End If
```

Here, a variable named PlayerAge is defined as an integer variable and assigned a value of 21. An If...Then code block is then set up that checks to see if the value assigned to PlayerAge is greater than or equal to 18, which of course it is, so the statement embedded within the code block is executed. Had the value of PlayerAge been less than 18, the statement embedded inside the code block would not have been executed.

The advantage of this form of the If...Then code block is that it lets you set up a conditional test to control the execution of one or more statements that will only execute if the condition being evaluated proves false. The disadvantage of this form of the If...Then code block is that in order to provide for the conditional execution of two separate sets of program code statements in the event the tested condition proves false, you must develop a second If...Then code block, as demonstrated here:

```
Define PlayerAge As Integer = 21

If PlayerAge >= 18 Then
    Print("OK, you can play.")
End If
If PlayerAge < 18 Then
    Print("Sorry, you are too young to play.")
End If
```

## Providing for Alternative Actions

If...Then code blocks can easily be expanded to allow you to specify an alternate set of statements that will be executed in the event the condition being tested evaluates as false by taking advantage of the optional Else keyword. An example of how this is done is provided here:

```
Define PlayerAge As Integer = 21

If PlayerAge >= 18 Then
    Print("OK, you can play.")
Else
    Print("Sorry, you are too young to play.")
End If
```

Here, either of two messages is displayed depending on the value assigned to PlayerAge. In addition to allowing for an alternate course of action, you can insert as many program code statements as necessary into both the upper and lower parts of the If...Then code block.

## Testing Alternative Conditions

Another useful form of the If...Then code block involves the addition of one or more instances of the Else If keyword, which lets you specify alternative conditions that should be tested in the event the If...Then code block's initial condition evaluates as false. An example of how to specify alternative conditional tests within an If...Then code block is provided here:

```
Define PlayerAge As Integer = 17

If PlayerAge >= 18 Then
    Print("OK, you can play.")
Else If PlayerAge >= 16 Then
    Print("You must have your parent's permission to play.")
Else If PlayerAge >= 15 Then
```

```
    Print("Come back next year.")
Else
    Print("Sorry, you are too young to play.")
End If
```

Here, the If…Then code block initially evaluates the value of PlayerAge to see if it is greater than or equal to 18 and if it is, displays a message telling the user that she can play the game. However, if the value assigned to PlayerAge is less than 18, a different condition is evaluated, this time checking to see if PlayerAge is greater than or equal to 16. If this evaluation proves False, a third condition is tested. If this test also evaluates as True, a message is displayed advising the player to come back next year. Otherwise, the Print statement associated with the optional Else keyword is displayed.

## Nesting If...Then Code Blocks

Another powerful feature of If…Then code blocks is that you can embed or *nest* them within one another in order to create complex conditional logic. This allows you to conditionally execute additional tests based on whether the previous test proved true. As an example of how to nest If…Then code blocks, look at the following statements.

```
Define FirstName As String = "Jerry"
Define MiddleName As String = "Lee"
Define LastName As String = "Ford"

If FirstName = "Jerry" Then
    If MiddleName = "Lee" Then
        If LastName = "Ford" Then
            Print("Welcome, Jerry. Would you like to play a game?")
        End If
    End If
End If
```

Here, a total of three If…Then blocks have been defined. The first If…Then block checks to see if the value of a variable named FirstName is equal to "Jerry". If it is not equal, all subsequent embedded code blocks are skipped. If, however, the first test evaluates as being True, the second test is performed, followed by the third test (if the second test proves True).

> **TRAP**
>
> There is no limit to how deeply you can nest If…Then code statements. However, the deeper you nest code blocks the more complicated your program code will be to understand and maintain. In general, you will not want to nest more than two or three levels deep.

**FIND IT ONLINE**

As you continue to work with Phrogram and begin writing your own applications from scratch, there will be times when you run into a problem that you are unable to figure out on your own. When this occurs, you need to reach out to others for help. One way of doing this is to reach out to Phrogram technical support, which is provided through the Phrogram Company website's online forums. The easiest way of getting to these forums when you are working with Phrogram is to click on the Technical Support option located on Phrogram's Help menu. When you do this, the window shown in Figure 4.8 displays.

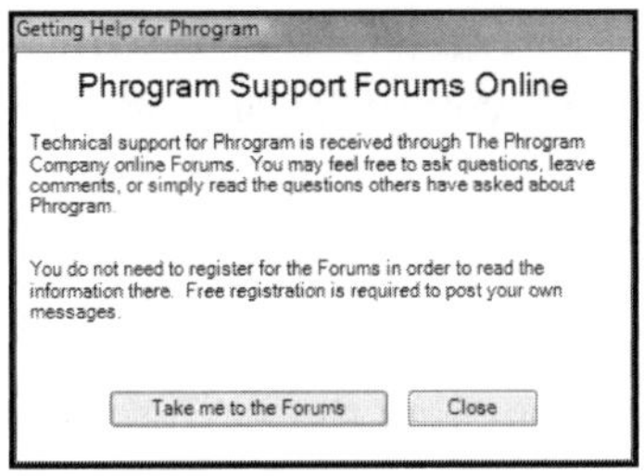


**FIGURE 4.8**

Accessing Phrogram Support Forums Online.

Click on the Take me to the Forums button and Phrogram will instruct your default web browser to open and display a list of forums where you can post questions and get help from Phrogram Technical Support as well as from its user community.

Take a few minutes to perform this process and to review postings published by other Phrogram programmers to get a feel for the kinds of problems that they are dealing with.

## USING THE SELECT...CASE CODE BLOCK

As an alternative to the `If...Then` code block, Phrogram also supports the `Select...Case` code block. The `Select...Case` code block allows you to compare a single value to a range of possible matching values and can be used to replace a series of `If...Then` statements designed to test different values resulting from the same expression. The syntax for the `Select...Case` statement is outlined here:

```
Select Expression

    Case Value
        Statements
    End Case

    Case Value
```

```
        Statements
    End Case

    Case Else
        Statements
    End Case

End Select
```

The Select…Case code block consists of a beginning Select statement and ends with an End Select statement. In between these statements you place one or more case statements, each of which has an accompanying End Case statement. You can also include an optional Case Else statement that will execute in the event that none of the case statements match the expression specified in the opening Select statement.

When executed, the statements nested within the first matching case statement are executed. If none of the case statements match, the statements associated with the Case Else statement are executed. If the Case Else statement is omitted and a match is not found with one of the case statements, nothing happens. If more than one case statement matches, only the statements associated with the first matching Case statement are executed.

To develop a better understanding of the logic involved in setting up a Select…Case statement, look at the following pseudo code example.

```
Select PlayerMove equals Rock
    Case If the computer's move is Rock
        Declare a tie
    End Case
    Case If the computer's move is Paper
        Declare the computer the winner
    End Case
    Case If the computer's move is scissors
        Declare the player the winner
    End Case
End Select
```

In this pseudo code example, three Case statements are specified, each representing one of three possible computer moves. A different action is then taken depending on which of the three Case statements results in a match. Since the value of each Case statement is compared to the value specified by the Select statement, the Select…Case code block is intuitively easier to read and understand than a series of separate `If…Then` code blocks designed to perform the same analysis.

To better understand the application of the `Select…Case` code block, consider the example provided here:

```
Define PlayerMove As String
Define ComputerMove As String

PlayerMove = "Rock"
ComputerMove = "Paper"

If PlayerMove = "Rock" Then
    Select ComputerMove
        Case "Rock"
            Print("Tie!")
        End Case
        Case "Paper"
            Print("The computer wins!")
        End Case
        Case "Scissors"
            Print("The player wins!")
        End Case
    End Select
End If
```

Here, the value assigned to `PlayerMove` is evaluated using three `Case` statements, each of which displays a different test message describing the result of the comparison.

## Exercises

**This chapter covered a lot of ground in its discussion of conditional programming logic. To further reinforce your understanding of these important concepts, complete the following hands-on exercises.**

1. **Using the Explorer window, open, review, and execute the following Phrogram programs, each of which provides further instructions and examples of how to work with `If…Then` code blocks.**

- **If-Then-Else.kpl located in the Phrogram examples folder.**
- **IfThenElseTemplate.kpl located in the 3) Phrogram templates folder.**
- **IfThenTemplate.kpl located in the 3) Phrogram templates folder.**

2. **Using the Explorer window, open, review, and execute the following Phrogram programs, each of which provides further instructions and examples of how to work with Select...Case code blocks.**
   - **Select Statement.kpl located in the Phrogram examples folder.**
   - **SelectStatementTemplate.kpl located in the 3) Phrogram templates folder.**
   - **Select Statement - Advanced.kpl located in the Times subfolder located in the 5) Advanced Learning Examples folder.**

## Different Ways of Comparing Data

As you have already seen, Phrogram allows you to perform many different types of comparisons using different comparison operators. For example, using the = operator you can compare two string or two numeric values to determine if they are equal to one another. Phrogram supports a number of additional operators that allow you to perform other types of comparisons. These operators are outlined in Table 4.1.

**Table 4.1 Phrogram Comparison Operators**

| Operator | Description |
|---|---|
| = | Equals |
| < | Less than |
| > | Greater than |
| <= | Less than or equal to |
| >= | Greater than or equal to |
| <> | Not equal |

To get a better feel as to how to work with these operators, look at the following example.

```
Define X As Integer = 5

//Check to see if X is equal to 5
```

```
If X = 5 Then
    Print("Match!")
End If

//Check to see if X is less than 10
If X < 10 Then
    Print("X is less than 10")
End If

//Check to see if X is greater than 3
If X > 3 Then
    Print("X is greater than 3")
End If

//Check to see if X is less than or equal to 5
If X <= 5 Then
    Print("X is less than or equal to 5")
End If

//Check to see if X is greater than or equal to 5
If X >= 5 Then
    Print("X is greater than or equal to 5")
End If

//Check to see if X is not equal to 10
If X <> 10 Then
    Print("X is not equal to 10")
End If
```

Using the comparison operators outlined in Table 4.1, you can set up comparison operations that are capable of performing comparisons that involve ranges of numbers. In addition, you can also use Phrogram's comparison operators to compare strings, as demonstrated in the following example.

```
If "He" = "She" Then
    ConsoleWriteLine("Match!")
End If

If "A" < "B" Then
```

```
    ConsoleWriteLine("A is less than B")
End If

If "Dog" > "Cat" Then
    ConsoleWriteLine("Dog comes after Cat")
End If

If "ABC" <= "EFG" Then
    ConsoleWriteLine("ABC is less than or equal to EFG")
End If
```

When executed, this example displays the results shown in Figure 4.9, demonstrating that Phrogram can perform an alphabetical comparison of strings.

FIGURE 4.9

Using comparison operators to compare string values.

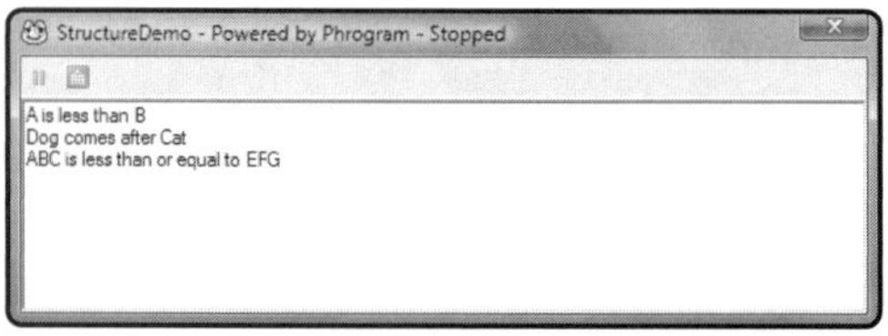


## DOING A LITTLE MATH

As you learned in Chapter 3, "Learning How to Work with Data," you can perform a host of mathematical operations using Phrogram and the `Math` library's built-in collection of mathematic methods. Phrogram supports addition, subtraction, multiplication, and division using the operators listed in Table 4.2.

TABLE 4.2 PHROGRAM MATHEMATIC OPERATORS

| Operator | Description | Example |
|---|---|---|
| + | Addition | x = 1 + 2 |
| – | Subtraction | x = 3 – 1 |
| * | Multiplication | x = 2 * 4 |
| / | Division | x = 6 / 3 |

For example, using the followings statements demonstrates how to add three numbers together using the addition operator.

```
Define X As Integer
X = 5 + 3 + 2
Print(X)
```

When executed this example displays a value of 10 on the console window. Phrogram allows you to work with numeric variables in place of numeric literal values, as demonstrated here:

```
Define X As Integer = 5
Define Y As Integer = 10
Define Z As Integer = 0

Z = X + Y

Print(Z)
```

When executed this example displays a value of 15 on the console window.

## Understanding the Order of Precedence

When performing mathematic calculations, Phrogram evaluates numeric expressions based on a specific set of rules, referred to as order of precedence. Table 4.3 outlines the rules that Phrogram follows when enforcing its order of precedence.

**Table 4.3 Phrogram's Order of Precedence**

| Operator | Description |
|---|---|
| *, / | Multiplication and division occur first on a left to right basis. |
| +, - | Addition and subtraction occur second on a left to right basis. |

To better understand how the order of precedence affects the manner in which Phrogram resolves numeric calculations, consider the following example.

```
Define X As Integer
X = 3 + 6 * 5 / 3 - 3 * 2
Print(X)
```

When executed, Phrogram assigns a value of 7 to X. it arrives at this value by following the steps outlined here:

1. Working from left to right, Phrogram performs all multiplication and division operations. So 6 is multiplied by 5 yielding a value of 30. This value is then divided by 3 yielding a value of 10. Next 3 is multiplied by 2 yielding a value of 6.
2. At this point, based on the calculations that have been performed, Phrogram has simplified as shown here:
   ```
   x = 3 + 10 - 6
   ```
3. Phrogram then performs addition and subtraction going from left to right, so 3 is added to 10 yielding a value of 13 from which 6 is subtracted. This results in a final value of 7, which is assigned to `X`.

### Controlling Precedence

If necessary, you can override the order in which Phrogram evaluates numeric expressions. This is accomplished using parentheses. When parts of numeric expressions are enclosed in parentheses, Phrogram evaluates those parts first and then uses the order of precedence to evaluate the rest of the expression. To see how this works, look at the following example.

```
x = (3 + 6) * (5 / 3 - 3) * 2
```

This statement is almost identical to the statement used in the previous section, the only difference being the addition of two pair of parentheses. As a result, Phrogram now evaluates the expression differently, arriving at a much different result as explained here:

1. Working from left to right Phrogram begins by evaluating the parts of the expression that are located inside parentheses. Therefore, 3 is added to 6 yielding 9 and then 5 is divided by 3 yielding a value of 1 from which 3 is then subtracted yielding a value of -2.
2. At this point, based on the calculations that have been performed, Phrogram has simplified as shown here:
   ```
   x = 9 * -2 * 2
   ```
3. Once everything within parentheses has been evaluated, multiplication and division are performed going from left to right. Therefore, 9 is multiplied by -2 yielding a value of -18, which is then divided by 2 yielding a final value of −36.

## Working with Logical Operators

In addition to mathematical and comparison operators, Phrogram also provides a group of operators referred to as logical operators. These logical operators are outlined in Table 4.4.

These logical operators give you the ability to combine different comparison operations, allowing you to develop program code statements that are more intuitive and easier to understand. For example, the following statements show an example that used a pair of `If...Then` code blocks to analyze two values and determine if a string should be displayed.

**Table 4.4 Phrogram's Logical Operators**

| Operator | Type | Example |
|---|---|---|
| and | A value of True is returned if both comparison operations evaluate as True | x > 1 and x < 5 |
| or | A value of False is returned if either of the comparison operations evaluate as True | x = 1 or x = 5 |
| not | Reverses the value returned by an expression | not (x = 0) |

```
Define X As Integer = 1
Define Y As Integer = 2

If X = 1 Then
    If Y = 2 Then
        Print("We have a match!")
    End If
End If
```

Using logical operators, you could rewrite this example as shown next, reducing the number of statements that are required.

```
Define X As Integer = 1
Define Y As Integer = 2

If X = 1 And Y = 2 Then
    Print("We have a match!")
End If
```

As you can see, the use of the `And` logical operator results in a code statement that is easier to understand. The `Or` logical operator is very similar to the `And` logical operator, except that it only requires one of its tested conditions to evaluate as being `True` for it to return a value of `True`, as demonstrated in the following example.

```
Define X As Integer = 1
Define Y As Integer = 2

If X = 1 Or Y = 3 Then
    Print("We have at least one match!")
End If
```

The `Not` logical operator is used by placing it before an expression, as demonstrated here:

```
Define X As Integer = 1

If Not X = 2 Then
    Print("X does not equal 2")
End If
```

When executed, it reverses the value of the expression, returning a value of `True` in place of a value of `False` and vice versa. In this example, `X` is not equal to 2, resulting in a value of `False`. Because the expression is preceded by the `Not` logical operator, a value of `True` is returned instead and the embedded print statement is executed.

## Review Questions

1. **What is conditional logic? What command do you use to implement it in Phrogram?**
2. **What is a code block?**
3. **What is a flow chart? What are the advantages of creating flowcharts?**
4. **Define the term pseudo code. List two benefits of developing pseudo code prior to beginning the coding process.**
5. **What is nesting? Does Phrogram place any limitations on how deeply you can nest code blocks? Are their any disadvantages to nesting?**
6. **What is the term that defines the order in which Phrogram evaluates numeric expressions?**
7. **List the order in which numeric expressions are evaluated.**
8. **Is there any way to override the order in which Phrogram evaluates numeric expressions?**
9. **Can comparison operators be used in conjunction with strings?**
10. **What is a logical operator? List three logical operators and explain how each works.**

# Back to the Rock, Paper, Scissors Game

Now it is time to return to this chapter's application project, the Rock, Paper, Scissors game. This game challenges the player to outguess the computer in a head-to-head battle based on the children's Rock, Paper, Scissors game. The development of this game will help to reinforce your understanding of conditional logic and will give you the opportunity to work more with both the `If...Then` and `Case...Select` code blocks.

## Designing the Game

To help keep things as simple as possible, this game will be created by following a series of steps, as outlined here:

1. Create a new program project.
2. Document your application.
3. Define a global constant.
4. Define method variables.
5. Configure the game's window.
6. Prompt the player for permission to begin.
7. Analyze the player's response.
8. Control game play.
9. Suggest the player play again another time.
10. Save and compile your new application.

### Step 1: Creating a New Phrogram Project

The first step in creating the Rock, Paper, Scissors game is to create a new program. To do so, start Phrogram and click on the New Program command located on the File menu. Next, assign a more meaningful name to the application by replacing the default program name of MyNewProgram with RockPaperScissors as the application's name on the first code statement.

The rest of the program code statements that make up the RockPaperScissors application are explained in the sections that follow and will be inserted between the program file's `Method Main()` and `End Method` statements.

### Step 2: Documenting Your New Program

Now it is time to add the program code statements that will make your new program come to life. Let's begin by adding the following comment statements to your program's code file.

```
//Program: RockPaperScissors.kpl
//Created: 12/26/2007
//Version: 1.0
```

```
//Author: Jerry Lee Ford, Jr.
//Description: This Phrogram game pits the player against the computer
//in a computerized implementation of the Rock, Paper, Scissors
//game.
```

As you can see, the purpose of these statements is to provide some high-level documentation about the program.

### Step 3: Defining a Global Constant

The name of the Rock, Paper, Scissors game is displayed in the titlebar at the top of the game's console window as well as in the titlebar of all the game's popup dialog windows. Instead of hard coding the game's name throughout the program file, let's define a constant and assign it the name of the game as its value. This is accomplished by adding the following statements to the beginning of the program file, immediately after the program statement and before the `Main()` method.

```
//Global constant used to store the name of the game
Constant GameTitle As String = "The Rock, Paper, Scissors Game"
```

Once added, you can refer to `cGameTitle` whenever you need to display the game's name.

### Step 4: Defining Method Variables

The next step in the creation of the Rock, Paper, Scissors game is to define a number of variables that will be used throughout the `Main()` method to keep track of different data, including player input, the player's moves, the computer's moves, and the game's randomly generated number. This is accomplished by adding the following statements to the `Main()` method.

```
Define Reply As Boolean = False     //Used to store player input
Define Move As String              //Stores player guesses
Define Msg As String                //Stores a display string
Define ComputerMove As String       //Stores computer moves
Define RandomNumber As Integer      //Stores the game's random #
Define Result As String             //Stores the game results
```

Comments have been added to the right of each variable definition that explains each variable's purpose.

### Step 5: Configuring the Game's Window

Now it is time to add the program code statements that are responsible for specifying configuration settings that control the appearance of the game's window. These statements, shown next, hide the window's toolbar, configure the window's size, and then display a text string of Rock, Paper, Scissors in the titlebar. Next, a background color of WhiteSmoke is set and the font style used to display text is set to bold.

```
HideToolbar()   //Prevent the window's toolbar from being displayed
SetScreenSize (600, 400)    //Set the screen size to 600x400 pixels
SetWindowTitle (GameTitle)  //Display the name of the game in the
                            //Window's titlebar

SetConsoleBackgroundColor(WhiteSmoke)        //Set background color

// Set console font style to Bold, non-italic and non-underline
SetConsoleFontStyle(True, False, False)
```

Each of these statements should be added to the Main() method, just after the comments statements that you added in the previous step.

### Step 6: Prompting the Player for Permission to Begin

Now it is time to add the program code statements responsible for displaying a message that welcomes the player and then pauses the game, waiting for the player to press a key on the keyboard before continuing.

```
//Outline the text of the game's welcome message
Msg = "Welcome To " + GameTitle + "!  Are You Ready To Play?"

//Display the game's welcome message in a popup dialog window and
//prompt the player to click on Yes to play the game or No to quit
Reply = Confirm(Msg, GameTitle)
```

These statements should be added to the Main() method, immediately following the set of statements that you added in the previous step.

### Step 7: Analyzing the Player's Response

The player's response to the popup dialog window displayed in the previous step must now be analyzed to determine which button the player clicked. This is accomplished by adding the following statements to the Main() method, immediately following the statements that you added in the previous step.

```
//Analyze the player's response
```

```
If Reply = True Then              //If Reply equals True then the
                                  //player clicked on the Yes button

Else    //Execute the following statements when the player clicks
        //on the No button

End If
```

These statements create the logical framework that controls the execution of the rest of the game. If the player clicks on the popup dialog window's Yes button, a value of `True` is assigned to `Reply`, in which case the program statements that you are going to insert in between the `If` and `Else` statements in Step 8 are executed. On the other hand, if the player clicks on the No button, the statements that you will place in between the `Else` and the `End If` statements (in Step 9) are executed.

## Step 8: Controlling Overall Game Play

The next set of program code statements to be added to the Rock, Paper, Scissors game are shown next and should be inserted into code statements that you just added to the `Main()` method. Specifically, you should insert these statements just after the `If` statement and just before the `Else` statement.

```
While True                      //Create a loop that runs forever

    ClearConsole()              //Clear the console

    //Prompt the player to enter a guess
    Move = ConsoleReadLine("Enter your move:", False)

    If Move = "ROCK" Or Move = "PAPER" Or Move = "SCISSORS" Then

        //Generate a number from 1 to 3
        RandomNumber = Random(1, 3)

        //Assign the random number to a valid game move
        Select RandomNumber
            Case 1
                ComputerMove = "ROCK"
            End Case
            Case 2
```

```
        ComputerMove = "PAPER"
    End Case
    Case 3
        ComputerMove = "SCISSORS"
    End Case
End Select

//Determine the results of the game
If Move = "ROCK" Then
    Select ComputerMove
        Case "ROCK"
            Result = "Tie!"
        End Case
        Case "PAPER"
            Result = "Computer wins!"
        End Case
        Case "SCISSORS"
            Result = "Player wins!"
        End Case
    End Select
End If

If Move = "PAPER" Then
    Select ComputerMove
        Case "ROCK"
            Result = "Player wins!"
        End Case
        Case "PAPER"
            Result = "Tie!"
        End Case
        Case "SCISSORS"
            Result = "Computer wins!"
        End Case
    End Select
End If

If Move = "SCISSORS" Then
    Select ComputerMove
```

```
        Case "ROCK"
            Result = "Computer wins!"
        End Case
        Case "PAPER"
            Result = "Player wins!"
        End Case
        Case "SCISSORS"
            Result = "Tie!"
        End Case
    End Select
End If

ClearConsole()                        //Clear the console

SetConsoleFontColor(DarkBlue)         //Set font color

// Set font to Courier New, point 14
SetConsoleFont("Courier New", 14)

//Display the game results
ConsoleWriteLine("")
ConsoleWriteLine("")
ConsoleWriteLine("")
ConsoleWriteLine(" Player Move:   " + ToUpperCase(Move))
ConsoleWriteLine("")
ConsoleWriteLine(" Computer Move: " + ComputerMove)
ConsoleWriteLine("")

SetConsoleFontColor(DarkRed)              //Set font color

ConsoleWriteLine(" Result:        " + Result)
ConsoleWriteLine("")
ConsoleWriteLine("")
ConsoleWriteLine("")
ConsoleWriteLine("")

// Set font to Courier New, point 12
SetConsoleFont("Courier New", 12)
```

```
        SetConsoleFontColor(Black)              //Set font color
        ConsoleWriteLine(" Press any key to play a new game.")

        ConsoleReadKey() //Wait for the player to press a key

    Else

        //The player has entered an invalid move
        Alert("Your move was invalid. Please try again.", GameTitle)

    End If

End While
```

With two exceptions, you should be familiar with all of the programming statements shown above. The first exception is the first and last statements, which set up a loop that repeats the execution of the game over and over again, allowing the player to play as many games as she wants. You will learn about loops and their operations in Chapter 5, "Using Loops to Process Data." The second exception is the use of the `ConsoleReadLine()` method in the sixth statement. This method displays a text prompt and retrieves user input entered into the console window's input area.

**HINT**

**The `Console` library's `ConsoleReadLine()` method retrieves text entered by the user into the console window's input area, using the following syntax.**

```
ConsoleReadLine(Prompt As String, EchoToConsole As Boolean) As String
```

***Prompt*** **represents a text string that is displayed at the bottom of the console window, just above a text field that is used to collect user input. `EchoToConsole` is a Boolean value that, when set to `True` instructs Phrogram to display the user's input on the console window.**

**For example, the following statement prompts the user to enter her first name and stores the user's input in a variable named `Username`.**

```
UserName = ConsoleReadLine("Enter your first name:", False)
```

Each time the `While` loop executes, a new round of play occurs and all of the program code statements listed within the loop are executed. The first statement executed clears the console window. Next the `ConsoleReadLine()` method displays a message at the bottom of the console window, prompting the player to enter a move. The player's move is stored in a string variable named `Move`. Next an `If…Then` code block is set up that begins by determining whether the player's input was valid. If the input is valid, game play continues. If the input was invalid, the code statements following the `If…Then` code block's `Else` keyword execute, displaying a popup dialog window that informs the user of the invalid move.

Each time a valid move is made, a random number in the range of 1 to 3 is generated using the `Random()` method and assigned to a variable named `RandomNumber`. Next, a `Select…Case` code block is set up for the purpose of assigning a move on behalf of the computer based on the value of the randomly generated number. Specifically, a value of 1 results in a computer move of `Rock`, a value of 2 results in a computer move of `Paper`, and a value of 3 results in a move of `Scissors`.

A set of three `If…Then` statement code blocks are executed next. Each of the three code blocks is designed to analyze a different type of player move. The first code block executes if the player's move was Rock. The second code block executes if the player's move was Paper, and the third code block executes only if the player entered a move of Scissors.

Within each `If…Then` code block is a `Select…Case` code block which determines the result of the game by comparing the player's move to the computer's assigned move. Once one of the `If…Then` code blocks has been executed, and the result of the game has been determined, the console window is cleared and the player is informed of the results and prompted to press a keyboard key to begin a new round of play.

## Step 9: Prompting the Player to Play Another Time

The last set of program code statements that need to be added to the Rock, Paper, Scissors game are shown next and should be added to the end of the `Main()` method, just after the `Else` statement and before the `End If` statement that you added in Step 7.

```
//Display a message in a popup window inviting the player to
//play again another time
Alert("OK. Perhaps another time.", GameTitle)
```

These statements execute only if the player decides not to play the game and clicks on the No button when prompted for permission to begin game play. When executed, these statements display a message that encourages the player to consider returning to play another time.

## Step 10: Saving and Compiling Your Application

That's it! If you have not done so, save your copy of the Rock, Paper, Scissors game by clicking on the Save All command located on the File menu. Once you have saved your new program, try compiling and running it by clicking on the Run the Program button located on the Phrogram toolbar. Once started, the Rock, Paper, Scissors game should run as previously described at the beginning of the chapter.

## The Final Result

Okay, at this point you should have all of the information you need to create the Rock, Paper, Scissors game. If you run into errors when developing your copy of this game, try using the error information provided by Phrogram to track down and fix any typos or mistakes you may have inadvertently made. Alternatively, you might want to open the copy of this game's source code from the book's accompanying CD and use it as a reference against which you can compare to see where things may have gone awry.

# Summary

In this chapter, you were introduced to the concepts of flowcharting and pseudo code. You were also introduced to conditional logic and learned how to apply it using the `If...Then` and `Case...Select` code blocks. You learned how to work with different forms of both of these statements and to embed code blocks in order to create more complex program logic. You learned more about Phrogram's support for mathematical operations, including how to override its order of precedence. You also learned how to work with Phrogram's comparison and logical operators.

Before you move on to Chapter 5, consider spending a little time improving the Rock, Paper, Scissors game by addressing the following list of challenges.

## Challenges

1. As currently written, the Rock, Paper, Scissors game makes the assumption that the player already knows how to play the game. However, you might want to consider displaying the rules for playing when the game is first started.
2. Forcing the player to make moves by typing in the words Rock, Paper, and Scissors leads to the possibility that the player may make typos. Consider allowing the player to enter R, P, or S instead. This will not only reduce the chances of a typo but will also speed up game play.
3. Consider keeping track of the number of games won, lost, and tied and displaying this information at the end of each game so that the player can gauge her overall performance against the computer.
4. Create a distribution package for your new game and share with a few friends, asking them to provide you with feedback.

CHAPTER 5

# Using Loops to Process Data

In the last chapter, you learned how to apply conditional logic when processing data to create Phrogram applications that could alter their execution based on the data they were presented with. Loops provide an efficient means of processing the data stored in arrays and can be used to streamline program code by providing the ability to process unlimited amounts of data using a minimum number of programming statements. More often than not, computer games involve the repeated execution of programming statements under the control of a loop. In this chapter, you will learn how to set up several different types of loops to repeat statement execution, manage animation sequences, and control the overall execution of game play. On top of all this, you will learn how to develop your next Phrogram application, the Slot Machine game.

Specifically, you will learn:

- How to set up `Loop...End Loop`, `For...Next`, and `While...End While` loops
- How to guard against endless loops
- How to break out of loops
- How to skip an iteration of a loop

## Project Preview: The Slot Machine Game

In this chapter, you will learn how to create a new Phrogram application known as the Slot Machine game. In this game, the player is presented with a Las Vegas-style three-dial slot machine and an account balance of $10. Rather than pulling a lever, the player starts the slot machine by pressing keys on the keyboard. Each time a spin occurs one of the following things happen.

- If three numbers match, the player wins $2.
- If two numbers match, the player wins $1.
- If no numbers match, the player loses $5.

Game play continues until the player decides to quit or until the player runs out of money and goes broke. Figure 5.1 shows the popup dialog window that appears when the game is first started.

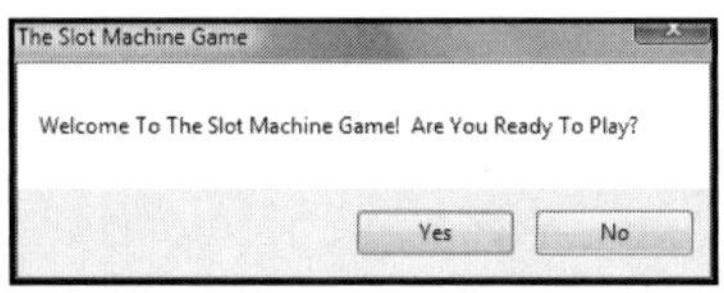


**Figure 5.1**

The player is welcomed to the game and prompted to begin playing.

If the player clicks on the No button, the game ends. If the player clicks on the Yes button, the window shown in Figure 5.2 displays.

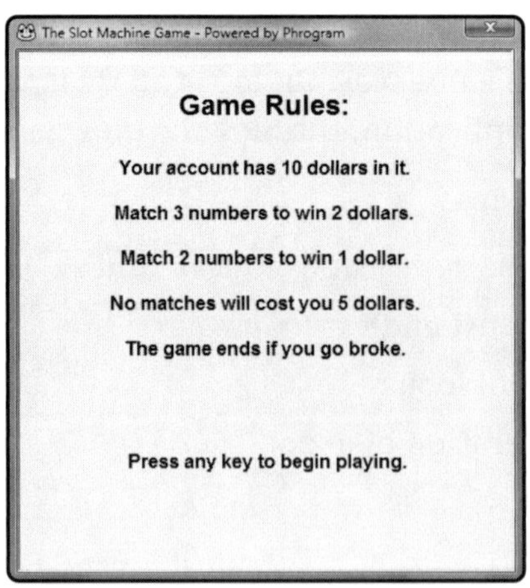


**Figure 5.2**

The player is given the opportunity to review the rules for playing the game.

To start playing, the player has to press a keyboard key at which time the screen clears and numbers, representing three slot machine dials display. Each number is randomly generated and is changed every 3/10 of a second, 11 times. The last set of numbers generated for each dial remains displayed, representing the results of the spin. At this point, the game analyzes the spin and determines whether money should be added or removed from the player accounts, as demonstrated in Figure 5.3.

**FIGURE 5.3**

Two numbers have been matched, resulting in the addition of $1 to the player's account.

Figure 5.4 shows an example of a spin in which the player has hit the jackpot, with a spin made up of three matching numbers.

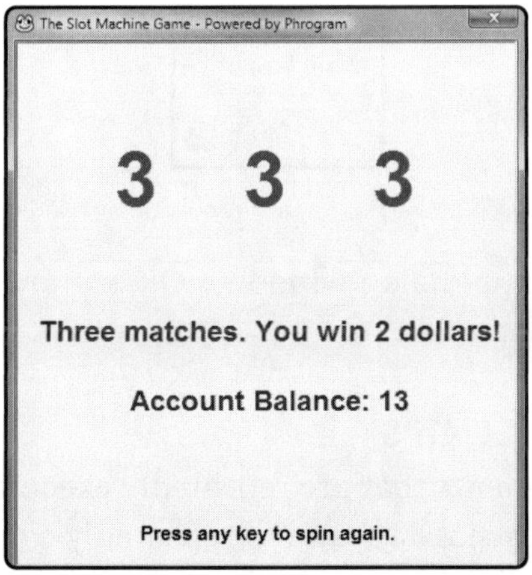


**FIGURE 5.4**

Three numbers have been matched resulting in the addition of $2 to the player's account.

As long as the player's account has money in it, the player can play as long as desired. To stop playing all the player has to do is to click on the Close button located in the upper-right corner of the game window. Game play automatically ends if the player goes broke, as demonstrated in Figure 5.5.

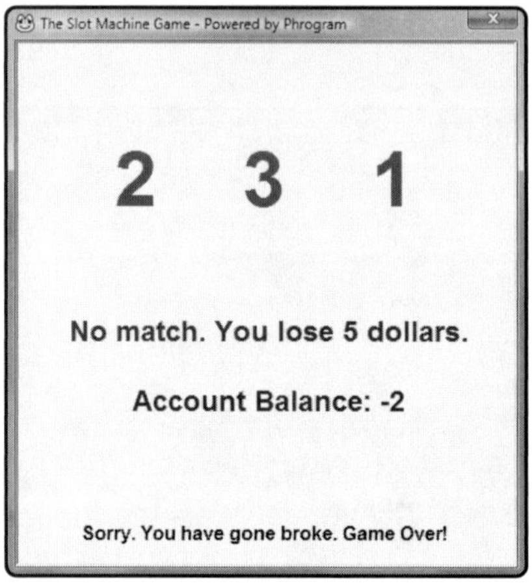


**FIGURE 5.5**

The player has gone bust.

Upon going broke, the player is presented with the results of the final spin and an explanation of what has happened. In the example shown in Figure 5.5, the player lost \$5 on the last spin, resulting in an account balance of -\$2. To wrap things up, the player is instructed to press any key, after which the popup dialog window shown in Figure 5.6 displays.

**FIGURE 5.6**

The game thanks the player for taking the time to play.

As soon as the player clicks on the popup dialog window's OK button, the game window is automatically closed and the application ends.

## GETTING WORK DONE WITH LOOPS

A *loop* is a block of programming statements that are repeatedly executed. Programmers use loops to efficiently process large amounts of data and to repeatedly control the execution of statements to accomplish repetitive tasks. Loops are a key component of computer games, providing the mechanism used to control animation sequences as well as manage the overall execution of most games.

Loops provide an essential means of controlling interactive and arcade-style computer games. Without loops, computer programs would become huge collections of repetitive statements. Loops help prevent this by allowing you to define all of the statements required to perform a particular task and then to execute all of the program statements that make up the loop's code block over and over again for as long as necessary.

To give you a better understanding of how loops can be used to stream program development, look at the following set of statements.

```
ConsoleWriteLine("1")
ConsoleWriteLine("2")
ConsoleWriteLine("3")
ConsoleWriteLine("4")
ConsoleWriteLine("5")
ConsoleWriteLine("6")
ConsoleWriteLine("7")
ConsoleWriteLine("8")
ConsoleWriteLine("9")
ConsoleWriteLine("10")
```

Here, 10 separate program code statements were needed to display a listing of numbers from 1 to 10. Suppose you want to display a list of numbers from 1 to 1000 or from 1 to 1000000. Clearly, things become unmanageable very quickly using individual program statements in this manner. A better way of addressing this challenge is to use a loop, as demonstrated here:

```
Define i As Integer = 1
Loop 10
    ConsoleWriteLine(i)
    i += 1
End Loop
```

Figure 5.7 shows the output that is produced when this example is executed. It is identical to the output that is produced by the 10 programming statements.

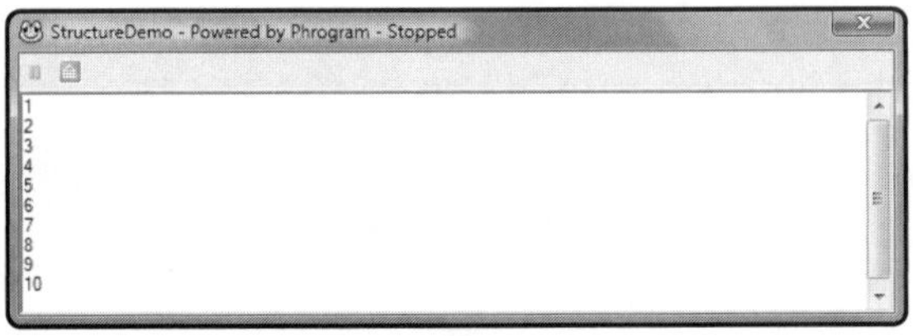


**FIGURE 5.7**

Using a Loop...End Loop to display a series of numbers.

As you can see, using a loop, this example is able to do in five code statements the same task that required 10 statements in the previous example. Better still, you would not have to add a single statement to count to 1,000 or 1,000,000. Instead, all you would need to do is change the second statement shown above to

```
Loop 1000
```

or

```
Loop 1000000
```

FIND IT ONLINE

Hungry for more Phrogram reading? Then check out *Learn to Program with Phrogram!*, a 100-plus page e-book designed to teach you basic Phrogram programming through the development of a computer game called UFO Escape! You can learn more about this book and purchase it online by visiting www.informit.com/store and searching on its title.

## Different Types of Loops Supported by Phrogram

Phrogram supports the execution of three different types of loops, each of which is outlined here:

- `Loop…End Loop`. Used to create a loop that executes a specific number of times.
- `For...Next`. Used to create a loop that repeats its execution a specified number of times based on an assigned start and end value.
- `While…End While`. Used to create a loop that repeats its execution as long as a tested condition is True.

You can use any of these loops to perform the same tasks. However, each of these loops has certain characteristics that make them applicable to performing certain types of tasks. You will learn how to work with each of these types of loops and the types of tasks to which they are suited throughout the rest of this book.

### Working with the Loop...End Loop Loop

Perhaps the simplest type of loop supported by Phrogram is its `Loop...End Loop` loop, which processes all of the program code statements in its code block a specified numbed of times. This type of loop is created using the syntax outlined here:

```
Loop Value
    Statements
End Loop
```

*Value* represents an integer value that specifies the number of times the loop will execute or iterate. *Statements* represents any number of program code statements that make up the loop's code block.

For example, the following statements demonstrate how to set up a `Loop...End Loop` loop that displays a list of numbers from 1 to 10.

```
Define i As Integer = 0

Loop 10
    i +=1
    ConsoleWriteLine(i)
End Loop
```

Here, an integer variable name `i` is defined and assigned a starting value of `0`. Then a `Loop... End Loop` loop is set up that iterates 10 times. Within the loop's code block, the value of i is incremented by 1 and then displayed on the console window each time the loop executes.

## Working with the For...Next Loop

The second type of loop supported by Phrogram is the `For...Next` loop, which executes a predetermined number of times over a range specified using starting and ending values using the following syntax.

```
For VariableName = Start To End [Step Value]
    Code Block Statements
Next
```

*VariableName* represents the name of an integer variable used to keep track of the number of times the loop is executed. *Start* represents a value that specifies the initial value assigned to *VariableName*. The value assigned to *VariableName* is incremented each time the loop finishes an iteration. By default, the value assigned to *VariableName* is incremented by 1. However, by specifying an optional *Step* value, you can increment or decrement the value assigned to *VariableName* by any value you want. The loop continues to iterate until the value of *VariableName* becomes equal to the value specified by *End*. If all this seems a bit overwhelming and difficult to grasp, don't worry; the following examples will clean things up.

```
Define i as Integer

ConsoleWriteLine("Counting with a For...Next Loop")
ConsoleWriteLine("")
```

```
For i = 1 to 10
  ConsoleWriteLine(i)
Next
```

In this example, an integer variable named i is defined. Next, a For...Next loop is set up that iterates two times. It does this by assigning a value of 1 to i on the loop's initial iteration. When it runs, the loop displays the value of i on the console window. The loop then repeats, automatically incrementing the value assigned to i by 1. The tenth time the loop executes, the value assigned to i is equal to 10. The loop ends after displaying this value on the console screen, as demonstrated in Figure 5.8.

**FIGURE 5.8**

Using a For...Next loop to count to 10.

As this example demonstrates, the For...Next loop can be used to accomplish the same type of tasks as the Loop...End Loop loop (e.g., looping a specified number of times).

## Looping in Reverse Order

The For...Next loop is a lot more flexible than the Loop...End Loop loop, allowing you to do many different things with it. For example, the following demonstrates how to set up a For...Next loop that displays a descending series of numbers instead of an ascending series of numbers.

```
For i = 10 To 1 Step -1
  ConsoleWriteLine(i)
Next
```

As you can see, the above loop uses the optional Step keyword to specify a value of -1. As a result, when executed, the value assigned to i is decremented by 1 upon each iteration of the loop. When executed, this example displays the following results.

```
10
9
8
7
6
```

```
5
4
3
2
1
```

### Skipping Loop Iterations

If you want, you can modify the value associated with the `Step` keyword, as demonstrated here, in effect displaying a list of odd numbers in the range of 1 to 10.

```
For i = 1 To 10 Step 2
  ConsoleWriteLine(i)
Next
When executed this example displays the following results.
1
3
5
7
9
```

### Iterating Through Arrays

One of the real advantages of the `For...Next` loop is the ability to use it to process the contents stored in arrays, as demonstrated in the following example.

```
Define VintageComputerCollection As String [10]
Define i As Integer

VintageComputerCollection [1] = "Atari 2600"
VintageComputerCollection [2] = "Atari 400"
VintageComputerCollection [3] = "Atari 800"
VintageComputerCollection [4] = "Atari 1200XL"
VintageComputerCollection [5] = "Atari 600XL"
VintageComputerCollection [6] = "Atari 800XL"
VintageComputerCollection [7] = "Atari 130XE"
VintageComputerCollection [8] = "Atari XEGS"
VintageComputerCollection [9] = "Atari 520ST"
VintageComputerCollection [10] = "Atari 1040ST"

ConsoleWriteLine("")
```

```
ConsoleWriteLine("Jerry's Vintage Computer Collection")
ConsoleWriteLine("")

For i = 1 To 10
     ConsoleWriteLine(VintageComputerCollection[i])
Next
```

Here, an array named `VintageComputerCollection` has been defined and populated with a list of 10 strings, each of which represents the name of a vintage computer system from the '70s, '80s, and early '90s. Next, a heading is displayed in the console window and a `For...Next` loop, consisting of just three statements, are used to iterate through the array and display each of the items stored in the array. Note that the first time the loop runs, the value of i is set to `1`. Therefore, when the embedded `ConsoleWriteLine()` method executes, the `VintageComputerCollection[i]` argument is converted to `VintageComputerCollection[1]` and then executed, displaying the first item stored in the array. Each time the loop repeats, the value of `i` is incremented by 1, resulting in a different array element being processed. When executed, this example displays the output shown in Figure 5.9.

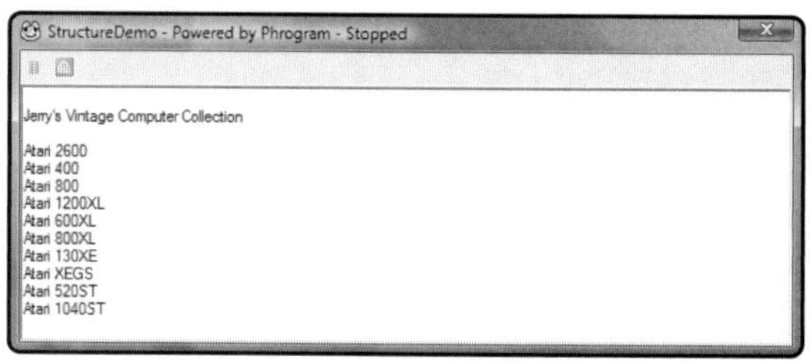


**FIGURE 5.9**

Using a `For...Next` loop to process the contents of an array.

## Determining an Array's Length

Instead of hard coding the size of the array in the previous example, you can use the `Shell` library's `ArrayLength()` method to retrieve the length of the array. You can also process the contents of an array in reverse order by reversing the value assigned to the loop's start and end values, as demonstrated in the following example.

**HINT** Whenever possible, you should avoid hard coding information in your Phrogram applications. This will make them easier to maintain. For example, using the `ArrayLength()` method, you can retrieve an integer value representing the length of the specified array. This method has the following syntax.

```
ArrayLength(List) As integer
```

Here, *List* is the name of the array whose length is being retrieved.

```
Define VintageComputerCollection As String [10]
Define i As Integer

VintageComputerCollection [1] = "Atari 2600"
VintageComputerCollection [2] = "Atari 400"
VintageComputerCollection [3] = "Atari 800"
VintageComputerCollection [4] = "Atari 1200XL"
VintageComputerCollection [5] = "Atari 600XL"
VintageComputerCollection [6] = "Atari 800XL"
VintageComputerCollection [7] = "Atari 130XE"
VintageComputerCollection [8] = "Atari XEGS"
VintageComputerCollection [9] = "Atari 520ST"
VintageComputerCollection [10] = "Atari 1040ST"

ConsoleWriteLine("")
ConsoleWriteLine("Jerry's Vintage Computer Collection")
ConsoleWriteLine("")

For i = ArrayLength(VintageComputerCollection) To 1 Step -1
    ConsoleWriteLine(VintageComputerCollection[i])
Next
```

Here, the `For…Next` loop has been set up to process the contents of an array named `VintageComputerCollection` in reverse order. To accomplish this, the loop has been set up to start at the end of the array as specified by assigning a start value of `ArrayLength(VintageComputerCollection)` and an end value of 1 with a `Step` value of -1.

As demonstrated next, you can use any of Phrogram's loops to process the contents of arrays. However, neither of the other two loops is as intuitive and will require more lines of code to implement.

```
Define VintageComputerCollection As String [10]
Define i As Integer

VintageComputerCollection [1] = "Atari 2600"
VintageComputerCollection [2] = "Atari 400"
VintageComputerCollection [3] = "Atari 800"
VintageComputerCollection [4] = "Atari 1200XL"
VintageComputerCollection [5] = "Atari 600XL"
VintageComputerCollection [6] = "Atari 800XL"
```

```
VintageComputerCollection [7] = "Atari 130XE"
VintageComputerCollection [8] = "Atari XEGS"
VintageComputerCollection [9] = "Atari 520ST"
VintageComputerCollection [10] = "Atari 1040ST"

ConsoleWriteLine("")
ConsoleWriteLine("Jerry's Vintage Computer Collection")
ConsoleWriteLine("")

Loop ArrayLength(VintageComputerCollection)
    i += 1
    ConsoleWriteLine(VintageComputerCollection[i])
End Loop
```

In this example, a `Loop...End Loop` loop has been set up to process the `VintageComputerCollection` array. As you can see, this example requires the use of five statements to process the contents of the array, as opposed to three statements when using a `For...Next` loop. In addition, unlike the `For...Next` loop, which automatically manages the incrementing or decrementing of the counter variable, Phrogram's other loops require that you manage the changing of the variable's value during loop execution.

## Working with the While...End While Loop

The last type of loop supported by Phrogram is the `While...End While` loop. This loop repeats the executions of a code block as long as a specified condition is `True`. The syntax for the `While...End While` loop is outlined here:

```
While BooleanExpression
    Code Block Statements
End While
```

*BooleanExpression* represents any expression that evaluates to a value of `True` or `False`. The loop executes only if the value of the tested expression evaluates as being `True`. Therefore, if the expression evaluates as `False` when first tested, the loop does not run and processing continues with the next statement in the program file following the loop.

When you use the `While...End While` loop, it is up to you to provide a means for terminating the loop's execution. For example, the following statements create a loop that counts to 10, halting when the value of i exceeds 10. In order to ensure that this happens, the value of `i` is incremented by a value of 1 at the end of each iteration of the loop.

```
Define i As Integer = 1

ConsoleWriteLine("Counting with a While…End While loop")
ConsoleWriteLine("")

While i <= 10
    ConsoleWriteLine(i)
    i += 1
End While
```

When executed, this loop displays the current value of `i`, which is initially set to 1. The loop stops executing when the value of `i` exceeds 10 (e.g., when the value of `i <= 10` ceases to evaluate as being `True`). When executed, this example displays the output shown in Figure 5.10.

**FIGURE 5.10**

Using a `While…End While` loop to count to 10.

As the preceding example demonstrates, the `While...End While` loop can be used to accomplish the same types of tasks as can be performed by the `Loop...End Loop` and `For...Next` loops. However, while the `Loop...End Loop` loop is better used to set up loops that execute a specific number of times, and the `For...Next` loop is better used when you need to process a range of values, the `While...End While` loop sets itself apart in its ability to execute for any number of iterations, stopping only when a predefined condition ceases to be `True`.

## Controlling Overall Game Execution

The `While...End While` loop is particularly well suited to game development. This loop is often used to control a game's main loop, which typically needs to execute an undetermined number of times. For example, the following statements provide a template that could be used to control the execution of a computer game.

```
Define GameOver As Boolean = False
Define Reply As Boolean

While GameOver = False
```

```
    //Statements

    Reply = Confirm("Do you wish to quit", "Game Demo")

    If Reply = True Then
        GameOver = True
    End If

End While
```

Here, two variables have been defined. The `GameOver` variable has been defined as `Boolean` and assigned a value of `False` and will be used to control the execution of a `While...End While` loop. The `Reply` variable has been set up as a Boolean variable and will be used to store player input. Next, a `While...End While` loop has been set up to execute for as long as the value of `GameOver` remains `False`. Within the loop a comment has been added representing the statements that control the execution of the game. For example, if this were a word guessing game, these statements might select a mystery word, manage the collection of player guesses, and determine when the game was won or lost, after which the player would be prompted to quit or start a new game by responding to a window prompt generated by the `Confirm()` method. If the player decides to quit and clicks on the popup dialog window's Yes button, the value of `GameOver` is set to `True`. As a result, the loop finishes its current execution and then stops running. If the player elects to keep playing by clicking on the popup dialog window's No button, the value assigned to `GameOver` remains unchanged and the loop iterates again, starting a new round of play.

## Controlling Loop Execution Using Keyboard Input

Starting in Chapter 6, you will begin learning how to develop interactive computer games that involve the use of graphics. The overall execution of these types of games is controlled by statements executing under the control of loops. Because of the fluid nature of arcade and other types of video games, it is not usually practical to pause game play at the end of each iteration of the main game loop to collect player input. Instead, player input is typically collected on the fly as the game executes. For example, in an arcade-style game, the player might use the keyboard's left and right arrow keys to control the movement of a space ship and the space key to control the firing of a gun.

The following example demonstrates how to control game termination by providing the player with the ability to terminate the game's loop at any time by pressing the Escape key.

```
Define i As Integer = 0

While True

    i += 1

    ConsoleWriteLine(i)

    If IsKeyDown("Escape") Then
        Break
    End If

End While
```

In this example, the game's loop includes an `If...Then` code block that checks to see if the player has pressed the Escape key each time the loop iterates. This is accomplished using the `Keyboard` library's `IsKeyDown()` method, which detects when a specified key has been pressed, using the following syntax.

```
IsKeyDown(Key As String) As Boolean
```

Here, *Key* represents the key pressed by the user. Phrogram provides you with the ability to determine when the user presses any of the keys listed in Table 5.1.

**TABLE 5.1 PHROGRAM KEYS LIBRARY CONSTANTS**

| | | |
|---|---|---|
| Back | F12 | Insert |
| Control | F2 | Left |
| Delete | F3 | PageDown |
| Down | F4 | PageUp |
| End | F5 | Pause |
| Enter | F6 | Right |
| Escape | F7 | Shift |
| F1 | F8 | Space |
| F10 | F9 | Tab |
| F11 | Home | Up |

Learning how to capture player input during game execution, as demonstrated in the previous example, is very important to the development of many different types of computer games. As such, you will see further examples of this in action as you make your way through the rest of this book.

**EXERCISES**

**It is helpful to keep your Program files organized to help keep things manageable. Before continuing, take a few minutes to get organized by completing the following exercises.**

1. **Using what you have learned about loops, create a Phrogram program that counts from 1 to 100. Modify the loop to count only odd numbers. Using the** `Delay()` **method, slow things down a bit so that the loop does not run too quickly. Next, modify your program so that you can stop its execution at any time by pressing the F3 key.**
2. **Create another new Phrogram program that contains a two-dimensional array. For each row in the array, store the name of a close friend or associate and their phone numbers. Then create a loop that uses the** `ConsoleReadLine()` **method to prompt you to enter a friend's name, and then use the loop to look up and display that person's phone number, before displaying another prompt that allows you to look up another person's name.**

## WATCHING OUT FOR ENDLESS LOOPS

Loops are extremely powerful and useful programming tools, allowing you to automate the execution of repetitive tasks, process huge amounts of data, and control the overall execution of computer games and applications. However, whenever you work with loops you run the risk of accidentally creating an endless loop. An *endless loop* is a loop that does not have a means for terminating its execution. As a result endless loops run forever, consuming computer resources.

For an example of an endless loop, look at the following example, which uses a `While…End While` loop to display a list of numbers on the console window.

```
Define GameOver As Boolean = False
Define i As Integer= 1

While GameOver = False
```

```
    ConsoleWriteLine(i)

    i += 1

End While
```

When executed, this example displays a list of numbers, starting at 1 on the screen. The number, represented by the variable `i`, is incremented by 1 upon each iteration of the loop. Because a provision has not been made for stopping the execution of the loop, it just keeps on displaying numbers. One way of addressing this situation would be to provide a simple means of terminating the execution of the loop. For example, you might modify the example to terminate when the value of i reaches some arbitrary value. Alternatively, you might modify the example as shown next to terminate the `While...End While` loop whenever the Escape key is pressed.

```
Define GameOver As Boolean = False
Define i As Integer= 1

While GameOver = False

    ConsoleWriteLine(i)

    i += 1

    If IsKeyDown("Escape") Then
        GameOver = True
    End If

End While
```

Here, the `IsKeyDown()` method is used to execute an `If...Then` code block in the event the Escape key is pressed. When this occurs, the value assigned to `GameOver` is set equal to `True`, terminating the loop at the end of its current execution.

**TRICK** From time to time every programmer accidentally sets up an endless loop. However, through proper testing, you should be able to detect any endless loops in your program. If during the development and testing of a Phrogram application you realize that your program is stuck in an endless loop, perhaps because it has become unresponsive or will not stop the repeated execution of a particular action, you can always halt the program's execution by pressing on the Stop the Running Program button located on the Phrogram IDE's toolbar.

If you are running your Phrogram program as a stand-alone application outside of the Phrogram IDE, you can halt the execution of your program using the Windows Task Manager. To do so, press the Ctrl + Alt + Del keys to open the Task Manager window and then select your program from the list of active applications that are displayed and click on the End Task button. In response, a popup dialog window displays asking you to confirm your action, after which the program's execution is terminated.

## Skipping an Iteration within a Loop

There may be instances where you want to skip the current iteration of a loop, allowing the loop to resume its execution with the subsequent iteration. For example, in a number guessing game controlled through the execution of a loop, you might want to keep count of every valid guess made by the player and reject any invalid guesses. One way of doing this is by skipping the iteration of any loop in which an invalid guess is made, disregarding any code block statements that would otherwise have been processed.

To interrupt the execution of the current iteration of a loop, you can execute the `Continue` keyword, which has the following syntax.

```
Continue
```

Once executed, the `Continue` keyword terminates the current iteration of the loop allowing the loop to skip to its next iteration, as demonstrated in the following example.

```
Define i As Integer = 0

Loop 10

    i += 1

    If i = 5 Then
        Continue
    End If

    ConsoleWriteLine(i)

End Loop
```

Here, the `Continue` keyword has been used to skip the fifth iteration of a `Loop...End Loop` loop. When executed, this example displays the output shown in Figure 5.11, demonstrating that the fifth execution of the loop was cut short.

**FIGURE 5.11**

Skipping the fifth iteration of a loop.

You can use the `Continue` keyword to skip an iteration in any of the loops supported by Phrogram.

## TERMINATING LOOPS EARLY

As has already been demonstrated, you can use the `Break` keyword to prematurely terminate the execution of a loop. To accomplish this, you need to use Phrogram's `Break` keyword, which has the following syntax.

```
Break
```

When executed, the `Break` keyword immediately terminates the loop in which it resides, allowing application execution to continue at the first program code statement following the loop, as demonstrated in the following example.

```
Define i As Integer = 0

Loop 10

    i += 1

    If i = 5 Then
        Break
    End If

    ConsoleWriteLine(i)

End Loop
```

Here, the `Break` keyword has been used to terminate the loop execution during its fifth iteration. When executed, this example displays the output shown in Figure 5.12, demonstrating the early termination of the loop.

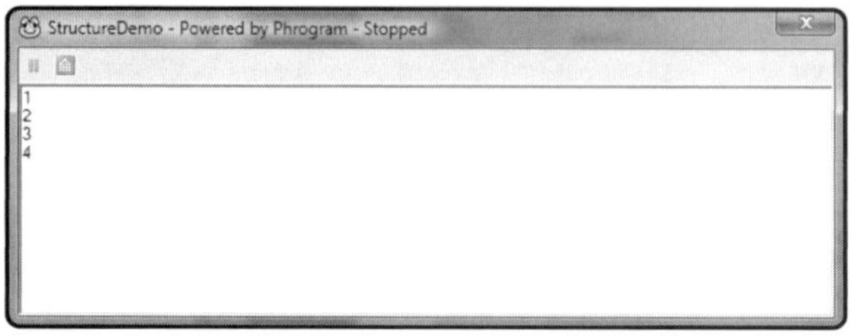


**FIGURE 5.12**

Prematurely terminating the execution of a loop.

> **HINT** If you use the `Break` keyword to terminate the execution of a loop that has been embedded within another loop, only the loop in which the `Break` keyboard resides is terminated. The output loop will continue normally.

## REVIEW QUESTIONS

1. **What is a loop? List three benefits provided by loops.**
2. **Which type of loop iterates for as long as a tested condition remains `True`?**
3. **Which type of loop executes a specified number of times?**
4. **Which type of loop repeats its execution based on an assigned start and end value?**
5. **Which method can be used to retrieve an integer value representing the length of the specified array?**
6. **Which type of loop is best suited to processing arrays?**
7. **What is an endless loop and how do they affect program execution?**
8. **What Phrogram keyword can be used to skip the iteration of a loop?**
9. **What Phrogram keyword can be used to force the immediate termination of a loop?**
10. **How can you terminate the execution of a Phrogram application that is stuck in an endless loop when the program is executed within the Phrogram IDE? How can you cancel a Phrogram application running as a stand-alone program?**

# BACK TO THE SLOT MACHINE GAME

Okay, it is time to begin working on this chapter's main project, the Slot Machine game. The development of this game will reinforce your understanding of how to work with the `While…End While` and `For…Next` loops and will further illustrate their importance in game development.

## Designing the Game

To help keep things as simple as possible, this game will be created in a series of 15 steps, as outlined here:

1. Create a new program project.
2. Document your application.
3. Define a global constant.
4. Define method variables.
5. Configure the game's window.
6. Prompt the player for permission to begin.
7. Analyze the player's response.
8. Display instructions for playing the game.
9. Set up a loop to control overall game play.
10. Display an animated series of dial numbers.
11. Generate a final spin.
12. Analyze spin results.
13. Display spin results.
14. Encourage the player to play another time.
15. Save and compile your new application.

As long as you follow along carefully with each of the steps outlined above, you'll have a new fully functional Phrogram game up and running in no time at all.

### Step 1: Creating a New Phrogram Project

Begin by creating a new Phrogram program by starting Phrogram and clicking on the New Program command located on the File menu. Next, assign a meaningful name to the application, by replacing `MyNewProgram` with `NumberGuess` as the application's name on the first code statement. All of the program code statements that make up the Slot Machine game are explained in the sections that follow and will be placed inside the program file's `Method Main()` and `End Method` statements.

### Step 2: Documenting Your New Program

Now that your new program file has been created, let's document the purpose of the application by adding the following code statements to the beginning of the program's code file.

```
//Program: SlotMachine.kpl
//Created: 01/04/2008
//Version: 1.0
//Author: Jerry Lee Ford, Jr.
//Description: This Phrogram game simulates a three-dial Las Vegas-style
//             casino slot machine.
```

### Step 3: Defining a Global Constant

The name of the Slot Machine game will be displayed in the application's titlebar, located on the game console window. It will also be displayed in the titlebar of each of the game's popup dialog windows. Instead of hard coding the game's name repeatedly throughout the program file, let's store the game's name in a global constant, making it available throughout the game whenever it needs to be referenced. This is accomplished through the addition of the following statements to the beginning of the program file, immediately after the program statement and before the `Main()` method.

```
//Global constant used to store the name of the game
Constant GameTitle As String = "The Slot Machine Game"
```

Once defined, you can use `cGameTitle` in place of the game's name any time you want to refer to the game's name.

### Step 4: Defining Method Variables

The next step in creating the Slot Machine game is to define a collection of variables with a method level scope for use throughout the `Main()` method. These variables will be used to keep track of different data used throughout program execution, including player input, randomly generated numbers representing dial spins, and the player's account balance. This is accomplished by adding the following statements to the `Main()` method.

```
Define Reply As Boolean = False        //Used to store player input
Define Msg As String                   //Stores a display string
Define Result As String                //Stores the game results
Define i As Integer                    //Controls loop execution
Define PlayerAccount As Integer = 10   //Player begins with $10
Define FirstDial As Integer      //Represents a slot machine dial
Define SecondDial As Integer     //Represents a slot machine dial
```

```
Define ThirdDial As Integer      //Represents a slot machine dial
Define Total As Integer          //Used in calculating spin results
Define Message As String         //Used to display console messages
```

As you can see, comments added just to the right of each variable explain each variable's usage in the application.

### Step 5: Configuring the Game's Window

Now it is time to add the code statements responsible for configuring the Slot Machine game's console window. These statements, which are shown next, hide the window's toolbar, configure the window's screen size, and display the name of the game in the window's titlebar. Next, a background color of `WhiteSmoke` is specified and the `SetConsoleFontStyle()` method is used to specify that all displayed text appears in bold. Finally, the `SetConsoleTextAlignment()` method is used to center the display of all text.

```
HideToolbar()   //Prevent the window's toolbar from being displayed
SetScreenSize(408, 400)    //Set the screen size to 600x400 pixels
SetWindowTitle(GameTitle)  //Display the name of the game in the
                           //Window's titlebar

SetConsoleBackgroundColor(WhiteSmoke)        //Set background color

// Set console font style to Bold, non-italic and non-underline
SetConsoleFontStyle(True, False, False)

SetConsoleTextAlignment("Center")    //Set text alignment to center
```

Insert each of these statements in the `Main()` method, immediately following the variable definition statements that you added in the previous step.

### Step 6: Prompting the Player for Permission to Begin

The next set of code statements that you need to add to the Slot Machine game are responsible for displaying a message prompt that welcomes the player and pauses game execution until the player clicks on one of the popup dialog's Yes or No buttons.

```
//Outline the text of the game's welcome message
Msg = "Welcome To " + GameTitle + "!  Are You Ready To Play?"

//Display the game's welcome message in a popup dialog window and
//prompt the player to click on Yes to play the game or No to quit
Reply = Confirm(Msg, GameTitle)
```

These statements should be added to the program file, immediately after the last set of statements that you just added.

### Step 7: Analyzing the Player's Response

The next step in the development of the Slot Machine game is to analyze the player's response to determine which button the player clicked on. This is accomplished by adding the following statements to the `Main()` method, immediately following the statements added in the previous step.

```
//Analyze the player's response
If Reply = True Then            //If Reply equals True then the
                                //player clicked on the Yes button


Else      //Execute the following statements when the player clicks
          //on the No button


End If
```

These statements set up a framework that will be used to control the execution of the rest of the application. Specifically, these statements control the execution of program statements that either manage the operation of the Slot Machine game or display a message that invites the player to return to play the game another time.

Statements that control the operation of the Slot Machine game will be placed in between the opening `If` statement and the `Else` keyword, as outlined in Steps 8 through 13, and the statements responsible for displaying the message that invites the player to return will be placed between the `Else` and the `End If` statements (in Step 14).

### Step 8: Displaying Game Instructions

Assuming that the player elects to play the game, the next task performed by the Slot Machine game is to display instructions for playing, which is accomplished by adding the following statements to the beginning of the `If…Then` code block that you set up in Step 7.

```
ClearConsole()              //Clear the console

SetConsoleFont("Arial", 18)         // Set font to Arial, point 18

//Begin displaying the rules for playing the game
ConsoleWriteLine("")
ConsoleWriteLine("Game Rules:")
```

```
ConsoleWriteLine("")

SetConsoleFont("Arial", 12)         // Set font to Arial, point 12

//Continue displaying the rules for playing the game
ConsoleWriteLine("Your account has 10 dollars in it.")
ConsoleWriteLine("")
ConsoleWriteLine("Match 3 numbers to win 2 dollars.")
ConsoleWriteLine("")
ConsoleWriteLine("Match 2 numbers to win 1 dollar.")
ConsoleWriteLine("")
ConsoleWriteLine("No matches will cost you 5 dollars.")
ConsoleWriteLine("")
ConsoleWriteLine("The game ends if you go broke.")
ConsoleWriteLine("")
ConsoleWriteLine("")
ConsoleWriteLine("")
ConsoleWriteLine("")
ConsoleWriteLine(" Press any key to begin playing.")

Console.ReadKey()           //Wait for the player to press a key
```

As you can see, the statements begin by clearing the console screen and then display a series of text strings using the `ConsoleWriteLine()` method.

### Step 9: Setting Up the Game's Main Loop

The operation of the Slot Machine game is controlled by a `While...End While` loop. This loop, outlined next, should be added to the program code file immediately following the statements you added in the previous step.

```
While True                  //Create a loop that runs forever

End While
```

The program code statements that you will insert into this loop, outlined in steps 10-13, will display an animated series of numbers that simulates the spinning of slot machine dials, generate a final set of numbers for each dial, determine the results of the spin, and then display those results after adjusting the player's account balance.

### Step 10: Displaying a Random Series of Dial Numbers

The first set of program code statements to be embedded within the While…End While loop are shown next. These statements begin by clearing the console window, after which a For…Next loop is used to display a series of three sets of randomly generated numbers, representing slot machine dials.

```
ClearConsole()

For i = 1 To 10  //Loop 19 times

    SetConsoleFont("Arial", 48)    // Set font to Arial, point 48
    SetConsoleFontColor(DarkRed)

    ConsoleWriteLine("")
    ConsoleWrite(Random(1, 3) + "     ")
    ConsoleWrite(Random(1, 3) + "     ")
    ConsoleWriteLine(Random(1, 3))

    Delay(300)

    ClearConsole()          //Clear the console

Next
```

Note that the first two dial numbers that are displayed are done so using the ConsoleWrite() method, which displays the numbers without executing a line feed operation. The third dial number is displayed using the ConsoleWriteLine() method, which displays the number and then executes a linefeed. The end result is that each time the For…Next loop iterates, a new set of randomly dialed numbers is displayed on the same line. Also note that the Delay() method pauses for three-tenths of a second between each iteration of the loop to ensure that the animated sequences does not occur at an unrealistic speed. Once the last set of numbers displays, the screen is cleared, preparing the game for the display of a final set of randomly generated numbers, as outlined in the next step.

### Step 11: Generating a Final Spin

This final set of randomly generated dial numbers is produced using the statements shown next, which should be added to the program file immediately after the statement you added in Step 10.

```
FirstDial = Random(1, 3)  //Display a random number in the 1st dial
SecondDial = Random(1, 3) //Display a random number in the 2nd dial
ThirdDial = Random(1, 3)  //Display a random number in the 3rd dial

//Add the results of all three spins together
Total = FirstDial + SecondDial + ThirdDial
```

The first three statements use the `Random()` method to generate three separate numbers, each of which is stored in a different variable. The last statement adds up the values stored in all three variables to a variable named `Total`. The value stored in `Total` will be used in the next step to analyze the role and determine its results.

### Step 12: Analyzing the Results of the Spin

To determine the results of the player's spin, the game must analyze the value stored in the `Total` variable. A value of three or nine indicates that a jackpot has occurred (three 1s or three 3s). A value of six means either a jackpot (three 2s) or a no match (three different values) has occurred. Any value other than three, six, or nine means that a pair of matching numbers was displayed.

```
//A value of 3 or 9 means that 2 dials match
If Total = 3 Or Total = 9 Then
    PlayerAccount = PlayerAccount + 2
    Message = " Three matches. You win 2 dollars!"
End If

//A value of 6 means either 3 matches or no matches
If Total = 6 Then       //Three 2s were generated
    If FirstDial = SecondDial Then
        PlayerAccount = PlayerAccount + 2
        Message = " Three matches. You win 2 dollars!"
    Else                //There were no matches
        PlayerAccount = PlayerAccount - 5
        Message = " No match. You lose 5 dollars."
    End If
End If

//A value other than 3, 6, or 9 means there were 2 matches
If Total <> 3 And Total <> 6 And Total <> 9 Then
    PlayerAccount = PlayerAccount + 1
```

```
    Message = " Two matches. You win 1 dollar!"
End If
```

When a jackpot occurs, $2 is added to the player's account. When a matching pair of numbers has been generated, $1 is added to the player's account. If no match occurs, $5 is subtracted from the player's account.

### Step 13: Displaying Spin Results

The last set of program code statements to be added to the `While...End While` loop is shown next. These statements display the results of the player's spin and adjust the player's account balance accordingly.

```
//Display the final spin
ConsoleWriteLine("")
ConsoleWriteLine(FirstDial + "     " + SecondDial + "     " + ThirdDial)
ConsoleWriteLine("")

SetConsoleFont("Arial", 18)          // Set font to Arial, point 18

SetConsoleFontColor(DarkBlue)        //Set font color to DarkBlue

ConsoleWriteLine(Message)            //Display spin results

//Continue displaying final spin
ConsoleWriteLine("")
ConsoleWriteLine(" Account Balance: " + PlayerAccount)
ConsoleWriteLine("")
ConsoleWriteLine("")
ConsoleWriteLine("")

SetConsoleFont("Arial", 12)          // Set font to Arial, point 12

SetConsoleFontColor(Black)           //Set font color to Black

//Game play ends if the player goes broke
If PlayerAccount <= 0 Then

    //Notify the player that the game is over
    ConsoleWriteLine("Sorry. You have gone broke. Game Over!")
```

```
        Console.ReadKey()    //Wait for the player to press a key

        //Thank the player for taking the time to play
        Alert("Thank you for playing!", GameTitle)

        Break   //Break out of the game loop to terminate application execution

    Else  //The player's account still has a positive balance

        //Display instructions
        ConsoleWriteLine(" Press any key to spin again.")

        Console.ReadKey()    //Wait for the player to press a key

    End If
```

When executed, these statements display the values representing the spin results and the value of the player's account balance. An `If…Then` code block is then used to analyze the value assigned to the `PlayerAccount` variable. If `PlayerAccount` is less than or equal to 0 a message is displayed informing the player that the game is over. Once the player presses a keyboard key, the `Alert()` method is used to display a popup dialog window that thanks the player for playing the game and then the `Break` keyword is used to terminate the execution of the game's `While…End While` loop, thus ending the game. However, as long as the player's account balance remains greater than zero, game play continues.

### Step 14: Inviting the Player to Play another Time

All that needs to be done to wrap up your work on the Slot Machine game is to add the program code statements that are responsible for displaying a message inviting the player to return to play another time in the event the player elects not to play the game when prompted in step 6. The statements that make this happen are shown next and should be added to the end of the `Main()` method, just after the `Else` statement and before the `End If` statement that you added in step 7.

```
//Display a message in a popup window inviting the player to
//play again another time
Alert("OK. Perhaps another time.", GameTitle)
```

### Step 15: Saving and Compiling Your Application

That's everything! If you have not already done so, now is the time to save your new Phrogram game by clicking on the Save All command located on the File menu. Once saved, compile and execute your new application by clicking on the Run the Program button located on Phrogram's toolbar. As long as you have not skipped any steps or made any typos, Phrogram should compile your new application and begin its execution. Once started, the Slot Machine game should run exactly as was described at the beginning of the chapter.

## The Final Result

Okay, hopefully your copy of the Slot Machine game is now ready to go. If you run into any trouble compiling it, use the Program IDE's error message to track down and fix any syntax errors and typos that you may have made along the way. Alternatively, you can download a complete copy of this game's source code from this book's companion CD and use it to compare against to determine where things have gone wrong.

# SUMMARY

In this chapter you learned how to set up different types of loops to control game play, perform repetitive tasks, and to process data stored in arrays. This includes learning how to work with the `Loop...End Loop`, `For...Next`, and `While...End While` loops. You learned how to skip an iteration within a loop using the `Continue` keyword and to prematurely terminate a loop's execution using the `Break` keyword. You also learned about the endless loops and how to halt the execution of your Phrogram program should it get stuck in an endless loop. Now, before you move on to Chapter 6, "Improving Program Organization with Procedures," consider spending a little time improving the Slot Machine game by addressing the following list of challenges.

## Challenges

1. Currently, the slot machine only generates numbers in the range of 1 to 3 for each dial. Consider expanding this range of numbers to increase the game's level of difficulty.
2. If you increase the range of numbers used by the game, you might also want to consider changing the amount of money subtracted and added to the player's account. Since it will become more difficult to generate a winning spin, the amount of money awarded to the player should probably be increased.
3. Consider keeping track of the previous spin and awarding double points when back-to-back jackpots occur (a jackpot is three matching dials).
4. Create a distribution package for your new game and share it with a few friends, asking them to provide you with feedback.

CHAPTER 6

# IMPROVING PROGRAM ORGANIZATION WITH PROCEDURES

As your Phrogram applications become larger and more sophisticated, it becomes more challenging to keep your program code well organized and manageable. Conditional logic code blocks and loops provide a means of grouping portions of your program code into efficient and manageable units. However, code blocks and loops only help to manage a portion of your program code statements. To take things to the next level and begin writing program code that is well organized and easier to maintain, you need to organize your Phrogram application code into procedures, each of which is designed to handle a specific task. In addition, you will learn your next computer application, the Crazy Eight Ball game.

Specifically, you will learn how to:

- Improve the organization of your Phrogram programs, making them more modular and easier to maintain
- Create methods and functions and use them to group related statements that can be called upon to be executed whenever necessary
- Pass data to methods and functions for processing as input
- Create functions that can return data back to calling statements
- Use the Phrogram IDE's Class Library Browser to locate built-in Phrogram methods and functions that you can use in your Phrogram applications

## Project Preview: The Crazy Eight Ball Game

This chapter's game project is the Crazy Eight Ball game. It works exactly like a child's Crazy Eight ball fortune telling toy except that instead of thinking of questions and then holding and shaking the eight -ball and waiting for an answer to appear, all you have to do is think of a question and click on a button. In response, the game will pause and then display an answer to your question.

Figure 6.1 shows the popup dialog window that is displayed when the game first starts, prompting the player for permission to begin game play.

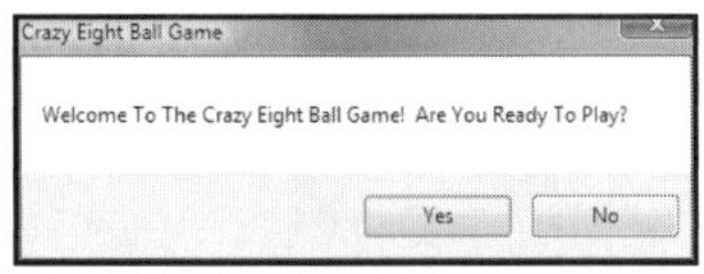


**Figure 6.1**

The player is given a chance to play or quit the game.

If the player decides not to play, another popup dialog window displays that suggests the player consider returning to play another time. If, on the other hand, the player elects to play the game, the image shown in Figure 6.2 displays.

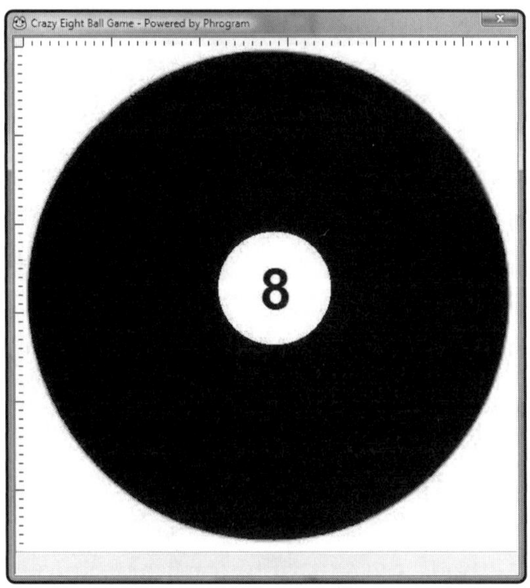


**Figure 6.2**

A graphic image representing an eight ball fortune-telling toy displays on the screen.

After a few moments pause, the popup dialog window shown in Figure 6.3 displays. The player is instructed to think of a question and then to click on the OK button. In order for the game to work properly, the player's questions must be formulated so that they can be answered with Yes/No type answers.

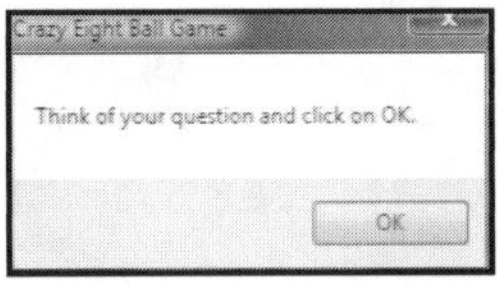


**FIGURE 6.3**

The player is prompted to think of a question and then to click on the OK button to see the game's answer.

As soon as the player thinks of a question and clicks on the OK button, the game pauses for one second and then displays an answer to the question, as demonstrated in Figure 6.4.

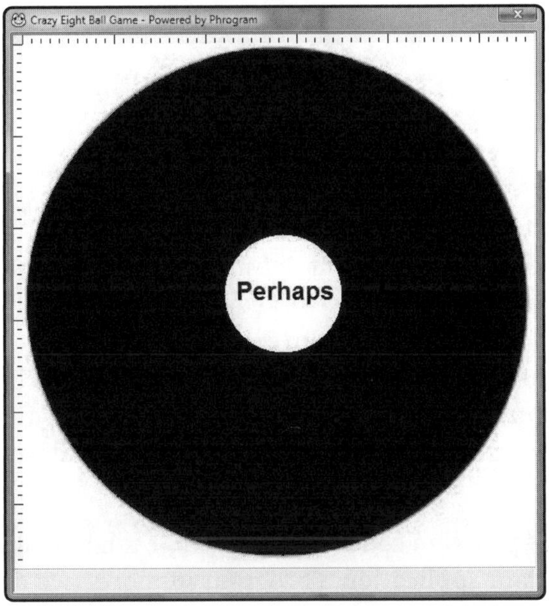


**FIGURE 6.4**

The Crazy Eight Ball game provides the player with a less than definitive answer.

The game's answer displays for three seconds after which a new popup dialog window displays, prompting the player to think of a new question for the eight ball to answer. Figure 6.5 shows the answer to the player's next question.

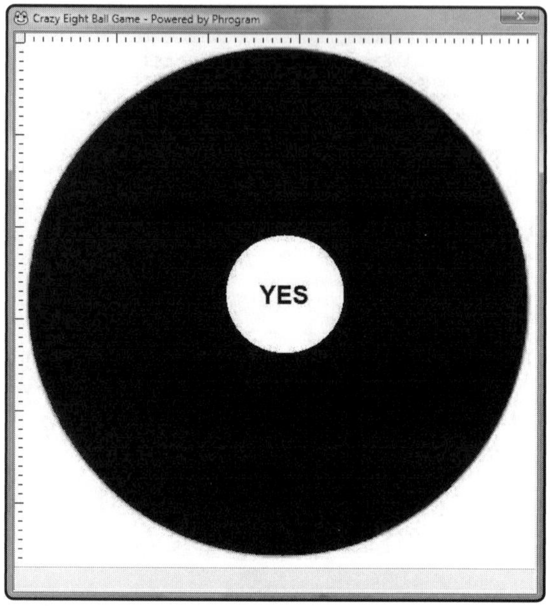


**FIGURE 6.5**

The Crazy Eight Ball game displays an answer of Yes.

In addition to Perhaps and Yes, the game's list of possible answers also includes Maybe and No.

## IMPROVING THE ORGANIZATION OF YOUR PHROGRAM APPLICATIONS

In every Phrogram application that you have worked on so far in this book, all of the application source code, except for a few global constant definitions, has been placed within the `Main()` method. As the applications that you have worked on have become larger and more complex, so has the size and complexity of the program code statements in the `Main()` method. Obviously, the larger the `Main()` method becomes, the more difficult your Phrogram applications will be to create and maintain. Fortunately, Phrogram provides a solution to this dilemma in the form of procedures, which you can use as the basis for developing modular programs.

A *procedure* is a named collection of program code statements that can be called on to execute from any location within a Phrogram application. Phrogram supports two different types of procedures: methods and functions. A *method* is a named collection of one or more program code statements that can be called upon to execute as a unit. A *function* is a named collection of program code statements that can be called upon to execute as a unit and which can return a value back to the statement that called upon the function to execute.

As you learned in Chapter 1, Phrogram applications begin by executing the first statement located in the `Main()` method and then process all remaining statements sequentially in the `Main()` method from top to bottom (although loops can be used to perform the repeated execution of code statements).

In Phrogram applications that consist of multiple methods and functions, all processing still begins with the first statement located in the `Main()` method and continues from top to bottom. However, if somewhere along the way a call is made to another method or a function, processing jumps to the specified method or function and continues with the first statements in that method or function and continues until the last statement has been executed, after which processing control returns back to the `Main()` method and continues with the statement that called upon the external method or function.

HINT Actually, any method and function can call upon any number of other methods or functions to execute. The methods and functions that are called can in turn call upon other methods and functions as needed. Every method or function that is called always returns processing control back to the statement that called upon it to execute. As such, all Phrogram applications begin by executing the first statement located in the `Main()` method and, regardless of how many methods and function calls are made, end after processing the last statement in the `Main()` method (unless the user closes the application first).

Procedures provide the ability to employ a building block approach to program development. They make application development easier by allowing program code statements to be grouped in methods and functions, each of which is designed to perform a specific task. Modular program development helps to reduce the overall size of the application by allowing you to group commonly executed sets of statements into methods and functions that can then be called upon to execute as many times as necessary from any point within the application. By improving overall application organization, procedures result in program files that are better organized and easier to maintain. This not only makes application development go smoother but can also help minimize the number of errors found in your programs.

## Using Methods to Manage Related Sets of Statements

As has been stated, a method is a named collection of program statements that can be called upon to execute as a unit. As such, a method is really just a named code block. Methods can be called upon to execute from any location within a Phrogram application and can even be set up to accept and process data passed to them as arguments. Because methods can be called upon to execute repeatedly, they help streamline the size and complexity of your Phrogram applications.

## Defining Methods

Methods begin with the `Method` keyword followed by the name assigned to the method and a list of optional parameters enclosed in parentheses and end with the `End Method` statement, using the syntax shown here:

```
Method MethodName(Parameter As Type, ...)
    Statements
End Method
```

*MethodName* represents the name assigned to the method. Methods can process any number of arguments passed to them when they are called to execute. To accept incoming arguments, each argument passed must be matched up against parameters defined within the opening `Method` statement. A method can support any number of parameters, provided that they are separated by commas and that each parameter includes a data type specification, as specified by *Type*.

**HINT**

An *argument* is a value, literal or variable, passed to a method or function for processing. A *parameter* is a variable defined as part of a method or function definition that identifies the order and type of arguments that must be passed to the method or function in order for it to execute.

Phrogram automatically matches up argument data passed to methods and functions against that method or function's parameter definitions. If you pass a method or function a number of arguments that do not match up one for one against its parameter definitions, an error will occur. In addition, the data types of all arguments passed to methods and functions must precisely match the data types of the method or function's defined data types or an error will occur.

When called upon to execute, methods process in a top-down order, returning control back to the statement that called upon them to execute once they are done.

**TRAP**

Like constants, variables, arrays, and structures, the names assigned to methods and functions must be unique throughout an application and must follow these rules.

- Method and function names must begin with a letter or the underscore character.
- Method and function names can only consist of letters, numbers, and the underscore characters.
- Method and function names cannot include blank spaces.
- Method and function names cannot be Phrogram language keywords.

The following example shows an example of a simple method, which displays a text string in a popup dialog window whenever it is called upon to execute.

```
Method WelcomeMsg()
    Alert("Hi", "Demo")
End Method
```

## Calling on Methods to Execute

To call upon a method to execute, type the name of the function followed by any required arguments (placed inside parentheses) using the syntax outlined here:

```
MethodName(Argument1, ... ArgumentN)
```

*MethodName* represents the name of the method being called. *Argument1...ArgumentN* represents any number of arguments that you may need to pass to the method for processing. If a method does not have any parameters defined, then all you have to do to call upon it to execute is to type its name followed by an empty set of parentheses, as shown here:

> **TRAP** Unlike some programming languages, you will get a syntax error if you try calling on a method to execute without including the required parentheses.

```
WelcomeMsg()
```

When executed, this statement calls upon a method named `WelcomeMsg()` to execute, without passing it any arguments.

## Passing Arguments to Methods for Processing

As has already been stated, you can define methods that are capable of processing any number of incoming arguments. To do so, you define parameters within the method definition that identify every argument the method can process as well as the data type required by each of those arguments. For example, the following statements define a method named `DisplayMsg()` that accepts and processes a single argument.

```
Method DisplayMsg("Msg As String")
    Alert(Msg, "Demo")
End Method
```

Here, the method requires that the calling statement pass it a text string, which the method then displays in a popup dialog window.

To execute this method, specify the method's name followed by a text string embedded within matching parentheses, as demonstrated here:

```
DisplayMsg(Well, hello there.)
```

This next example demonstrates how to set up a method that processes three incoming arguments, representing the user's first name, last name, and age.

```
Method DisplayMsg(FirstName As String, LastName As String, Age As Integer)

    Define Msg As String

    Msg = "Hello " + FirstName + " " + LastName + ". "
    Msg = Msg + "You are " + Age + " years old. "

    Alert(Msg, "Demo")

End Method
```

To call upon this method to execute, pass it three required arguments, in the order defined by the method, as demonstrated here:

```
DisplayMsg("William", "Ford", 8)
```

## Exiting Out of Methods

When called, a method processes in a top-down order, returning control back to the statement that called it. However, there may be times in which you determine there is a need to terminate a method's execution early. You can do this at any time using the `Return` keyword, which has the following syntax.

```
Return
```

For example, suppose you were working on a new Phrogram application that includes a method named `GreetPlayer()` whose purpose is to display a text message in a popup dialog window that greets the player by name and that the player's name is collected through the use of the `ConsoleReadLine()` method, as demonstrated here:

```
Program GreetingProgram

    Method GreetPlayer(Name As String)

        If Length(Name) = 0 Then
```

```
            Alert("Invalid input!", "Demo")
            Return
        End If

        Alert("Hi " + Name, "Demo")

    End Method

    Method Main()

        Define Input As String

        While True

            Input = ConsoleReadLine("What is your name?", False)

            GreetPlayer(Input)

        End While

    End Method

End Program
```

As currently written, there is nothing in the `Main()` method that prevents the player from simply clicking on the Submit button when prompted by the `ConsoleReadLine()` method to enter her name. Therefore, there is no guarantee that when this program is executed that anything other than an empty string will be passed to the `GreetPlayer()` method. Rather than allow the method to process the invalid input, the `GreetPlayer()` method uses an `If... Then` code block to analyze the argument that is passed to it to make sure that it is valid and displays an error message if it is not. Next, the `Return` keyword is used to force the immediate termination of the `GreetPlayer()` method, thus preventing it from processing its remaining statement.

**TRICK** Using this example as a template, you can easily develop methods that can perform a host of data validation checks to ensure that everything is in order before running.

## Using Functions to Process and Return Data

A function is a named collection of program statements that can be called upon to execute as a unit. Like methods, functions are really just named code blocks. Functions can be called from any location within a program file and can be set up to accept and also process any amount of data passed to them as arguments. Unlike methods, functions can also return data back to calling statements.

### Defining Functions

Functions are almost identical to methods, except that functions can also be used to return a value back to a calling statement. Phrogram functions have the following syntax.

```
Function FunctionName(Parameter As Type, ...) As Type
    Statements
    Return Value
End Function
```

*FunctionName* represents the name assigned to the function. Like methods, you can define any number of function parameters. All functions return a value back to the statement that calls upon them to execute. This value is returned using the `Return` keyword followed by the *Value* to be returned. *Type* is a placeholder representing the data type of the value returned to the statement that calls on the function to execute.

The following statements provide an example of an application that includes a function named `GetRandomNo()` that when called returns a random number in the range of 1 to 3 back to the statement that called upon it.

```
Program RandomNumberDemo

    Function GetRandomNo() As Integer

        Define RandomValue As Integer

        RandomValue = Random(1, 3)

        Return RandomValue

    End Function

    Method Main()
```

```
        Define RandomNumber As Integer

        RandomNumber = GetRandomNo()

        Alert("The random number is " + RandomNumber, "Random Number Demo")

    End Method

End Program
```

Here, a variable named `RandomNumber` is defined in the `Main()` method and a method named `GetRandomNo()` is then called. This method returns a random value, which is then assigned to RandomNumber, and then displays in a popup dialog window.

The `GetRandomNo()` function, which is located just above the `Main()` method, executes only when explicitly called. It defines an integer value named `RandomValue` and then assigns a random value to it, generated using the `Math` library's `Random()` function. The randomly generated number is then returned back to the calling statements in the `Main()` method.

## Calling on Functions to Execute

As was demonstrated in the previous example, you can call on a function to execute using the syntax outlined here:

```
VariableName = FunctionName()
```

Alternatively, you can call upon a function by simply embedding its name within an expression, as demonstrated in the following example.

```
Program RandomNumberDemo

    Function GetRandomNo() As Integer

        Define RandomValue As Integer

        RandomValue = Random(1, 3)

        Return RandomValue

    End Function

    Method Main()
```

```
        Define RandomNumber As Integer

        Alert("The random number is " + GetRandomNo(), "Random Number Demo")

    End Method

End Program
```

Here, instead of explicitly calling upon the function to execute and assigning the value that it returns to a variable, which can then be displayed, the function call is embedded inside the `Alert()` method statement (as shown above in bold).

> **HINT** You can also call upon methods to execute by embedding them inside expression statements.

## Breaking Out of Functions

In addition to returning data back to calling statements, you can use the `Return` keyword within functions to force the early termination of that function, as demonstrated here:

```
Program RandomNumberDemo

    Function GetRandomNo(RndNo As Integer) As Integer

        Define RandomNumber As Integer

            If RndNo < 0 Or RndNo > 5 Then
                Return 0
            End If

        RandomNumber = Random(1, RndNo)

        Return RandomNumber

    End Function

    Method Main()

        Define RandomNumber As Integer
        Define Input As Integer
```

```
        While True
            Input = ConsoleReadInt("Enter a number from 1 to 5", False)
            RandomNumber = GetRandomNo(Input)
            Alert("The random number is " + RandomNumber, "Demo")
        End While

    End Method

End Program
```

Here, a function named `GetRandomNo()` has been defined. Within the function, an `If…Then` code block, shown above in bold, has been set up to analyze the value of the argument passed. If the value that is passed is less than 0 or greater than 5, it is rejected by the function, which returns a value of 0 instead of a random number. However, if a valid argument is passed, the `If…Then` code block is not executed and the rest of the function proceeds to execute normally.

FIND IT ONLINE

This chapter has covered the basics of how to create custom methods and functions. To learn more, visit www.phrogram.com and perform a search on "methods" and "functions." In response, dozens of postings addressing different aspects of working with methods and functions are displayed, including advanced topics not covered in this chapter such as passing arguments by reference and by value.

## Exercises

**To help further your understanding of how to improve Phrogram application structure, perform the following exercises, each of which is designed to reinforce your understanding of how to work with methods and functions.**

1. **Create a new copy of the Number Guessing game which you developed in Chapter 3.**
2. **Reorganize this new copy of the Number Guessing game's program file into methods and functions, creating functions to manage the generation of random numbers, collect player guesses, validate player input, and analyze game results. Use methods to organize and manage other related processes.**

## Leveraging Phrogram's Built-in Library of Methods and Functions

From the very beginning of this book, you have been developing Phrogram applications using methods and functions provided by Phrogram. These methods and functions are provided as part of Phrogram's Class Library. Examples of these functions and methods include the `ConsoleWrite()` and `ConsoleWriteLine()` methods and the `Random()` and `Confirm()` functions. By taking advantage of these predefined methods and functions, you have been able to significantly reduce the size and complexity of your Phrogram applications. As such, you are also able to cut down on development time and produce more reliable programs.

Phrogram provides access to these methods and functions, as well as to properties and constants through its Class Library. Within the Class Library, methods and functions are organized into a hierarchy. At the top or *root* of the hierarchy is a collection of libraries. Within these libraries, you will find large collections of methods and functions that you can incorporate into your Phrogram applications. You will also find class definitions, which support object-oriented programming. If you drill down into the class definitions, you will find class methods and functions. You can browse Phrogram's class library using the Class Library Browser window, as demonstrated in Figure 6.6.

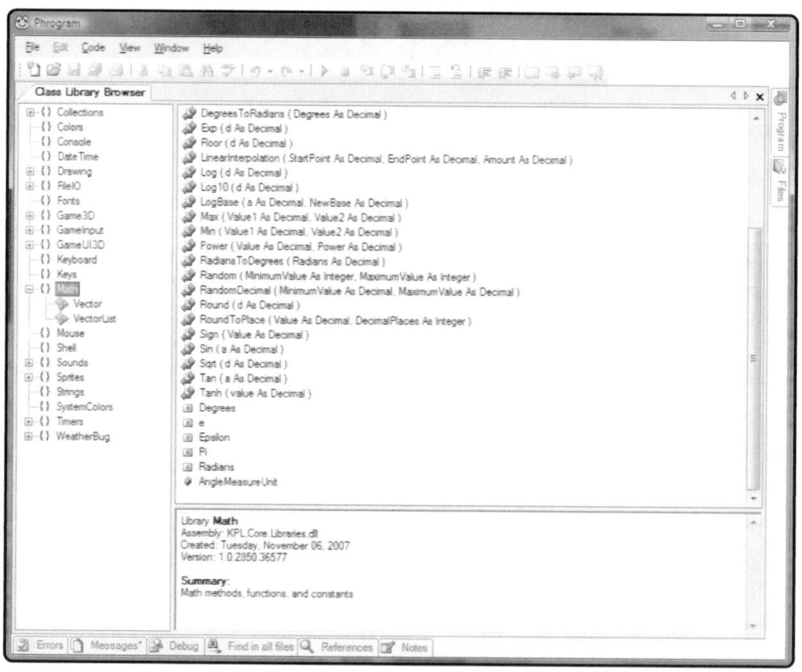


**Figure 6.6**

Viewing functions provided by the Math Library.

If you drill down into Phrogram's Class Library, you will find collections of methods and functions. For example, in Figure 6.6, functions belonging to the Math Library are displayed. You can click on any of these functions to view its purpose and syntax. After spending a little time browsing Phrogram's Class Library, you will come to appreciate the intuitive manner in which the library is organized. As such, it is relatively easy to figure out which library you need to browse in order to see if Phrogram provides a method or function that solves a problem or performs a task that you need to do, saving you the time and effort required to solve the problem yourself. Likewise, syntax and usage description is provided for each method and function, which makes figuring out how to work with a given method or function a snap.

HINT You will learn more about Phrogram's Class Library in Chapter 7, "Getting Comfortable with Object-Oriented Programming."

## Review Questions

1. **What is a procedure? List at least two advantages of using procedures.**
2. **Define the term method.**
3. **Define the term function.**
4. **What is the difference between a method and a function?**
5. **What is a parameter? Create a small method named `ProcessNames()` and set it up so that it has two parameters, representing the user's first and last name. Within the method, display a popup dialog window that displays the first and last name that is passed to it as arguments.**
6. **What is an argument? How are arguments passed to methods and functions?**
7. **Write a statement that demonstrates how to call on a method named `ProcessNames()`, passing it your first and last name as arguments.**
8. **What is the name of the Phrogram keyword that you can use to prematurely exit from a method?**
9. **What is the name of the Phrogram keyword that you can use to pass data back from a function? Write a statement that demonstrates how to pass back the value (belonging to a variable named `PlayerTotalScore()`) from a function.**
10. **What is the name of the Phrogram window that you can use to browse Phrogram class methods and functions?**

# Back to the Crazy Eight Ball Game

Now it is time to turn your attention back to the development of this chapter's application project, the Crazy Eight Ball game. This game will rely heavily upon the development of methods and functions in order to manage the organization of program statements. The end result will be a modularly organized Phrogram application that is easy to understand and maintain.

## Designing the Game

As has been the case with all of the other Phrogram applications that you have created in this book, the Crazy Eight Ball game will be developed in 10 steps, as outlined here:

1. Download and add graphic files to Phrogram's images subfolder.
2. Create a new Phrogram program.
3. Document your program file.
4. Define the application's global variables.
5. Add controlling logic to the `Main()` method.
6. Add the `ConfigureWindow()` method.
7. Add the `LoadImageFiles()` method.
8. Add the `GenerateRandomNo()` method.
9. Add the `DisplayAnswer()` method.
10. Save and compile your application.

As long as you follow along carefully and make sure that you do not make any typing errors along the way, you should have a fully functional copy of the Crazy Eight Ball game in no time at all.

### Step 1: Downloading and Adding Graphic Files

The Crazy Eight Ball involves the display of a number of graphic image files, representing different views of the eight ball. Figure 6.7 displays a view of the five eight-ball images used by the game.

In order to create your own copy of this game, you need to download these graphic files from the book's companion CD included with this book. In total there are five eight-ball images files that are needed, as outlined here:

- **EightBall.jpg.** An eight-ball image displayed when the game is first started and redisplayed in between player questions.
- **MaybeBall.jpg.** An eight-ball image displayed whenever the game selects Maybe as the answer to the player's question.

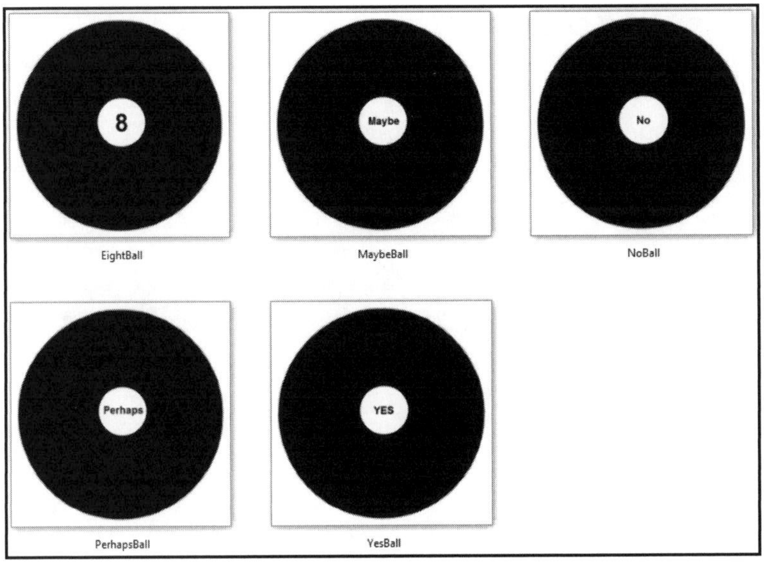


**Figure 6.7**

The Crazy Eight Ball game displays different JPEG graphic files representing different views of the eight ball.

- **NoBall.jpg.** An eight-ball image displayed whenever the game selects No as the answer to the player's question.
- **PerhapsBall.jpg.** An eight-ball image displayed whenever the game selects Perhaps as the answer to the player's question.
- **YesBall.jpg.** An eight-ball image displayed whenever the game selects Yes as the answer to the player's question.

Once downloaded to your computer, you must copy these files into Phrogram's Images subfolder located in (Documents/My Phrogram Files/Media Files/Images).

**TRICK** After copying the Crazy Eight Ball game's graphic files, you can verify that you put them in the right place by opening the Picture Browser window and verifying that the images are now visible.

### Step 2: Creating a New Phrogram Project

The next step in the creation of the Crazy Eight Ball game is to create a new program. Do so by clicking on the File menu's New Program command. Once you have done this, assign Crazy8Ball as the name of the application. The rest of the program statements that will make up the Crazy Eight Ball application are outlined in the sections that follow.

### Step 3: Documenting Your New Program

Now that you have created a new program with which to begin working on the Crazy Eight Ball application, let's add the following program statements to the beginning of the program file, immediately following the opening `Program` statement.

```
//Program: Crazy8Ball.kpl
//Created: 01/11/2008
//Version: 1.0
//Author: Jerry Lee Ford, Jr.
//Description: This Phrogram game simulates the operation of a Crazy
//             Eight Ball fortune telling toy, providing randomly selected
//             answers to players' questions.
```

As you can see, these comment statements provide a little high-level documentation about the program and its purpose.

### Step 4: Defining the Application's Global Variables

Now it is time to define a global constant and a number of global variables that will be used throughout the application. The constant will be used to store a text string containing the name of the application and the variables will be used to store references to objects representing five graphic images. The program statements that manage the definitions are shown next and should be added to the beginning of the program file, immediately following the comment statements that you added in the previous step and before the beginning of the `Main()` method.

```
//Global constant used to store the name of the game
Constant GameTitle As String = "Crazy Eight Ball Game"

//Global variables used to store references to different graphic images
Define EightBall As Sprite
Define YesBall As Sprite
Define NoBall As Sprite
Define MaybeBall As Sprite
Define PerhapsBall As Sprite
```

Later in the game, you will refer to these variable names when you need to display or hide the display of the game's graphic image files.

**HINT** Each of the five previous variable definitions set up object references to the image files used by the application. For example, the first statement defines a variable named `EightBall` and assigns it a data type of `Sprite`. A *sprite* is a two-dimensional image that represents an object used within the game. In the case of the Crazy Eight Ball game, each sprite represents a different eight-ball image. You will learn more about sprites in Chapter 8, "Working with Graphics and Animation."

### Step 5: Adding Controlling Logic to the Main() Method

The Crazy Eight Ball game relies heavily on the use of methods and functions to store most of its program code. This modular approach helps to make the application easier to maintain and update. The glue that helps bind all of the application's methods and functions together are the programming statements located in the `Main()` method, which are responsible for the overall execution of the game.

```
//Primary method used to control game play
Method Main()

    //Define method variables used in the main() method
    Define Reply As Boolean = False //Used to store player input
    Define Msg As String            //Stores a display string
    Define RandomNumber As Integer  //Stores a randomly generated number

    //Call on the method that configures Window attributes
    ConfigureWindow()

    //Outline the text of the game's welcome message
    Msg = "Welcome To The " + GameTitle + "!  Are You Ready To Play?"

    //Display the game's welcome message in a popup dialog window and
    //prompt the player to click on Yes to play the game or No to quit
    Reply = Confirm(Msg, GameTitle)

    //Analyze the player's response
    If Reply = True Then            //If Reply equals True then the
                                    //player clicked on the Yes button

        //Call on the method that preloads image files into memory
        LoadImageFiles()

        //Call on the method that displays an image of an eight ball
        EightBall.Show()
```

```
        //Call on the built-in Delay() method to pause execution
        Delay(1000)

        While True                  //Create a loop that runs forever

            //Prompt the player to think of a question
            Alert("Think of your question and click on OK.", GameTitle)

            //Call on the built-in Delay() method to pause execution
            Delay(1000)

            //Call on the function that generates and returns a random
            //number from 1 to 4
            RandomNumber = GenerateRandomNo()

            //Call on the method that displays an answer to the player's
            //question based on a random numeric value passed to it as
            //an argument
            DisplayAnswer(RandomNumber)

            //Call on the built-in Delay() method to pause execution
            Delay(1000)

        End While

    Else    //Execute the following statements when the player clicks
            //on the No button

        //Display a message in a popup window inviting the player to
        //play again another time
        Alert("OK. Perhaps another time.", GameTitle)

    End If

End Method
```

These statements should be inserted in the `Main()` method exactly as shown. The first of these statements defines a number of method variables which are used within the `Main()` method to store player input, the game's opening message, and a randomly generated number that is used as the basis for determining how the player's questions should be answered.

The next statement in the `Main()` method calls upon the `ConfigureWindow()` method, which is responsible for configuring settings that control the appearance of the game's window. The `Confirm()` method is then used to display a popup dialog window that prompts the player for permission to begin game play. An `If...Then` code block is then used to determine whether the player clicked on the popup dialog window's Yes or No buttons and reacts accordingly.

If the player elects to play the game, the `LoadImageFiles()` method is called. This method is responsible for pre-loading each of the image files used by the application into memory. Next, the EightBall.jpg file is displayed in the application's window using the `Sprite` class's `Show()` method and then the application's execution is paused for one second using the `Delay()` method.

> **HINT** The `Sprite` class's `Show()` method is used to make the image file associated with a sprite visible. To use it, simply specify the variable name representing the sprite followed by a period and then the method name.

Next, a `While...End While` loop is set up to execute forever. The loop is responsible for managing the eight ball's interaction with the player. The loop begins by using the `Alert()` method to display a message in a popup dialog window that instructs the player to think of a question and then to click on the window's OK button. Once the player responds to the popup dialog window, the game's execution is paused for one second after which the `GenerateRandomNo()` function is called. This function generates a random number from 1 to 4 and returns the random number, which is then stored in the `RandomNumber` variable. Finally, the `DisplayAnswer()` method is called and passed the value stored in `RandomNumber` as an argument. Using the randomly generated number as input, the `DisplayAnswer()` method selects and then displays an answer to the player's questions. The loop ends by using the `Delay()` method to pause execution for one second, after which the loop iterates, permitting the player to ask the game a new question.

If the player elected not to play the game when prompted by the popup dialog window, the statements that follow the `Else` keyword in the `If...Then` code block are executed, and the `Alert()` method is used to display a popup dialog window with a text message that encourages the player to return and play another time.

### Step 6: Developing the ConfigureWindow() Method

The `ConfigureWindow()` method, whose program statements are shown next, is responsible for configuring the game's application window. When creating this method, place it inside the opening `Program` statement and before the closing `End Program` statement, either just before or just after the `Main()` method.

```
//This method configures Window attributes
Method ConfigureWindow()

    HideToolbar()   //Prevent the window's toolbar from being displayed
    SetScreenSize(560, 570)     //Set the screen size to 560x570 pixels
    SetWindowTitle(GameTitle)  //Display the name of the game in the
                               //Window's titlebar

End Method
```

When called upon to execute, this method hides the window's toolbar, sets the screen size for the application's window, and then displays the name of the game in the application window's titlebar.

### Step 7: Developing the LoadImageFiles() Method

The `LoadImageFiles()` method, shown next, is responsible for loading each of the image files used by the application into memory. When adding this method to your program file, place it just underneath the `ConfigureWindow()` method which you created in the previous step.

```
//This method pre-loads graphic images displayed during game play
Method LoadImageFiles()

    //Load images into memory representing different views of the eight
    //ball
    EightBall.Load("EightBall.jpg")
    YesBall.Load("YesBall.jpg")
    NoBall.Load("NoBall.jpg")
    MaybeBall.Load("MaybeBall.jpg")
    PerhapsBall.Load("PerhapsBall.jpg")

End Method
```

This method uses the `Sprite` class's `Load()` method to load a graphic image into memory using the following syntax.

`Load(`*`FileName`*` As String)`

*FileName* represents the name of the image file to be loaded into memory. By pre-loading the game's image files into memory, the game is able to instantly display them on the screen.

## Step 8: Developing the GenerateRandomNo() Method

The `GenerateRandomNo()` method, shown next, is responsible for generating and then returning a random number from 1 to 4. When adding this method, place it immediately after the `LoadImageFiles()` method that you created in Step 7.

```
//This method generates and returns a random number in the range of
//1 to 4
Function GenerateRandomNo() As Integer

    //Define a method variable used to store a randomly generated number
    Define RandomNumber As Integer

    //Call on the built-in Random function in order to generate a
    //random number between 1 and 4
    RandomNumber = Random(1, 4)

    //Return the value of the randomly generated number back to the
    //calling statement
    Return RandomNumber

End Function
```

This method defines an integer variable named `RandomNumber`, to which it assigns a randomly generated number, generated using the `Random()` method. The value stored in `RandomNumber` is then passed back to the calling statements using the `Return` keyword.

## Step 9: Developing the DisplayAnswer() Method

The `DisplayAnswer()` method, shown next, is generating the eight ball's response, based on a random number passed to it as an argument. This is accomplished using a `Case...Select` code block, which compares the value of `RandomNumber` against a series of values (1, 2, 3, or 4). The statements belonging to the matching `Case` statements are then executed. These statements use the `Sprite` class's `Show()` method to display an image file for three seconds, after which the `Sprite` class's `Hide()` method is used to suppress the display of the image file.

```
//This method generates and displays a graphic image answering the
//player's question based on numeric values passed to it as an
```

```
//argument
Method DisplayAnswer(RandomNumber As Integer)

    //Retrieve an answer based on the value of the random number
    Select RandomNumber

        Case 1    //Execute block statements if RandomNumber equals 1
            YesBall.Show()  //Display an eight-ball image with a Yes answer
            Delay(3000)     //Pause execution for three seconds
            YesBall.Hide()    //Hide the display of the image
        End Case

        Case 2    //Execute block statements if RandomNumber equals 2
            NoBall.Show()   //Display an eight-ball image with a No answer
            Delay(3000)       //Pause execution for three seconds
            Noball.Hide()     //Hide the display of the image
        End Case

        Case 3    //Execute block statements if RandomNumber equals 3
            MaybeBall.Show()  //Display an eight-ball image with a Maybe
                              //answer
            Delay(3000)       //Pause execution for three seconds
            MaybeBall.Hide()  //Hide the display of the image
        End Case

        Case 4    //Execute block statements if RandomNumber equals 4
            PerhapsBall.Show() //Display an eight-ball image with a Perhaps
                               //answer
            Delay(3000)        //Pause execution for three seconds
            PerhapsBall.Hide() //Hide the display of the image
        End Case

    End Select

End Method
```

**HINT** The `Sprite` class's `Hide()` method hides an image file. To use it, simply specify the variable name representing the sprite followed by a period and then the method name.

When creating this method, place it immediately after the `GenerateRandomNo()` method which you created in step 8.

## Step 10: Saving and Compiling Your Application

At this point your copy of the Crazy Eight Ball game should be ready to go. If you have not done so yet, save your new application by clicking on the Save All command located on the File menu. Now close and reopen your program. Once displayed, the program statements that are stored in all of the program's methods and functions are automatically collapsed or folded, leaving only the name of the methods and functions visible, as demonstrated in Figure 6.8.

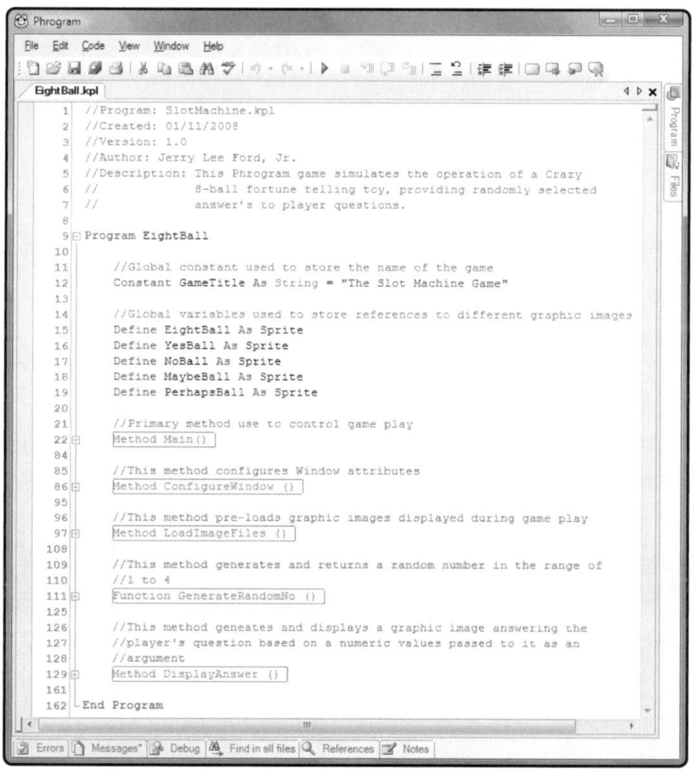


**FIGURE 6.8**

The Phrogram IDE automatically collapses program code statements stored in methods and functions.

Now move the pointer over the `ConfigureWindow()` method. As shown in Figure 6.9, you can view the program statements belonging to the method without having to expand it in the IDE. If the number of statements in the method is too numerous to be displayed in the tool tip window that is displayed, an ellipse is displayed at the bottom-left corner of the tool tip. To see all of the statements that make up the method, you will have to click on the plus sign located just to the left of the method name to expand the method.

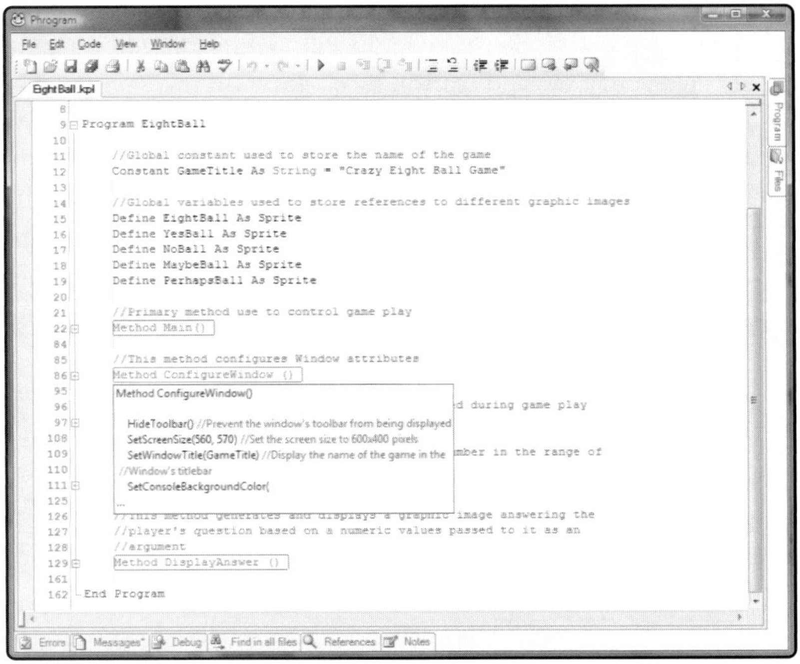

**FIGURE 6.9**

You can peek at the code statements belonging to any method or function without opening it by moving the pointer over the method or function name.

As you can see, folded methods and functions reduce the overall size of your program files, allowing you to navigate your program files more quickly, selectively opening and closing methods and functions when necessary.

All right, if you have not done so yet, compile and execute your application by clicking on the Run the Program button. As long as you did not skip any steps or make any typos along the way, Phrogram will launch your new application within a few moments. Once started, the Crazy Eight Ball game executes exactly as described at the beginning of the chapter.

## The Final Result

All right! Hopefully, you have finished working on your copy of the Crazy Eight Ball game. If, however, you experience problems, you should try using the information presented in any error messages displayed to track down and fix any typos or mistakes you may have accidentally made when keying in program code statements. Alternatively, you can download a copy of the source code for this application from the book's companion CD.

## Summary

This chapter taught you how to improve the organization of your Phrogram applications through the use of custom methods and functions. This included learning how to define and call on methods and functions to execute as well as how to pass data to them as arguments for processing. You learned how to create functions that can return data back to the statements that called upon them to execute. This chapter also showed you how to break out of methods early. In addition to all this, you learned how to work with the Class Library Browser and to use it to learn more about Phrogram's built-in library of methods and functions.

Before you move on to Chapter 7, consider spending a little time improving the Crazy Eight Ball game by addressing the following list of challenges.

### Challenges

1. **As currently written, the Crazy Eight Ball game only has four possible responses to choose from when answering player questions. As such, it does not take the player very long to begin to see the repetition. Consider increasing the number of responses that the game has to choose from to 6, 8, or 10 choices. You will need to create corresponding graphic images for each new answer that you add to the game.**
2. **The Crazy Eight Ball game does not provide the player with much in the way of instructions that explain how to play the game. Consider modifying the opening popup dialog window to provide the player with a few instructions that explain in advance how the game operates.**
3. **Create a distribution package for your new game and share it with a few friends, asking them to provide you with feedback.**

# Part III

# Advanced Programming Topics

CHAPTER 7

# Getting Comfortable with Object-Oriented Programming

Phrogram is an object-oriented programming language. It provides you with access to all sorts of object-oriented resources, in the form of properties, methods, and functions provided by the Phrogram Class Library. In addition, Phrogram allows you to define and implement custom classes, from which you can then create objects based on those classes. This chapter will teach you how to define custom classes and to create objects based on those classes. This chapter will also provide an overview of Phrogram's support for object-oriented programming. In addition, you will learn how to create your next Phrogram application, the Doodle game.

Specifically, you will learn:

- About a number of fundamental object-oriented terms and concepts
- How to define your own custom classes and add variables, properties, methods, and functions to them
- How to create new objects based on the classes you define
- How to limit access to class variables, properties, methods, and functions

## Project Preview: The Doodle Game

This chapter's game project is a Windows paint application called the Doodle game. The development of this Phrogram application provides the opportunity to apply many of the object-oriented programming concepts and programming techniques that are covered in this chapter. In addition, you will also learn how to work with a number of new Phrogram classes, executing methods that draw and setting properties that control line size and color.

Figure 7.1 shows the message that is displayed in the application's opening popup dialog window, which welcomes the player and explains how to display instructions for playing the game.

**Figure 7.1**

Instructions can be displayed at any time by pressing the F10 key.

After clicking on the popup dialog window's OK button, the popup window closes, leaving the window shown in Figure 7.2 displayed on the screen. The status bar at the bottom of the window displays a text string showing the current color setting that will be used when the player begins drawing.

To draw, the player presses and holds down one of the mouse's buttons and moves the mouse around on the console window. Drawing stops whenever the player releases the mouse button. The player can select from different colors at any time by pressing one of the following letters on the keyboard.

- R — Red
- Y — Yellow
- P — Purple
- G — Green
- B — Blue
- W — White
- O — Orange

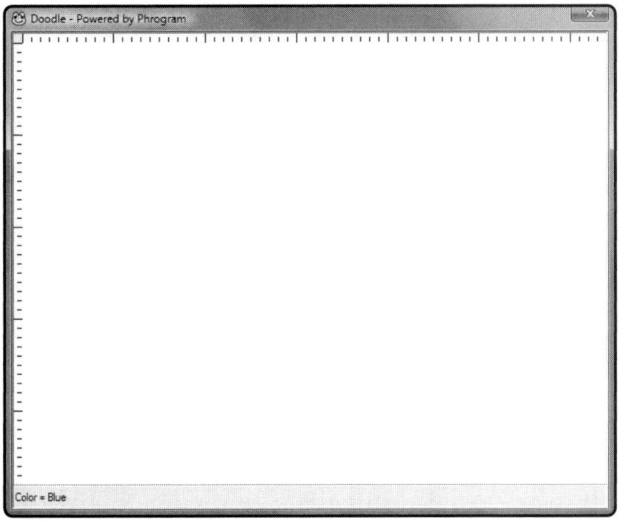


**FIGURE 7.2**

The Doodle game's console window provides a virtual canvas for the player to draw on.

The player can also choose from any of three line sizes by pressing the following keys.

- F1 — 6 Point
- F2 — 9 Point
- F3 — 12 Point

Figure 7.3 shows an example of a picture drawn using different line sizes and colors.

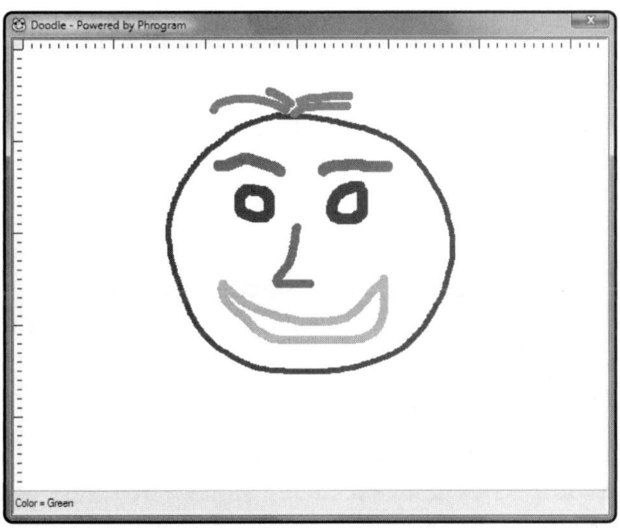


**FIGURE 7.3**

An example of a smiling face drawn using the Doodle game.

The player can clear the drawing area (console window) at any time by pressing the F4 key. In addition, by pressing the F10 key, the player can display the game's instructions, as demonstrated in Figure 7.4.

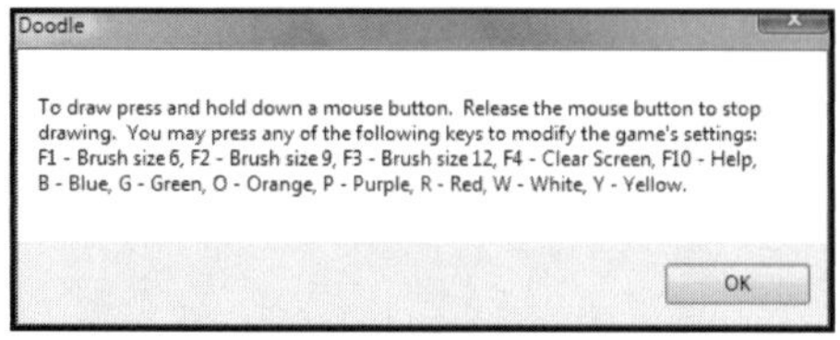


**FIGURE 7.4**

Viewing the Doodle game's instructions.

# WHAT IS OBJECT-ORIENTED PROGRAMMING?

Object-oriented programming (OOP) is a form of application development based on the definition of objects, representing real world concepts like cars, tanks, planes, and people. In OOP, objects are assigned specific attributes or properties, along with methods and functions that are required to interact with and control the operation of the objects.

In OOP, program code statements are grouped into related collections in order to form *class* definitions. A *class* is a blueprint or template that defines the variables, properties, methods, and functions used as a basis for creating objects. For example, a class defining the characteristics (properties) of a car and the actions (methods and functions) that the car can perform could be used to programmatically create any number of instances of cars within an application. Thus, OOP supports code re-use. Each new instance of a car that is programmatically created or *instantiated* is associated with a unique variable name. By referencing individual cars, you can manipulate their object's properties, making some red and others blue or making some two-door while some are four-door. Using object methods, you can programmatically control the operations of each car that you have defined. Examples of actions that cars might be made to perform in a computer game include moving, turning right or left, and stopping.

In OOP, the programmer's focus begins with the identification of the different objects required to solve a problem or perform a task, followed by the specification of each object's attributes and the types of operations that the object can perform. Object-oriented programs store object data as well as the methods and functions required to control the object as part of the object itself. As such, objects are very much self-contained.

OOP applications solve problems and perform tasks by creating and manipulating objects and then manipulating object properties and executing object methods and functions. Because access to object data is controlled through methods and functions, you can add program code to object procedures that validate any data that is passed to them and take steps to ensure that any actions executed by objects are appropriate to the context in which the object is being used. By properly defining the classes upon which objects are based, you can develop Phrogram applications that are more reliable and easier to maintain and update.

## Key OOP Concepts and Terms

One of the keys to understanding how OOP works is to understand that in an OOP language, everything is viewed as an object. An example of a commonly referenced object in most Phrogram applications is the console object, which represents the console window in which Phrogram applications execute. Examples of other types of objects that computer programs deal with include text files, sound files, folders, and graphics.

There are two ways of accessing objects within Phrogram programs. First, as you have been doing since the beginning of this book, you can access any of the different types of objects defined in Phrogram's Class Library. Phrogram automatically makes these objects available to your Phrogram applications, so you can reference them from within your program files. The second way to work with objects is to define your own custom objects.

HINT

Phrogram supports both procedural and OOP programming styles. A procedural program is organized in a modular fashion using methods and functions. OOP programs also use methods and functions, only within the context of classes and objects. Phrogram's Class Library provides you with access to all of the language's methods and functions, both procedural and OOP. Using the Class Library Browser window you can view all of Phrogram's methods and functions. You will find the procedural method and functions are stored at the root of the Class Library. Phrogram's OOP methods and functions are stored inside class definitions at levels below the root level. Because Phrogram is so flexible, you can use procedural and OOP methods and functions interchangeably. However, like most modern programming languages, plans for the future development of Phrogram will continue to move it towards OOP and away from procedural programming.

All objects are derived from classes. A *class* is a definition or blueprint that outlines the variables, properties, methods, and functions that together form a template from which objects can be generated. Phrogram has already defined the class definitions for all kinds of helpful objects like the console and shell objects. Using the properties, methods, and functions belonging to the console object for example, you can set different console properties that affect console size and color. Using console methods and functions, you can clear the screen and display data on it. To view the impressive set of predefined classes that Phrogram automatically puts at your fingertips, open the Class Browser window.

**HINT**

A *property* is an object attribute that describes some characteristics of the object. For example, an object might have properties that you can use to effect the color and size of the object. Object methods and functions are methods and functions defined within an object's class definition, specifically designed to interact with or control the object in some manner.

## Major Features of Object-Oriented Programming Languages

All object-oriented programming languages are based on two primary concepts, abstraction and inheritance, which you will learn about in the next two sections. In addition, many programming languages expand their support of OOP to include additional advanced concepts that include inheritance and polymorphism. Phrogram does not support inheritance or polymorphism and instead limits itself to basic fundamental OOP concepts. The result is a powerful programming language that is easy to learn, allowing first time programmers to learn the basics of object-oriented programming without getting overwhelmed, while at the same time preparing new programmers with a foundation which will prepare them to make the jump to more robust professional OOP languages like Visual Basic, C#, and C++.

**HINT**

*Inheritance* is an object-oriented programming concept in which one class is derived from another (parent) class. With inheritance, the child class inherits all of the features of the parent class and can then be modified through the addition of new property, method, and function definitions. Inheritance can be used to reduce the number and complexity of class definitions within applications by allowing new classes to be generated from existing classes. Inheritance comes in handy in situations in which you need to work with multiple objects that are closely related but not identical to one another. In Phrogram, since you cannot use inheritance, you must manually define any new class definitions.

*Polymorphism* is an object-oriented programming concept in which programmers add two or more like named methods or functions with different sets of parameter definitions to the same class definition. When objects based on the classes are called upon to execute, the actual method or function that is executed depends on which ones parameter definitions match up against the arguments that are passed. Using polymorphism, you can define objects that are able to accept different sets of arguments and alter their execution accordingly. Since Phrogram does not support polymorphism, you must create a new method or function (each with a unique name) in order to handle all of the different possible sets of arguments that you many need for an object to be able to process.

### Abstraction

*Abstraction* is a term used to refer to a programming language's ability to define a logical representation of a real world concept in the form of a class. Using variables and properties, you can define attributes that describe different characteristics such as the height, width, and color of the class and any objects that are based on it. Using methods and functions, you can provide the class with program code that allows it to perform whatever actions you see fit.

To better understand the concept of abstraction, let's consider as an example an application in which a class called `Automobile` is used as the basis for creating different cars to be used in a racing game. You might choose to define class properties for color, model, and any number of other attributes that describe the appearance of an automobile. In addition to properties, the class definition should include a number of methods or functions that can be called upon to control the operation of automobiles. For example, you might add methods that control speed and direction. Having abstracted all of the essential qualities of an automobile into a class definition, you can then use the class within the game to create as many cars as needed to play the game, assigning each car to a unique variable (referred to as an object variable), allowing each car to be individually referenced and operated.

### Encapsulation

*Encapsulation* is the process of simplifying application development by hiding as much as possible the complexity and inner workings of a class from the programs that use it. The complexity of the program code that makes up each of Phrogram's built-in classes is encapsulated and hidden from you. You can call upon class methods and functions to run at any time without concerning yourself as to the inner workings of those procedures. They are simply there if you need them. As such, encapsulation helps simplify application development. As you will learn later in this chapter, you can implement encapsulation yourself by defining variables, properties, methods, and functions within the custom class definitions that restrict access to class resources.

## Defining Classes and Creating Objects

Phrogram lets you create your own custom classes, which you then use to create objects. An *object* is just an instance of a given class. To help better understand the relationship between classes and objects think of the relationship between a cookie mold and a cookie. The mold defines the shape and size and other attributes. Once cookie dough is pored into the mold and baked, a new instance of a cookie is created that takes on the basic qualities of the mold.

### Creating a Custom Class

Phrogram lets you create and define your own custom classes by placing variable, property, method, and function definitions within the `Class` and `End Class` statements, using the syntax outlined here:

```
Class ClassName

   Statements

End Class
```

*ClassName* is the name assigned to the class and *Statements* represents any number of variable, property, method, and function definitions.

When you add a custom class definition to a Phrogram file, you place it outside of the `Main()` method or any other method. The following statements demonstrate how to create a simple class named `MessageBoard`.

```
Program ClassDemo

    Class MessageBoard

    End Class

    Method Main()

    End Method

End Program
```

At the moment, the class does not do anything, since you have not added any variables, properties, methods, or functions to it.

## Defining Class Variables

You may recall from Chapter 3, "Learning How to Work with Data," that Phrogram supports three types of variable scope, as outlined here:

- **Global.** Variables defined within the Program code block. These variables are accessible from any location within a program file.
- **Method.** Variables that are defined within a method or its parameter lists. These variables are accessible only within the methods where they are defined.
- **Class.** Variables defined within a class block. These variables are accessible only within the class where they are defined.

The following example demonstrates how to add a class variable named `MessageText` to the `MessageBoard` class.

```
Program ClassDemo

    Class MessageBoard
        Define MessageText As String
    End Class

End Program
```

By default, all class variables are accessible to all objects that you instantiate based on the class that defines them. However, as you will learn later in this chapter, you can restrict access to class variables by making them private, in which case they can only be accessed indirectly through class properties.

**TRICK**

By default, you cannot access global variables from within any classes that you define. However, using the `Global` prefix you can override this behavior and access any global variable as demonstrated in the following example.

```
Program ClassDemo

    Define GameName As String = "Wambam"

    Class DemoClass

        Method Display()
            ConsoleWriteLine(Global.GameName)
        End Method

    End Class

    Method Main()
        Define TestObject As DemoClass
        TestObject.Display()

    End Method

End Program
```

Here, a global variable named `GameName` has been defined. In order to reference it from within the `DemoClass`, the `Global` prefix is used. If the `Global` prefix were omitted, a syntax error would occur.

## Defining Class Properties

Rather than allow direct access to class variables, you may instead want to make them private and control access to a variable's value through the implementation of class properties. Class properties can be set and retrieved. To define a property within a class, you begin by declaring the variable as private. This prevents the variable from being accessed outside of the class itself. Access to the variable can then be provided via the property, whose definition includes the following pair of property procedures.

- **Get.** Returns the value assigned to a variable.
- **Set.** Assigns a value to a variable.

The following example demonstrates how to modify the `MessageBoard` class through the addition of a property that provides access to the `MessageText` variable.

```
Class MessageBoard

    Private Define MessageText As String
    Property Msg As String

        Get
            Return MessageText
        End Get

        Set(Value As String)
            MessageText = Value
        End Set

    End Property

End Class
```

Note that the keyword `Private` has been added to the beginning of the definition of the `MessageText` variable. As a result, this variable can no longer be accessed directly. Instead, to set or retrieve the variable's value, you must work through the class's `Msg` property.

Any time a property's value is modified, its `Set` procedure is executed and the value that is being assigned is automatically passed to the `Set` procedure as an argument. As you can see in the previous example, when the `MessageBoard` class's `Msg` property is modified and its `Set` procedures executed, the value assigned to the `MessageText` variable is modified using the argument passed to the `Set` procedure. Any time a property's value is retrieved, its `Get` procedure executes. As you can see in the previous example, when the MessageBoard class's Msg property is retrieved, the Get procedure returns the value assigned to the MessageText variable.

The whole reason for defining a class is so that you can use it as the basis for creating objects. In order to work with an object, you must instantiate it. The following example demonstrates how to create a new object named WhiteBoard that is based on the MessageBoard class.

```
Define WhiteBoard As MessageBoard
```

Once instantiated, you can access its properties, as demonstrated here:

```
WhiteBoard.Msg = "Well, hello there."
ConsoleWriteLine(WhiteBoard.Msg)
```

The first statement uses dot notation to access the WhiteBoard object's Msg property and assigns it a value. The second statement retrieves and displays the value of the object's Msg property.

TRICK

You may be wondering why you should bother defining class properties given that class variables are so easy to work with. The advantage of setting up properties to control access to private class variables is that properties give the opportunity to perform data validation before any changes are made to a variable's value. For example, take a look at the following property definition, whose Set procedure has been modified to validate the length of the data passed to it to ensure that it is a minimum of two characters long before any change is made to the variable that it is associated with.

```
Property Text As String
    Get
       Return Message
    End Get
    Set(Value As String)
        If Len(Value) > 2 Then
            Message = Value
        End If
    End Set
End Property
```

## Adding Class Methods and Functions

In addition to defining variables and properties, you can also add your own methods and functions to your custom classes. To add a method or function, all you have to do is add a Method or Function, as demonstrated here:

```
Program ClassDemo

    Class MessageBoard

        Private Define MessageText As String

        Property Msg As String

            Get
                Return MessageText
            End Get

            Set(Value As String)
                MessageText = Value
            End Set

        End Property

        Method Display()
            ConsoleWriteLine(Msg)
        End Method

    End Class

    Method Main()
        Define WhiteBoard As MessageBoard
        WhiteBoard.Msg = "Well, hello there."
        WhiteBoard.Display()
    End Method

End Program
```

Here, a method named `Display()` has been added to the `MessageBoard` class. In addition, a statement has been added to the `Main()` method that calls on the `Display()` method to execute.

**FIND IT ONLINE**

This chapter has taught you the basics of how to define your own custom classes. You can learn more about Phrogram's support for object-oriented programming and find information about undocumented class features supported by Phrogram by reading the Unofficial Undocumented Features Guide. This guide is a small PDF file, which you can download for free at http://phrogram.com/forums/post/2452.aspx.

## Restricting Access to Class Variables, Properties, Methods, and Functions

As has been demonstrated throughout this chapter, variables defined within classes are publicly accessible to any objects that you define based on that class. For example, consider the following example.

```
Program ClassAccessExample

    Class Greeting
        Define Message As String = "Hello World!"
    End Class

    Method Main()
        Define Notify As Greeting
        Print(Notify.Message)
    End Method

End Program
```

Here, a class named `Greeting`, containing a variable named `Message`, is defined. This class is then used to define an object named `Notify` in the `Main()` method. Once created the `Notify` object displays the value assigned to the `Message` variable. This works because `Message` is by default, publicly available.

### Explicitly Making Class Resources Public

If you want to be more explicit, you can specify the `Public` keyword when defining class variables, as demonstrated here:

```
Program ClassAccessExample

    Class Greeting
        Public Define Message As String = "Hello World!"
    End Class

    Method Main()
        Define Notify As Greeting
        Print(Notify.Message)
```

```
    End Method

End Program
```

The addition of the `Public` keyword is for your benefit only and has no effect on the way the example works. Like variables, you can also add the `Public` keyword to class methods and functions. Again, this has no effect on an object's ability to access class methods and functions, since they are publicly accessible by default. For example, the following Phrogram application adds a method named `Display()` to the `Greeting` class.

```
Program ClassAccessExample

    Class Greeting

        Define Message As String = "Hello World!"

        Public Method Display()
            ConsoleWriteLine(Message)
        End Method

    End Class

    Method Main()
        Define Notify As Greeting
        Notify.Display()
    End Method

End Program
```

The `Display()` method has been made accessible to all objects based on that class. You could rewrite the statements that define the `Display()` by removing the `Public` keyword as shown next and it would not have any effect on an object's ability to access the method.

```
Public Method Display()
    ConsoleWriteLine(Message)
End Method
```

## Limiting Access to Class Resources

If you want, you can limit access to class variables, methods, and functions using the `Private` keyword, as demonstrated here:

```
Program ClassAccessExample

    Class Greeting

        Private Define Message As String = "Hello World!"

        Private Method Display()
            ConsoleWriteLine(Message)
        End Method

        Public Method Show()
            Display()
        End Method

    End Class

    Method Main()

        Define Notify As Greeting
        Notify.Show()

    End Method

End Program
```

Here, the `Private` keyword has been used to restrict access to the `Message` variable and the `Display()` method, preventing them from being accessed by objects based on that class. However, a new method named `Show()` has been added to the class, which is publicly available. When called, the `Show()` method executes, calling upon the private `Display()` method, allowing indirect access to it.

## Exercises

To help you become better acquainted with classes, set aside a few minutes to perform the following exercises, which are designed to reinforce your understanding of how to define and work with classes.

1. Create a new Phrogram application and add a class to it named `Animal`.
2. Add a number of variables to this class that define different animal features. For example, you should create variables to store animal name, type, and color.
3. Add a method to the class that when called, displays a text string representing the type of noise that a specified animal would make.
4. Instantiate an object in the `Main()` method based on the `Animal` class and then prompt the user to enter the name of one of the animals supported by the game.
5. Based on the user's input, display a string that identifies the name, type, and color of the animal and then tell the user what the animal sounds like.

## Review Questions

1. In your own words, explain object-oriented programming.
2. Define class and object. What is the relationship of objects to classes?
3. What purpose do properties serve in custom classes?
4. What is the difference between private and public variables?
5. List and explain the three types of variable scope supported by Phrogram.
6. What do you have to do to be able to reference a global variable from within a class?
7. What two procedures are needed to support the definition of a class property? Explain what each type of procedure is used for.
8. What does the term abstraction mean?
9. What does the term encapsulation mean?
10. Where does Phrogram store its built-in collection of predefined classes?

# Back to the Doodle Game

Okay, it is time to turn your attention back to the development of this chapter's application project, the Doodle game. The design of this application includes the use of a custom class as well as an assortment of object properties and methods made available through Phrogram's Class Library. The end result will be a paint program that supports the use of different colors and line sizes.

Before you begin working on the development of this game, there are a few things you need to understand about how Phrogram manages the placement of graphics on the console window and how drawing operations occur. For starters, graphics are displayed on the console screen, which is a virtual canvas, using a system of coordinates. This system of coordinates consists of an X and Y axis that originates in the upper-left corner of the console window at coordinates (0, 0), as demonstrated in Figure 7.5.

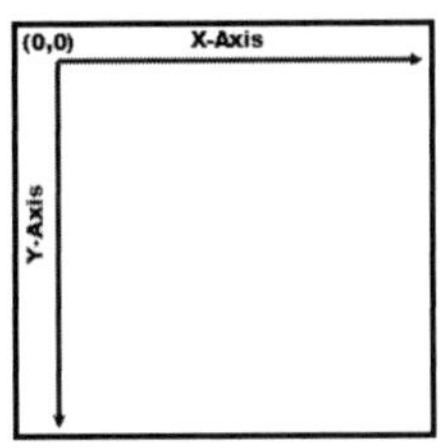


**Figure 7.5**

Graphics are drawn on the console screen at a specific location based on a specified set of coordinates.

The further to the right you go on the console screen the larger the value of the X axis. Similarly, the further down you go on the console screen the higher the value on the Y axis. Figure 7.6 shows an example of how this coordinate system maps out on the Phrogram console window.

Each coordinate on the console screen represents a pixel. A *pixel* is the smallest addressable area on the console window to which you can draw. Phrogram's coordinate system is pixel based, meaning that a console window with a screen size of 640x480 consists of 640 columns by 480 rows of pixels. Drawings are made using a virtual pen by specifying different sets of coordinates along with pen and brush settings. You can affect the operation of the pen using different drawing methods that allow you to change its color and width.

## Designing the Game

The design of the Doodle game is pretty straightforward and will be completed in a series of steps, as outlined here:

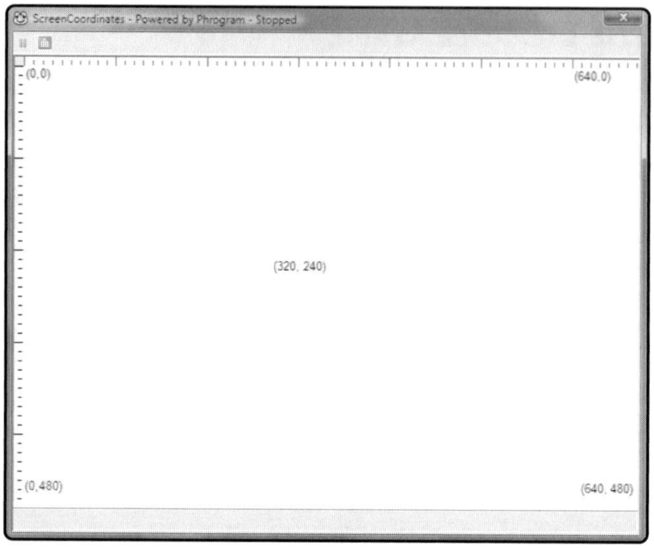


**FIGURE 7.6**

By specifying different sets of coordinates, you can place graphics at any location on the console screen.

1. Create a new Phrogram program.
2. Document your program file.
3. Define the global constants and variables.
4. Add controlling logic to the `Main()` method.
5. Define the `MessageManager` class.
6. Add the `SetProgramDefaults()` method.
7. Add the `ConfigureWindow()` method.
8. Add the `DisplayWelcomeMsg()` method.
9. Add the `AdjustPenSize()` method.
10. Add the `ClearTheScreen()` method.
11. Add the `DisplayInstructions()` method.
12. Add the `ApplyColorSetting()` method.
13. Add the `CollectInputAndDraw()` method.
14. Add the `RefreshScreenOutput()` method.
15. Save and compile your application.

### Step 1: Creating a New Phrogram Project

The first step in the creation of the Doodle game is to create a new program. Do so by clicking on the File menu's New Program command. Next, assign Doodle as the name of the application. The rest of the program statements that will make up the game are outlined in the sections that follow.

### Step 2: Documenting Your New Program

Now that you have created a new program, let's add the following program statements to the beginning of the program file, just before the opening Program statement.

```
//Program: Doodle.kpl
//Created: 01/17/2008
//Version: 1.0
//Author: Jerry Lee Ford, Jr.
//Description: This Phrogram application is a basic paint program that
//             allows the player to use the mouse to draw pictures using
//             an assortment of colors and line sizes.
```

### Step 3: Defining the Application's Global Constants and Variables

Now it is time to define a global constant and a number of global variables used throughout the application. The constant will be used to store a string containing the application's name and the variables will be used throughout the application. The program statements that define the constant and variables are shown next and should be added to the beginning of the program file, immediately following the Program statement.

```
//Global constant used to store the name of the application
Constant GameTitle As String = "Doodle"

//Define a global variable used to keep track of when drawing operations
//should occur
Define StartDrawing As Boolean = False

//Define pen and circle objects
Define ApplicationPen As Pen
Define ApplicationCircle As Circle
```

### Step 4: Defining the MessageManager Class

The Doodle game needs to display text messages in popup dialog windows at the beginning of the game and on demand throughout the execution of the game in order to display the game's instructions. To facilitate this requirement, let's add a custom class named MessageManager to the code file that can be used to store and display these text messages.

```
//This class is used as the basis for instantiating objects that need
//to set and display messages in popup dialog windows
Class MessageManager
```

```
    //Define a variable and restrict its access to inside the class
    Private Define Message As String

    //Define a property representing a text string
    Property Text As String

        //Allow the property to be retrieved
        Get
            Return Message
        End Get

        //Allow the property's value to be set
        Set(Value As String)
            Message = Value
        End Set

    End Property

    //Add a method that displays the value of the Message variable
    Method Display()
        Alert(Message, "Doodle")
    End Method

End Class
```

As you can see, the `MessageManager` class contains a variable definition, a property along with a corresponding `Get` and `Set()` code block, and a method. The class property has been declared private to prevent it from being accessed from anywhere outside the class. Access to the data stored in the variable, which is used to store text strings that the program needs to display, is provided through the `Text` property definition and its `Get` and `Set()` code block.

The text string stored in the `Message` variable is displayed whenever the class's `Display()` method is called to execute. When called, this method uses the `Alert()` method to display the value of `Message`.

## Step 5: Adding Controlling Logic to the Main() Method

The overall controlling logic for the Doodle game is contained in its `Main()` method. The `Main()` method consists of a collection of calls to different methods and a `While...End While` loop, which is responsible for the overall execution of the game.

```
//This method controls overall application execution
Method Main ( )

    //This method sets default pen and color settings
    SetProgramDefaults()

    //This method configures window attributes
    ConfigureWindow()

    //This method welcomes the player and explains how to display
    //game instructions
    DisplayWelcomeMsg()

    //This loop controls player interaction and drawing operations
    While True

        //This method checks to see if the player wants to change
        //pen size
        AdjustPenSize()

        //This method clears the console window
        ClearTheScreen()

        //This method displays the game's instructions
        DisplayInstructions()

        //This method checks to see if the player wants to change color
        ApplyColorSetting()

        //This method tracks mouse movement and manages drawing
        CollectInputAndDraw()

        //This method updates the display of the player's drawing on
        //the console window
        RefreshScreenOutput()

    End While

End Method
```

The first method called establishes the game default pen and color settings. The next method configures settings that effect the display of the console window. The DisplayWelcomeMsg() method displays the game's welcome message and explains how to display the game's instructions. The remainder of the methods called are located inside the While…End While loop. These methods adjust the pen settings whenever the player decides to change them, clears the console window allowing the player to start over with a new drawing, displays the game's instructions, adjusts the color setting, tracks mouse movements, handles drawing operations, and then displays the player's drawing.

### Step 6: Developing the SetProgramDefaults() Method

The SetProgramDefaults() method, shown next, is responsible for setting the game's default pen width and color settings.

```
//This method sets default pen and color settings
Method SetProgramDefaults()

    //Set the line width for the pen
    ApplicationPen.LineWidth = 6

    //Set circle's line width, filled status, and radius
    ApplicationCircle.LineWidth = 6
    ApplicationCircle.Filled = True
    ApplicationCircle.Radius = 3

    //Set the application's default color to blue
    ApplicationPen.Color = Blue
    ApplicationCircle.Color = Blue

    //Display the name of the current color on the window's status bar
    Status("Color = Blue")

End Method
```

Pen width is set using the Pen class's LineWidth() method. This method sets the pixel width of the line that the pen draws. The Circle class's LineWidth, Filled, and Radius properties are then set. Next, the Pen and Circle class's Color() properties are used to specify the color to be used when drawing. Finally, the Shell class's Status() method is used to post a message on the console window's status bar, showing the currently selected color setting.

HINT

Drawing operations are done using a virtual pen and various drawing methods and properties. One of these properties is the `LineWidth` property, which specifies the width, in pixels, of the line drawn by the pen.

There are a number of properties that you need to be familiar with when working with the `Circle` class, including, the `LineWidth` property, which specifies the width, in pixels, of the line used to draw a circle. The `Filled` property is a Boolean value that when set to `True` instructs Program to fill in the circle when drawn. The `Radius` property specifies the Circle's radius (e.g., the distance from the center of the circle to its outside edge).

Both the `Pen` and the `Circle` classes have a `Color` property, which specified the color to be used when drawing.

The `Shell` class's `Status()` method is used to post messages on the console window's status bar using the following syntax.

```
Status(Text)
```

*Text* represents the message that is to be displayed.

## Step 7: Developing the ConfigureWindow() Method

The `ConfigureWindow()` method, shown next, is responsible for configuring the size and appearance of the console window, which it does by hiding the toolbar, setting the screen size to 640 x 480, and then displaying the name of the game in the console window's titlebar.

```
//This method configures Window attributes
Method ConfigureWindow()

   HideToolbar()   //Prevent the window's toolbar from being displayed
   SetScreenSize(640, 480)    //Set the screen size to 640x480 pixels
   SetWindowTitle(GameTitle)  //Display the name of the game in the
                              //Window's titlebar

End Method
```

## Step 8: Developing the DisplayWelcomeMsg() Method

The `DisplayWelcomeMsg()` method, shown next, is responsible for displaying the game's welcome message and explains to the player how to access the game instructions.

```
//This method displays the game's welcome message and explains how to
//display instructions
Method DisplayWelcomeMsg()
```

```
    //Create an object based on the MessageManager class
    Define Msg As MessageManager

    //Use the MessageManager class's Text property to store the game's
    //welcome message
    Msg.Text = "Welcome to " + GameTitle + "!  Press F10 to instructions."

    //Use the MessageManager class's Display() method to display a
    //welcome message
    Msg.Display()

End Method
```

The first statement in the code block defines an object named `Msg`, based on the `MessageManager` class. A text string is then formatted and assigned to the `Msg` object's `Text` property and then displayed by executing the `Msg` object's `Display()` method.

## Step 9: Developing the AdjustPenSize() Method

The `AdjustPenSize()` method, shown next, is responsible for changing the `Pen` object's line width and the `Circle` object's radius.

```
//This method is responsible for changing pen and brush size
Method AdjustPenSize()

    //Change pen and circle settings when the F1 key is pressed
    If IsKeyDown("F1") Then
        ApplicationPen.LineWidth = 6
        ApplicationCircle.Radius = 3
    End If

    //Change pen and circle settings when the F2 key is pressed
    If IsKeyDown("F2") Then
        ApplicationPen.LineWidth = 8
        ApplicationCircle.Radius = 4
    End If

    //Change pen and circle settings when the F3 key is pressed
    If IsKeyDown("F3") Then
        ApplicationPen.LineWidth = 12
```

```
        ApplicationCircle.Radius = 6
    End If

End Method
```

This method consists of three sets of If…Then code blocks, each of which is set up to execute when the player clicks on a function key. The first code block uses the Keyboard class's IsKeyDown() method as a trigger, executing when the player presses the F1 key. When this occurs, a value of 6 (representing pixels) is assigned to the Pen object's LineWidth property and the Circle object's Radius is set to 3.

HINT

The Keyboard class's IsKeyDown() function detects when a key on the keyboard is pressed and returns a Boolean value of True when the key is detected in a pressed state. This function has the following syntax.

IsKeyDown(*Key*)

*Key* represents the key to monitor.

## Step 10: Developing the ClearTheScreen() Method

The ClearTheScreen() method, shown next, is responsible for clearing the console window so that the player can begin drawing a new picture. When executed, this method executes an If…Then code block that executes only in the event that the player presses the F4 key.

```
//This method is responsible for clearing the console window (e.g. the
//drawing area)
Method ClearTheScreen()

    //Set the console window's background color to white, effectively
    //clearing the window when the F4 key is pressed
    If IsKeyDown("F4") Then
        ClearBackground(White)
    End If

End Method
```

When the F4 key is pressed, the If…Then code block executes the Drawing library's ClearBackground() method, passing it an argument of white, filling the screen with white and effectively erasing anything the player may have previously drawn.

HINT

The `ClearBackground()` method fills the console window with the specified color, erasing anything that may already be displayed on it. This method uses the following syntax.

`ClearBackground(`*`Color`*`)`

`Color` represents one of the 140 constant colors supported by Phrogram.

## Step 11: Developing the DisplayInstructions() Method

The `DisplayInstructions()` method, shown next, is responsible for displaying the game's instructions in a popup dialog window when called. It consists of a single `If…Then` code block that executes only when the player presses the F10 key.

```
//This method is responsible for displaying the game's instructions
Method DisplayInstructions()

    //Display game instructions when the F10 key is pressed
    If IsKeyDown("F10") Then

        //Define a method variable to hold the display string
        Define Msg As String

        //Create an object based on the MessageManager class
        Define MsgOutput As MessageManager

        //Format the message string containing the game's instructions
        Msg = "To draw press and hold down a mouse button.  "
        Msg = Msg + "Release the mouse button to stop drawing.  "
        Msg = Msg + "You may press any of the following keys to modify "
        Msg = Msg + "the game's settings:  "
        Msg = Msg + "F1 - Brush size 6, "
        Msg = Msg + "F2 - Brush size 9, "
        Msg = Msg + "F3 - Brush size 12, "
        Msg = Msg + "F4 - Clear Screen, "
        Msg = Msg + "F10 - Help, "
        Msg = Msg + "B - Blue, "
        Msg = Msg + "G - Green, "
        Msg = Msg + "O - Orange, "
        Msg = Msg + "P - Purple, "
        Msg = Msg + "R - Red, "
```

```
        Msg = Msg + "W - White, "
        Msg = Msg + "Y - Yellow."

        //Use the MessageManager class's Text property to store the game's
        //instructions
        MsgOutput.Text = Msg

        //Use the MessageManager class's Display() method to display a
        //welcome message
        MsgOutput.Display()

    End If

End Method
```

The first statement in the code block defines a string variable that will be used to store a text string containing the game's instructions. Next, an object named `MsgOutput` is created based on the `MessageManager` class. A series of assignments are then executed that create a single string representing the game's instructions. This string is then assigned to the `MsgOutput` object's `Text` property and then displayed by executing the `MsgOutput` object's `Display()` method.

### Step 12: Developing the ApplyColorSetting() Method

The `ApplyColorSetting()` method, shown next, is responsible for changing the color used when drawing. The player signals color instructions by pressing letters on the keyboard. For example, pressing the letter `R` sets the drawing color to red and pressing the letter `P` sets it to purple.

```
//This method is responsible for changing the color used when drawing
Method ApplyColorSetting()

    //Set the color to red when the R key is pressed
    If IsKeyDown("R") Then
        ApplicationPen.Color = Red
        ApplicationCircle.Color = Red
        Status("Color = Red") //Display text in the status bar
    End If

    //Set the color to yellow when the Y key is pressed
```

```
If IsKeyDown("Y") Then
    ApplicationPen.Color = Yellow
    ApplicationCircle.Color = Yellow
    Status("Color = Yellow") //Display text in the status bar
End If

//Set the color to purple when the P key is pressed
If IsKeyDown("P") Then
    ApplicationPen.Color = Purple
    ApplicationCircle.Color = Purple
    Status("Color = Purple") //Display text in the status bar
End If

//Set the color to green when the G key is pressed
If IsKeyDown("G") Then
    ApplicationPen.Color = Green
    ApplicationCircle.Color = Green
    Status("Color = Green") //Display text in the status bar
End If

//Set the color to blue when the B key is pressed
If IsKeyDown("B") Then
    ApplicationPen.Color = Blue
    ApplicationCircle.Color = Blue
    Status("Color = Blue") //Display text in the status bar
End If

//Set the color to white when the W key is pressed
If IsKeyDown("W") Then
    ApplicationPen.Color = White
    ApplicationCircle.Color = White
    Status("Color = White") //Display text in the status bar
End If

//Set the color to orange when the O key is pressed
If IsKeyDown("O") Then
    ApplicationPen.Color = Orange
    ApplicationCircle.Color = Orange
```

```
        Status("Color = Orange") //Display text in the status bar
    End If

End Method
```

This method consists of seven nearly identical `If…Then` code blocks. The first `If…Then` code block uses the `Keyboard` class's `IsKeyDown()` function to capture player keystrokes. In the event that the `R` key is pressed, then the `Pen` and `Circle` class's `Color()` property is set to read and the `Shell` class's `Status()` method are executed. The `Status()` method is used to display a string identifying the current color setting on the console window's status bar.

Each of the six methods that follow is essentially the same as the first method, the only difference being that each of these methods is designed to assign a different system color.

> **HINT** You can assign either the integer value or the string value of one of the 140 color constants supported by Phrogram when assigning the value of the `Pen` and `Circle` object's `Color` property.

### Step 13: Developing the CollectInputAndDraw() Method

The `CollectInputAndDraw()` method, shown next, is responsible for tracking the movement of the mouse and the status of its buttons. When the player presses the mouse button, this method draws on the console window. When the player releases the mouse button, drawing stops.

```
//This method tracks mouse movement and handles drawing operations
Method CollectInputAndDraw()

    //Prepare the game for drawing whenever a mouse button is pressed
    If MouseEvent = "ButtonDown" Then

        //Set variable value to indicate that it is time to draw
        StartDrawing = True

        //Set the location where the current drawing operation
        //should begin
        ApplicationPen.MoveTo(MouseX, MouseY)

    End If

    //Drawing should stop when the player lets go of the mouse button
```

```
    If MouseEvent = "ButtonUp" Then

        //Set variable value to indicate that it is time to stop drawing
        StartDrawing = False

    End If

    //Begin drawing as the player moves the mouse
    If StartDrawing = True And MouseEvent = "Move" Then

        //Draw line beginning at the pointer's starting position and
        //ending at the current pointer location
        ApplicationPen.DrawTo(MouseX, MouseY)

        //Draw a circle at the end of each line in order to give it a
        //rounded edge
        ApplicationCircle.Center.X = MouseX
        ApplicationCircle.Center.Y = MouseY
        ApplicationCircle.Draw()

        //Pause 2/1000 of a second to allow for smoother drawing effect
        Delay(2)

    End If

End Method
```

This method is organized into three separate `If…Then` code blocks. The first code block checks the value assigned to the `MouseEvent` property to see if it is equal to `ButtonDown`, which indicates that the player is currently holding down the mouse button. If this is the case, the value of `StartDrawing` is set equal to `True` and the location of the mouse is used to position the `Pen` object by assigning its X and Y coordinates (provided by the `Mouse` class's `MouseX` and `MouseY` properties).

**HINT** The `Mouse` class provides access to a collection of methods and properties that identify the status of the mouse. The `MouseEvent` property, which detects mouse button events, can be set to one of the following values.

- **ButtonDown.** The mouse's button is currently pressed.
- **ButtonUp.** The mouse's button is not being pressed.
- **Move.** The mouse is being moved.
- **Wheel.** The mouse's wheel, if present, is being moved.

The second `If…Then` code block checks the value assigned to the `Mouse` class's `MouseEvent` property to see if it is equal to `ButtonUp`. If it is, then the value assigned to `StartDrawing` is set equal to false, indicating that no drawing operations should occur.

The third `If…Then` code block checks the value assigned to `StartDrawing` and `MouseEvent`. If `StartDrawing` is equal to `True` (in which case the player is holding down a mouse button) and `MouseEvent` is equal to move (in which case the player is moving the mouse over the console window), then the following actions are taken. First, the `Pen` class's `DrawTo()` method is executed in order to draw a line on the screen. The line is drawn from the pen's last position to the pointer's current location. The `Circle` class's `X` and `Y` coordinates are then set to the pointer's current location and the `Circle` class's `Draw()` method is executed, drawing a circle at the end of the line, giving it a rounded appearance. Finally, a delay of 2/1000 of a second occurs.

HINT

The `Pen` Class's `DrawTo()` method draws a line on the screen using the following syntax.

```
DrawTo(X, Y)
```

The line that is drawn is drawn from the `Pen` object's previous location (0,0 by default), to *X*, *Y*, which specify the line's endpoint.

The `Circle` class's `Draw()` method draws a circle on the screen using the following syntax.

```
Circle()
```

### Step 14: Developing the RefreshScreenOutput() Method

The `RefreshScreenOutput()` method, shown next, is responsible for redrawing the contents of the console window. It accomplishes this by executing the `Shell` class's `RefreshScreen()` method, which refreshes all graphics drawn on the console window.

```
//This method updates the display of the player's drawing
Method RefreshScreenOutput()


    //Redraw the screen in order to show the player's artwork
```

```
    RefreshScreen()

End Method
```

NOTE

The `RefreshScreen()` method does not take any argument nor does it return anything. This method has the following syntax.

```
RefreshScreen()
```

### Step 15: Saving and Compiling Your Application

All right, your copy of the Doodle game should be ready to go. If you haven't done so recently, save your new application by clicking on the Save All command located on the File menu. While you are at it, check the Errors window to see if your copy of the Doodle application has any syntax errors, and if any are reported, go back to the appropriate step and see where you may have made a typo or skipped a statement.

## The Final Result

At this point, your copy of the Doodle game should be error free and should run exactly as described at the beginning of this chapter. Assuming that this is the case, spend a little time putting the Doodle game through its paces. Make sure that each of the game's seven color settings work and that you can switch between the three supported line sizes. Also, do not forget to test the ability to clear the drawing area and to display the game's instructions.

HINT

If you are pressed for time and cannot create your own copy of the Doodle game from scratch, you can download a copy of the game's source code from the book's companion CD.

# Summary

In this chapter you learned the basic concepts behind object-oriented programming. You learned how to define your own custom classes, complete with variables, properties, methods, and functions. You learned how to restrict access to class properties, methods, and functions. You also learned how to create new objects based on your custom classes and then to manipulate those objects by interacting with their properties, methods, and functions. On top of all this, you also learned how to work with the methods and properties belonging to a number of additional Phrogram classes and in doing so learned how to create the Doodle game.

Before you move on to Chapter 8, "Working with Graphics and Animation," consider spending a little time improving the Doodle game by addressing the following list of challenges.

## Challenges

1. As currently written, the Doodle game supports only a small subset of the 140 colors made available by Phrogram's Colors Library. Consider modifying the game to provide the player with access to a greater range of colors.
2. As currently written, the Doodle game only supports three different sized lines. Consider providing the player with additional choices. For example, you might modify the game to use the F9 key to clear the screen, thus freeing up the F4 through F8 keys for additional line size specifications.
3. Create a distribution package for your new game and share with a few friends, asking them to provide you with feedback.

CHAPTER 8

# WORKING WITH GRAPHICS AND ANIMATION

The real power and fun of working with Phrogram comes from the programming language's support for graphics, animation, and video game development. This chapter will teach you the basics of how to programmatically draw and work with graphics. You will learn how to display graphic images and to move them around the console window as sprites. You will also learn how to make them appear and disappear and to programmatically detect when they collide with one another. Using this information, which is fundamental to the development of arcade-style computer games, you will learn how to create your next computer application, the PCPong game.

Specifically, you will learn how to:

- Work with different Phrogram methods and properties required to draw graphics
- Display and control the movement of graphic images using sprites
- Control sprite visibility
- Determine when sprites collide with one another

## Project Preview: The PCPong Game

This chapter's game project is the PCPong game. It is based upon the original Atari Pong game that made its debut back in the 1970s. In this game, two players compete in a ping-pong style game, using electronic paddles to hit an electronic ball that bounces back and forth across the screen. Due to the size and complexity of this game, its development will be completed in two parts, with the first part being completed in this chapter and the second part in Chapter 9.

The game begins by displaying a popup dialog window, welcoming the players to the game, as shown in Figure 8.1.

**Figure 8.1**

The PCPong game's welcome message.

As soon as one of the players clicks on the popup dialog window's OK button, a second popup dialog window displays. This window shows the starting score for both players, as demonstrated in Figure 8.2.

**Figure 8.2**

Both players begin the game with no points.

To win the game a player must accumulate 21 points. To play, both players must use their paddles, which are controlled via the keyboard, to hit a blue ball that bounces around the screen. A point is scored whenever a player misses the ball. As Figure 8.3 demonstrates, game play always begins with the ball displayed in the middle of the screen.

Player 1 uses the Shift key to move the paddle up and the Control key to move it down. Similarly, Player 2 uses the Up and Down keys to perform these same tasks. During game play, the ball bounces all over the screen, as demonstrated in Figure 8.4, bouncing off the player's paddles and the top and bottom of the screen.

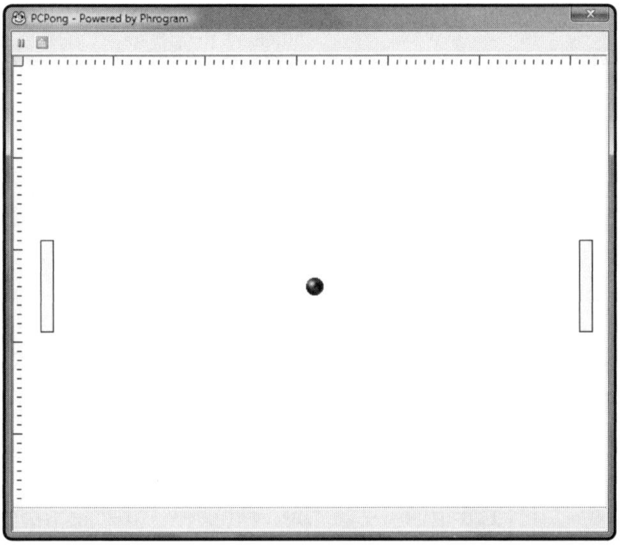


**FIGURE 8.3**

Each new point begins with the player's paddles and the ball centered on the screen.

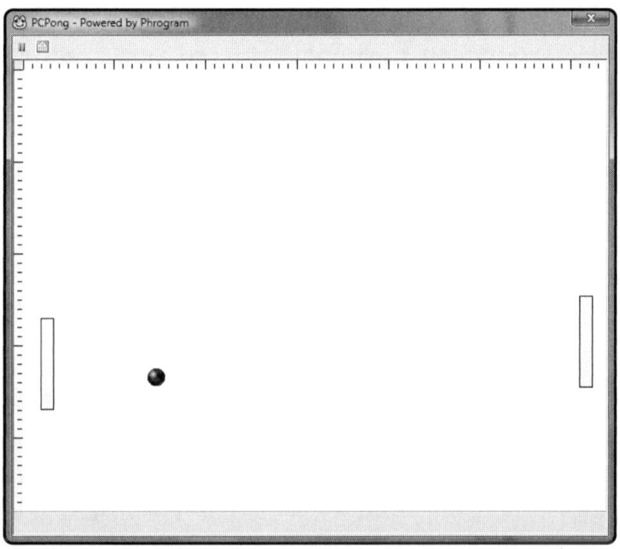


**FIGURE 8.4**

The speed at which the ball moves during a point constantly increases to make things more challenging.

Game play ends when one of the player scores 21 points, at which time the console window is cleared and the popup dialog window shown in Figure 8.5 displays.

**FIGURE 8.5**

Player 1 has won the game 21 to 14.

## AN INTRODUCTION TO DRAWING AND WORKING WITH GRAPHICS

Until recently, the development of computer games and animation was restricted to the realm of professional programming and required advanced programming knowledge and experience working with programming languages like C and C++. In addition, a technical understanding of DirectX was also required. However, new programming languages like Phrogram are changing the playing field by providing a whole new generation of programmers with a simplified programming environment capable of supporting sophisticated graphics and game development that does not require years of technical experience just to master the basics. Instead, Phrogram manages all of the complex interaction with DirectX for you, allowing you to keep your focus on the programming logic required to make your Phrogram games and applications work.

Phrogram was designed from the ground up to support the creation and development of graphics and computer games. It provides the ability to programmatically draw and provides you with access to a host of methods, functions, and properties that help make drawing simple and fast. In addition, Phrogram makes it equally easy for you to incorporate the use of graphics files, such as .jpg, .gif, .png, etc., into your applications and games, allowing you to create sharp, graphically stylish games and computer animation.

## DRAWING TEXT

When you think of drawing on the computer you probably think of lines and various shapes and colors that you need to use to render whatever type of image you plan on drawing. However, you probably do not think of writing text as being part of drawing, such as when you signed your name to the bottom of a picture or painting you just created. From Phrogram's perspective, text is also drawn on the console window, which acts as a virtual canvas.

**TRAP**

Some Phrogram methods, such as the `ConsoleWrite()` and `ConsoleWriteLine()` methods and the `ConsoleReadKey()` and `ConsoleReadLine()` methods are specifically designed to display text and retrieve text using the console window. These methods, and the other methods and functions provided by the `Console` library, are designed specifically to support these tasks, which are not compatible with any of the drawing operations supported by Phrogram. Therefore, you cannot use `Console` library methods in conjunction with the `Drawing` library or any of its subclasses. Instead, if you need to display text on the console screen when drawing, you need to use one of the methods belonging to the Drawing library. These methods are listed here:

- `Print()`. Displays text at the current Pen location followed by a blank space.
- `PrintInRectangle()`. Displays text within a rectangular area, wrapping text as necessary to fit within the specified set of coordinates forming the rectangle.
- `PrintLine()`. Displays text at the current Pen location and then wraps it when necessary to begin a new line.

In order to incorporate text into any drawing, you need to use the Drawing library's Print(), PrintInRectangle(), and PrintLine() methods, as demonstrated in the following example.

```
//Print a blank line
PrintLine("")

//Print a text string
Print("Once upon a time, ")

//Turn the pen off
Pen(False)

//Move the pen to a new location
MoveTo(120, 100)

//Print some more text
Print("there was a little boy")

//Turn the pen off
Pen(False)

//Move the pen to a new location
MoveTo(250, 200)

//Print some more text inside a rectangle
PrintInRectangle("whose name was Alexander.", 250, 200, 120, 100)
```

You have already worked with the `Print()` and `PrintLine()` methods on a number of occasions. However, unlike this example, you have not worked with the `PrintInRectangle()` method. This method displays a text string inside an invisible rectangle using the following syntax.

```
PrintInRectangle(Text, X, Y, Width, Height)
```

*`Text`* represents the text that is to be displayed and *`X`* and *`Y`* represents the coordinates of the upper-left corner of the rectangle. *`Width`* specifies the length of the rectangle and *`Height`* specifies how tall the rectangle is. Text is automatically wrapped within the specified dimension of the rectangle. The rectangle itself is not displayed. If the amount of text to be displayed exceeds the amount of space available in the rectangle, some of the text will be cut short.

When executed, the preceding example draws the output shown in Figure 8.6.

**FIGURE 8.6**

Drawing text in the console window.

> **HINT**
>
> The preceding example also used the `Drawing` library's `Pen()` and `MoveTo()` methods. By passing the `Pen()` method a Boolean value of `True`, you enable drawing. By passing the method a value of `False`, you disable the pen's ability to draw. The `MoveTo()` method moves the pen to a new location, using the following syntax.
>
> `MoveTo(X, Y)`

## WORKING WITH THE PEN CLASS

One method of displaying graphics on the screen is to programmatically draw them. To do so you can use Phrogram's `Pen` class. Depending on what you want to do, there are many different ways of working with the methods, functions, and properties defined by the Pen class. One basic way of drawing it is to use the Pen class as the basis for defining a Pen object within your application and then calling upon the different Pen class methods, functions, and properties as necessary to draw. The first step in this approach is to declare a Pen object as demonstrated here.

```
Define DemoPen As Pen
```

Here, an object named DemoPen has been declared as a Pen object. Once instantiated, you can begin drawing with the DemoPen object, as demonstrated here:

```
Define DemoPen As Pen

DemoPen.LineWidth = 4
DemoPen.Color = Green
DemoPen.MoveTo(100, 240)
DemoPen.DrawTo(550, 240)
```

Here, a Pen object name DemoPen is instantiated. Next, the Pen object's Color property is set to Green.

> **HINT**
>
> To work with the Pen object's color property you must use the syntax outline shown here:
>
> *ObjectName*.Color = *Value*
>
> Here, *ObjectName* is the name of the Pen object that you have instantiated and *Value* is one of the 140 color constants supported by Phrogram.

Next, the Pen object's MoveTo() method, which is used to move the Pen object around the console window, is used to move the virtual pen to a specified set of coordinates.

> **HINT**
>
> The Pen object's MoveTo() method provides the ability to programmatically reposition the pen to any location on the console window using the following syntax.
>
> *ObjectName*.MoveTo(*X*, *Y*)
>
> Here, *ObjectName* is the name of the Pen object that you have instantiated and *X* and *Y* represent the coordinate to which the Pen is moved.

The last statement in the example used the Pen object's DrawTo() method to draw a line on the console screen. The line is drawn from the Pen object's current location to a location specified by coordinates passed as arguments to the DrawTo() method.

HINT

The Pen object's DrawTo() method draws a line from the current Pen location to the specified set of coordinates using the following syntax.

```
DrawTo(X, Y)
```

Here, *X* and *Y* represent the coordinates to which the line is drawn.

## WORKING WITH DIFFERENT DRAWING CLASSES

In Phrogram, the graphics can be drawn using a combination of dots, lines, and other types of shapes on the console window. As was explained in Chapter 7, "Getting Comfortable with Object-Oriented Programming," graphics are laid out using the Phrogram coordinate system where the origin starts in the left-hand corner at location (0,0).

By default, graphics are drawn on the console window's white background. Using methods and functions provided by different classes stored within the Drawing library, you can perform a host of different drawing operations.

### Drawing a Point

The smallest addressable area to which you can draw on the console window is a pixel. Using the Point class's DrawPoint() method, you can draw a colored dot at any pixel position on the console window. To work with the Point class, you must first define a variable and use it to instantiate Point objects, as demonstrated here:

```
Define PointObject As Point
```

Once instantiated, you can draw a point (pixel) anywhere on the console window using the methods and properties belonging to the Point class, as demonstrated here:

```
Define PointObject As Point

PointObject.X = 320
PointObject.Y = 240

PointObject.Color = Black

PointObject.Draw()
```

Here, a variable named PointObject has been instantiated. Its coordinates are set to (320, 240) using the Point class's X and Y properties. Its color is set to Black using the Point class's Color property. Lastly, the dot is drawn using the Point class's Draw() method.

## Drawing a Line

By stringing a series of points together, you can draw pretty much anything you want. However, drawing detailed shapes and images a point at a time involves a considerable amount of work. To help simplify things, Phrogram's `Line class` provides access to a number of methods, functions, and properties that you can use to draw lines.

Like `Point` objects, you must first instantiate a `Line` object before you can access different `Line` methods, functions, and properties. The following example demonstrates how to draw a series of purple lines, each of which is of a different thickness.

Program MyNewProgram

```
    Define LineObject As Line

    Method Main()

        Linemaker(4, 100, 150, 300, 150)
        Linemaker(8, 100, 200, 400, 200)
        Linemaker(12, 100, 250, 500, 250)
        Linemaker(16, 100, 300, 600, 300)

    End Method

    Method LineMaker(Width As Integer,
      StartX As Integer, StartY As Integer, EndX As Integer, EndY As Integer)

        LineObject.Color = Purple
        LineObject.LineWidth = Width

        LineObject.StartPoint.X = StartX
        LineObject.StartPoint.Y = StartY
        LineObject.EndPoint.X = EndX
        LineObject.EndPoint.Y = EndY

        LineObject.Draw()

    End Method

End Program
```

Here, a series of four lines are drawn by calling on a custom method named `LineMaker()`. In order to draw a line, this method is passed five pieces of data, all of which are integer values. The first value passed specifies the width of the line to be drawn. The next two values specify the line's starting coordinate and the last two values specify the line's ending coordinate.

As you can see, before being drawn using the `Draw()` method, the statements in the `LineMaker()` method set the Line class's `Color` and `LineWidth` properties. In addition, the X and Y coordinate of the `StartPoint` and `EndPoint` properties are set.

As you can see, the `LineMaker()` method is called upon four times to draw four different lines. When executed, this example displays the outline shown in Figure 8.7.

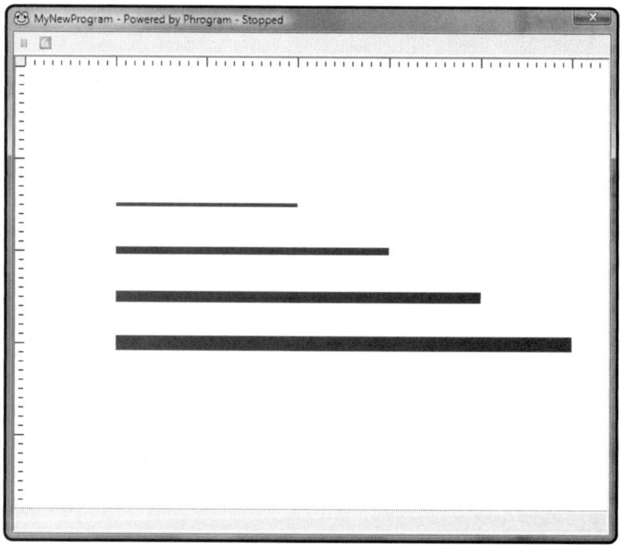


**FIGURE 8.7**

Drawing a series of lines using methods and properties belonging to the `Line` class.

## Drawing a Rectangle

Another geometric shape that you can easily draw is a rectangle. One way of doing so is to use methods, functions, and properties belonging to the `Rectangle` class. `Rectangle` objects, like `Line` objects, must first be instantiated before you can access different `Rectangle` class methods, functions, and properties. The following example demonstrates how to draw a pair of rectangles. The first rectangle is drawn as an outline and then a second filled in rectangle is drawn inside the first rectangle.

```
Define RectangleObject As Rectangle

RectangleObject.LineWidth = 4
RectangleObject.Color = Red

RectangleObject.X = 175
RectangleObject.y = 150

RectangleObject.Width = 300
RectangleObject.Height = 200

RectangleObject.Draw()

RectangleObject.X = 200
RectangleObject.y = 175

RectangleObject.Width = 250
RectangleObject.Height = 150

RectangleObject.Filled = True

RectangleObject.Draw()
```

Here, a `Rectangle` object named `RectangleObject` has been instantiated. Its `LineWidth` and `Color` properties are then set and the object's coordinates are specified. The `Width` and `Height` properties are set and the outline of a rectangle is then drawn. Next, a second rectangle is drawn. This time, in addition to specifying the rectangle's coordinates and width and height, the `Rectangle` class's `Filled` property is set equal to `True`, resulting in the drawing of a filled in rectangle.

Figure 8.8 shows how the pair of rectangles look when drawn on the console window.

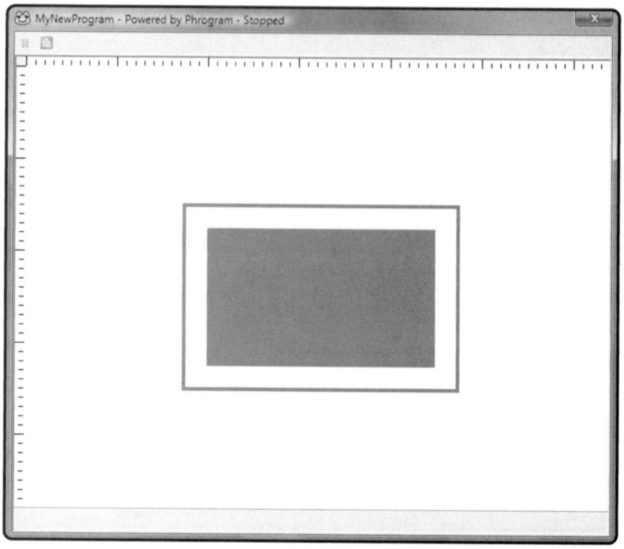


**FIGURE 8.8**

Using methods and properties belonging to the `Rectangle` class to draw a pair of rectangles.

## Drawing a Circle

Phrogram also makes drawing circles a snap through the use of methods, functions, and properties belonging to the `Circle` class, which draws a circle based upon a specified center coordinate, using the circle's Radius property value. The following example demonstrates how to work with the `Circle` class. Here, two circles are drawn side by side. The first circle is drawn as an outline and then a second circle is filled in.

```
Define CircleObject As Circle

CircleObject.LineWidth = 4
CircleObject.Color = Blue

CircleObject.Center.X = 200
CircleObject.Center.Y = 230
CircleObject.Radius = 100

CircleObject.Draw()

CircleObject.Center.X = 450
CircleObject.Center.Y = 230
CircleObject.Radius = 100
```

```
CircleObject.Filled = True

CircleObject.Draw()
```

As you can see, a variable named `CircleObject` is used to set up an instance of the `Circle` class. The first of two circles is prepared for drawing by setting the object's `LineWidth` and `Color` properties as well as the coordinates of its `Center` property, followed by its `Radius` property (specifying the distance from the center of the circle to its outside edge). The circle is then drawn using the object's `Draw()` method. Next, a second circle is drawn, only this time the `Circle` class's `Filled` property is set equal to `True` before the second circle is drawn. As a result, the second circle is drawn as a solid blue circle. Figure 8.9 shows how the pair of circles look when drawn on the console window.

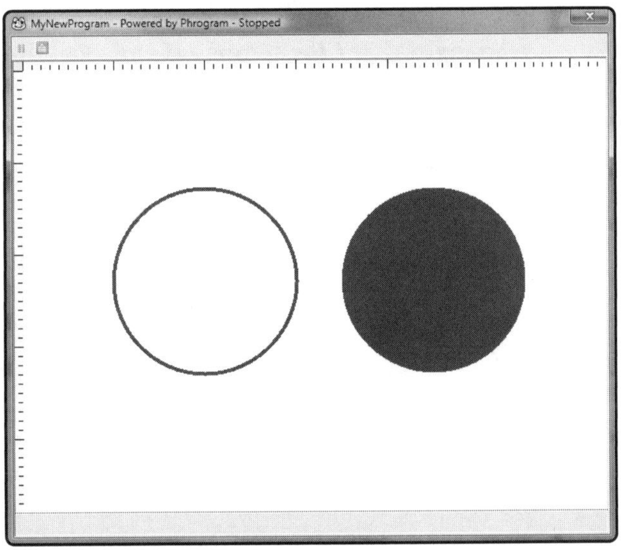


**FIGURE 8.9**

Using methods and properties of the `Circle` class method to draw a pair of circles on the console window.

## Other Shapes

In addition to points, lines, rectangles, and circles, Phrogram also supplies classes for drawing polygons. A *polygon* is a multi-sided figure. A triangle is an example of a three-sided polygon. You can create a polygon using methods and properties provided by the `Polygon` class. In addition to providing you with methods that you can use to draw various shapes, you can mix and match the usage of all of Phrogram's different drawing classes to create an unlimited number of shapes and drawings. If you can imagine it, you can draw it!

HINT

In addition to all of the different object-oriented drawing classes covered in this chapter, Phrogram also provides access to a collection of procedural methods and functions located in the `Drawing` library, which can be used to draw various shapes. However, whenever possible, use of the OOP methods and functions provided through the various drawing classes is strongly recommended.

## EXERCISES

**Phrogram's `Drawing` library provides a collection of classes that provide access to methods, functions, and properties that you can use to draw all kinds of shapes including points, lines, rectangles, and circles. To help further your understanding of how to work with these classes perform the following exercises.**

1. **Using the `Polygon` class, draw a triangle that fills in most of the available area in the console screen.**
2. **Using the `Rectangle()` class, draw the outline of a square around the triangle.**
3. **Using the `Line()` class draw a horizontal line on the console window, placing the end of the line at the tip of the triangle.**

# WORKING WITH GRAPHIC FILES

Most new games being developed today are 3D and Phrogram provides strong support for 3D programming. However, an understanding of two-dimensional programming is fundamental to any programmer's education. In two-dimensional computer games the player moves things like cars, planes, space ships, and people around the screen when interacting with the game. Each of these types of characters, as well as the objects that they interact with within the game is managed as sprites.

A *sprite* is a 2D bitmap drawn as an image on a transparent background, which can be moved around the console window. As sprites move, any underlying background color or images are automatically redrawn. Only the pixels that make up the sprite's graphic image are displayed. This allows the background behind the sprite to remain visible.

FIND IT ONLINE

Phrogram provides access to over 180 graphics files located in the My Phrogram File\Media Files\Image folder. The files are readily visible using the Picture browser window and provide a greater collection of starter graphics. Of course, you can always use your favorite graphics application to create your own graphics and then add them to My Phrogram File\Media Files\Image folder. You can also download graphic files from the download area at the www.phogram.com website, which includes free collections of 2D and 3D graphic files.

## Displaying Graphic Files

In addition to providing everything you need to draw graphic images from scratch, Phrogram provides the ability to display graphic files. To do so, you need to define a new type of object called a sprite. Sprites provide access to a host of methods, functions, and properties that you can use to manipulate and work with graphic files. As the following example demonstrates, you can define and then use a sprite to display any graphic file.

```
Define FlowerPic As Sprite

FlowerPic.Load("Flowers.jpg")
SetScreenSize(FlowerPic.Width, FlowerPic.Height)
FlowerPic.Show()
```

Here, a new sprite is defined and assigned a variable name of `FlowerPic`. Sprites are created from images files. Therefore, the first step involved in displaying the graphic image is to tell Phrogram the name of the graphic file to associate with the `Sprite` object. This is accomplished using the `Sprite` class's `Load()` method. Next, the `Shell` library's `SetScreenSize()` method is used to set the size of the console window equal to the width and height of the sprite's graphic file using the `Sprite` class's `Width` and `Height` properties.

HINT Phrogram can work with many different types of graphic files including JPG, BMP, GIF, and PNG files.

With the sprite now defined and assigned a graphic file and the console window's size set equal to the size of the image to be displayed, all that remains is to execute the `Sprite` class's `Show()` method to display the graphic file.

When executed, this example produces the output shown in Figure 8.10.

**FIGURE 8.10**

Using sprites to display a graphic file on the console window.

HINT

The `Sprite` class's `Load()` method has the following syntax.

*SpriteName*.Load(*FileName*)

*SpriteName* represents the name of the sprite. *FileName* identifies the graphic file to be assigned to the sprite. Once defined, a sprite can be moved around the console screen without requiring that any portion of the screen over which it moves be redrawn. Sprites provide the basis for many computer games. In the case of this chapter's game project, the PCPong game, sprites will be used to control the movement of the game's ball and paddles.

The `Sprite` class's `Show()` method has the following syntax.

*SpriteName*.Show()

*SpriteName* represents the name of the sprite to be displayed and made visible on the console window.

## Learning How to Move Sprites

Now that you know how to define, load, and display sprites, the next step in learning how to use them to create computer games is to learn how to move them around the console window, as demonstrated in the following example.

```
Define Counter As Integer
Define Ball As Sprite

Ball = LoadSprite("BigPurpleBall.png")
```

```
Ball.MoveTo(100, 0)
Ball.Show()

While True

    For Counter = 1 To 460 Step 4
        Ball.MoveTo(100, Counter)
        Delay(10)
    Next

    For Counter = 460 To 1 Step -4
        Ball.MoveTo(100, Counter)
        Delay(10)
    Next

End While
```

Here, a sprite named `ball` is defined. Then a graphic image of a purple ball stored in a file named `BigPurpleBall.png` is loaded. Note that this `Sprites` library's `LoadSprite()` function is used to load the sprite this time.

> **HINT**
>
> The `LoadSprite()` function tells Phrogram which image file to load as the sprite and uses the following syntax.
>
> `LoadSprite(`*`FileName`*`)`
>
> *`Filename`* is the name of the graphic file to be loaded.

Once loaded, the sprite is displayed at coordinates (100, 0) on the console screen. The rest of the example is controlled by a `While...End While` loop that has been set up to run forever. Within the loop are two `For...Next` loops. The first of these two loops iterates from 1 to 40, stepping by 4 at the end of each iteration. Each time the loop runs it uses the `MoveTo()` method to move the location of the sprite on the screen down by four pixels. Because loops process so quickly, a delay of 10/1000 of a second has been added to slow things down a bit. The end result is that as this loop executes, the sprite image of the purple ball is shown moving down from the top to the bottom of the console window.

The second `For...Next` loop reverses the direction of the ball, moving back upwards towards the top of the console window –4 pixels at a time, pausing every 10/1000 of a second until the top of the window is reached. As soon as the loop's last iteration is processed, the `While...End While` loop runs again.

When executed, this example displays a bouncing purple ball on the console window, as demonstrated in Figures 8.11 and 8.12.

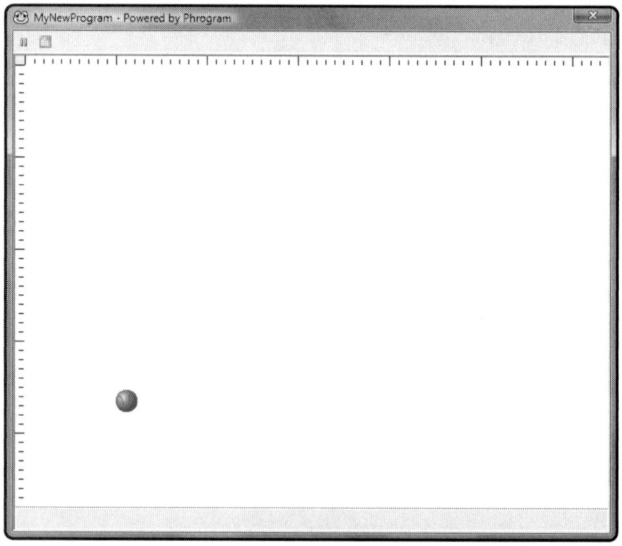


**FIGURE 8.11**

An example of the purple ball on its way down the screen.

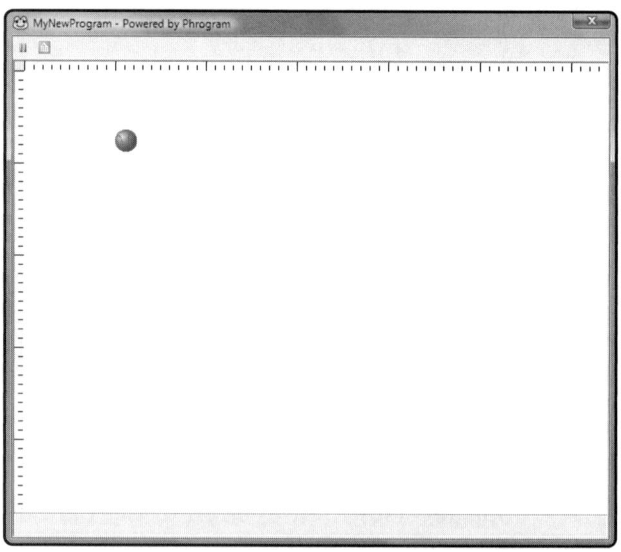


**FIGURE 8.12**

An example of the purple ball bounding back towards the top of the screen.

## Moving Sprites Around the Console Window

Instead of simply moving a sprite up and down or left and right, many games need to be able to move sprites in all directions. An example of how this might be done is provided next. When executed, this example moves the ball around the console window, bouncing it off each side of the console whenever contact is made.

```
Define RedGameBall As Sprite

Define RedSpeedX As Integer = 4
Define RedSpeedY As Integer = 4

Define RedBallX As Integer = ScreenWidth() / 2
Define RedBallY As Integer = ScreenHeight() / 2

RedGameBall.Load("BigRedBall.png")

RedGameBall.MoveTo(RedBallX, RedBallY)

RedGameBall.Show()

    While True

        RedBallX += RedSpeedX
        RedBallY += RedSpeedY

        RedGameBall.MoveTo(RedBallX, RedBallY)

        If RedBallX > ScreenWidth() -30 Then
            RedSpeedX *= -1
        End If

        If RedBallX < 0 Then
            RedSpeedX *= -1
        End If

        If RedBallY > ScreenHeight() -30 Then
            RedSpeedY *= -1
        End If
```

```
        If RedBallY < 0 Then
            RedSpeedY *= -1
        End If

        Delay(20)

    End While
```

Here, a sprite named RedGameBall has been defined and then a pair of variables, named RedSpeedX and RedSpeedY are defined and assigned a value of 4. The values assigned to these variables will be used later in the example to move a red ball by four pixels upon each iteration of a loop. The next two statements set the starting coordinates of the game's ball.

The next three statements load a graphic image representing a red ball, move it to the center of the console window, and display it. The rest of the statements in the example are controlled by a While…End While loop. Each time the loop iterates, the location of the game's ball is moved by four pixels along both the X-axis and Y-axis.

Next, four If…Then code blocks are executed. The first code block checks to see if the sprite's X coordinate has exceeded the width of the screen (less 30 pixels). This keeps the red ball from disappearing off of the edge of the console window. If this is the case, the value of RedSpeedX is multiplied by −1, effectively reversing the direction the ball is traveling on the X-axis.

The second code block checks to see if the sprite's X coordinate is less than 0, in which case the ball has reached the left-hand edge of the console window. If this is the case, the ball's direction is reversed. The next two code blocks reverse the direction that the ball is traveling on the Y-axis whenever the ball makes contact with the bottom of the top of the console window. Because of the pace at which the loop executes, the Delay() method is then used to slow things down a bit by pausing the loop's execution by 20/1000 of a second.

## Creating Animation Sequences

In addition to working with different types of image files like JPG and GIF files, Phrogram also supports the use of animated GIF files. An animated GIF file is a GIF file that is made up of two or more frames, each of which can be displayed in sequences when the GIF file is made visible. You can create animated GIF files using a number of popular graphics applications. Phrogram includes a number of animated GIF files in the Images folder. One such GIF is named Animated.gif. You can use the Picture Browser window to preview Animated.gif, as demonstrated in Figure 8.13.

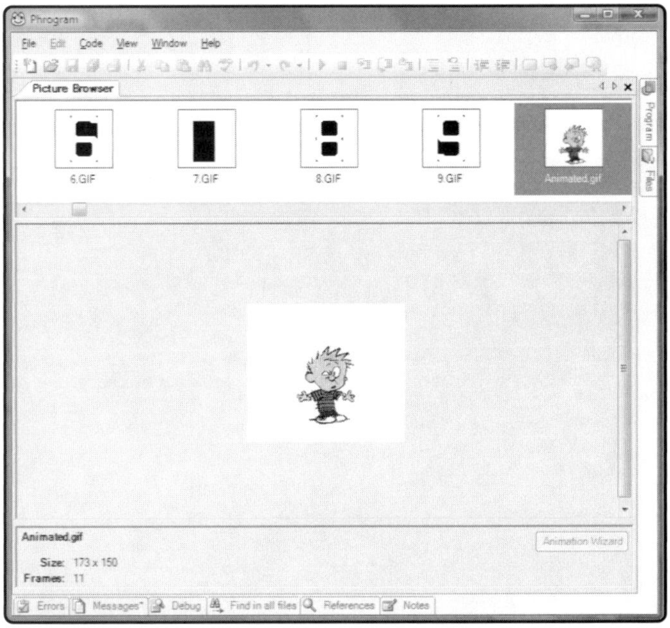


**FIGURE 8.13**

Previewing an animated GIF file using Phrogram's Picture Browser window.

The Animated.gif file consists of 11 separate images or frames, each of which shows a different image of a little boy. Once opened in the Picture Browser window, each of the 11 frames is placed in sequence. In addition, if you look at the bottom of the Picture Browser window, you will see the name of the file, its size (in pixels), and a count of the number of frames it is comprised of.

Using an array and a loop, you can easily use animated GIF files as the basis for creating all sorts of animation. As the following example demonstrates, animated GIF files can be used as the basis for creating small cartoons, video comics, graphic presentations, and for generating sophisticated game graphics.

```
Define Explosion As Sprite
Define ComicSequence As Integer [11]

Explosion.Load("Animated.gif")

Explosion.MoveTo(ScreenWidth() / 2 - Explosion.Width / 2, ScreenHeight() / 2 -
Explosion.Height / 2)

Explosion.Show()
```

```
ComicSequence[1] = 250
ComicSequence[2] = 250
ComicSequence[3] = 250
ComicSequence[4] = 500
ComicSequence[5] = 500
ComicSequence[6] = 500
ComicSequence[7] = 2000
ComicSequence[8] = 250
ComicSequence[9] = 250
ComicSequence[10] = 250
ComicSequence[11] = 250

Explosion.AnimationTimeline = ComicSequence

While TickCount() < 5500
    RefreshScreen()
End While
```

Here, a sprite is defined and assigned to a variable named `Explosion`. Next, an array named `ComicSequence` is defined and assigned a size of 11 elements. The Animated.gif file is the loaded into the sprite, positioned in the middle of the screen, and displayed.

**HINT** Note that in order to center the display of the GIF file, the values returned by the `ScreenWidth()` and `ScreenHeight()` functions are then divided by two, giving you the center coordinates for the console window. If you were to use these coordinates when displaying the GIF file, the GIF file would be displayed such that its upper-left corner was in the middle of the console window. To center the file in the console window, you need to determine the file's width and height and then divide them by two and subtract the resulting values from the window's width and height coordinates. This has been accomplished in this example using the `Sprite` class's `Width` and `Height` properties, which are used to retrieve the size of the GIF file and are then divided by two and finally subtracted from the console window's center width and height coordinates.

If you were to stop and run this example at this point, only the first of the 11 frames that make up the GIF file would be displayed. In order to display all 11 of the frames that make up the GIF file, this example uses the `ComicSequence` array (which consists of one item for each frame in the GIF file) and assigns a value to each array item specifying how long its associated frame should be displayed.

Next, Phrogram needs to be told to associate each array entry with a frame in the GIF file. This is accomplished by specifying the `Sprite` class's `AnimationTimeline` property and setting it equal to the `ComicSequence` array. With this linkage now established, all that needs to be done to display the entire series of frames is to set up a loop. As you can see, in this example a `While...End While` loop has been set up to run for as long as `TickCount()` is less than 5500.

`TickCount()` is a property belonging to the `Timers` library. It returns a value representing the length of time that a program has run. The value of 5500 represents the accumulated values of all of the times stored in the `ComicSequence` array plan and an additional 250/1000 of a second. This value ensures that the loop will run just long enough to display every frame of the GIF file.

Take note that every time the `While...End While` loop runs, it executes the `Shell` library's `RefreshScreen()` method. This method takes no argument and when executed instructs Phrogram to refresh the display of any sprites and graphics displayed on the console window.

Figures 8.14 through 8.17 show examples of 4 of the 11 frames displayed as the animation sequences play out on the console screen.

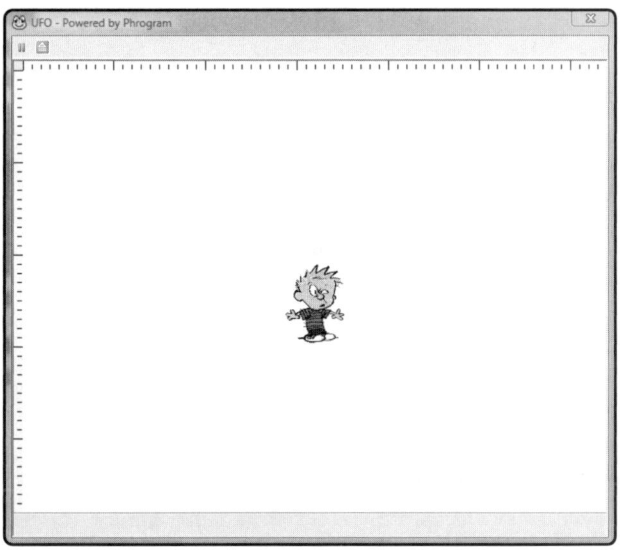


FIGURE 8.14

A confused little boy is shown in the middle of the console window.

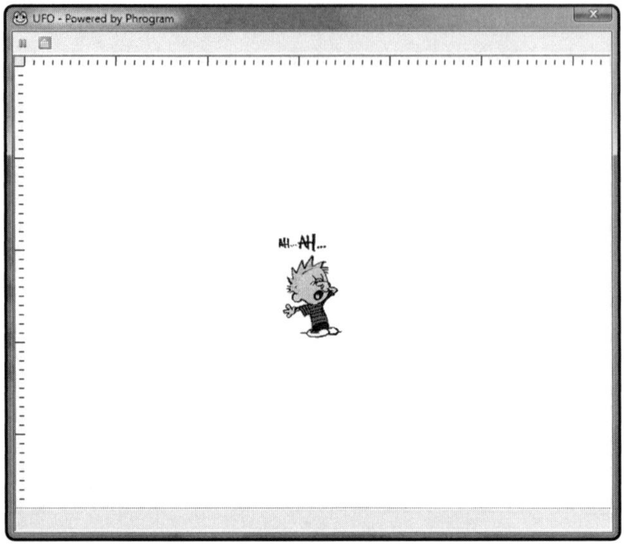


**FIGURE 8.15**

The little boy looks like he may be about to sneeze.

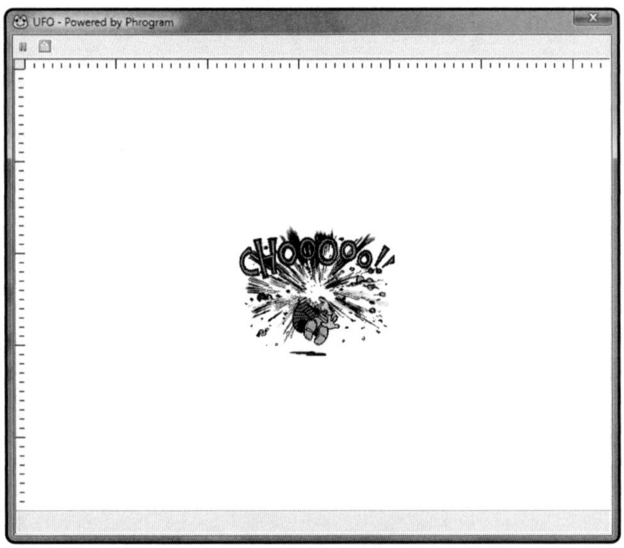


**FIGURE 8.16**

The little boy's sneeze creates an explosion.

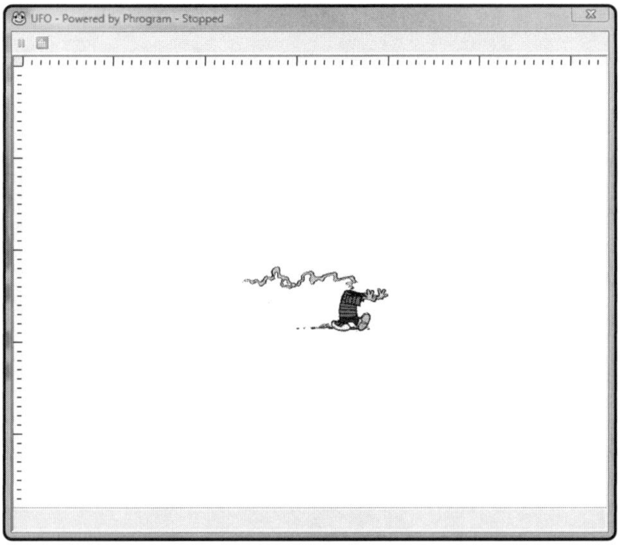


**FIGURE 8.17**

The little boy's head has been blown off his body.

## DETECTING SPRITE COLLISIONS

One key requirement of most computer games that use sprites is to be able to detect when two sprites collide with one another such as would be the case in a game where, for example, the player was required to navigate a space ship through a field of flying asteroids. In order to determine when collisions occur, you can use the `Sprite` class's `Intersects` function, which has the following syntax.

```
FirstSprite.Intersects(SecondSprite)
```

Here, *FirstSprite* represents the name of a sprite for which you want to see if a collision has occurred with *SecondSprite*. If a collision has occurred a Boolean value of `True` is returned.

As an example of how to work with the `Intersects()` function, look at the following example.

```
Program BouncingRedBallDemo

    Define Collision As Boolean = False

    Define RedGameBall As Sprite
    Define YellowGameBall As Sprite

    Define RedSpeedX As Integer = 4
    Define RedSpeedY As Integer = 3
```

```
Define YellowSpeedX As Integer = 5
Define YellowSpeedY As Integer = 2

Define RedBallX As Integer = ScreenWidth() / 2
Define RedBallY As Integer = ScreenHeight() / 2

Define YellowBallX As Integer
Define YellowBallY As Integer

Method Main()

    RedGameBall.Load("BigRedBall.png")
    YellowGameBall.Load("BigYellowBall.png")

    RedGameBall.MoveTo(RedBallX, RedBallY)
    YellowGameBall.MoveTo(YellowBallX, YellowBallY)

    RedGameBall.Show()
    YellowGameBall.Show()

    While Collision = False

        RedBallX += RedSpeedX
        RedBallY += RedSpeedY
        YellowBallX += YellowSpeedX
        YellowBallY += YellowSpeedY

        RedGameBall.MoveTo(RedBallX, RedBallY)
        YellowGameBall.MoveTo(YellowBallX, YellowBallY)

        HandleCollisions()
        BounceTheRedBall()
        BounceTheYellowBall()

        Delay(20)

    End While
```

```
End Method

Method HandleCollisions()

    If RedGameBall.Intersects(YellowGameBall) Then
        Alert("C R A S H !", "Collision Demo")
        Collision = True
    End If

End Method

Method BounceTheRedBall()

    If RedBallX > ScreenWidth() -30 Then
        RedSpeedX *= -1
    End If
    If RedBallX < 0 Then
        RedSpeedX *= -1
    End If
    If RedBallY > ScreenHeight() -30 Then
        RedSpeedY *= -1
    End If
    If RedBallY < 0 Then
        RedSpeedY *= -1
    End If

End Method

Method BounceTheYellowBall()

    If YellowBallX > ScreenWidth() -30 Then
        YellowSpeedX *= -1
    End If
    If YellowBallX < 0 Then
        YellowSpeedX *= -1
    End If
    If YellowBallY > ScreenHeight() -30 Then
        YellowSpeedY *= -1
```

```
        End If
        If YellowBallY < 0 Then
            YellowSpeedY *= -1
        End If

    End Method

End Program
```

Here, two sprites are defined representing a red and a yellow ball. The sprites are initially placed at different locations on the console window and are then bounced around the screen under the control of a `While...End While` loop. Each time the loop runs it updates the location of the two balls and then calls on three methods. The `HandleCollisions()` method, which is highlighted in the above example, uses the `Intersects()` method to determine whether the `RedGameBall` sprite has collided with the `YellowGameBall` sprite. The `BounceTheRedBall()` and `BounceTheYellowBall()` methods are responsible for moving the red and yellow ball around the console window.

Figure 8.18 shows an example of how the two balls look as they bounce around the console window.

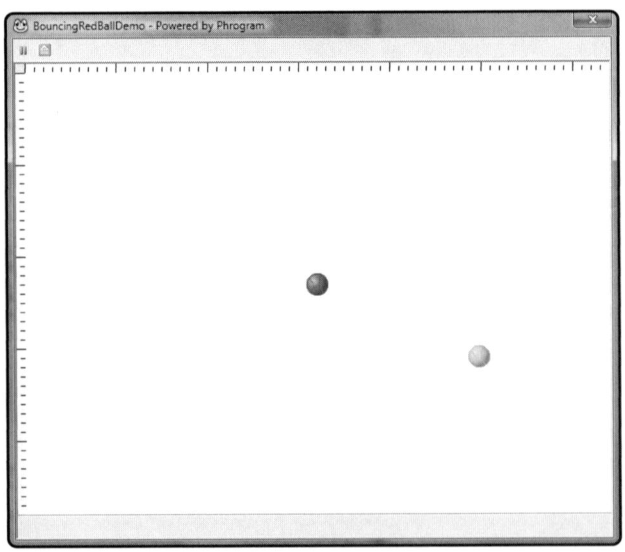


**FIGURE 8.18**

Two balls bouncing around the console window.

Figure 8.19 shows the popup dialog window that displays when the two balls collide.

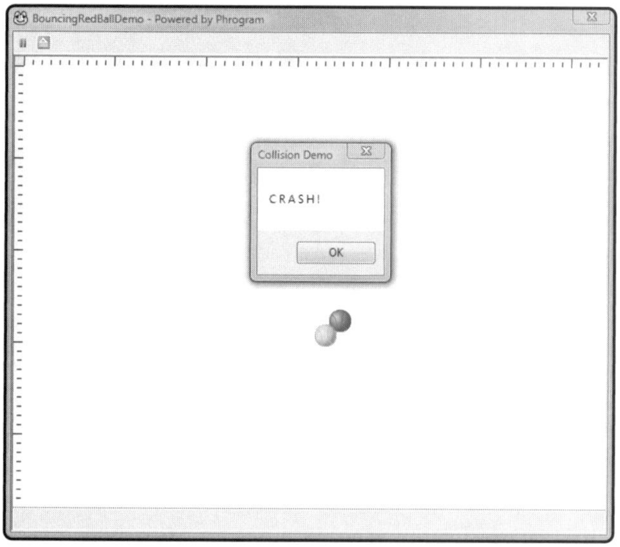


**FIGURE 8.19**

A collision occurs when the two balls run into one another.

## REVIEW QUESTIONS

1. **List three methods that you could use to draw text on the console window. What class do these methods belong to?**
2. **Name two classes that provide methods and functions that support drawing operations.**
3. **Define the term sprite.**
4. **What advantages do sprites provide?**
5. **List three types of graphic files supported by Phrogram.**
6. **What is a collision? What method can be used to detect sprite collisions? What class does this method belong to?**
7. **List two methods that can be used to assign a graphic file to a sprite.**
8. **List three drawing shapes supported by Phrogram and identify the methods that can be used to draw them.**
9. **List three different ways that a square could be drawn.**
10. **What is an animated GIF? In your own words, describe the basic steps involved in using an animated GIF as the basis for creating animation in a Phrogram application.**

# BACK TO THE PCPONG GAME

Okay, now it is time to turn your attention back to the development of this chapter's application project, the PCPong game. The PCPong game is a Windows version of the original Atari *Pong* game. Because of its size and complexity, you will complete its development in two parts. Part 1 is covered in this chapter and part 2 will be covered in Chapter 9, "Integrating Sound and Working with Input Devices." The development of this game relies on the use of sprites and will help to reinforce everything that you have learned in this chapter.

## Designing the Game

The first part of the PCPong game will be developed in 14 steps, as outlined here:

1. Download and add graphics files to Phrogram's Images subfolder.
2. Create a new Phrogram program.
3. Document your program file.
4. Define the application's constants, global variables, and sprites.
5. Add controlling logic to the `Main()` method.
6. Add the `ConfigureWindow()` method.
7. Add the `StartANewPoint()` method.
8. Add the `ProcessPlayerMoves()` method.
9. Add the `UpdateBallPosition()` method.
10. Add the `ProcessPlayerMisses()` method.
11. Add the `ManageVerticalCollisions()` method.
12. Add the `ProcessPlayerHits()` method.
13. Add the `DisplayResults()` method.
14. Save and compile your application.

### Step 1: Downloading Graphics Files Needed by the Game

The PCPong game involves the use of sprites representing player paddles and the game ball. For the game ball, you will use one of the graphic files supplied in Phrogram's /Media Files/ Images folder. However, the graphic image that will be used to represent player paddles, named PongPaddle.gif, must be downloaded from this book's companion CD. Once downloaded, you will need to copy the PongPaddle.gif file into Phrogram's Images subfolder located in Documents/My Phrogram Files/Media Files/Images.

### Step 2: Creating a New Phrogram Program

The second step in the development of the PCPong game is to create a new Phrogram program file. Do so by clicking on the File menu's New Program command. Once you have done this, assign PCPong as the name of the application. The rest of the program statements that make up the PCPong application are outlined in the sections that follow.

### Step 3: Documenting Your New Program

The next step in the development of the PCPong application is to add the following comment statements to the beginning of the program file, just before the opening `Program` statement.

```
//Program: PCPong.kpl
//Created: 01/22/2008
//Version: 1.0
//Author: Jerry Lee Ford, Jr.
//Description: This Phrogram game is based on the original Pong
//             computer game that pits two players against one
//             another in a ping-pong style video game.
```

### Step 4: Defining the Application's Constants, Global Variables, and Sprites

Now it's time to define the constants, global variables, and sprites that will be used throughout the PCPong application by adding the following statements to the beginning of the program file, immediately following the comment statements that you added in the previous step and before the beginning of the `Main()` method.

```
//Global constant used to store the name of the application
Constant GameTitle As String = "PCPong"

//Global variables used throughout the game
Define PongBall As String = "BlueBall.png"      //Ball
Define PlayerPaddle As String = "PongPaddle.gif"    //Paddle

//Define variables that control the speed and direction of the ball
Define MoveX As Integer
Define MoveY As Integer

//Define global variables in which to store player scores
Define Player1Score As Integer
Define Player2Score As Integer

//Specify the number of points required to win the game
Define WinningScore As Integer = 21
```

```
//Define a variable that will be used to control the game's primary loop
Define GameOver As Boolean = False

//Definition of sprite objects used to play the game
Define Player1Paddle As Sprite   //Player 1's paddle
Define Player2Paddle As Sprite   //Player 2's paddle
Define GameBall As Sprite   //The game ball
```

As you can see, these statements define constants containing the game's name, a series of variable definition statements used to store references to the image files used by the game, the coordinates of the game ball, player scores and the number of points required to win the game, and a Boolean variable named `GameOver`, which will be used to control the execution of the game loop. Lastly, three sprites are defined, representing player paddles and the game ball.

### Step 5: Adding Controlling Logic to the Main() Method

The PCPong game relies heavily on methods and functions to organize its program code. The glue that binds everything together is the programming statements in the `Main()` method, shown next, which are responsible for the overall execution of the game.

```
//This method is responsible for the overall execution of the game
Method Main()

    //Define a variable to be used to keep track of how long a point
    //has lasted
    Define Duration As Integer

    //Define a variable to
    Define LastCheck As Integer

    //Define a Timer object to be used to control the pace of the game
    Define GameTimer As Timer

    //Display the game's welcome message and explain how to view
    //instructions
    Alert("Welcome to " + GameTitle + "!", GameTitle)

    ConfigureWindow() //This method sets the console window's default
                      //settings
```

```
GameTimer.Start() //Turn on the game's Timer object

StartANewPoint() //Call method in order to start the game's first point

While GameOver = False  //This loop controls overall game play

    //Keep track of how long the game has been running
    Duration = TickCount()

    //Ensure 30/1000 of a second has passed before doing anything
    If Duration - LastCheck > 30 Then

        ProcessPlayerMoves()  //Call on the method that processes
                              //player moves

        UpdateBallPosition()  //Call on the method that moves the ball

        ProcessPlayerMisses() //Call on the method that handles player
                              //misses

        //Perform the following methods as long as neither player has
        //earned 21 points
        If GameOver = False Then

            //Call on the method that handles collisions with the top
            //and bottom of the screen
            ManageVerticalCollisions()

            //Call on the method that handles collisions with player
            //paddles
            ProcessPlayerHits()

        End If

        LastCheck = Duration  //Reset the timer in order to start a new
                              //30 second count

    End If
```

```
    End While

    //The game is over. It is time to display the final result.
    DisplayResults()

End Method
```

The `Main()` method begins by defining several variables that will be used to keep track of time. Take note of the third variable definition, which defines an object based on the `Timers` library, which provides access to methods and objects used to keep track of the passing of time within applications. An opening welcome message is displayed next, followed by the execution of three methods that configure the game window, enable the execution of the game's time, and start the play of a new point.

The actual play of the point as well as the playing of all remaining points is managed by a `While...End While` loop. This loop uses the `Timers` library's `TickCount()` function to determine how long the program has been running. This information is issued to ensure that at least 30/1000 of a second have passed since the last execution of the loop. This forces the loop to iterate over and over again until 30/1000 has passed, before any of the statements in the loop are processed again.

> **HINT** Use of the `Timers` library and the `Timer` class to control the game loop is essential to ensure the smooth operational flow of the game. By ensuring the consistent passage of at least 30/1000 of a second between executions of the statements within the game's loop, the pace of game play is controlled and kept at a reasonable speed.

Each time the loop executes, it calls on methods that process any player moves that may have been made, updates the position of the ball as it bounces around the console windows, and updates the score when a point is made. In addition, an `If...Then` code block is continuously executed to manage the direction of the ball's movement after it collides with the top or bottom of the console window or with one of the player paddles. Game play continues until one of the players scores 21 points, at which time the game's loop stops executing and a method named `DisplayResults()` is executed, displaying the game's final score.

### Step 6: Developing the ConfigureWindow() Method

The code statements that make up the `ConfigureWindow()` method are shown next. These statements are responsible for configuring the game's application window, including its screen size, titlebar message, and background color.

```
//This method configures Window attributes
Method ConfigureWindow()

    SetScreenSize(640, 480)    //Set the screen size to 640x480 pixels
    SetWindowTitle(GameTitle)  //Display the name of the game in the
                               //Window's titlebar
    Color(White)    //Set the console window's background color to white

End Method
```

### Step 7: Developing the StartANewPoint() Method

The code statements that make up the `StartANewPoint()` method are shown next. These statements are responsible for starting a new point.

```
//This method initiates the start of a new point
Method StartANewPoint()

    //Define a variable to be used when displaying the score
    Define Msg As String

    //Format the output text
    Msg = "Player 1:  " + Player1Score + " points             "
    Msg = Msg + "        Player 2: " + Player2Score + " points"

    //Displays the score
    Alert(Msg, GameTitle)

    //Load graphics representing the sprites for player paddles and

    //the ball
    Player1Paddle.Load(PlayerPaddle)
    Player2Paddle.Load(PlayerPaddle)
    GameBall.Load(PongBall)

    //Set the starting point on the X-axis for both players' paddles
    Player1Paddle.X = 20
    Player2Paddle.X = 610

    //Set the starting point on the Y-axis for both players' paddles
```

```
    Player1Paddle.Y = ScreenHeight() / 2 - 50
    Player2Paddle.Y = ScreenHeight() / 2 - 50

    //Start the GameBall off in the middle of the screen
    GameBall.X = ScreenWidth() / 2 - 10
    GameBall.Y = ScreenHeight() / 2 - 10

    //Display players' paddles and the ball
    Player1Paddle.Show()
    Player2Paddle.Show()
    GameBall.Show()

    //Pause for one second to give both players time to get ready
    Delay(1000)

    //Begin game play by moving the ball between 4 - 6 pixels on the X-axis
    MoveX = Random(5, 7)

    //Move the ball between 2 to 5 pixels on the Y-axis
    MoveY = Random(2, 5)

End Method
```

As you can see, the method begins by displaying the game's current score in a popup dialog window. The sprites representing the players' paddles and the game ball are then loaded and vertically centered on the console window, with the game ball centered in the middle of the screen and then made visible. Next, a one-second pause is made and then the ball begins to move. The coordinates of the ball's next location are determined by setting the value of the ball's `X` and `Y` coordinates equal to a pair of randomly selected coordinates. Note that the ball location does not actually change until the `UpdateBallPosition()` method executes.

**HINT** In this version of the PCPong game, the game ball also begins moving downward and to the right at the beginning of each new point. The exact angle and speed at which the ball moves is randomly adjusted using the `Random()` method to retrieve X and Y coordinate values using different ranges of numbers.

### Step 8: Developing the ProcessPlayerMoves() Function

The code statements that make up the `ProcessPlayerMoves()` method are shown next. These statements are responsible for moving the players' paddles up and down the console window based on player input.

```
//This method controls the movement of the game paddles
Method ProcessPlayerMoves()

    //Move Player 1's paddle up when the Shift key is pressed
    If IsKeyDown("Shift") Then
        //Do not let the paddle go off the top of the console window
        If Player1Paddle.Y > 1 Then
            //Prepare to move the paddle up by 8 pixels on the Y-axis
            Player1Paddle.Y -= 8  //The higher the number the faster the
                                  //paddle moves
        End If
    End If

    //Move Player 1's paddle down when the Control key is pressed
    If IsKeyDown("Control") Then
        //Do not let the paddle go off the bottom of the console window
        If Player1Paddle.Y < (ScreenHeight() - Player1Paddle.Height) Then
            //Prepare to move the paddle down by 8 pixels on the Y-axis
            Player1Paddle.Y += 8  //The higher the number the faster the
                                  //paddle moves
        End If
    End If

    //Move Player 2's paddle up when the Up key is pressed
    If IsKeyDown("Up") Then
        //Do not let the paddle go off the top of the console window
        If Player2Paddle.Y > 1 Then
            //Prepare to move the paddle up by 8 pixels on the Y-axis
            Player2Paddle.Y -= 8  //The higher the number the faster the
                                  //paddle moves
        End If
    End If
```

```
    //Move Player 2's paddle down when the Down key is pressed
    If IsKeyDown("Down") Then
        If Player2Paddle.Y < (ScreenHeight() - Player2Paddle.Height) Then
            //Prepare to move the paddle down by 8 pixels along the Y-axis
            Player2Paddle.Y += 8    //The higher the number the faster the
                                    //paddle moves
        End If

    End If
    //Move player paddles as instructed by the player to their new
    //coordinates
    Player1Paddle.MoveTo(Player1Paddle.X, Player1Paddle.Y)
    Player2Paddle.MoveTo(Player2Paddle.X, Player2Paddle.Y)

End Method
```

This method begins with four `If…Then` code blocks. The first two code blocks control the movement of Player 1's paddle. They do this by using the `IsKeyDown()` method to determine when the Shift and Control keys are being pressed. Each time one of these keys is pressed, the `Y` property, representing the location of Player 1's paddle on the Y-axis is increased or decreased by eight pixels. Similarly, the last two code blocks manage the movement of Player 2's paddle by monitoring the Up and Down keys. Finally, the last two statements in the method use the `MoveTo()` method to reposition the player paddle on the Y-axis.

## Step 9: Developing the UpdateBallPosition() Method

The code statements that make up the `UpdateBallPosition()` method are shown next. These statements are responsible for updating the location of the game ball as it bounces around the console window.

```
//This method is responsible for moving the ball around the console window
Method UpdateBallPosition()

    GameBall.X += MoveX  //Adjust the ball's location on the X-axis
    GameBall.Y += MoveY  //Adjust the ball's location on the Y-axis

    GameBall.Show()      //Display the ball at its new location

End Method
```

As you can see, when called this method updates the display of the game ball by adding the values stored in MoveX and MoveY to the X and Y properties of the GameBall sprite. Once the sprite's location has been modified, the Show() method is executed, updating the game ball's location on the console window.

### Step 10: Developing the ProcessPlayerMisses() Method

The ProcessPlayerMisses() method, shown next, is responsible for determining when players miss the ball with their paddle, allowing their opponent to score a point.

```
//This method determines when points are scored
Method ProcessPlayerMisses()

    //Player 2 loses the point if the ball reaches the right edge of
    //the window
    If GameBall.X > ScreenWidth() - 20 Then

        Player1Score += 1  //Increment Player 1's score by one point

        //Check to see if Player 1 has won the game
        If Player1score = WinningScore Then
            GameOver = True
        End If

        GameBall.Unload()    //Unload the game ball

        If GameOver = False Then  //If the game is not over, start a new
                                  //point
            StartANewPoint()
        End If

    Else
        //Player 1 loses the point if the ball reaches the left edge of
        //the window
        If GameBall.X < 0 Then

            Player2Score += 1  //Increment Player 2's score by one point

            //Check to see if Player 1 has won the game
            If Player2Score = WinningScore Then
```

```
                GameOver = True
            End If

            GameBall.Unload()  //Unload the game ball

            If GameOver = False Then  //If the game is not over, start
                                      //a new point
                StartANewPoint()
            End If

        End If
    End If

End Method
```

As you can see, this method consists of a single `If…Then` code block and begins by checking if the location of the game's ball on the X-axis is greater than `ScreenWidth() -20`, in which case the ball has gotten past Player 2's paddle. If this is the case, Player 1's score is incremented, and depending on whether Player 1 has 21 points, the game either ends or a new point is started by executing the `StartANewPoint()` method. The second half of the `If…Then` code block is almost identical to the first half, the only difference being that this time it checks to see if the ball has gotten past Player 1's paddle.

## Step 11: Developing the ManageVerticalCollisions() Method

The `ManageVerticalCollisions()` method, shown next, is responsible for deflecting the ball whenever it makes contact with the top or bottom of the console window.

```
//This method deflects the ball when it hits the top or bottom of the
//window
Method ManageVerticalCollisions()

    //Detect the ball when it collides with the bottom of the screen
    If GameBall.Y > (ScreenHeight() - 20) Then
        MoveY = MoveY * -1      //Reverse the ball's direction on the Y-axis
    Else  //Detect the ball when it collides with the top of the screen
        If GameBall.Y < 10 Then
           MoveY = MoveY * -1  //Reverse the ball's direction on the Y-axis
        End If
```

```
    End If

End Method
```

This method begins by checking the location of the `GameBall` sprite's location on the Y-axis to see if it is within 20 pixels of the top of the screen. If this is the case the ball's direction on the Y-axis is reversed by multiplying the value assigned to `MoveY` by -1. Likewise, the remainder of the `If…Then` code block checks to see if the ball has reached the bottom of the console window.

> **HINT** Remember that in Phrogram's coordinates system the origin begins at (0, 0). As you increase the value of a sprite's `Y` property, the sprite is moved down the screen, and if you decrease the value of the sprite's `Y` property it will move up towards the top of the screen. When set to a positive value, any addition to a sprite's Y property moves it downward. When you multiply this value by –1 and then begin adding new values to it, the sprite will begin to move back upwards. Likewise, if you once again multiply the value of the sprite's `Y` property by –1, it will reverse the sprite's movement back to its original direction.

### Step 12: Developing the ProcessPlayerHits() Method

The `ProcessPlayerHits()` method, shown next, is responsible for deflecting the ball whenever it is hit by one of the player's paddles.

```
//This method deflects the ball whenever it collides with a paddle
Method ProcessPlayerHits()

    //Look for a collision between the ball and one of the paddles
    If GameBall.Intersects(Player1Paddle) Or
         GameBall.Intersects(Player2Paddle) Then

        //Let's speed things up a bit every time the ball hits a paddle
        If MoveX > 0 Then
            MoveX += 1   //Speed up the movement of the ball on the X-axis
        End If

        MoveX *= -1  //Reverse the direction of the ball on the X-axis

        //Manage collision with Player 1's paddle
        If GameBall.Intersects(Player1Paddle) Then
            MoveY -= Random(0, 2)
```

```
        End If

        //Manage collision with Player 2's paddle
        If GameBall.Intersects(Player2Paddle) Then
            MoveY -= Random(0, 2)
        End If

        GameBall.X += MoveX  //Adjust the ball's location on the X-axis
        GameBall.Y += MoveY  //Adjust the ball's location on the Y-axis

        //Move the ball to the specified set of coordinates
        GameBall.MoveTo(GameBall.X, GameBall.Y)

    End If

End Method
```

In order to determine if the ball has collided with one of the player's paddles, the method begins by using `Sprite` class's `Intersects()` function to determine if either player's paddle has made contact with the ball. If this is the case, the first thing that happens is that the value assigned to `MoveX` (e.g., representing the number of pixels that the `GameBall` sprite moves each time its location is updated) is incremented by 1. You should note that the value of `MoveX` is only incremented when it is moving towards the right-hand side of the console window. As such, the `GameBall` sprite's speed is only updated every other time it is hit.

Next, the `GameBall` sprite's direction is changed by multiplying its `X` property by −1. In addition, the angle at which the `GameBall` sprite is moving is randomly changed. Once new coordinates for the game ball have been calculated, the `GameBall` sprite's `X` and `Y` properties are updated and the sprite is moved to its new coordinates.

### Step 13: Developing the DisplayResults() Method

The game's last method is `DisplayResults()`. It is called at the end of the game, once one of the two players has gotten 21 points. When called, it formats a string that shows both players' scores, displays the text string "G A M E O V E R!" next to the game's name in the popup dialog window's titlebar, and hides the display of the game's paddles.

```
//This method does a little clean up and notifies the player when the end
//of the game is reached
Method DisplayResults()
```

```
    //Define a variable to be used when displaying the score
    Define Msg As String

    //Format the output text
    Msg = "Player 1:  " + Player1Score + " points            "
    Msg = Msg + "       Player 2: " + Player2Score + " points"

    //Displays the score
    Alert(Msg, GameTitle + "  -  G A M E  O V E R!")

    //The game has ended so remove both paddles from the screen
    Player1Paddle.Hide()
    Player2paddle.Hide()

End Method
```

### Step 14: Saving and Compiling Your Application

Okay, at this point you have everything you need to complete this part of the development of the PCPong game. If you have not done so, save your new application by clicking on the Save All command located on the File menu. Next, do a quick check to see if Phrogram is reporting any syntax errors and fix any that are reported by following the instructions provided in the previous steps.

## The Final Result

Assuming that you have followed along carefully, your copy of the PCPong game should be ready and should run as described at the beginning of the chapter. If you do not have the time to key in your own copy of this application, you can download a copy of the source code for this application from the book's companion CD.

**HINT** In Chapter 9, you will learn how to make a number of changes and improvements to the PCPong game. These modifications include the addition of sound effects, a less intrusive means of displaying player scores, the ability to apply a little "English" when hitting the ball with the corner of the paddles, and the display of a snazzier end of game message.

## Summary

This chapter has provided you with a solid review of Phrogram's support for graphics and animation. You learned how to draw and create an assortment of different shapes. You learned how to display graphic files and to use sprites as a means of controlling the display and movement of graphics on the console window. You also learned to control sprite visibility and to determine when sprite collisions occur.

Before you move on to Chapter 9, consider spending a little time improving the PCPong game by addressing the following list of challenges.

### Challenges

1. The PCPong game is by far the most complex project that you have worked on so far. Although extensively documented, there is still plenty of room for improvement. Spend a little time going through the program file, modifying and adding to the documentation to better explain what is going on.
2. To better learn how to control the movement of the game ball and its paddle, spend a little time experimenting with the program code that affects the movement of the game ball and paddles to see how it affects game play. For example, try altering the number of pixels that are used when moving paddles and modifying the ranges of numbers used to randomly alter the game ball's trajectory.
3. Create a distribution package for your new game and share with a few friends, asking them to provide you with feedback.

CHAPTER 9

# Integrating Sound and Working with Input Devices

Up to this point of the book, all of the applications that you have worked on have been mute, meaning that they have not used any sounds effects. In addition, most of the games that you have worked on have made very limited use of the mouse, depending instead on the computer keyboard as the primary source of input and game control. In this chapter, you will learn how to enhance your applications through the addition of sound. You will also learn more about how to interact with the computer keyboard and mouse and how to use joysticks as input devices. On top of everything mentioned above, this chapter will guide you through the development of the second part of the PCPong game.

Specifically, you will learn:

- How to improve your programs by adding sound effects and music playback
- New ways of working with the keyboard and mouse as input devices
- How to detect when joysticks are connected to the computer and to uniquely identify them
- How to track joystick movement and direction and use joysticks to control the movement of sprites

## Project Preview: The PCPong Game

This chapter's game project involves the modification and completion of the PCPong game. This improved version of PCPong will feature a number of enhancements, as listed here:

- A new graphical end of game message.
- Sound effects that play whenever the ball is deflected off of a paddle, or the top or bottom of the console window, and when points are scored.
- An enhancement of the program logic that controls ball movement at the beginning of each new point, allowing for random changes in the direction and angle at which the ball initially moves.
- An enhancement of the program logic used to control the trajectory of the ball when it makes contact with the upper or lower end of player paddles, allowing the player to apply a little "English" to the ball when hitting it back to the other player (giving players added influence over the direction at which the ball is deflected).
- The replacement of popup dialog windows with display of text in the console window's status bar for reporting player scores, providing a less intrusive means of displaying player scores.

As shown in Figure 9.1, the PCPong game still looks and feels very much the same as it did in Chapter 8, with the ball and paddles centrally placed at the beginning of each point; only now, instead of pausing game play to display scores in a popup dialog window every time a point is scored, player scores are displayed in the status bar located at the bottom of the console window.

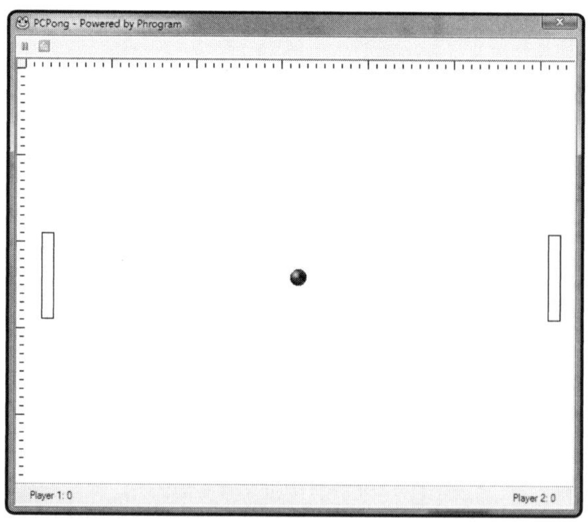


**FIGURE 9.1**

Player scores are displayed on the status bar at the bottom of the console window.

Figure 9.2 shows an example of a point being played. Players move the ball around the console window by deflecting it off of their paddles. In this updated version of the PCPong game, players can now apply a little "English" when hitting the ball to influence the angle at which the ball travels on its way back at the other player.

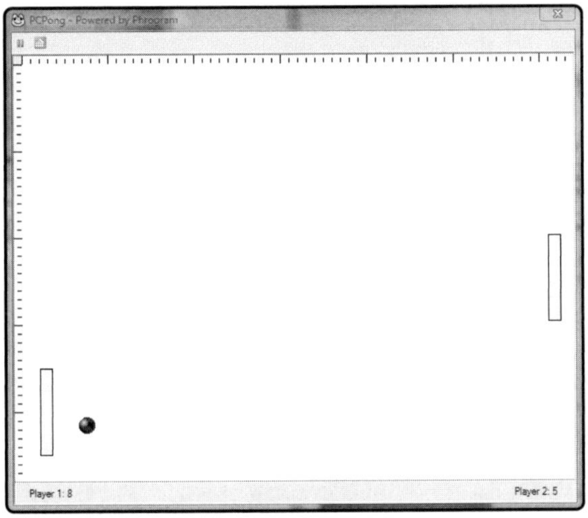


**FIGURE 9.2**

The game ball bounces around the console window using a wider range of angles.

Since player scores are now displayed in the status bar, there is no longer a need to use popup dialog windows to display player scores or the game's "Game Over!" message. As such, when the end of the game is reached, the graphic message shown in Figure 9.3 displays on the console window in place of a popup dialog window.

**FIGURE 9.3**

A sprite is used to display a stylish graphic at the end of the game.

## Capturing Player Input

To work with any computer application or game, the user needs to be able to input instructions and commands for processing. Depending on the application or game, input may be provided through a number of different means, including the keyboard, mouse, or joystick. For example, a word guessing game might be controlled by the keyboard, whereas a computer video game might be controlled by the mouse or a joystick, if one is available. Phrogram supports all three of these types of devices through methods, functions, and properties provided by the `Keyboard` and `Mouse` libraries and the `Joystick`, and `JoystickValue` classes.

## Collecting Input from the Keyboard

As you have already learned, you can interact with the user from the console window using methods and functions provided by the `Console` library, such as `ConsoleReadKey()` and `ConsoleReadLine()` functions. You can also interact with the user and collect input using the `Shell` library's `Alert()` method and `Confirm()` functions. In addition to working with the `Console` library, you can also capture user input using the following methods and functions provided by the `Keyboard` library.

- `GetKey()`. Returns the last key that was pressed.
- `IsKeyDown()`. Detects when a key is pressed and returns its value.
- `ClearKeyboardEvents()`. Clears out any characters stored in the process queue.

### Capturing Individual Keystrokes

As you have already learned, you can capture user keyboard input using the `ConsoleReadKey()` and `ConsoleReadLine()` functions. However, the problem with these functions is that they temporarily halt or block the execution of your Phrogram application while waiting for the user to key in input. This behavior is fine for many types of games and applications. However, for action-driven games, you need to be able to collect player input on the fly without bringing the game to a screeching halt. One way of doing this is through the use of the `Keyboard` library's `GetKey()` method.

The `GetKey()` method is non-blocking, meaning that it can be used to collect user keyboard input, a key at a time, without halting the program execution. The syntax required to use this method is outlined here:

```
UserInput = GetKey()
```

*UserInput* is a variable used to store the key retrieved by the `GetKey()` function. By using this function inside a loop, you can capture most keystrokes.

To help give you a better understanding of how to work with the GetKey() method, take a look at the following example.

```
Define UserInput As String

While True

    UserInput = GetKey()

    If UserInput <> "" Then
        Status("You typed: " + UserInput)
    End If

End While
```

Here, a While...End While loop has been set up to run forever. Each time the loop repeats, it executes the GetKey() method. If the user has pressed a keyboard key since the last iteration of the loop ended, it is captured and stored in the UserInput variable and then displayed at the bottom of the console window, as demonstrated in Figure 9.4.

FIGURE 9.4

Capturing user input without blocking an application's execution.

## Capturing Special Keys

The GetKey() method is useful for capturing most keyboard keystrokes. Most computer keyboards have 104 or more keys, not all of which can be captured using this method. For example, using the GetKey() method you cannot capture special keystrokes like #, $, and %. Nor can it determine when a function key has been pressed. One way of capturing keystrokes that cannot be detected by the GetKey() function is by using the IsKeyDown() function.

Table 9.1 provides a listing of all the special keystrokes that you can capture using the IsKeyDown() function.

You have already seen the IsKeyDown() function in action. For example, it is used to capture player input and control paddle movement in the PCPong game. As a quick refresher on how to work with the IsKeyDown() function, take a look at the following example.

**Table 9.1 Keystrokes That Can Be Captured Using the IsKeyDown() Function**

| | | | |
|---|---|---|---|
| Back | Control | Delete | Down |
| End | Enter | Escape | F1 |
| F10 | F11 | F12 | F2 |
| F3 | F4 | F5 | F6 |
| F7 | F8 | F9 | Home |
| Insert | Left | PageDown | PageUp |
| Pause | Right | Shift | Space |
| Tab | Up | | |

```
While IsKeyDown("Q") = False
    If IsKeyDown("F1") Then
        Status("Setting game level to beginner.")
    End If
    If IsKeyDown("F2") Then
        Status("Setting game level to intermediate.")
    End If
    If IsKeyDown("F3") Then
        Status("Setting game level to advanced.")
    End If
    If IsKeyDown("F4") Then
        Status("Setting game level to expert")
    End If
End While
```

As you can see, the `IsKeyDown()` function has been used in four separate `If…Then` code blocks to control the display of text strings in the console window's status bar. Figure 9.5 shows an example of the output produced by this example when the F3 key is pressed.

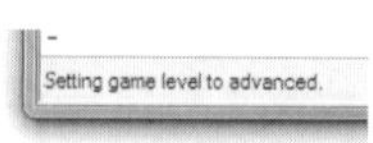


**Figure 9.5**
Capturing special keyboard keys.

## Clearing Out the Process Queue

In order to collect and process keyboard data, you must set up a loop to poll the keyboard. As the user types, keystrokes are stored in a process queue. Phrogram provides the ability to programmatically retrieve items from the process queue. When you execute the `GetKey()` function, you retrieve and remove keystrokes from this queue. If you want, you can clear out all of the keystrokes stored in the process queue by executing the `ClearKeyBoardEvents()` method, which has the following syntax.

```
ClearKeyboardEvents()
```

As an example of how to work with this method, take a look at the following statements.

```
PrintLine("Type the letters Q W E R T Y and then press the F3 key.")
PrintLine("")

While IsKeyDown(F3) = False

End While

Print("You typed: ")

Print(GetKey())
Print(GetKey())
Print(GetKey())
Print(GetKey())
ClearKeyboardEvents()
Print(GetKey())
Print(GetKey())
```

Here, a text message is displayed on the console window instructing the user to type the letters `QWERTY`. Since the process queue starts out empty when the application is executed, the only keystrokes stored in it will be those typed in by the user. The user is then instructed to press the F3 key. The `GetKey()` function is used to retrieve the first four keystrokes (qwer) stored in the process queue, each of which is then displayed on the console window. Next, the `ClearKeyBoardEvents()` method is executed, clearing out the contents of the process queue. As a result, when the next two statements attempt to retrieve keystrokes from the process queue, there is nothing left to retrieve and display.

**HINT** Note that the `IsKeyDown()` function has no effect on the process queue. When executed, it is able to detect and respond to keystrokes but does not remove them from the process queue.

Figure 9.6 shows the output that is displayed when this example is executed.

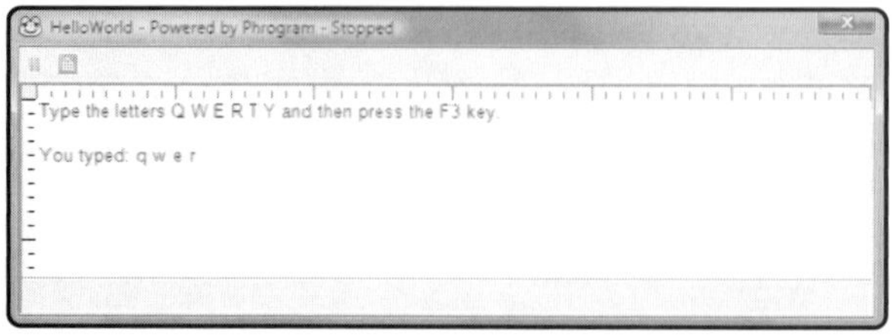


**FIGURE 9.6**

Clearing out keystrokes stored in the process queue.

**TRICK** The process queue is also automatically cleared any time you execute the `Shell` library's `Alert()` method.

## USING THE MOUSE TO COLLECT PLAYER INPUT

Just as there are many different types and shapes of keyboards, there are many different types of mouse devices. Some mice have a small wheel in between their buttons. Touch pad, pen, and track ball devices can also be regarded as different types of mice. Each of these devices provides input that specifies the `X` and `Y` coordinates of the pointer. They also provide data showing when their buttons are pressed. As such, any of these devices can be used to drive a car, fly a plane, or move a character around the console window.

In order to help you work with and control the computer's mouse, Phrogram's `Mouse library` supplies a number of properties, as shown in Table 9.2, that you can use to retrieve information about mouse movement and to capture information about button clicks.

**TABLE 9.2 MOUSE LIBRARY PROPERTIES**

| Property | Description |
|---|---|
| `MouseButton` | Returns an integer representing the button that has been pressed (1 = left, 2 = right, 3 = middle). |
| `MouseClicks` | Returns an integer indicating whether the mouse has been clicked or double-clicked (1 = clicked, 2 = double-clicked). |
| `MouseEvent` | Returns a string value indicating one of the following events: "ButtonUp", "ButtonDown", "Move", or "Wheel". |
| `MouseLocation` | Returns coordinates showing the pointer's current location. |
| `MouseWheel` | Returns a value indicating whether the mouse's wheel is being moved. A value of 0 indicates no movement, a positive value indicates the wheel is being moved upward, and a negative value indicates the wheel is being moved downward. |
| MouseX | Returns an integer representing the pointer's `X` coordinate. |
| MouseY | Returns an integer representing the pointer's `Y` coordinate. |

## Tracking Mouse Movement

The primary use of the mouse in most applications and games is to move the pointer around the screen. Using the `Mouse` library's `MouseX` and `MouseY` properties, you can track mouse movement. The `MouseX` method retrieves the location of the pointer on the X-axis. The `MouseY` method retrieves the pointer's location on the Y-axis.

The following example demonstrates how to use the `MouseX` and `MouseY` properties to track and report on the location of the pointer, whenever it is positioned somewhere over the console window.

```
Define Msg As String

While True

    Msg = MouseX + ", " + MouseY

    Status(Msg)

    Delay(10)

End While
```

Here, a `While...End While` loop has been set up to continuously display the current location of the mouse in a text string displayed in the console window's status bar. Figure 9.7 shows an example of the output displayed when this example is executed.

**FIGURE 9.7**

Capturing and reporting the co-ordinates of the pointer on the console window.

## Keeping an Eye on Mouse Clicks

In addition to keeping track of the pointer as the user moves it around the console window, you also need to be able to programmatically determine when the user clicks on mouse buttons. This will enable you to develop applications and games that use mouse button clicks to control sprite behavior. For example, you might create a Space Invaders-style game that shoots a missile at incoming space monsters whenever the left mouse button is clicked.

To determine when a mouse button is clicked, you must set up a loop to repeatedly check on the value of the `MouseButton` property. A value of 1 indicates that the left mouse button has been clicked, and a value of 2 indicates that the right mouse button has been clicked. If the mouse has a third button, a value of 3 indicates when the middle button has been clicked.

As a quick demonstration of how to detect when a mouse's buttons are clicked, look at the following example.

```
While True

    If MouseButton = 1 Then
        ClearBackground(Red)
        Status("Red")
    Else If MouseButton = 2 Then
        ClearBackground(Yellow)
        Status("Yellow")
    Else
        ClearBackground(White)
        Status("")
    End If

    Delay(10)

End While
```

In this example, the console window's background color is briefly cleared and set to red whenever the left mouse button is clicked and set to yellow when the right button is clicked. If neither button is pressed, the console window's background is set back to white.

**HINT** A little later in this chapter you will see an example of how to use the `MouseButton`, `MouseX`, and `MouseY` properties to determine when the user clicks on buttons drawn on the console window.

## Using Joysticks as Input Devices

In addition to the keyboard and mouse, Phrogram is also capable of using joysticks as input and control devices. Joysticks are essential to the operation of game consoles like Xbox 360 and PlayStation 3. However, joysticks are not nearly as commonly used on personal computers. Regardless, for some games joystick control is an absolute requirement. Thankfully, Phrogram provides robust support for working with joysticks. Like a mouse, joysticks provide a stream of input reflecting `X`, `Y` coordinates. Modern joysticks also typically support more than one button, perhaps as many as 6 to 10.

## Determine if Any Joysticks Are Attached to the Computer

In order to work with joysticks, you first need to determine how many, if any, joysticks are attached to the computer and to uniquely identify each one. Today's modern joysticks connect to the computer via USB ports, allowing Microsoft Windows to automatically detect them and make them available to desktop applications. Phrogram is able to access this information, which it uses to automatically populate a special array named `Joystick`, with a list of all joysticks that are currently connected to the computer.

In order to work with the information stored in the `Joystick` array, you need to set up an array of your own and populate it with the information that is stored in the `Joystick` array. Once populated, you can process your array and display information about any joysticks connected to the computer, as demonstrated in the following example.

```
Define aStick As Joystick[10]
Define I As Integer

For I = 1 To 10

    If aStick[I].IsConnected Then

        PrintLine("")
        Print("Joystick " + I + " is a " + aStick[I].MakeAndModel + ". ")
        PrintLine("It has " + aStick[I].NumberOfButtons + " buttons")

    End If

Next
```

This example begins by setting up an array named `aStick`, based on Phrogram's built-in `Joystick` array. By setting `aStick` to `Joystick[10]`, you can retrieve information about the first 10 joysticks (if that many are connected). A `For...Next` loop is then set up to iterate through `aStick` to see if the computer has any joysticks connected. If this is the case, the `Joystick` class's `MakeAndModel` and `NumberOfButtons` properties are used to display information about the joystick(s). By the time this example finishes executing, a list of all the joysticks connected to the computer will be displayed on the window console, as demonstrated in Figure 9.8.

**TRICK**

By default, you can use the `Joystick` class's `Stick1` and `Stick2` properties to reference and work with the first two joysticks connected to the computer. You will see an example of how to work with these two properties a little later in this chapter.

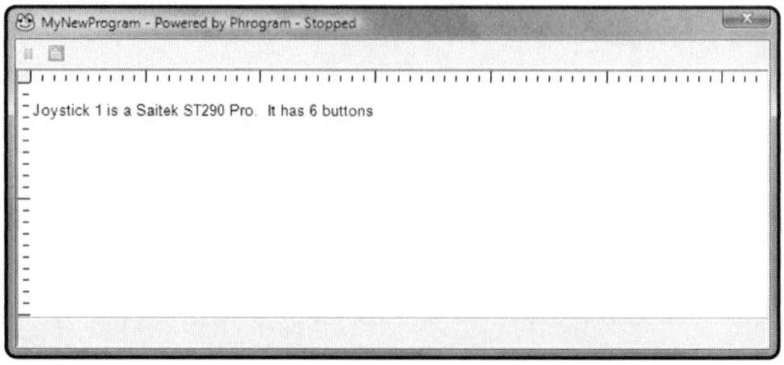


**FIGURE 9.8**

Programmatically detecting when one or more joysticks are connected.

## Identifying Joysticks

In order to be able to use a joystick in a computer game, your application must be able to uniquely identify it. One way of doing this is to prompt the player to select a joystick and press one of its buttons while at the same time iterating through the list of joysticks connected to the computer looking for one that has a button pressed. Once your application has identified the joystick selected by the user, you can programmatically interact with that joystick throughout the rest of the game. To see an example of how you might implement this logic, look at the following example.

```
Define aStick As Joystick[10]
Define I As Integer
Define NoOfButtons As Integer
Define SelectionMade As Boolean = False
Define Msg As String
Define UserInput As Boolean
Define SelectedStick As Integer

Msg = "This game can be played with either the keyboard or a joystick. "
Msg = Msg + "If your computer has a joystick and you wish to play the "
Msg = Msg + "game using it, click on Yes. Otherwise, click on No to "
Msg = Msg + "play the game using your keyboard."

UserInput = Confirm(Msg, "Joystick Demo")

If UserInput = True Then

    Alert("Click on OK and then press a joystick button.", "Joystick Demo")

    While SelectionMade = False
        For I = 1 To 10
```

```
            If aStick[I].IsConnected Then
                For NoOfButtons = 1 To aStick[I].NumberOfButtons
                    If aStick[I].IsButtonPressed(NoOfButtons) Then

                        SelectedStick = I

                        Msg = "You have selected joystick number " + I
                        Msg = Msg + " - " + aStick[I].MakeAndModel

                        Alert(Msg, "Joystick Demo")
                        SelectionMade = True

                    End If
                Next
            End If
        Next
    End While
End If
```

Here, a message is displayed informing the player that the game can be played using either the keyboard or a joystick. The message prompts the player to click on the popup dialog window's Yes button to play the game using a joystick. Next, the player is instructed to press any button on the joystick (so that the game can identify it). A `While...End While` loop is then set up to iterate through an array named `aStick` to look for the joystick whose button is being pressed. To ensure that the state of every button on every joystick is checked, a second `For...Next` loop has been set up to loop from 1 to the value of `NumberOfButtons`. As soon as the player's joystick is identified, a confirmation message is displayed, as demonstrated in Figure 9.9.

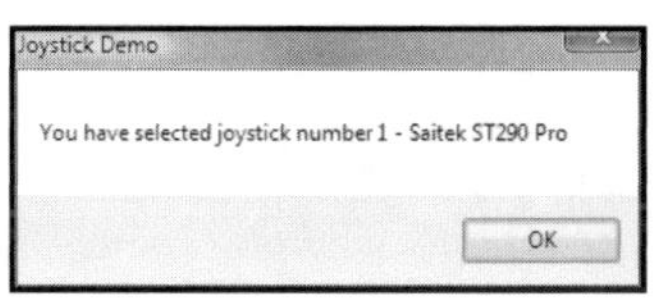


**FIGURE 9.9**

Presenting the player an option of using a joystick and detecting the joystick to be used.

## Tracking Joystick Button Clicks

Once your Phrogram application has identified which joystick the player is using, it needs to begin monitoring the joystick's status. This means monitoring and reacting to joystick button clicks and movement. As demonstrated in this next example, Phrogram applications can detect and react to joystick button clicks using the Joystick class's `IsButtonPressed()` function, which returns a value of `True` if a specified joystick button is pressed.

```
Define I As Integer
Define aStick As Joystick[10]

While True

    For I = 1 To 10

        If aStick[I].IsConnected Then

            If aStick[I].IsButtonPressed(1) Then
                Console.WriteLine("Firing phasers!")
            End If
            If aStick[I].IsButtonPressed(2) Then
                Console.WriteLine("Firing photon torpedoes!")
            End If
            If aStick[I].IsButtonPressed(3) Then
                Console.WriteLine("Firing mega-ton cannon!")
            End If
            If aStick[I].IsButtonPressed(4) Then
                Console.WriteLine("Firing heat seeking missile!")
            End If

        End If

    Next

    Delay(50)

End While
```

As you can see, this example loops through an array named `aStick`, checking to see if any of the first four buttons on the joystick are being pressed. As demonstrated in Figure 9.10, a message is displayed on the console window each time a joystick button is pressed.

## Tracking Joystick Location and Movement

Now that you know how to identify joysticks and to detect when their buttons are pressed, you need to know how to track joystick movement, as demonstrated in the following example.

**FIGURE 9.10**

Executing program statements based on which joystick buttons are pressed.

```
Define Stick As Joystick[5]
Define I As Integer
Define NoOfButtons As Integer
Define SelectionMade As Boolean = False
Define Msg As String
Define UserInput As Boolean
Define SelectedStick As Integer

Msg = "This game can be played with either the keyboard or a joystick. "
Msg = Msg + "If your computer has a joystick and you wish to play the "
Msg = Msg + "game using it, click on Yes. Otherwise, click on No to "
Msg = Msg + "play the game using your keyboard."

UserInput = Confirm(Msg, "Joystick Demo")

If UserInput = True Then

    Alert("Click on OK and then press a joystick button.", "Joystick Demo")

    While SelectionMade = False
        For I = 1 To 5
            If Stick[I].IsConnected Then
                For NoOfButtons = 1 To Stick[I].NumberOfButtons
                    If Stick[I].IsButtonPressed(NoOfButtons) Then

                        SelectedStick = I

                        Msg = "You have selected joystick number " + I
                        Msg = Msg + " - " + Stick[I].MakeAndModel

                        Alert(Msg, "Joystick Demo")
```

```
                        SelectionMade = True

                    End If
                Next
            End If
        Next
    End While
End If

While True

    Msg = "X Coordinate: " + Stick[SelectedStick].Stick1.X + "      "
    Msg = Msg + " Y Coordinate: " + Stick[SelectedStick].Stick1.Y

    Status(Msg)
    Delay(10)

End While
```

Here, the player is prompted to select a joystick and to press one of its buttons. This allows the example to identify the selected joystick and then, using a `While...End While` loop, to track and report on the value of the joystick's `X` and `Y` coordinates.

**HINT** Unlike the mouse, which reports on the physical location of the pointer on the console window, a joystick's `X` and `Y` coordinates represent joystick movement and direction and not its location. Figure 9.11 depicts the coordinate system that Phrogram uses when working with joysticks.

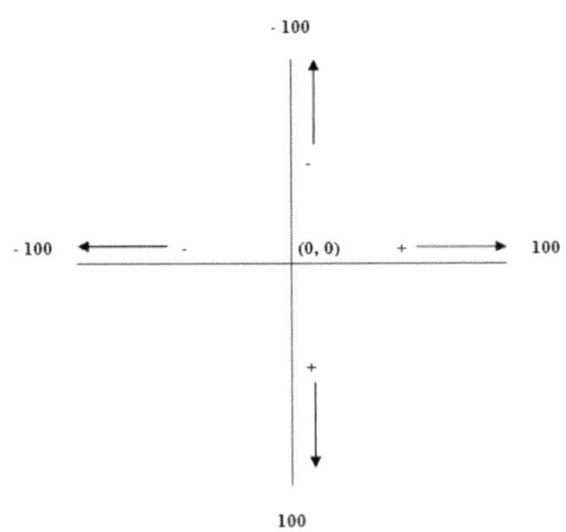


**FIGURE 9.11**

Coordinate (0, 0) lies at the center of the joystick coordinate system.

As Figure 9.11 shows, joysticks use a totally different coordinate system. As you can see, the maximum range of values used to track joystick movement is from −100 to 100 on both axes.

Figure 9.12 shows an example of the output that is generated when the previous example is executed.

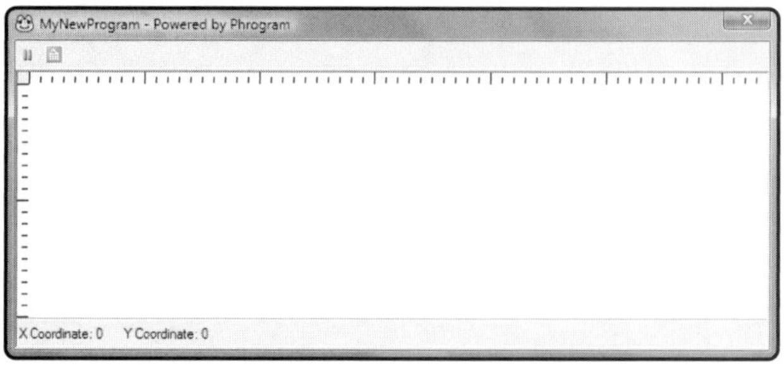


**FIGURE 9.12**

Tracking joystick movement.

## Using a Joystick to Control Sprite Movement

As the following example demonstrates, you can easily use a joystick to control the movement of a sprite in a computer application. In this example, a sprite representing a blue bird can be moved in any direction on the console window. Of course, this example could easily be modified to move a space ship, tank, or a robot.

```
Define Joystick As Joystick

Define Bird As Sprite

Bird.Load("BlueBird.gif")

Bird.X = ScreenWidth() / 2 - Bird.Width / 2
Bird.Y = ScreenHeight() / 2 - Bird.Height / 2

Bird.Show()

While True

    Status("X: " + Joystick.Stick1.X + "     " + "Y: " + Joystick.Stick1.Y)

    If Joystick.Stick1.X < 0 Then
```

```
        Bird.MoveRight(5)
    End If

    If Joystick.Stick1.X > 0 Then
        Bird.MoveLeft(5)
    End If

    If Joystick.Stick1.Y < 0 Then
        Bird.Back(5)
    End If

    If Joystick.Stick1.Y > 0 Then
        Bird.Forward(5)
    End If

    Delay(10)

End While
```

This example begins by displaying the sprite representing the blue bird in the middle of the console window. Next, a `While…End While` loop repeatedly executes a series of four `If…Then` code blocks, which move the sprite around the console window. The sprite is moved by five pixels by calling on the `Sprite` class's `MoveRight`, `MoveLeft`, `Forward`, and `Back` methods. Figure 9.13 shows an example of this program in action.

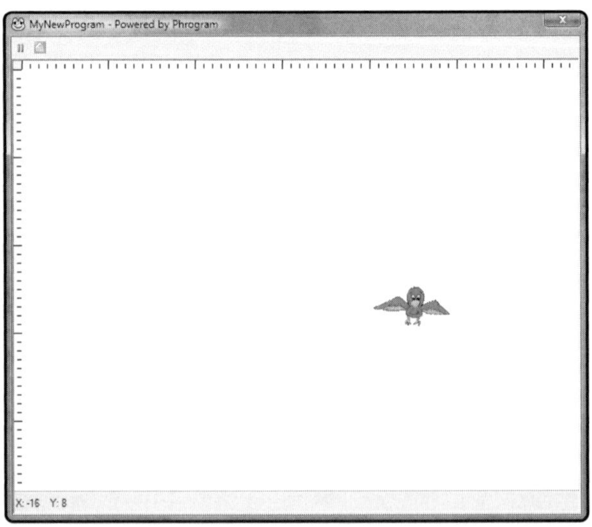


**FIGURE 9.13**

Using a joystick to control the movement of a sprite.

**Exercises**

**To help you become better acquainted with how to work with the keyboard, mouse, and joystick as input and control devices, take a few minutes to complete the following exercises.**

1. **Using the preceding example as a starting point, modify the program so that the blue bird's movement can be controlled using the keyboard's Up, Down, Left, and Right arrow keys.**
2. **Modify the program so that the blue bird's movement can be controlled using the mouse.**
3. **Now modify the program so that a second sprite, using the Spider.gif image file located in Phrogram's Image folder, is displayed and can be controlled using a second joystick.**

## Breathing Life into Applications with Sound Effects

So far all of the applications that you have developed have had one thing in common: they have been mute. However, sound is a very important component in many types of applications, especially games. Phrogram provides the ability to add sound effects and music playback to your applications through methods supplied by the `Sound` class, which are listed here:

- **LoadFile.** Loads a wave file but does not play it.
- **Play.** Plays a previously loaded wave file.
- **PlayLoop.** Repeatedly plays a loaded wave file.
- **Stop.** Terminates the playback of a wave file.

HINT

A *wave* file is a file that supports the storage and playback of audio on personal computers.

### Loading a Sound File

The first step involved in working with a sound file is to load it. Once loaded, you can control its playback in a number of ways. To load a sound file, you can use the `LoadFile()` method, which has the following syntax.

```
ObjectName.LoadFile("FileName")
```

*ObjectName* is the name of a previously defined instance (object) of the `Sound` class. *FileName* specifies the name of a wave (.WAV) file that you want to load.

The following statement demonstrates how to load a wave file, using the `LoadFile()` method.

```
Define ExplodeWav As Sound
ExplodeWav.LoadFile("Explode.wav")
```

Here, a wave file named `Explode.wav` has been loaded, making it available for playback.

## Playing a Sound File

Once loaded, a wave file can be played using the `Play()` method, which has the following syntax.

```
ObjectName.Play()
```

*ObjectName* is the name of a previously defined instance of the `Sound` class. When executed, it plays a previously loaded wave file and can be used as a means of adding sound effects to your Phrogram applications.

As an example of how to work with this method, take a look at the following statements.

```
Define ExplodeWav As Sound
ExplodeWav.LoadFile("Explode.wav")
ExplodeWav.Play()
Delay(2000)
```

When executed, this example loads and then pauses for two seconds in order to give the application time to play the `Explode.wav` wave file.

> **HINT** You will find the Explode.wav file along with a host of other wave files in Phrogram's Sound folder located in My Programs\Media Files\Sounds.

## Repeating Sound File Playback

If you want, you can repeatedly play a wave file using the `PlayLoop()` method. The `PlayLoop()` method has the following syntax.

```
ObjectName.PlayLoop()
```

*ObjectName* is the name of a previously defined instance of the `Sound` class. When executed, it plays a previously loaded wave file.

The following example demonstrates how to repeatedly play a wave file for 10 seconds.

```
Define ExplodeWav As Sound
ExplodeWav.LoadFile("Explode.wav")
ExplodeWav.PlayLoop()
Delay(10000)
```

## Stopping Sound File Playback

You can stop sound playback at any point by executing the `Sound` class's `Stop()` method, which has the following syntax.

```
ObjectName.Stop()
```

*`ObjectName`* is the name of a previously defined instance of the `Sound` class. When executed, it terminates the playback of a wave file.

The following statement demonstrates how to execute this method.

```
ExplodeWav.Stop()
```

FIND IT ONLINE

Phrogram comes equipped with 70 wave files that you can use when developing new applications. You can browse the files, which are located in My Programs \Media Files\Sounds using the Files Explorer window.

In addition to the sound files supplied with Phrogram, there are hundreds of additional sound files available for free download from the Phrogram website at http://phrogram.com/files/folders/soundfiles/default.aspx.

# Playing More than One Sound at a Time

This chapter has taught you the basics of how to integrate sound playback into your Phrogram applications. In addition, you have learned how to exercise detailed control over the keyboard, mouse, and joysticks. To help bring together your understanding of these programming concepts, look at the following example, which demonstrates how to control the playback of multiple wave files.

```
Program WavePlayer

    Define ExplodeWav As Sound
    Define TargetLockWav As Sound
    Define MissileWav As Sound

    Method Main()

        SetScreenSize (600, 175)
```

```
    ExplodeWav.LoadFile("Explode.wav")
    TargetLockWav.LoadFile("TargetLock.wav")
    MissileWav.LoadFile("Missile.wav")

    Define Rect1 As Rectangle
    Define Rect2 As Rectangle
    Define Rect3 As Rectangle

    TargetLockWav.PlayLoop()

    DrawButton(100, 50)
    DrawButton(250, 50)
    DrawButton(400, 50)

    DrawText()

    While True
        CheckButtons()
        Delay(10)
    End While

End Method

Method DrawButton(StartX As Integer, StartY As Integer)

    Define RectangleObject As Rectangle

    RectangleObject.Color = Black
    RectangleObject.X = StartX
    RectangleObject.y = StartY
    RectangleObject.Width = 100
    RectangleObject.Height = 50
    RectangleObject.Draw()

    RectangleObject.Color = Gray
    RectangleObject.X = StartX + 1
    RectangleObject.y = StartY + 1
    RectangleObject.Width = 99
```

```
        RectangleObject.Height = 49
        RectangleObject.Filled = True
        RectangleObject.Draw()

    End Method

    Method DrawText()

        Pen(False)
        MoveTo(123, 65)
        Print("Explode")
        MoveTo(275, 65)
        Print("Missile")
        MoveTo(430, 65)
        Print("Stop")

    End Method

    Method CheckButtons()

        If MouseButton = 1 Then
            If MouseY >= 50 And MouseY <=100 Then
                If MouseX >= 100 And MouseX <= 200 Then
                    ExplodeWav.Play()
                End If
                If MouseX >= 250 And MouseX <= 350 Then
                    MissileWav.Play()
                End If
                If MouseX >= 400 And MouseX <= 500 Then
                    ExplodeWav.Stop()
                    MissileWav.Stop()
                End If
            End If
        End If

    End Method

End Program
```

This example begins by defining three global variables representing sound objects. Next, three statements in the `Main()` method load three different wave files, one for each variable. Three separate `Rectangle` objects are then instantiated and then the `Sound` class's `PlayLoop()` method is used to play one of the wave files over and over again as the application's background sound.

Next, three square gray rectangles are drawn on the console window by calling on a custom method named `DrawButton()`. Each of these rectangles represents a button control. Text is then drawn on top of each rectangle by calling on another custom method named `DrawTest()`.

The first two buttons are used to initiate the playback of different wave files. When clicked, the third button pauses playback of the wave files played when the other two buttons are clicked. Both of these wave files are relatively small and it only takes a couple seconds to complete their playback. If the Stop button is clicked when neither of these sound files is being played, nothing happens. However, if either one or both of these sound files are being played, their playback is immediately halted.

A `While…End While` loop is then set up to repeatedly execute a custom method named `CheckButtons()`. Each time it is called, this method checks to see if the user has clicked on the application's three buttons. If this is the case, a check is then made to determine if the pointer was positioned over the first button (e.g., the rectangle labeled `Explode`) and if this is the case, a wave file is played. Similarly, a second check is performed to see if the player clicked on the second button, in which case a different wave file is played. A third check is also performed to see if the player has clicked on the third button, in which case the playback of the wave files associated with each of the other two buttons is haulted.

Figure 9.14 shows an example of how this application looks when executed. A background sound is continuously played and up to two additional wave files can also be simultaneously played by clicking on the first two button controls.

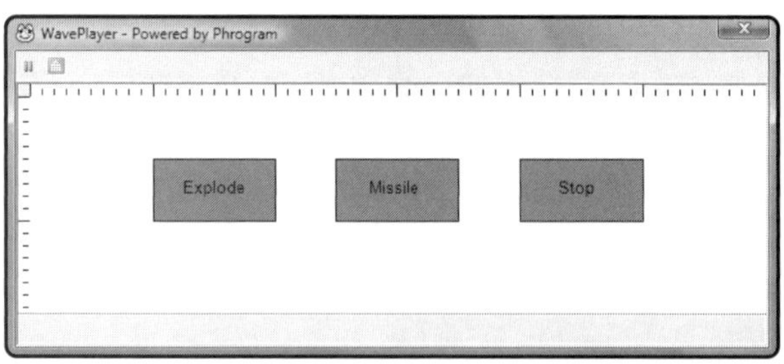


**FIGURE 9.14**

Playing more than one sound at a time.

## Review Questions

1. **What function can you use to retrieve keystrokes from the process queue? What class does this function belong to?**
2. **What function can you use to capture function key keystrokes? What class does this function belong to?**
3. **What is the process queue? What method can you use to clear out the process queue?**
4. **Identify the types of values returned by the following mouse properties:** `MouseButton`, `MouseX`, **and** `MouseY`. **How might you use these properties in a Phrogram application?**
5. **List and define at least three additional** `Mouse` **library properties and provide examples of how they might be used.**
6. **How are modern joysticks connected to computers?**
7. **Is the coordinate system used by joysticks the same as the coordinate system used by the mouse? If not, how do they differ?**
8. **Earlier in this chapter an example was provided that demonstrated the use of the** `Sprite` **class's** `MoveRight`, `MoveLeft`, `Forward`, **and** `Back` **methods. Using the Class Library Browser, look up and define the purpose of each of these methods.**
9. **What type of sound file does Phrogram support?**
10. **List and define four** `Sound` **class methods that support the playback and management of sound files?**

# Back to the PCPong Game

It's time to turn the focus of this chapter back to the development of part 2 of the PCPong game. As stated at the beginning of this chapter, this version of the PCPong game features a number of enhancements, including sound effects, enhanced player control over the movement of the game ball, and improved reporting of player scores. By the time you have finished updating the PCPong game, you will have a full featured computer game that you can really be proud of and brag to your friends about.

## Designing the Game

The development of part 2 of the PCPong game involves the application of a number of changes to the first part of the game, which you created in Chapter 8. Most, though not all, of the application's methods will require some sort of modification. To keep things as simple as possible, the development of part 2 of the PCPong game will still be outlined in a series of steps. Any parts of the program file that contain new or modified code statements will be explained and the new or modified statements will be highlighted in bold to make them stand out. In total, part 2 of the PCPong game will be developed in 15 steps, as outlined here:

1. Download and add graphics files to Program's Images subfolder.
2. Create a new Phrogram program.
3. Document your program file.
4. Define the application's constants, global variables, and sprites.
5. Add controlling logic to the `Main()` method.
6. Add the `ConfigureWindow()` method.
7. Add the `StartANewPoint()` method.
8. Add the `ProcessPlayerMoves()` method.
9. Add the `UpdateBallPosition()` method.
10. Add the `ProcessPlayerMisses()` method.
11. Add the `ManageVerticalCollisions()` method.
12. Add the `ProcessPlayerHits()` method.
13. Add the `DisplayResults()` method.
14. Create the `DisplayScore()` Method.
15. Save and compile your application.

### Step 1: Downloading Graphic Files

Part 2 of the PCPong game includes an enhancement at the end of the game that displays a snazzy graphic image showing a "Game Over!" message. In order to include this new feature in your copy of the game, you must download the PongGameOver.gif file from this book's companion CD and then add it to Phrogram's Images folder.

### Step 2: Creating a New Copy of the PCPong Game

Do not begin work on Part 2 of the PCPong game by making changes to your current copy of the game. Instead, make a backup copy of the game and then make all changes to this new copy of the application. This way, if something goes wrong, you will not break your current copy of the game and, if necessary, you can always create another copy and try again.

### Step 3: Modifying High Level Program Documentation

Once you have created a new copy of your program file to work with and have downloaded the new graphic file needed by the game and placed it in Phrogram's Images folder, it is time to begin modifying the application's source code. Let's begin by modifying the comment statements highlighted here:

```
//Program: PCPong.kpl
//Created: 01/28/2008
//Version: 1.1
//Author: Jerry Lee Ford, Jr.
//Description: This Phrogram game is based on the original Pong
//             computer game that pits two players against one
//             another in a ping-pong style video game.
```

As you can see, these statements reflect a new modification date and version number for this new copy of the PCPong game.

### Step 4: Adding New Global Variables

This new version of the PCPong game requires the definition of a number of new variables representing the new image files used in the application, the inclusion of two Sound objects, which will be used to play sound effects, and a sprite used to display the new "Game Over!" message. To set all this up, you need to add all of the new statements shown next in bold to the beginning of the program file.

```
//Global constant used to store the name of the application
Constant GameTitle As String = "PCPong"

//Global variables used throughout the game
Define PongBall As String = "BlueBall.png"      //Ball
Define PlayerPaddle As String = "PongPaddle.gif"    //Paddle
Define GameOverImage As String = "PongGameOver.gif" //Game ending graphic

//Define variables that control the speed and direction of the ball
Define MoveX As Integer
Define MoveY As Integer

//Define global variables in which to store player scores
Define Player1Score As Integer
Define Player2Score As Integer

//Specify the number of points required to win the game
Define WinningScore As Integer = 21

//Define a variable that will be used to control the game's primary loop
Define GameOver As Boolean = False
```

```
//Definition of sprite objects used to play the game
Define Player1Paddle As Sprite   //Player 1's paddle
Define Player2Paddle As Sprite   //Player 2's paddle
Define GameBall As Sprite          //The game ball
Define GameOverMsg As Sprite        //Game ending graphic message

//Define sound objects to be used to play sound effects
Define CollisionSound As Sound
Define ScorePointSound As Sound
```

### Step 5: Reviewing the Main() Method

Although many of its methods require extensive modification, the overall controlling logic outlined in the game's `Main()` method remains unchanged except for the addition of statements required to load the game sound effect wave file, as shown below in bold:

```
//This method is responsible for the overall execution of the game
Method Main()

    //Define a variable to be used to keep track of how long a point
    //has lasted
    Define Duration As Integer

    //Define a variable to
    Define LastCheck As Integer

    //Define a Timer object to be used to control the pace of the game
    Define GameTimer As Timer

    //Load the sound files to be used to play sound effects
    CollisionSound.LoadFile("TargetLock.wav")
    ScorePointSound.LoadFile("PulseWave.wav")

    //Display the game's welcome message and explain how to view
    //instructions
    Alert("Welcome to " + GameTitle + "!", GameTitle)

    ConfigureWindow() //This method sets the console window's default
                      //settings
```

```
GameTimer.Start() //Turn on the game's Timer object

StartANewPoint() //Call method in order to start the game's first point

While GameOver = False  //This loop controls overall game play

    //Keep track of how long the game has been running
    Duration = TickCount()

    //Ensure 30/1000 of a second has passed before doing anything
    If Duration - LastCheck > 30 Then

        ProcessPlayerMoves()  //Call on the method that processes
                              //player moves

        UpdateBallPosition()  //Call on the method that moves the ball

        ProcessPlayerMisses() //Call on the method that handles player
                              //misses

        //Perform the following methods as long as neither player has
        //earned 21 points
        If GameOver = False Then

            //Call on the method that handles collisions with the top
            //and bottom of the screen
            ManageVerticalCollisions()

            //Call on the method that handles collisions with player
            //paddles
            ProcessPlayerHits()

        End If

        LastCheck = Duration  //Reset the timer in order to start a new
                              //30 second count

    End If
```

```
    End While

    //The game is over. It is time to display the final result.
    DisplayResults()

End Method
```

## Step 6: Reviewing the ConfigureWindow() Method

The code statements that make up the `ConfigureWindow()` method, which is responsible for configuring the application's console window attributes, remain unchanged in this version of the PCPong game.

```
//This method configures Window attributes
Method ConfigureWindow()

    SetScreenSize(640, 480)    //Set the screen size to 640x480 pixels
    SetWindowTitle(GameTitle)  //Display the name of the game in the
                               //Window's titlebar
    Color(White)    //Set the console window's background color to white

End Method
```

## Step 7: Updating the StartANewPoint() Method

Changes made to the `StartANewPoint()` method are outlined next in bold print. The first statement shown in bold calls on the `DisplayScore()` method, which is a new method that you will add to the program file later in Step 13, to update the display of player scores in the console window's status bar. This method call replaces a call to the `Alert()` method, which was used in part 1 of the PCPong game to display player scores in a popup dialog window.

```
//This method initiates the start of a new point
Method StartANewPoint()

    DisplayScore()  //Call on the method that displays player scores

    //Load graphics representing the sprites for player paddles and
    //the ball
    Player1Paddle.Load(PlayerPaddle)
    Player2Paddle.Load(PlayerPaddle)
    GameBall.Load(PongBall)
```

```
    //Set the starting point on the X-axis for both players' paddles
    Player1Paddle.X = 20
    Player2Paddle.X = 610

    //Set the starting point on the Y-axis for both players' paddles
    Player1Paddle.Y = ScreenHeight() / 2 - 50
    Player2Paddle.Y = ScreenHeight() / 2 - 50

    //Start the GameBall off in the middle of the screen
    GameBall.X = ScreenWidth() / 2 - 10
    GameBall.Y = ScreenHeight() / 2 - 10

    //Display players' paddles and the ball
    Player1Paddle.Show()
    Player2Paddle.Show()
    GameBall.Show()

    //Pause For one second to give both players time to get ready
    Delay(1000)

    //Begin game play by moving the ball between 4 - 6 pixels on the X-axis
    MoveX = Random(5, 7)

    //Move the ball between 2 to 5 pixels on the Y-axis
    MoveY = Random(2, 5)

    //By default the ball always begins by moving down and to the right.
    //The following code blocks randomly override this behavior
    If Random(0, 1) = 0 Then  //Reverse direction if the random number = 0
        MoveX *= -1  //Reverse direction
    End If

    //Set the initial direction of the ball on the Y-axis
    If Random(0, 1) = 0 Then  //Reverse direction if the random number = 0
        MoveY *= -1  //Reverse direction
    End If

End Method
```

The last set of changes to be made to the `StartANewPoint()` method, which is located at the end of the method, ensures that the game ball moves in a random direction at the start of each new point. By default, the game ball is set to move down and to the left. Now, two `If…Then` code blocks have been added that randomly modify the game ball's direction.

### Step 8: Reviewing the ProcessPlayerMoves() Method

The code statements that make up the `ProcessPlayerMoves()` method, which is responsible for controlling the movement of player paddles, remain unchanged in this version of the PCPong game.

```
//This method controls the movement of the game paddles
Method ProcessPlayerMoves()

    //Move Player 1's paddle up when the Shift key is pressed
    If IsKeyDown("Shift") Then
        //Do not let the paddle go off the top of the console window
        If Player1Paddle.Y > 1 Then
            //Prepare to move the paddle up by 8 pixels on the Y-axis
            Player1Paddle.Y -= 8  //The higher the number the faster
                                  //the paddle moves
         End If
    End If

    //Move Player 1's paddle down when the Control key is pressed
    If IsKeyDown("Control") Then
        //Do not let the paddle go off the bottom of the console window
        If Player1Paddle.Y < (ScreenHeight() - Player1Paddle.Height) Then
            //Prepare to move the paddle down by 8 pixels on the Y-axis
            Player1Paddle.Y += 8  //The higher the number the faster
                                  //the paddle moves
        End If
    End If

    //Move Player 2's paddle up when the Up key is pressed
    If IsKeyDown("Up") Then
        //Do not let the paddle go off the top of the console window
        If Player2Paddle.Y > 1 Then
            //Prepare to move the paddle up by 8 pixels on the Y-axis
            Player2Paddle.Y -= 8  //The higher the number the faster
```

```
                                    //the paddle moves

        End If
    End If

    //Move Player 2's paddle down when the Down key is pressed
    If IsKeyDown("Down") Then
        If Player2Paddle.Y < (ScreenHeight() - Player2Paddle.Height) Then
            //Prepare to move the paddle down by 8 pixels along the Y-axis
            Player2Paddle.Y += 8    //The higher the number the faster
                                    //the paddle moves
        End If
    End If

    //Move player paddles as instructed by the player to their new
    //coordinates
    Player1Paddle.MoveTo(Player1Paddle.X, Player1Paddle.Y)
    Player2Paddle.MoveTo(Player2Paddle.X, Player2Paddle.Y)

End Method
```

### Step 9: Reviewing the UpdateBallPosition() Method

The code statements that make up the `ProcessPlayerMoves()` method, which is responsible for moving the ball around the console window, remain unchanged in this version of the PCPong game.

```
//This method is responsible for moving the ball around the console window
Method UpdateBallPosition()

    GameBall.X += MoveX  //Adjust the ball's location on the X-axis
    GameBall.Y += MoveY  //Adjust the ball's location on the Y-axis

    GameBall.Show()      //Display the ball at its new location

End Method
```

### Step 10: Modifying the ProcessPlayerMisses() Method

The code statements that make up the `ProcessPlayerMisses()` method, shown next, remain largely unchanged except for the addition of two statements that play a sound effect indicating that one of the players has scored a point.

```
//This method determines when points are scored
Method ProcessPlayerMisses()

  //Player 2 loses the point if the ball reaches the right edge of
  //the window
  If GameBall.X > ScreenWidth() - 20 Then

    Player1Score += 1  //Increment Player 1's score by one point

    //Check to see if Player 1 has won the game
    If Player1score = WinningScore Then
      GameOver = True
    End If

    ScorePointSound.Play() //Play a sound indicating impact with the
                           //side of the screen or a paddle
    GameBall.Unload()    //Unload the game ball

    If GameOver = False Then  //If the game is not over, start a
                              //new point
      StartANewPoint()
    End If

  Else
    //Player 1 loses the point if the ball reaches the left edge of
    //the window
    If GameBall.X < 0 Then

      Player2Score += 1  //Increment Player 2's score by one point

      //Check to see if Player 1 has won the game
      If Player2Score = WinningScore Then
        GameOver = True
      End If

      ScorePointSound.Play() //Play a sound indicating impact with
                             //the side of the screen or a paddle
```

```
            GameBall.Unload()  //Unload the game ball
            If GameOver = False Then  //If the game is not over, start
                                      //a new point
                StartANewPoint()
            End If

        End If
    End If

End Method
```

## Step 11: Updating the ManageVerticalCollisions() Method

The code statements that make up the `ManageVerticalCollisions()` method have been modified to include two new statements that play a sound effect indicating when the game ball collides with the top or bottom of the console window.

```
//This method deflects the ball when it hits the top or bottom of
//the window
Method ManageVerticalCollisions()

    //Detect the ball when it collides with the bottom of the screen
    If GameBall.Y > (ScreenHeight() - 20) Then
        MoveY = MoveY * -1     //Reverse the ball's direction on the Y-axis
        CollisionSound.Play()  //Play a sound indicating a deflection
    Else  //Detect the ball when it collides with the top of the screen
        If GameBall.Y < 10 Then
            MoveY = MoveY * -1 //Reverse the ball's direction on the Y-axis
            CollisionSound.Play()  //Play a sound indicating a deflection
        End If
    End If

End Method
```

## Step 12: Updating the ProcessPlayerHits() Method

Three sets of code modifications are required in the `ProcessPlayerHits()` method. The first change is the playing of a wave file whenever one of the players hits the game ball with a paddle.

The next two sets of changes are nearly identical and are responsible for fine tuning player control of the game ball's movement whenever it is struck by a paddle. The first of these sets of statements compares the location of the game ball's `Y` coordinate to see if it made contact with the upper portion of Player 1's paddle (e.g., the first 20 pixels) and if it has, the game ball is deflected back in the general direction that it came from. If this is not the case then a second check is made to see if the game ball has collided with the bottom of Player 1's paddle (e.g., the last 20 pixels) and modifies the game ball's direction on the Y-axis accordingly.

If, however, the game ball hits any other part of Player 1's paddle, the direction that the game ball is moved on the Y-axis is reversed. The overall result of these changes is that by hitting the game ball with the top or bottom edge of the of the paddle, Player 1 can attempt to apply a little "English," sending the game ball back in the same direction that it came from (as opposed to always deflecting it away at a randomly opposing angle). The last set of statements manages the game ball's movement when hit by Player 2's paddle, allowing Player 2 to apply a little "English" as well.

```
//This method deflects the ball whenever it collides with a paddle
Method ProcessPlayerHits()

    //Look for a collision between the ball and one of the paddles
    If GameBall.Intersects(Player1Paddle) Or
           GameBall.Intersects(Player2Paddle) Then

        CollisionSound.Play()  //Play a sound indicating a deflection
                               //with a paddle

        //Let's speed things up a bit every time the ball hits a paddle
        If MoveX > 0 Then
            MoveX += 1   //Speed up the movement of the ball on the X-axis
        End If

        MoveX *= -1  //Reverse the direction of the ball on the X-axis

        //Manage collision with Player 1's paddle
        If GameBall.Intersects(Player1Paddle) Then

            //If the ball hits the upper end of the paddle, reverse its
            //direction on the Y-axis
            If GameBall.Y < Player1Paddle.Y + 20 Then
```

```
        MoveY = Random(-4, 2)
    //If the ball hits the lower end of the paddle, reverse
    //its direction //on the Y-axis
    Else If GameBall.Y > Player1Paddle.Y + 80 Then
        MoveY = Random(2, 4)
    //If the ball hits the middle of the paddle, make a slight
    //change of the ball's direction On the Y-axis
    Else
        MoveY -= Random(0, 2)
    End If

End If

//Manage collision with Player 2's paddle
If GameBall.Intersects(Player2Paddle) Then

    //If the ball hits the upper end of the paddle, reverse its
    //direction  on the Y-axis
    If GameBall.Y < Player2Paddle.Y + 20 Then
        MoveY = Random(-4, 2)
    //If the ball hits the lower end of the paddle, reverse its
    //direction on the Y-axis
    Else If GameBall.Y > Player2Paddle.Y + 80 Then
        MoveY = Random(2, 4)
    //If the ball hits the middle of the paddle, make a slight
    //change of the ball's direction on the Y-axis
    Else
        MoveY -= Random(0, 2)
    End If

End If

GameBall.X += MoveX  //Adjust the ball's location on the X-axis
GameBall.Y += MoveY  //Adjust the ball's location on the Y-axis

//Move the ball to the specified set of coordinates
GameBall.MoveTo(GameBall.X, GameBall.Y)
```

```
    End If

End Method
```

### Step 13: Updating the DisplayResults() Method

The code statements that make up the `DisplayResults()` method have undergone considerable change, as shown next. Instead of displaying player scores in a popup dialog window that interrupts the flow of the game, the method now calls on the `DisplayScore()` method to handle the display of player scores. In addition, statements have been added to the end of the method to load and then show a sprite that displays an end of game message.

```
//This method does a little clean up and notifies the player when the end
//of the game is reached
Method DisplayResults()

    DisplayScore()  //Call on the method that displays player scores

    //The game has ended so remove both paddles from the screen
    Player1Paddle.Hide()
    Player2paddle.Hide()

    //Load the graphic message displayed at the end of the game
    GameOverMsg.Load(GameOverImage)

    //Center the display of the graphic image
    GameOverMsg.MoveTo(ScreenWidth() / 2 - 122, ScreenHeight() / 2 - 45)

    //Display the graphic image
    GameOverMsg.Show()

End Method
```

### Step 14: Creating the DisplayScore() Method

The last of the modifications to be made to the PCPong game occur in the form of a new method named `DisplayScore()` that when called displays player scores at the bottom of the console window in its status bar. The statements that make up this method are shown next and should be added to the end of the program's code file.

```
//This method displays the current scores in the console window
```

```
//status bar
Method DisplayScore()

    //Define method variable used to display player scores in the
    //status bar
    Define ScoreString As String

    //Format the text string showing player scores
    ScoreString = "     Player 1: " + Player1Score + "                    "
    ScoreString = ScoreString + "                                         "
    ScoreString = ScoreString + "                                         "
    ScoreString = ScoreString + "                                         "
    ScoreString = ScoreString + "                                         "
    ScoreString = ScoreString + "       Player 2: " + Player2Score

    //Display the formatted string in the status bar
    Status(ScoreString)

End Method
```

Take note of the manner in which the string stored in the `ScoreString` variable is formatted. Larger amounts of blank space are repeatedly concatenated to the end of the variable's value to ensure that Player 2's score is displayed on the right-hand side of the status bar.

### Step 15: Saving and Compiling Your Application

At this point you should have all the instructions you need to wrap up work on the PCPong game. If you have not done so yet, save your work by clicking on the Save All command located on the File menu. Check to see if Phrogram is reporting any syntax errors and track down and fix any errors that may be reported.

## The Final Result

That's it. Your copy of the PCPong game should be ready for testing and should execute as described at the beginning of this chapter. If you experience any problems, use the error messages that are displayed to track down and fix any typos or mistakes you may have accidentally made. Of course, you can always download a copy of the source code for this application from the book's companion CD.

## Summary

In this chapter you learned the ins and outs of interactively collecting user input. Specifically, you learned how to work with methods and functions provided by the `Keyboard` library to collect non-blocking input as well as methods and functions provided by the `Mouse` library that allow you to track mouse location and button clicks. You also learned how to integrate joystick support into your Phrogram games. On top of all this, you learned how to liven up your applications through the addition of sound effects.

Before you move on to Chapter 10, "Debugging Your Applications," consider spending a little time improving the PCPong game by addressing the following list of challenges.

### Challenges

1. **Using the information presented in this chapter for incorporating joystick support into Phrogram applications, modify the PCPong game to check for the presence of multiple joysticks and when found, give the players the option of playing the game using either the keyboard or joystick.**
2. **Modify the game so that it displays an additional message at the end of the game allowing the players to start a new game by pressing the F3 key and then modify the game to allow the players to play as many games as they want.**
3. **Create a distribution package for your new game and share with a few friends, asking them to provide you with feedback.**

CHAPTER 10

# Debugging Your Applications

Up to this point in the book you have been advised to double check your typing whenever you have run into problems working on any of the game projects. In the event that this did not solve your problem, you were advised to do your best to discern the meaning of any error messages that were displayed and if all else failed, to download a copy of the book's source code for each game project to have something to compare your work against. The goal of this chapter is to provide you with more assistance when it comes to understanding, tracking down, and fixing application errors. You will also receive tips to prevent errors from occurring in the first place. On top of all this, you will be guided through the development of the book's final game project, the Tic-Tac-Toe game.

Specifically, you will learn how to:

- Deal with syntax, logical, and run-time errors
- Work with Phrogram's debugger
- Set and clear breakpoints
- Monitor variable values during program execution
- Exercise detailed control over program statement execution

## Project Preview: The Tic-Tac-Toe Game

This book's final application project is the development of the Tic-Tac-Toe game. This implementation of Tic-Toe-Toe is a two-player version. The game is played using the mouse, with both players taking turns under the direction of the game. Figure 10.1 shows what the game board looks like when the game is first started. As you can see, it consists of nine squares organized by four lines drawn vertically and horizontally across the console window.

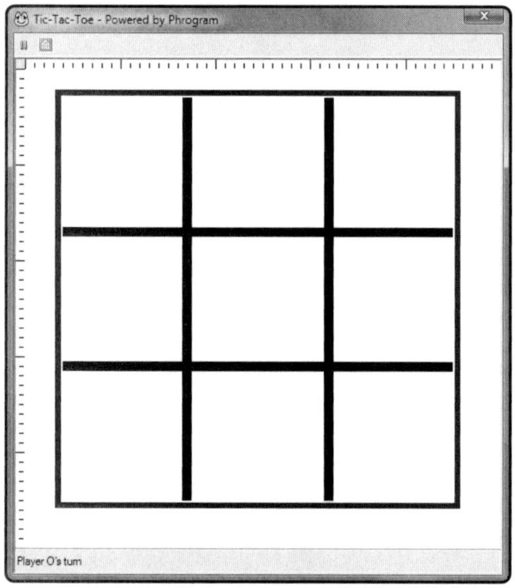


**Figure 10.1**

The Tic-Tac-Toe game board consists of nine squares organized into three columns with three rows.

To play the game, players click on the game board squares. When a player clicks on a square, that player's assigned letter is displayed in the square. Player X always goes first. To select a square the square must be blank. Attempts to select a square that has already been assigned are ignored.

As shown in Figure 10.2, the game automatically keeps track of whose turn it is and displays a text message at the bottom of the console window to ensure that players know when to switch turns. Game play ends when one of the players wins by lining up three game board squares in a row, vertically, horizontally, or diagonally. Game play may also end with a tie, in which case all nine game board squares are selected without either planner having managed to line up three in a row.

Figure 10.3 shows an example of the popup dialog window that is displayed at the end of each game. In this example, Player O has won the game.

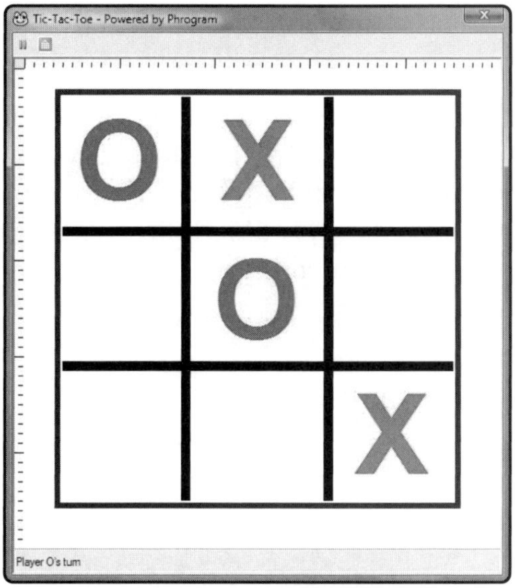


**Figure 10.2**

Players move by clicking on an open square.

**Figure 10.3**

The game monitors player moves and automatically determines when someone has won.

Upon dismissing this popup dialog window by clicking on its OK button, the popup dialog window shown in Figure 10.4 displays. The players are allowed to play as many games as they want.

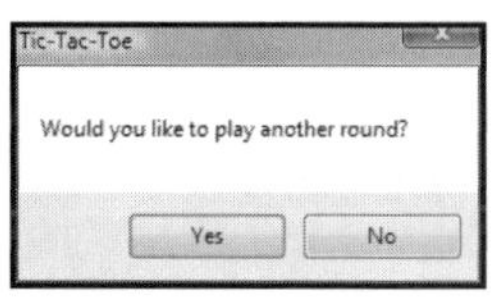


**Figure 10.4**

Players are prompted to play again at the end of each game.

## Coping with Application Errors

When it comes to application development, errors are inevitable. Even the most talented and experienced programmers have to deal with errors all of the time. It is therefore important that you learn how to deal with them, which is the purpose of this chapter. Some errors may cause unexpected results, while other application errors may force the immediate termination of a program's execution.

Application errors are often referred to as bugs and your job as a programmer is to seek out and exterminate all the bugs from your applications. Of course, the best way of dealing with program errors is to take steps to prevent them from occurring in the first place. Start the development of new Phrogram applications by spending a little time planning the steps involved in developing new programs. You might consider creating a flowchart or writing a pseudo code outline of the logic involved.

Make sure that you write your program code in a series of steps, thoroughly testing as you go. Organize your program code into methods and functions to break your application into manageable chucks, each of which performs a specific tasks. As you become more comfortable with OOP, begin developing your own custom classes and use them to create objects that can then be used to organize and control the execution of application functionality.

When testing your application, make sure that you test using both good and bad data to ensure that your application properly handles it and add additional programming logic where necessary to manage any unhandled errors. In addition to following all of these tips, make sure that you also follow each of the following good programming practices.

- Make liberal use of comments to thoroughly document code statements in your program files.
- Develop clear instructions for the proper operation of your applications and provide them to your users.
- Implement a consistent naming standard for all your variables, constants, arrays, structures, methods, functions, and classes and adhere to it at all times.

## Three Basic Types of Errors

Phrogram, like all programming languages, is subject to three basic types of errors, as listed here.

- Syntax errors
- Logical errors
- Run-time errors

Each of these types of errors is examined in detail in the sections that follow. In addition, to see examples of each of these types of errors and learn what makes these types of errors distinct from one another, you will receive helpful advice on how to deal with them when they occur.

## Tracking Down Syntax Errors

The most common type of error that you are going to run into is syntax errors. A *syntax error* is an error that occurs when you fail to follow Phrogram's syntax requirements when formulating the code statements that make up your applications. Perhaps the biggest cause of syntax errors is simply typing mistakes. For example, suppose that you forgot to supply the required closing right parenthesis when working with the `Print()` method, as demonstrated here:

```
Print("Hello World!"
```

Phrogram will not compile an application if it contains any syntax errors. If you attempt to compile an application that contains a syntax error, Phrogram will display an error message, as demonstrated in Figure 10.5.

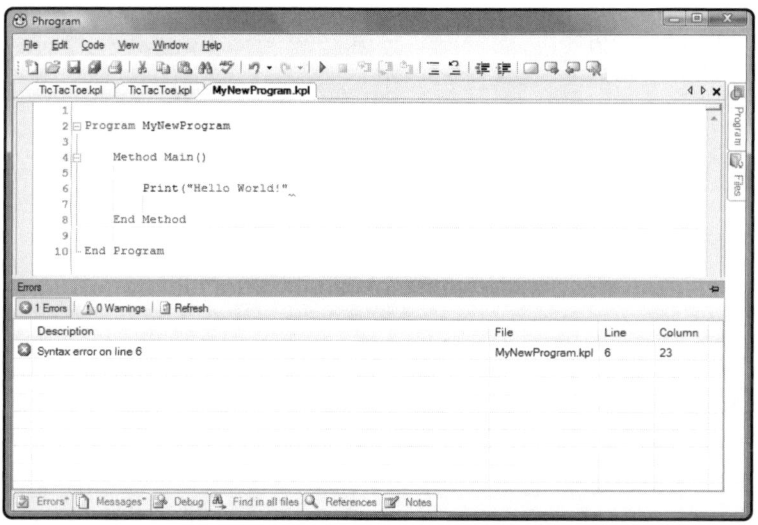


**FIGURE 10.5**

A syntax error generated because of an improperly formatted statement.

Of course, if you are in the habit of checking the Errors window while you are working, you'll see a running list of any syntax errors that Phrogram has identified and can thus fix them before trying to compile your applications. Phrogram also identifies syntax errors by underlining them with a red squiggly line, helping you to quickly spot and fix them as you are keying in your application's statements.

In addition to typos, syntax errors will occur if you fail to precisely follow a method or function's syntax, as outlined in Phrogram's Class Library Browser window. Phrogram's syntax error messages provide an explanation of the error and the line number in which the error was detected. Unfortunately, as you have no doubt learned, some of Phrogram's syntax error messages are a little cryptic and take some getting used to.

> **TRICK** Typically, a syntax error message tells you everything you need to know to track down and eliminate a syntax error. However, if you are unable to figure out what's wrong with a given statement, open the Class Library Browser window and look up the syntax of the function or method with which you are working to verify the proper use of its syntax.

## Fixing Logical Errors

Another type of error that all computer applications are subject to is logical errors. A *logical error* is an error that occurs when the programmer implements faulty programming logic that does not perform the desired task. Logical errors can be all too easily made while at the same time being extremely difficult to track down and fix. As an example of how easy it is to accidentally set up a logical error, consider the following example.

```
Define Player1Score As Integer = 10
Define Player2Score As Integer = 10
Define AverageScore As Decimal

AverageScore = (Player1Score + Player2Score ) * 2

Print("The average score for both players is " + AverageScore)
```

The intent of this example is to calculate the average of two players' scores. However, instead of dividing the combined total of the two players' scores by two, this value is multiplying by two, yielding a useless result. The problem in dealing with logical errors is that they do not prevent your applications from compiling and you do not know that they are present until you realize that the application is misbehaving in some manner. The best way to track down and fix logical errors is through careful and extensive testing that includes the validation of application output.

## Eliminating Run-time Errors

A third type of error that you need to be aware of is run-time errors. Run-time errors occur when applications attempt to perform an illegal action of some type. For example, a run-time error will occur if an application attempts to load a sound or graphic file that cannot be found. If this happens, Phrogram will display an error message as demonstrated in Figure 10.6, which most users will not understand or be able to do anything about and the application will terminate. Obviously, the last thing you want is to let your users encounter this type of problem when running one of your applications.

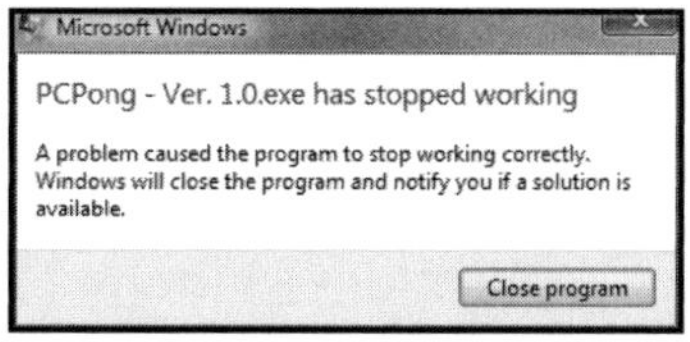


**FIGURE 10.6**

An error produced when a stand-alone copy of a Phrogram application experiences a run-time error.

The problem with run-time errors is that Phrogram's compiler cannot detect them. Run-time errors are often buried deep inside methods and functions and unless you thoroughly test every part of your application, run-time errors can easily slip by you unnoticed. Often, it helps to have others assist in testing your applications. The more people you get to help you test, the better. The following statement demonstrates how easy it is to create a run-time error.

```
Define X As Integer
X = 10 / 0
```

Division by zero is illegal, but Phrogram's compiler will not be able to detect this error. As a result, a run-time error will occur. If an application containing this statement is executed from within the Program IDE, the error message shown in Figure 10.7 will be displayed. As you can see, in addition to the run-time error message, Phrogram also highlights the statements where the errors occurred in the code editor.

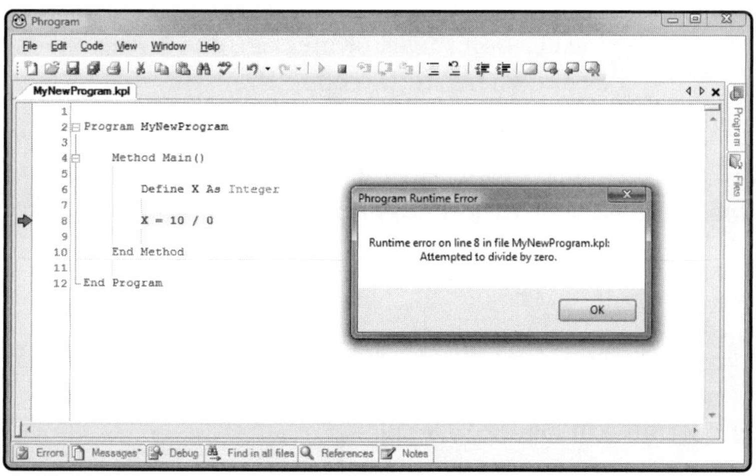


**FIGURE 10.7**

Attempting to divide a number by zero generates a run-time error.

Run-time errors occur for all kinds of reasons, such as faulty data and invalid user input. To overcome these types of errors, you can add data and input validation logic to your applications. A well-worded custom error message displayed in a popup dialog window, providing the user with instruction on the proper format to use when keying input can also go a long way towards helping to eliminate run-time errors.

No application is perfect and with hard drive crashes, unpredictable users, and a host of other possible problems, you can never make your applications a hundred percent error proof. Still, to keep your hard-earned reputation as an expert programmer intact, you will want to take every possible precaution to make your applications as reliable as possible.

FIND IT ONLINE

Throughout this book, you have learned how to create a number of computer games culminating in games like PCPong and Rock, Paper, Scissors. Phrogram also comes equipped with the source code for a number of other great games. For example, you can use the Files Explorer window to look in My programs\games and toys (2D) where you will find the source code for games like Asteroids, KPLong3D, and Maze. In addition to these games, you can download the source code for a number of computer games from http://phrogram.com/files/. Among the games that you will find are Billiards, Checkers, Missile Command, Pinball, Tetris, and Minesweeper.

## Examining Errors Reported by Phrogram

When run from within the Phrogram IDE, error messages provide information that you can use to track down and find errors. All error messages display an explanation of the error that has occurred. Error messages also list the line number where the error was discovered. By correlating this reported line number with the line number displayed on the right-hand side of the Phrogram code editor window, you can track down the statement where the error was detected. Alternatively, you can double click on the error message and Phrogram will jump to and display the corresponding code statement in the code editor window.

Phrogram makes error information available for viewing in the Errors window, which by default is displayed in the Message pane located at the bottom of the Phrogram IDE. For example, suppose that you were working with an application that contains the following statement.

```
Alrt("Hello World!", "Demo Program")
```

This statement contains a syntax error. Specifically, `Alert()` has been mistyped as `Alrt()`. Phrogram automatically reports on the error by displaying the following error message in the Errors window, as demonstrated in Figure 10.8.

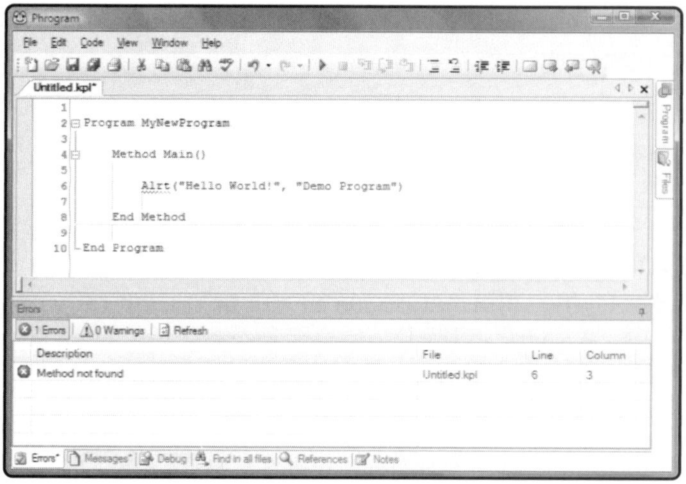

**FIGURE 10.8**

Error messages are visible in the Errors window.

Phrogram also identifies syntax errors by underlining any syntax that it does not understand with a red squiggly line. If you place the pointer of an error in the IDE, Phrogram displays error information in a popup dialog window, as demonstrated in Figure 10.9.

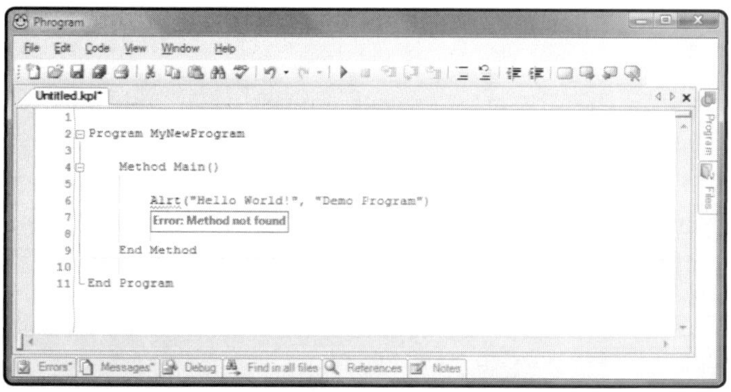

**FIGURE 10.9**

If you place the pointer of an error in the IDE, Phrogram displays error information in a popup dialog window.

## KEEPING A WATCHFUL EYE ON APPLICATION EXECUTION

When developing and testing an application using the Phrogram IDE, error messages help you to quickly home in on and locate statements containing errors. However, logical errors can be a lot more difficult to track down. For example, if you have an application that is incorrectly reporting on the player's score and the score is modified throughout the program in a number of different places, it can sometimes be challenging to determine in which of the locations the problem lies. However, by strategically inserting statements that display the value of the variable used to store the player's score at different locations within the program file, you can keep an eye on what is going on and determine the part of the program file where the variable's value is being incorrectly set.

Similarly, if you suspect that the logical execution within a program file may not be occurring in the order you expect, you can strategically add statements throughout the program file that let you know when different parts of the program are executing.

## Displaying Tracking Information

One quick and easy way of displaying information about the operation of your Phrogram applications is by using the `Alert()` method in statements inserted at key locations within your program file. This will allow you to keep abreast of when certain events occur, such as when methods or functions are executed, as demonstrated in the following example.

```
Alert("Method - ProcessPlayerMoves() now executing", "Debug Message")
```

By placing this statement at the beginning of the `ProcessPlayerMoves()` method, you can alert yourself whenever this method is executed. Placing similar statements in all of the other methods and functions in your applications, you can easily monitor the logical flow of your application as it executes. By placing statements similar to the following statement in your Phrogram applications, you can also monitor the value of key variables.

```
Alert("Variable - PlayerOneScore = " + PlayerOneScore, " Debug Message ")
```

Of course, the problem with using the `Alert()` method as previously demonstrated, is that your program's execution is blocked each time the method executes, requiring you to click on the OK button of the popup dialog window that is generated to continue. A less intrusive way of accomplishing the same thing is to substitute the `Status()` method in place of the `Alert()` method, as demonstrated here:

```
//Monitoring execution flow
Status("Method - ProcessPlayerMoves() now executing")

//Monitoring variable value
Status("Variable - PlayerOneScore = " + PlayerOneScore)
```

## Generating Trace Message Output

Another option for keeping an eye on the logical execution of Phrogram applications and variable values is through the use of the `Shell` library's `Trace()` method. This method displays text messages in the Messages window. This method has the following syntax.

```
Trace(Text)
```

*Text* represents the text string that is to be displayed in the Messages window.

The advantage of using this option over the `Alert()` and `Status()` method is that a history of output messages remains available, allowing you to scroll through it to study and evaluate the application's execution. For example, the following statement could be used to write a text string to the Messages window when a method named `ProcessPlayerMoves()` is executed. Figure 10.10 shows how this message looks once written to the Messages window.

```
Trace("Method - ProcessPlayerMoves() now executing")
```

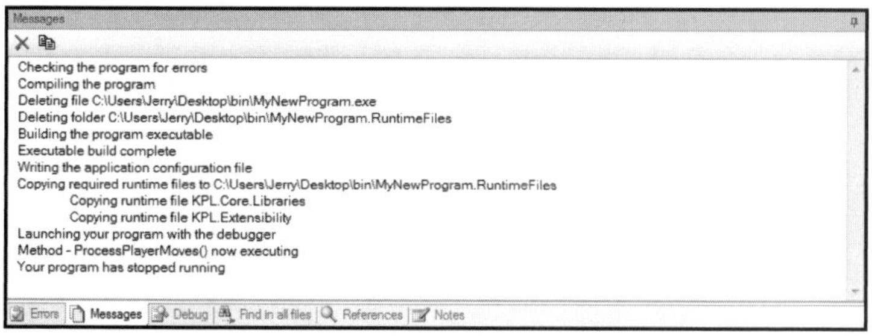


**FIGURE 10.10**

Writing trace messages to the Messages window.

# DEBUGGING YOUR PHROGRAM APPLICATIONS

For some run-time errors, using the debugging techniques previously discussed in this chapter can be time-consuming and laborious. In especially lengthy and complex applications, these debugging techniques may prove completely inadequate. Fortunately, Phrogram comes equipped with a built-in debugger that you can use in these situations to track down and fix even the most difficult to find program bugs.

A *debugger* is a software program you can use to run a computer program in a special mode that allows you to take complete control over the program's execution. A debugger also provides the ability to examine variable values and to keep an eye on them as your program executes. Using Phrogram's debugger, you can literally control the execution of every statement in your application to validate the order in which statements are being processed, while at the same time pausing program execution whenever necessary to keep an eye on variable values to ensure that they are being properly set.

## Pausing Application Execution with Breakpoints

To use Phrogram's debugger, you first need to set breakpoints inside your program file, identifying points at which the debugger should pause when executing the application and then turn control over to you. A *breakpoint* is a line marker that when reached instructs the debugger to pause application execution and await your instruction.

> **HINT** Breakpoints do not have any effect on the execution of the stand-alone version of your applications. Breakpoints only affect the execution of your application when it is executed within the Phrogram IDE.

To set a breakpoint within a program file, use your mouse to click the left-hand column in the code editor window just to the left of the statement at which you want Phrogram to pause, as demonstrated in Figure 10.11. As you can see, in addition to highlighting the statement at which the breakpoint has been set, Phrogram also places a red dot just to the left of the statement.

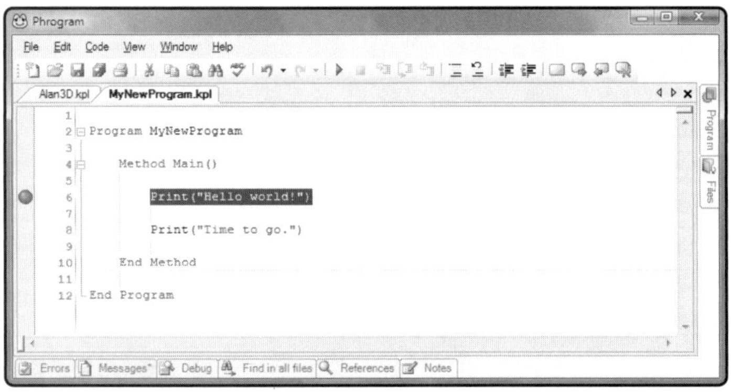


**FIGURE 10.11**

A red dot indicates when a breakpoint has been set.

There is no limit to the number of breakpoints that you can set in a program file. Once set, a breakpoint can be removed by clicking on its associated red dot.

> **HINT** The View menu provides access to a number of commands that affect breakpoints. These commands include Toggle Bookmark, Go to Next Bookmark, Go to Previous Bookmark, and Remove All Bookmarks.

## Monitoring Variable Values

If you think that something is going wrong with the way variable values are being managed within an application, you can use the Debug window, as demonstrated in Figure 10.12, to keep an eye on variable values whenever you pause the application's execution in the debugger.

As Figure 10.12 shows, Phrogram places a yellow arrow on top of the statement at which Phrogram pauses execution, identifying the next statement to be executed. When paused, the name, value, and data type of every variable that Phrogram currently knows about in your application is displayed. If your application has more variables than can be displayed at one time, you can scroll down to view the others.

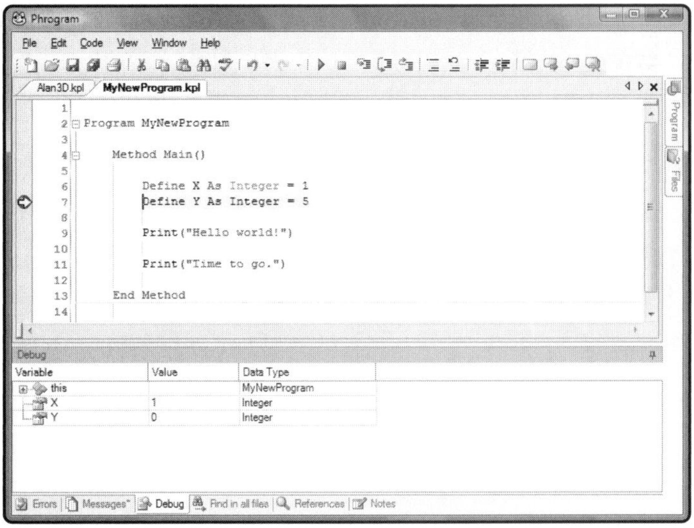


**FIGURE 10.12**

Once paused, you can use the Debug window to examine the value assigned to any application variables.

HINT This is a special type of Phrogram value that represents the program itself.

## Taking Control of Statement Execution

Once paused as a breakpoint, you can instruct Phrogram how to proceed by clicking on one of three buttons located on the Phrogram IDE toolbar, as depicted in Figure 10.13.

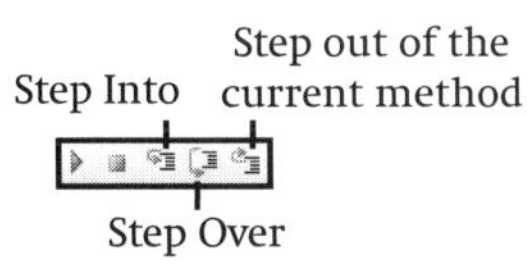


**FIGURE 10.13**

The Phrogram IDE's debug control buttons.

Ordinarily, these three debug buttons are disabled and grayed out so that you cannot access them. However, they are automatically enabled whenever a breakpoint is processed. The functionality provided by each of the buttons is outlined here:

- **Step Into.** Instructs Phrogram to execute the next program statement. If that statement is a function or a method, Phrogram is instructed to pause on the first statement within the method or procedure and to wait for further instruction.
- **Step Over.** Instructs Phrogram to process any remaining statements without pausing (unless another breakpoint is found). This command also instructs Phrogram to enter and process the code statements located in methods and functions without pausing.

- **Step out of the current method.** When inside a method or function, this command instructs Phrogram to execute any statements remaining in the method or function and then to pause program execution at the first statement following the method or function.

## A Debugging Demo

To help you gain a better appreciation of how to work with Phrogram's debugger, let's step through a quick debugging exercise. In this exercise, you will work with a small Phrogram program that is supposed to count from 1 to 10. To get started, create a new Phrogram application as shown here:

```
Program MyNewProgram

    Method Main()

        Define I As Integer
        Define KeepRunning As Boolean = True

        SetScreenSize (600, 100)
        SetConsoleFont("Arial", 18)

        ConsoleWriteLine("")
        ConsoleWrite("Watch me count to 10.   ")

        While KeepRunning = True

            ConsoleWrite("  " + I)

            If I = 10 Then
                KeepRunning = False
            End If

            Delay(500)

        End While

    End Method

End Program
```

Once you have typed in this example, go ahead and run it. It shouldn't take long to realize that the program is not operating like it is supposed to. Instead of counting to 10, an endless series of zeros is being displayed on the console window. Obviously something is amiss. Press the Stop the running program button to terminate the program's execution.

Let's run the program using Phrogram debugger to figure out what is going on here. Let's begin by first setting a breakpoint on the line that contains the opening statement for the loop's `While...End While` loop. Once set, go ahead and click on the Run the program button on the Phrogram IDE's toolbar.

In response, the application will begin running and its application window will display, although no text is displayed at this point. Within the IDE, the line containing the breakpoint should be highlighted in red.

Next, click on the Debug tab at the bottom of the console window to display the Debug window in the Messages pane. A list of the program's variables should be visible. The value of `I` should be set to `0` and the value of `KeepRunning` should be set to `True`.

Now that we know what the application's initial variable values are being set to, click on the Step Into button. The first statement in the loop should not be highlighted. Click on the Step Into button five more times. This will begin a new execution of the loop. Now, check on the value assigned to I in the Debug window and you'll see that it is still set to 0. As should be obvious at this point, the value of I was not incremented like it should have been. To fix this problem, modify the example as shown here:

```
Program MyNewProgram

    Method Main()

        Define I As Integer
        Define KeepRunning As Boolean = True

        SetScreenSize (600, 100)
        SetConsoleFont("Arial", 18)

        ConsoleWriteLine("")
        ConsoleWrite("Watch me count to 10.   ")

        While KeepRunning = True

            ConsoleWrite("   " + I)
```

```
            If I = 10 Then
                KeepRunning = False
            End If

            I += 1

            Delay(500)

        End While

    End Method

End Program
```

As you can see, a new statement has been added near the end of the `While...End While` loop that increments the value of `I`. To see how things work now, remove the program's breakpoint and run it again normally. This time, things should look a lot better and you should see a series of numbers from 1 to 10 displayed on the console window.

One problem still remains. The program is supposed to count from 1 to 10 and not from 0 to 10. While the program is small enough for you to determine where the problem lies without using the debugger, let's pretend that you do not know where the problem lies and run the program in the debugger again, after first resetting the breakpoint.

Once started, the program will automatically pause when it reaches the breakpoint. Once paused, look at the value of the `I` variable by moving the pointer over it in the text editor area by opening the Debug window. Either way, you should see that the value assigned to `I` is equal to zero. Click on the Step Into button six times. This instructs Phrogram to execute every statement in the loop and to pause at the beginning of the loop upon its second iteration.

Look at the application console window and you should see that the number `0` has been displayed. Obviously what is going on here is that the value of `I` is not being set equal to 1 before being displayed by the first iteration of the loop. To fix this, modify the application as shown here:

```
Program MyNewProgram

    Method Main()

        Define I As Integer
        Define KeepRunning As Boolean = True
```

```
        SetScreenSize (600, 100)
        SetConsoleFont("Arial", 18)

        ConsoleWriteLine("")
        ConsoleWrite("Watch me count to 10.   ")

        While KeepRunning = True

            I += 1

            ConsoleWrite("  " + I)

            If I = 10 Then
                KeepRunning = False
            End If

            Delay(500)

        End While

    End Method

End Program
```

As you can see, the `I += 1` statement has been moved from the end to the beginning of the loop. To see the effect of this change, run the application again. It will begin executing and then pause at the beginning of the `While...End While` loop. Click on the Step Into button two times and then check on the value assigned to `I`. You should see that it is now equal to 1. Click on the Step Out of the Current Method button to allow the application to continue running normally. At this point, the application is now fully debugged and should display the output shown in Figure 10.14.

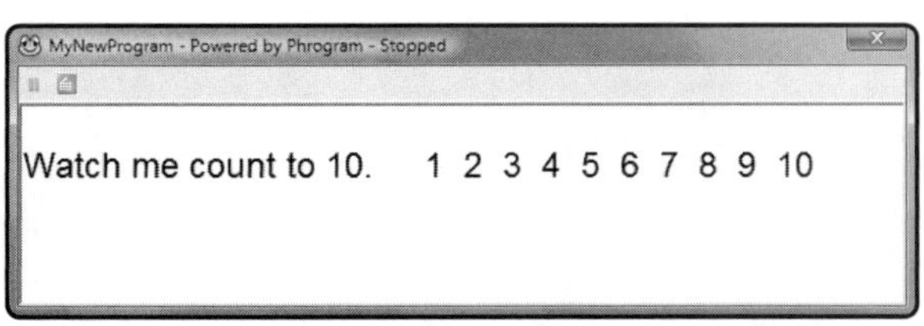


**FIGURE 10.14**

Now that the program has been debugged everything works like it is supposed to.

## Exercises

**Learning how to take full advantage of Phrogram's built-in debugger takes time and lots of practice. To help you gain more experience working with this power tool, complete the following exercises.**

1. **Visit http://phrogram.com/files/folders/beginner_examples/entry5118.aspx. This will bring up a download page for a sample Phrogram application named DeBugDaBug. Download the Zip file containing this application and extract its contents to a folder on your computer.**
2. **The DeBugDaBug application was created by the Phrogram development team specifically for the purpose of providing an interactive debugging exercise. Follow the instructions provided inside the application (as comments) to complete the debugging exercise.**

# A Few Quick Words about 3D Programming

All of the computer games that you have worked on in this book have been 2D programming projects. However, Phrogram also provides strong support for 3D programming through classes stored in the Game3D library, as shown in Figure 10.15.

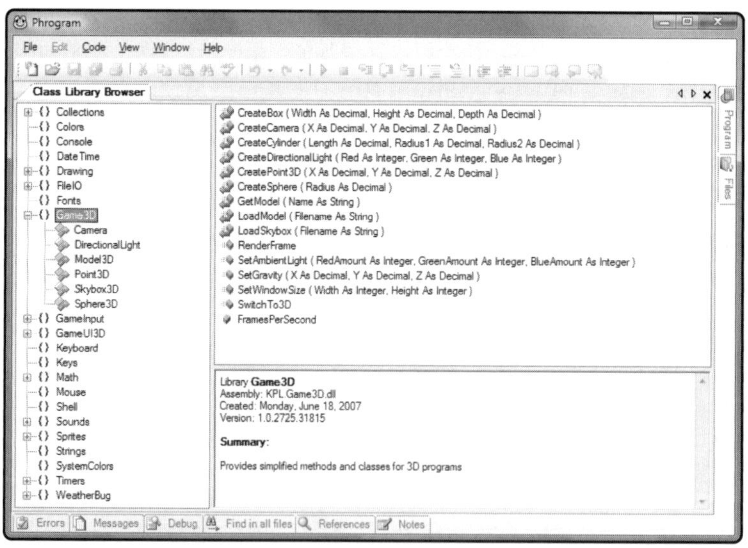


**Figure 10.15**

Phrogram provides a robust collection of methods, functions, and properties in support of 3D programming.

Phrogram's support for 3D programming includes advanced support for programming features like cameras and lights. Using virtual cameras, you can create 3D applications that are able to provide different views from different angles. Like real cameras, you can also zoom in and out. Using lighting, you can illuminate and darken different parts of a 3D game as necessary to set up changing moods and scenery.

Unlike 2D applications that are based on a two-coordinate system with an X and a Y axis with coordinates (0, 0) residing in the upper-left hand corner, 3D applications are built around a three-dimensional coordinate system that includes an additional axis, as depicted in Figure 10.16.

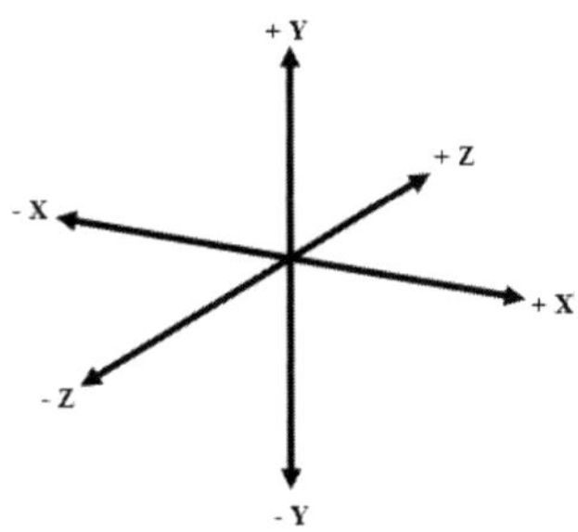


**FIGURE 10.16**

A depiction of the coordinates system used in 3D programming.

To make this 3D coordinate system easier to visualize, the image shown in Figure 10.16 has been rotated slightly to make the new Z axis easier to visualize. If it were lined up properly, the Z axis runs straight back and forth making it difficult to visualize.

Phrogram provides access to a number of 3D programming examples. For example, if you look in the Files Explorer window you will find the source code for a game called KPLong3D. As shown in Figure 10.17, KPLong3D is a single-player version of Pong that pits the player against the computer.

Another 3D programming example that you will want to look at is Alan3D. As shown in Figure 10.18, Alan3D lets you fly a space ship around in a 3D world. Amazingly the entire application consists of just 38 code statements.

To learn more about Phrogram's support for 3D programming, spend a little time reviewing the methods, functions, and properties provided by the Game3D library and then visit http://phrogram.com/forums/ and begin by searching on the term Game3D Library.

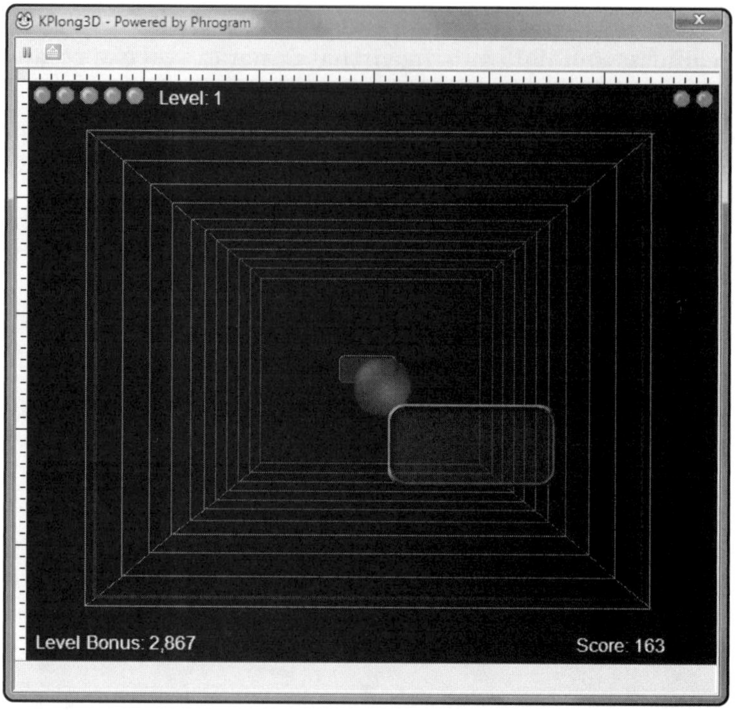


**FIGURE 10.17**

Kplong3D is a great example of Phrogram's ability to support the development of 3D computer games.

**FIGURE 10.18**

Alan3D is a 3D flight simulator program.

## Review Questions

1. List at least three good programming practices that you can follow to help make your Phrogram applications less prone to error.
2. What is a syntax error? What is the most common cause of syntax errors? List three ways of identifying syntax errors.
3. What is a logical error? What is the best way of tracking down and eliminating logical errors?
4. What is a run-time error? What makes run-time errors challenging to discover?
5. What is the most effective way of tracking down and identifying run-time errors?
6. List two methods that you can use to keep track of the logical flow of statements and variable values within Phrogram applications.
7. What method can be used to write text output to the Messages window? What class does this method belong to?
8. What is a debugger? What do you have to do to pause program execution and begin a debug session?
9. List and explain the three types of commands that you can execute within the debugger to control program statements' execution.
10. What is the difference between the coordinate systems used in 2D and 3D applications?

## Back to the Tic-Tac-Toe Game

Okay, it is time to turn your attention back to the development of this book's final application project, the Tic-Tac-Toe game. This game will make use of all of the programming concepts that you have learned in this book, including the use of variables, constants, sprites, methods, functions, and so on. To set up this game, you will need to programmatically draw the application's game board, dividing it into a series of nine distinct logical squares. Figure 10.19 provides a detailed outline of the layout of the game board and the coordinates that delineate each of its major areas.

You may want to bookmark this page to be able to quickly return to it as you work on the rest of the code statements that make up the program file.

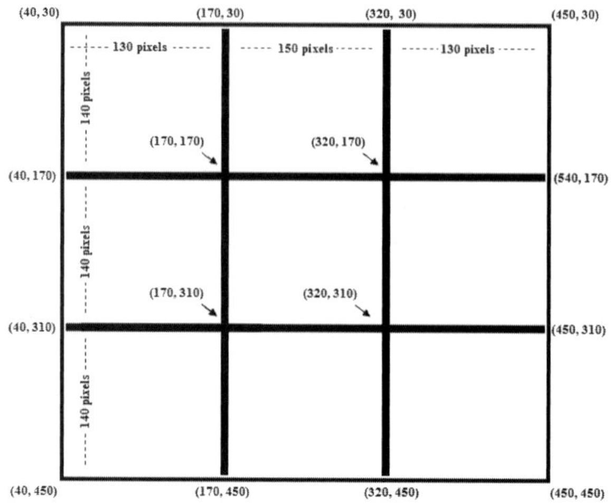


**FIGURE 10.19**

An overview of the coordinates that make up the Tic-Tac-Toe game.

## Designing the Game

Before you begin work on this game, you need to add a pair of graphic files to Phrogram's Images folder. These graphic files will be used during game play to display graphical letters (X and O) on top of game board squares as the players play the game. You will find copies of these files on the book's companion CD. Once you have completed this task, you will be ready to begin work on the Tic-Tac-Toe game that will be developed in a series of steps, as outlined here:

1. Create a new Phrogram program.
2. Document your program file.
3. Define global variables, constants, and sprites.
4. Add controlling logic to the `Main()` method.
5. Add the `ConfigureWindow()` method.
6. Add the `DrawGameBoard()` method.
7. Add the `ProcessPlayerMoves()` method.
8. Add the `SwitchPlayerTurn()` method.
9. Add the `CheckForGameOver()` function.
10. Add the `ClearBoard()` method.
11. Save and compile your application.

### Step 1: Creating a New Phrogram Project

The first step in the development of the Tic-Tac-Toe game is to create a new program, which you can do by clicking on the File menu's New Program command. Once created, assign TicTacToe.kpl as the name of your new application. The program statements that make up this application are outlined in the sections that follow.

### Step 2: Documenting Your New Program

The next step in the development of the Tic-Tac-Toe application is the addition of high-level comment statements that document the application and its purpose. These statements are outlined next and should be added to the beginning of the program file.

```
//Program: TicTacToe.kpl
//Created: 02/07/2008
//Version: 1.0
//Author: Jerry Lee Ford, Jr.
//Description: This Phrogram application is a two-player implementation
//             of the Tic-Tac-Toe game.
```

### Step 3: Defining Global Variables, Constants, and Sprites

The Tic-Tac-Toe game makes use of a number of global variables, constants, and sprites. The statements that define these constants, variables, and sprites are shown next and should be added to the beginning of the program file, immediately following the `Program` statement.

```
//Global constant used to store the name of the game
Constant GameTitle As String = "Tic-Tac-Toe"

//Global variable used to keep track of whose turn it is
Define CurrentPlayer As String = "X"

//Global variable used to keep count of the number of moves made
Define NoMoves As Integer

//Global variables used to keep track of game board square assignments
Define SquareA1 As String
Define SquareA2 As String
Define SquareA3 As String
Define SquareB1 As String
Define SquareB2 As String
Define SquareB3 As String
Define SquareC1 As String
Define SquareC2 As String
Define SquareC3 As String

//Sprites associated with each of the game board squares
Define A1 As Sprite
```

```
Define A2 As Sprite
Define A3 As Sprite
Define B1 As Sprite
Define B2 As Sprite
Define B3 As Sprite
Define C1 As Sprite
Define C2 As Sprite
Define C3 As Sprite
```

These statements begin by declaring a constant used to store a string containing the game's name followed by two variables that are used to keep track of which player's turn it is and the total number of moves made by both players in each game. Next, nine variables, representing the nine squares that make up the Tic-Tac-Toe game board are defined. Lastly, nine sprites are defined. These sprites will be used later in the application to display graphic images containing a red X or a green O, when players click on squares to select them during game play.

### Step 4: Reviewing the Main() Method

The overall controlling logic for the Tic-Tac-Toe game is contained in its `Main()` method. This method consists of a collection of calls to different methods and a `While…End While` loop, which is responsible for the overall execution of the game.

```
//This method is responsible for the overall execution of the game
Method Main()

    ConfigureWindow()  //This method configures the console window

    //This loop controls overall game play
    While True

        DrawGameBoard()        //This method draws the game board

        ProcessPlayerMoves()  //This method processes player moves

        Delay(10)              //Briefly pause game play

    End While

End Method
```

The first method that is called configures settings that effect the display of the console window. The rest of the method calls reside within a `While…End While` loop. When called, the `DrawGameBoard()` method draws the Tic-Tac-Toe game board on the console window. The `ProcessPlayerMoves()` method is then called to collect and process player moves.

## Step 5: Reviewing the ConfigureWindow() Method

The `ConfigureWindow()` method, shown next, configures the size of the console window, setting the screen size to 500 × 500. The name of the game is then displayed in the console window's titlebar. Lastly, a message is displayed at the bottom of the screen informing the player whose turn it is, as stored in the global `CurrentPlayer` variable.

```
//This method is responsible for configuring the console window
Method ConfigureWindow()

    SetScreenSize(500, 500)    //Set the screen size to 500×500 pixels
    SetWindowTitle(GameTitle)  //Display the name of the game in the
                               //Window's titlebar

    Status("Player " + CurrentPlayer + "'s turn")  //Display player turn

End Method
```

## Step 6: Creating the DrawGameBoard() Method

The `DrawGameBoard()` method, shown next, is responsible for drawing the game board. An outline of the game board is drawn after setting the color to Dark Blue and the pen width to 6. Next, the color is set to Black and the pen width to 10, after which a pair of lines is drawn vertically up and down the game board. Finally, two more lines are drawn horizontally.

```
//This method is responsible for drawing the game board
Method DrawGameBoard()

    //Define a rectangle object and line object
    Define RectangleObject As Rectangle
Define LineObject As Line

    //Specify the rectangle object's color and line width
    RectangleObject.Color = DarkBlue
    RectangleObject.LineWidth = 6
```

```
//Specify the rectangle object's beginning coordinate
RectangleObject.X = 35
RectangleObject.y = 25

//Specify the rectangle object's width and length
RectangleObject.Width = 420
RectangleObject.Height = 430

RectangleObject.Draw()  //Draw the rectangle

//Specify the line object's color and line width
LineObject.Color = Black
LineObject.LineWidth = 10

//Draw the Tic-Tac-Toe board's first vertical line
LineObject.StartPoint.X = 170
LineObject.StartPoint.Y = 30
LineObject.EndPoint.X = 170
LineObject.EndPoint.Y = 450
LineObject.Draw()

//Draw the Tic-Tac-Toe board's second vertical line
LineObject.StartPoint.X = 320
LineObject.StartPoint.Y = 30
LineObject.EndPoint.X = 320
LineObject.EndPoint.Y = 450
LineObject.Draw()

//Draw the Tic-Tac-Toe board's first horizontal line
LineObject.StartPoint.X = 40
LineObject.StartPoint.Y = 170
LineObject.EndPoint.X = 450
LineObject.EndPoint.Y = 170
LineObject.Draw()

//Draw the Tic-Tac-Toe board's second horizontal line
LineObject.StartPoint.X = 40
LineObject.StartPoint.Y = 310
```

```
    LineObject.EndPoint.X = 450
    LineObject.EndPoint.Y = 310
    LineObject.Draw()

End Method
```

## Step 7: Creating the ProcessPlayerMoves() Method

The next method that you need to add to the application is the `ProcessPlayerMoves()` method, which is shown next. This method is responsible for processing player moves. Players move by clicking on squares on the game board. Once selected, a square displays an X or O, depending on which player selected it. Of course, the same square cannot be selected twice in the same game.

```
//This method is responsible for accepting and processing player moves
Method ProcessPlayerMoves()

    //Method variable used to keep track of when the game has ended
    Define GameStatus As Boolean = False

    //Method variable used to store player input
    Define PlayerReply As Boolean

    //Execute only when a player is pressing the left mouse button
    If MouseButton = 1 Then

        //Execute only when the pointer is within the bounds of the
        //first column
        If MouseX >= 40 And MouseX <= 165 Then

            //Execute only when the pointer is within the bounds of the
            //first row
            If MouseY >= 30 And MouseY <= 165 Then

                //A player has clicked on the A1 game board square. If it
                //is not already assigned, the player can have it.
                If SquareA1 = "" Then
                    SquareA1 = CurrentPlayer    //Assign the square
                    //Load a graphic image representing the player's letter
                    A1.Load(CurrentPlayer + ".jpg")
```

```
            A1.X = 45   //Position the display of the graphic image
            A1.Y = 35   //so that it appears in the A1 square
            A1.Show()   //Display the image
            NoMoves += 1  //Add one to the number of moves made
        Else  //The square is already assigned
            Return  //Do not make an assignment
        End If

    End If

    //Execute only when the pointer is within the bounds of the
    //second row
    If MouseY >= 175 And MouseY <= 305 Then

        //A player has clicked on the A2 game board square. If it
        //is not already assigned, the player can have it.
        If SquareA2 = "" Then
            SquareA2 = CurrentPlayer    //Assign the square
            //Load a graphic image representing the player's letter
            A2.Load(CurrentPlayer + ".jpg")
            A2.X = 45   //Position the display of the graphic image
            A2.Y = 180  //so that it appears in the A2 square
            A2.Show()   //Display the image
            NoMoves += 1  //Add one to the number of moves made
        Else  //The square is already assigned
            Return  //Do not make an assignment
        End If

    End If

    //Execute only when the pointer is within the bounds of the
    //third row
    If MouseY >= 315 And MouseY <= 450 Then

        //A player has clicked on the A3 game board square. If it
        //is not already assigned, the player can have it.
        If SquareA3 = "" Then
            SquareA3 = CurrentPlayer    //Assign the square
```

```
            //Load a graphic image representing the player's letter
            A3.Load(CurrentPlayer + ".jpg")
            A3.X = 45   //Position the display of the graphic image
            A3.Y = 320  //so that it appears in the A3 square
            A3.Show()   //Display the image
            NoMoves += 1  //Add one to the number of moves made
        Else  //The square is already assigned
            Return  //Do not make an assignment
        End If

    End If

End If

//Execute only when the pointer is within the bounds of the
//Second column
If MouseX >= 175 And MouseX <= 315 Then

    //Execute only when the pointer is within the bounds of the
    //first row
    If MouseY >= 30 And MouseY <= 165 Then

        //A player has clicked on the B1 game board square. If it
        //is not already assigned, the player can have it.
        If SquareB1 = "" Then
            SquareB1 = CurrentPlayer    //Assign the square
            //Load a graphic image representing the player's letter
            B1.Load(CurrentPlayer + ".jpg")
            B1.X = 190  //Position the display of the graphic image
            B1.Y = 35   //so that it appears in the B1 square
            B1.Show()   //Display the image
            NoMoves += 1  //Add one to the number of moves made
        Else  //The square is already assigned
            Return  //Do not make an assignment
        End If

    End If
```

```
//Execute only when the pointer is within the bounds of the
//second row
If MouseY >= 175 And MouseY <= 305 Then

    //A player has clicked on the B2 game board square. If it
    //is not already assigned, the player can have it.
    If SquareB2 = "" Then
        SquareB2 = CurrentPlayer    //Assign the square
        //Load a graphic image representing the player's letter
        B2.Load(CurrentPlayer + ".jpg")
        B2.X = 190  //Position the display of the graphic image
        B2.Y = 180  //so that it appears in the b2 square
        B2.Show()   //Display the image
        NoMoves += 1  //Add one to the number of moves made
    Else  //The square is already assigned
        Return  //Do not make an assignment
    End If

End If

//Execute only when the pointer is within the bounds of the
//third row
If MouseY >= 315 And MouseY <= 450 Then

    //A player has clicked on the B3 game board square. If it
    //is not already assigned, the player can have it.
    If SquareB3 = "" Then
        SquareB3 = CurrentPlayer    //Assign the square
        //Load a graphic image representing the player's letter
        B3.Load(CurrentPlayer + ".jpg")
        B3.X = 190  //Position the display of the graphic image
        B3.Y = 320  //so that it appears in the B3 square
        B3.Show()   //Display the image
        NoMoves += 1  //Add one to the number of moves made
    Else  //The square is already assigned
        Return  //Do not make an assignment
    End If
```

```
        End If

    End If

    //Execute only when the pointer is within the bounds of the
    //third column
    If MouseX >= 325 And MouseX <= 450 Then

        //Execute only when the pointer is within the bounds of the
        //first row
        If MouseY >= 30 And MouseY <= 165 Then

            //A player has clicked on the C1 game board square. If it
            //is not already assigned, the player can have it.
            If SquareC1 = "" Then
                SquareC1 = CurrentPlayer    //Assign the square
                //Load a graphic image representing the player's letter
                C1.Load(CurrentPlayer + ".jpg")
                C1.X = 330  //Position the display of the graphic image
                C1.Y = 35   //so that it appears in the C1 square
                C1.Show()   //Display the image
                NoMoves += 1  //Add one to the number of moves made
           Else  //The square is already assigned
               Return  //Do not make an assignment
            End If

        End If

        //Execute only when the pointer is within the bounds of the
        //second row
        If MouseY >= 175 And MouseY <= 305 Then

        //A player has clicked on the C2 game board square. If it
        //is not already assigned, the player can have it.
        If SquareC2 = "" Then
            SquareC2 = CurrentPlayer    //Assign the square
            //Load a graphic image representing the player's letter
            C2.Load(CurrentPlayer + ".jpg")
```

```
            C2.X = 330  //Position the display of the graphic image
            C2.Y = 180  //so that it appears in the C2 square
            C2.Show()   //Display the image
            NoMoves += 1  //Add one to the number of moves made
        Else  //The square is already assigned
            Return  //Do not make an assignment
        End If
    End If

    //Execute only when the pointer is within the bounds of the
    //third row
    If MouseY >= 315 And MouseY <= 450 Then

        //A player has clicked on the C3 game board square. If it
        //is not already assigned, the player can have it.
        If SquareC3 = "" Then
            SquareC3 = CurrentPlayer    //Assign the square
            //Load a graphic image representing the player's letter
            C3.Load(CurrentPlayer + ".jpg")
            C3.X = 330  //Position the display of the graphic image
            C3.Y = 320  //so that it appears in the C3 square
            C3.Show()   //Display the image
            NoMoves += 1  //Add one to the number of moves made
        Else  //The square is already assigned
            Return  //Do not make an assignment
        End If
    End If

End If

//Call the method responsible for determining when the game is over
GameStatus = CheckForGameOver()

//Prompt the players to play a new game if the current game has ended
If GameStatus = True Then
    PlayerReply = Confirm("Would you like to play another round?", GameTitle)

    If PlayerReply = True Then //The Players have elected to play
```

```
            ClearBoard()         //Reset the game board
         Else                    //The players have elected to stop playing
            Stop()               //Terminate the application
         End If
         Else
            SwitchPlayerTurn() //Switch player turns if the game is not over
         End If

      End If

   End Method
```

As you can see, this method is pretty large. It begins by defining two method variables used to keep track of when the game ends and to store player input. Next an `If…Then` code block is set up that executes only when one of the players presses the left mouse button. The code statements that make up this code block are organized into four groups. The first group of statements is controlled by an `If…Then` code block that executes only when one of the players moves the pointer over the first column on the game board. Within this code block are three additional `If…Then` code blocks, each of which is associated with a different game board square in the first column. Statements in each of these three code blocks are designed to respond when one of the players clicks on a square. If the square has not been selected yet, it is assigned to the player that selected it and a graphic image showing that player's letter is displayed on the square. However, if the player attempts to select a square that has already been assigned, the player input is ignored, forcing the player to pick a different square. The second and third major groups of code are nearly identical to that of the first group, the only difference being that they are designed to process player input when the second and third columns are clicked.

The fourth major group of code statements is located at the end of the method. These statements call upon the `CheckForGameOver()` function. If this function returns a value of `True`, then the game has ended and the players are prompted to play again. If the players decide to play again, the `ClearBoard()` method is called to ready the game for a new round of play. If the players decide not to play, then the `Stop()` method is executed, terminating the application execution.

**HINT**

`Stop()` is a method provided by the `Shell` library. When executed, this method closes the application's console window and then terminates the application's execution. This method has the following syntax.

```
Stop()
```

## Step 8: Creating the SwitchPlayerTurn() Method

The code statements that make up the `SwitchPlayerTurn()` subroutine are shown next and should be added to the end of the program file.

```
//This method is responsible for handling the switching of player turns
Method SwitchPlayerTurn()

    //If Player X just moved then make it Player O's turn
    If CurrentPlayer = "X" Then
        CurrentPlayer = "O"  //Swap player turns
        Status("Player " + CurrentPlayer + "'s turn")  //Notify the players
        Return
    End If

    //If Player O just moved then make it Player X's turn
    If CurrentPlayer = "O" Then
        CurrentPlayer = "X"  //Swap player turns
        Status("Player " + CurrentPlayer + "'s turn")  //Notify the players
        Return
    End If

End Method
```

This method is made up of two `If…Then` code blocks. The first code block executes if Player X just made a move, assigning a value of "O" to `CurrentPlayer`. If, on the other hand, Player O was the last player to make a move, the first code block is skipped and the second `If…Then` code block is executed, assigning "X" to `CurrentPlayer`. By toggling the value of `CurrentPlayer` from X to O and vice versa, the game is able to keep track of and control whose turn it is.

## Step 9: Creating the CheckForGameOver() Function

The code statements for the `CheckForGameOver()` function are shown next. This method is responsible for determining if the current player has won the game.

```
//This function is responsible for determining if the current game has been
//won, lost, or tied
Function CheckForGameOver() As Boolean

    //Check vertically for a winner on the first column
```

```
  If SquareA1 = CurrentPlayer And SquareA2 = CurrentPlayer And SquareA3 =
  CurrentPlayer Then
      //Notify the player that the game is over
      Alert("Player " + CurrentPlayer + " has won!", GameTitle)
      Status("") //Clear the status bar
      Return True
  End If

  //Check vertically for a winner on the second column
  If SquareB1 = CurrentPlayer And SquareB2 = CurrentPlayer And SquareB3 =
  CurrentPlayer Then
      //Notify the player that the game is over
      Alert("Player " + CurrentPlayer + " has won!", GameTitle)
      Status("") //Clear the status bar
      Return True
  End If

  //Check vertically for a winner on the third column
  If SquareC1 = CurrentPlayer And SquareC2 = CurrentPlayer And SquareC3 =
  CurrentPlayer Then
      //Notify the player that the game is over
      Alert("Player " + CurrentPlayer + " has won!", GameTitle)
      Status("") //Clear the status bar
      Return True
  End If

  //Check horizontally for a winner on the first row
  If SquareA1 = CurrentPlayer And SquareB1 = CurrentPlayer And SquareC1 =
  CurrentPlayer Then
      //Notify the player that the game is over
      Alert("Player " + CurrentPlayer + " has won!", GameTitle)
      Status("") //Clear the status bar
      Return True
End If

  //Check horizontally for a winner on the second row
  If SquareA2 = CurrentPlayer And SquareB2 = CurrentPlayer And SquareC2 =
  CurrentPlayer Then
```

```
    //Notify the player that the game is over
    Alert("Player " + CurrentPlayer + " has won!", GameTitle)
    Status("")  //Clear the status bar
    Return True
End If

//Check horizontally for a winner on the third row
If SquareA3 = CurrentPlayer And SquareB3 = CurrentPlayer And SquareC3 =
CurrentPlayer Then
    //Notify the player that the game is over
    Alert("Player " + CurrentPlayer + " has won!", GameTitle)
    Status("")  //Clear the status bar
    Return True
End If

//Check diagonally for a winner from the top-left corner to the
//bottom-right corner
If SquareA1 = CurrentPlayer And SquareB2 = CurrentPlayer And SquareC3 =
CurrentPlayer Then
    //Notify the player that the game is over
    Alert("Player " + CurrentPlayer + " has won!", GameTitle)
    Status("")  //Clear the status bar
    Return True
End If

//Check diagonally for a winner from the bottom-left corner to the
//top-right corner
If SquareA3 = CurrentPlayer And SquareB2 = CurrentPlayer And SquareC1 =
CurrentPlayer Then
    Alert("Player " + CurrentPlayer + " has won!", GameTitle)
    Status("")  //Clear the status bar
    Return True
End If

//If none of the other possible combinations has resulted in a winner
//check to see if all nine squares have been selected and declare a tie
If NoMoves = 9 Then
    //Notify the player that the game is over
```

```
        Alert("The game has ended in a tie!", GameTitle)
        Status("")  //Clear the status bar
        Return True
    End If

    Return False  //The game has not been won so game play continues

End Function
```

This function consists of nine different If…Then code blocks. The first three If…Then code blocks check to see if the current player has won the game by lining up three consecutive squares vertically in one of the game board's columns. The next three If…Then code blocks look to see if the current player has won the game by lining up three squares in a row horizontally. The next two If…Then code blocks look for a winner diagonally. If any of these conditional tests prove True, the Alert() method is used to display a popup dialog window notifying the players that the game has been won. If none of the conditional checks evaluate as being True, then a final If…Then code block looks to see if all nine game board squares have been selected and declares a tie if this is the case. If any of these nine conditional tests evaluate as being True, the function returns a value of True back to the statement that called upon the function to execute. Otherwise, a value of False is returned.

## Step 10: Creating the ClearBoard() Method

The last method to be added to the program file is the ClearBoard() method whose statements are shown next. When called, this method readies the game for a new round of play by hiding any image files displayed on the game board and then setting the value of NoMoves and CurrentPlayer back to their default starting values.

```
//This method sets the game board back to its initial state
Method ClearBoard()

    //Un-assign any game board square that was selected in the last
    //game and hide the sprite that was displayed on it
    If SquareA1 <> "" Then
        SquareA1 = ""
        A1.Hide()
    End If
    If SquareA2 <> "" Then
        SquareA2 = ""
        A2.Hide()
```

```
    End If
    If SquareA3 <> "" Then
        SquareA3 = ""
        A3.Hide()
    End If
    If SquareB1 <> "" Then
        SquareB1 = ""
        B1.Hide()
    End If
    If SquareB2 <> "" Then
        SquareB2 = ""
        B2.Hide()
    End If
    If SquareB3 <> "" Then
        SquareB3 = ""
        B3.Hide()
    End If
    If SquareC1 <> "" Then
        SquareC1 = ""
        C1.Hide()
    End If
    If SquareC2 <> "" Then
        SquareC2 = ""
        C2.Hide()
    End If
    If SquareC3 <> "" Then
        SquareC3 = ""
        C3.Hide()
    End If

    NoMoves = 0   //Reset the number of player moves to zero

    CurrentPlayer = "X"  //Make Player X the default player

    //Update the status bar
    Status("Player " + CurrentPlayer + "'s turn")

End Method
```

### Step 11: Saving and Compiling Your Application

Assuming that you have followed along carefully and finished typing in the code statements that make up the Tic-Tac-Toe game, everything should be ready to go. Save your new application by clicking on the Save All command located on the File menu. Don't forget to take a moment to look at the Errors window to make sure that Phrogram has not identified any syntax errors, and if it has, go ahead and fix them.

## The Final Result

Okay, it's time to run your copy of the Tic-Tac-Toe game and see how things go. Barring any typing errors, everything should work as described at the beginning of this chapter. If, however, you run into some trouble, it may be time to put some of the troubleshooting and debugging techniques covered in this chapter to the test. Of course, as with every other application that has been covered in this book, you can find a copy of the source code for this application on the book's companion CD and work with it instead of re-keying your own copy of the application.

## Summary

In this chapter, you reviewed the three basic types of errors that all computer programs are subject to. You received tips for writing program code that is less subject to errors. You were introduced to different ways of keeping track of program execution flow and variable values. In addition, you learned how to set breakpoints and to work with Phrogram's built-in debugger. Using the debugger, you learned how to monitor variable values and to exercise detailed control over program statement execution. Using all of this new information, you walked through a sample debugging session. With this new information, you should be able to track down and fix even the most pesky application bug.

Now, before you put down this book, consider spending a little time improving the Tic-Tac-Toe game by addressing the following list of challenges.

## Challenges

1. Consider updating the game to keep track of the total number of games played as well as the total number of games that each player has won and lost and display this information at the bottom of the console window in the status bar.
2. Consider adding sound effects to the Tic-Tac-Toe game for each of the following situations: an available square is selected, an unavailable square is selected, the game has been won, and the game has ended in a tie.
3. Create a distribution package for your new game and share with a few friends, asking them to provide you with feedback.

# Part IV

## Appendices

APPENDIX A

# What's on the CD?

In order to become an effective programmer, you must continue to dedicate yourself to the task of learning as much as possible about computer programming. As you continue on your journey and begin tackling larger and more complex projects, it helps to have access to a good collection of source code that you can reference and find examples of how to perform different tasks.

The folders located in Phrogram's Files window provide you with ready access to a number of sample programs. Assuming that you have been re-creating all of the computer game projects that have been presented at the end of each chapter in this book, then you also have access to a second collection of source code. By continuing to study these examples you can learn a great deal about how to program. Better yet, you can find working examples of code statements that can perform various tasks and then copy and paste these statements into new Phrogram programs, modifying them as necessary to fit into your existing program code. This saves you the trouble of having to reinvent the wheel and lets you focus on solving new challenges.

In the event that you read this book selectively, focusing only on chapters that were of particular interest, then you are no doubt missing at least some of the source code for one or more of the games developed in this book. However, there is no reason to let this stand in your way. You will find copies of all of this book's projects, including graphics and source code, available on this book's accompanying CD, just waiting for you to download them.

## Phrogram Project Source Code

Table A.1 provides an overview of all the Phrogram game projects that you will find on the CD.

**Table A.1 Phrogram Projects Available on the CD**

| Chapter | Project File | Overview |
|---|---|---|
| Chapter 1 | KidsJokes.kpl | This Phrogram game displays a series of jokes, demonstrating the steps involved in controlling the display and appearance of text. |
| Chapter 2 | StoryTime.kpl | This Phrogram game generates a mad-lib-styled story in which player input is used in unexpected ways to generate a humorous story. |
| Chapter 3 | NumberGuess.kpl | This Phrogram game demonstrates how to generate random numbers and how to use variables as a means of storing and processing data collected during game play. |
| Chapter 4 | RockPaperScissors.kpl | This Phrogram game pits the player against the computer in a computerized implementation of the Rock, Paper, Scissors game. |
| Chapter 5 | SlotMachine.kpl | This Phrogram game simulates a Las Vegas-style casino slot machine. |
| Chapter 6 | Crazy8ball.kpl | This Phrogram game simulates the operation of a Crazy 8-ball fortune telling toy, providing randomly selected answers to player questions. |
| Chapter 7 | Doodle.kpl | This Phrogram game demonstrates how to work with different drawing classes in order to create a Windows point like drawing program. |
| Chapter 8 | PCPong - Ver.1.0.kpl | This Phrogram game is based on the original Pong computer game that pits two players against one another in a ping-pong-style video game. |
| Chapter 9 | PCPong – Ver.1.1.kpl | This version of the PCPong game includes a number of enhancements, including sound effects, better ball control, and enhanced score reporting. |
| Chapter 10 | Tic-Tac-Toe.kpl | This game is a two-player implementation of the classic children's game, Tic-Tac-Toe. |

APPENDIX B

# What Next?

Learning how to become a good programmer takes a lot of commitment, time, and effort. By making it to the end of this book, you have demonstrated all of these qualities. While this book has covered a lot of ground, there is plenty left to learn. This book has provided you with a strong programming foundation and a good introduction to 2D programming. However, there is still a lot more to be learned about both 2D and 3D programming.

If you are interested in becoming a world-class programmer, then you need to continue your programming education. This means spending time developing new Phrogram applications, experimenting, and learning how things work. Therefore, you should think of this book as the beginning rather than as the end of your programming education. To help you continue to further your programming knowledge, this appendix provides a list of resources that you can explore to learn more about Phrogram, Windows programming, DirectX, and the .NET Framework.

## Locating Phrogram Resources Online

There is plenty of good information available on the internet about Phrogram. By keeping an eye on the websites identified in the sections that follow, you can stay on top of the latest happenings in the Phrogram community and continue to expand your understanding of the Phrogram programming language. To help get you started, this appendix provides an essential starter list of websites.

## The Phrogram Company Website

The best and most important place to regularly visit is the Phrogram Company website located at http://www.phrogram.com, as shown in Figure B.1.

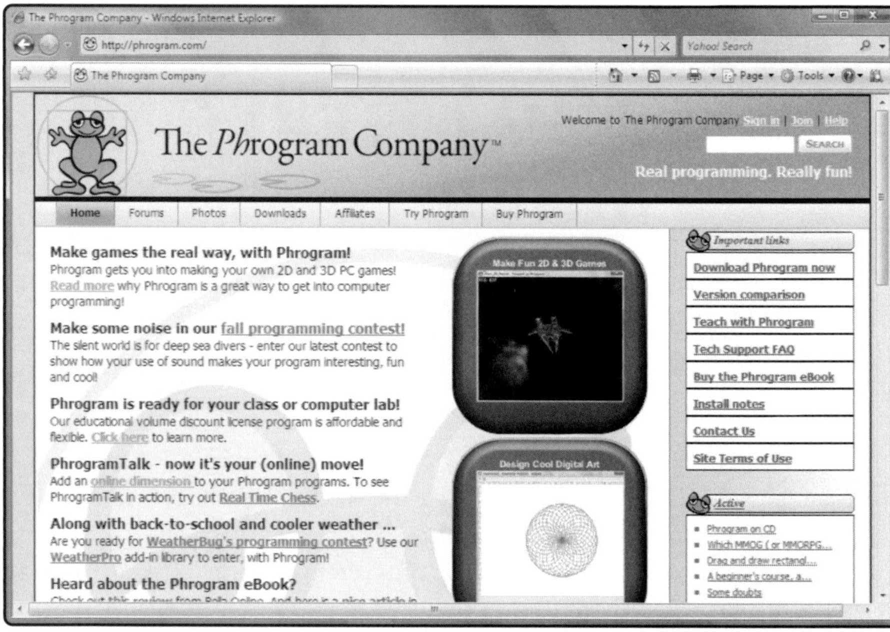


**FIGURE B.1**

The home page of the Phrogram Company website.

This site is the ultimate author on all things Phrogram. From here, you can download and install the latest release of Phrogram as well as download PDF documentation files. You will also find no shortage of code examples, not to mention graphics and audio files.

## Wikipedia's Phrogram Page

Another way to keep abreast of what is happening with Phrogram is to keep an eye on Wikipedia's Phrogram page located at http://en.wikipedia.org/wiki/Phrogram, as shown in Figure B.2.

Here you will find a community-maintained encyclopedia of information on Phrogram. You will also find a collection of links to other Phrogram resources.

## Jamey's Phrogram Programs

Another good site to visit is Jamey's Phrogram Programs website, located at http://jameyfriend.com/Phrogram/index.html, as shown in Figure B.3.

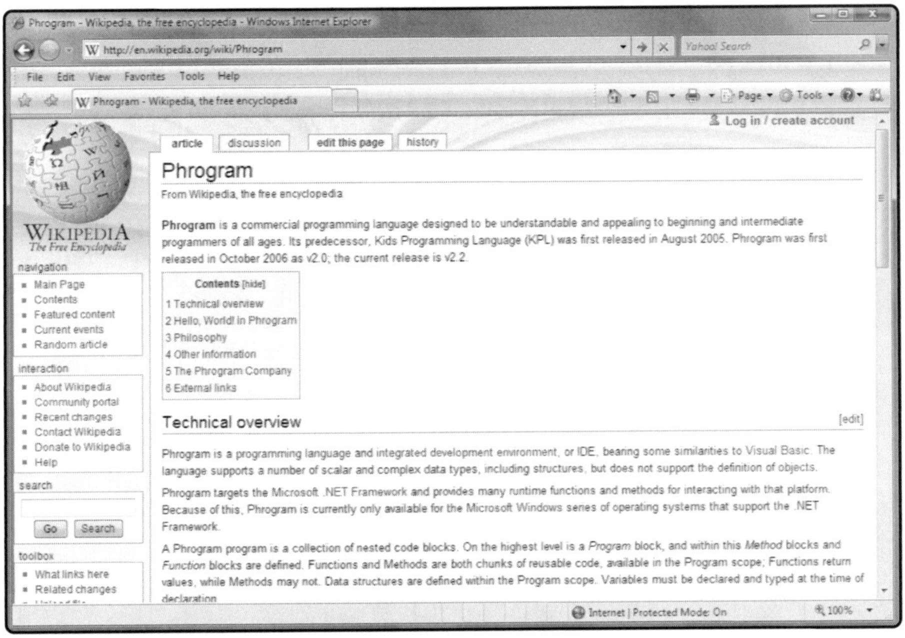


**FIGURE B.2**

Wikipedia's Phrogram page.

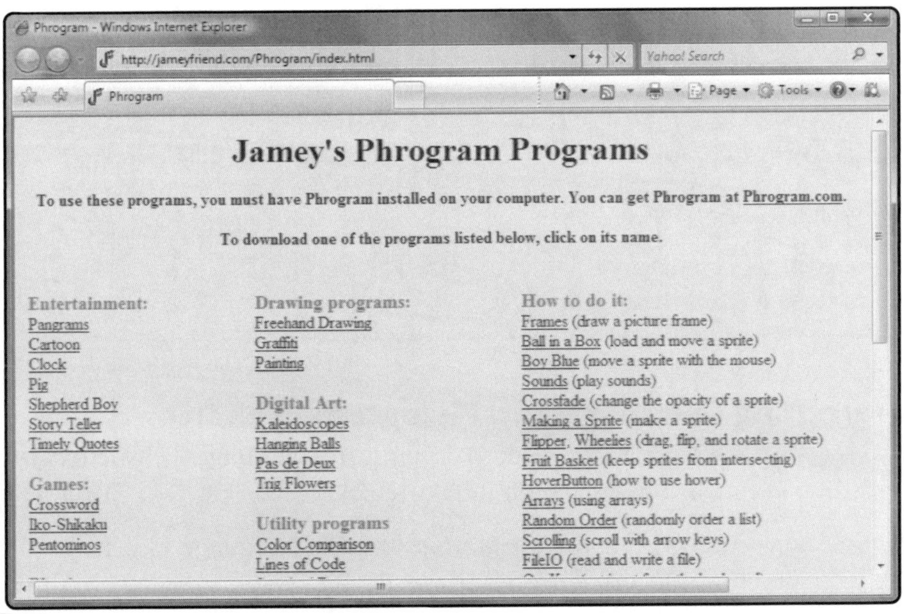


**FIGURE B.3**

The Jamey's Phrogram Programs website is packed with sample programs that are free for download and modification.

Sample programs and resources available at the Jamey's Phrogram Programs website include games, drawing programs, and examples of how to perform an assortment of specific programming tasks like working with arrays and file input and output.

## The Kid's Programming Language Video at Channel 9

If you would like to meet and listen to some of the developers behind Phrogram, then you should view the Kids Programming Language video available from Microsoft's Channel 9 website located at http://channel9.msdn.com/ShowPost.aspx?PostID=166995, as shown in Figure B.4.

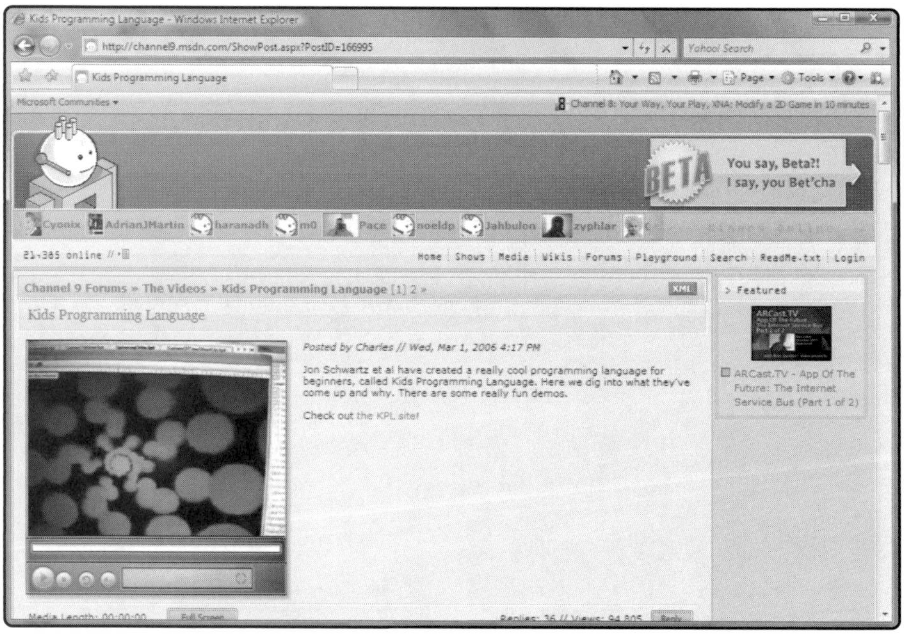

**FIGURE B.4**

The Kids Programming Language Video provides you with the chance to hear about Phrogram in the words of its creators.

## The Kid's Programming Language and Phrogram Website

Another site to visit at least once is the original Kids programming language website located at http://kidsprogramminglanguage.com, as shown in Figure B.5.

Although it is not being updated any more, the Kid's Programming Language website is still a useful resource packed with information.

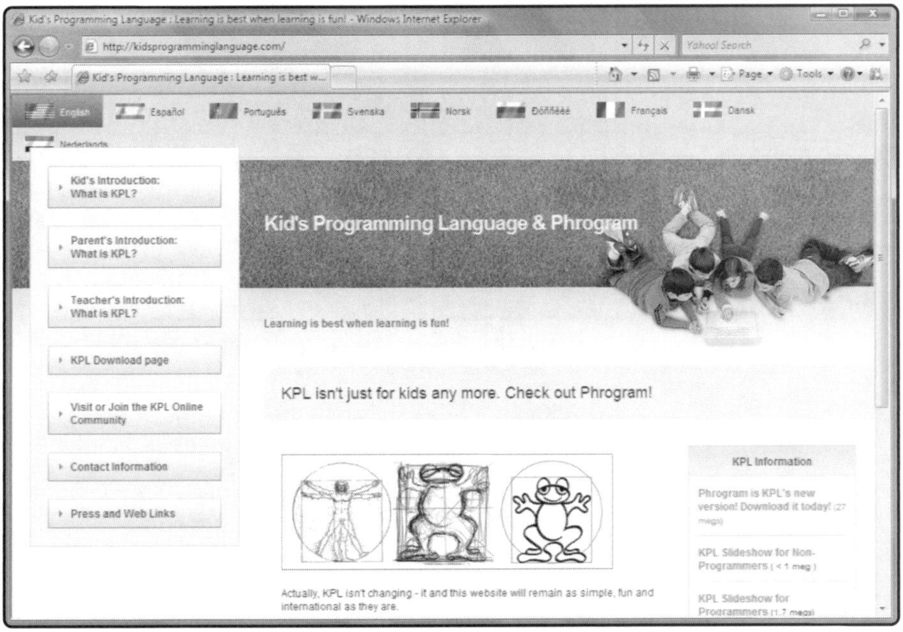


**Figure B.5**

The original Kid's Programming Language website.

## .NET Resources

In order to run Phrogram or a Phrogram application on a Windows computer, Microsoft .NET version 2.0 or higher must be installed. As such, it is a good idea to learn about .NET and how it works. The next three sections identify a number of excellent websites that you can visit to learn all about the .NET Framework.

### The Microsoft .NET Homepage

The best place to start learning about the .NET Framework is Microsoft's .NET homepage, which is located at http://www.microsoft.com/net/, as shown in Figure B.6.

This web page provides a great overview of the .NET Framework and operations on Windows computers. You will also find links to other online .NET resources and can also download and install .NET.

### The .NET Framework Developer Center

If after visiting the Microsoft .NET homepage, you find yourself hungry for more technical information about the inner workings of .NET, you should visit the .NET Framework Developer Center located at http://msdn2.microsoft.com/en-us/netframework, as shown in Figure B.7.

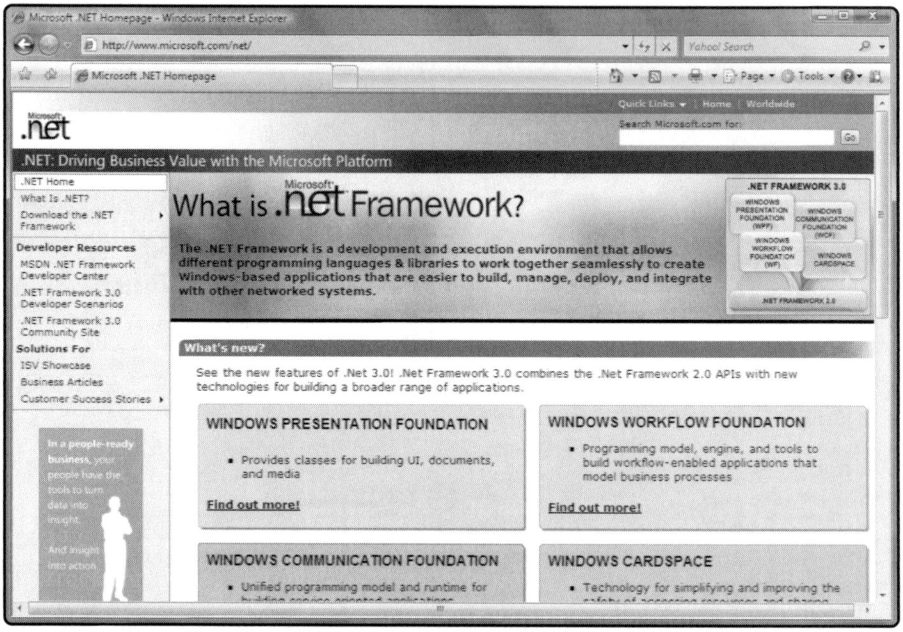


**FIGURE B.6**

The Microsoft .NET Framework homepage.

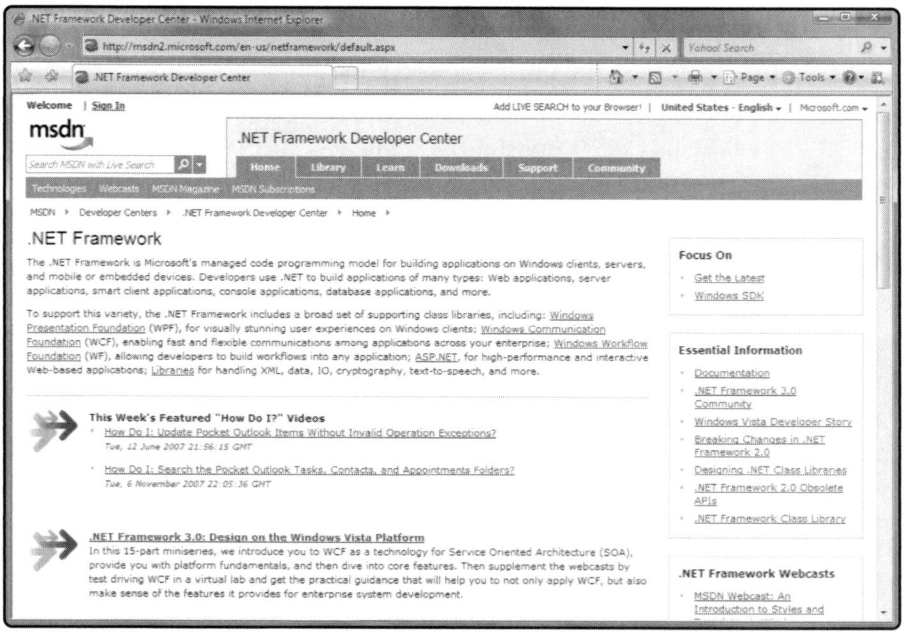


**FIGURE B.7**

The .NET Framework Developer Center web page.

This website provides access to .NET documentation as well as to tons of .NET Framework technical articles. You will also get easy access to current .NET patches and updates.

## The Wikipedia .NET Framework Page

If you are interested in finding a basic overview of the .NET Framework and do not want to wade through tons of technical articles to find it, try the .NET Framework pages at Wikipedia. As shown in Figure B.8, you will find this page located at http://en.wikipedia.org/wiki/.NET_Framework.

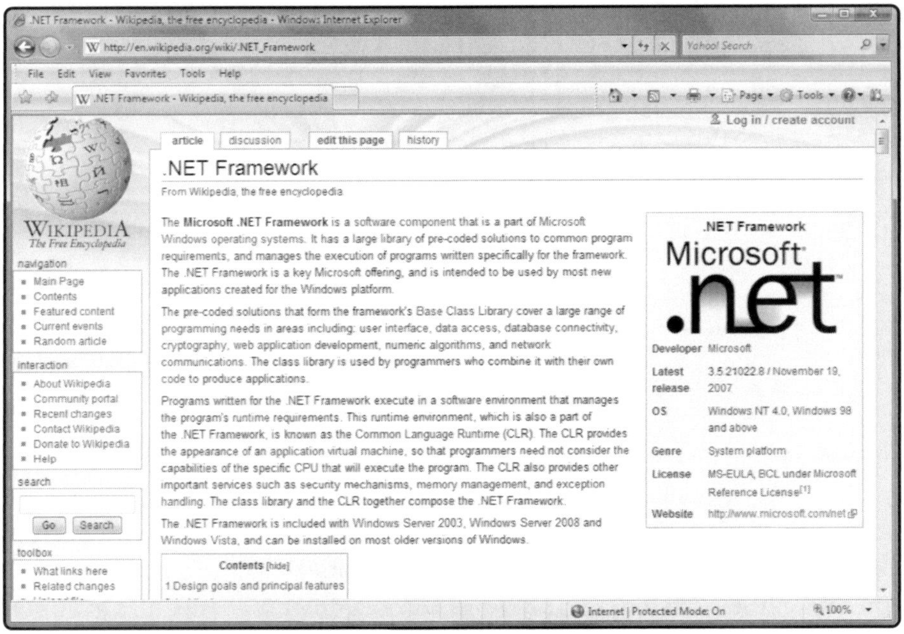


FIGURE B.8
The Wikipedia .NET Framework page.

# DIRECTX RESOURCES

In addition to the Microsoft .NET Framework, Phrogram also requires Microsoft DirectX for rendering 3D graphics and for managing interaction with hardware devices like joysticks. Therefore, it is a good idea to spend a little time learning more about DirectX and what it does behind the scenes to support game development on computers running Microsoft Windows. The next several sections identify a number of good websites that you can visit to learn everything you would ever want to know about DirectX.

## The DirectX Home Page

The single best place to go to learn about DirectX is Microsoft's DirectX web page located at http://www.gamesforwindows.com/en-US/AboutGFW/Pages/Directx10-a.aspx, as shown in Figure B.9.

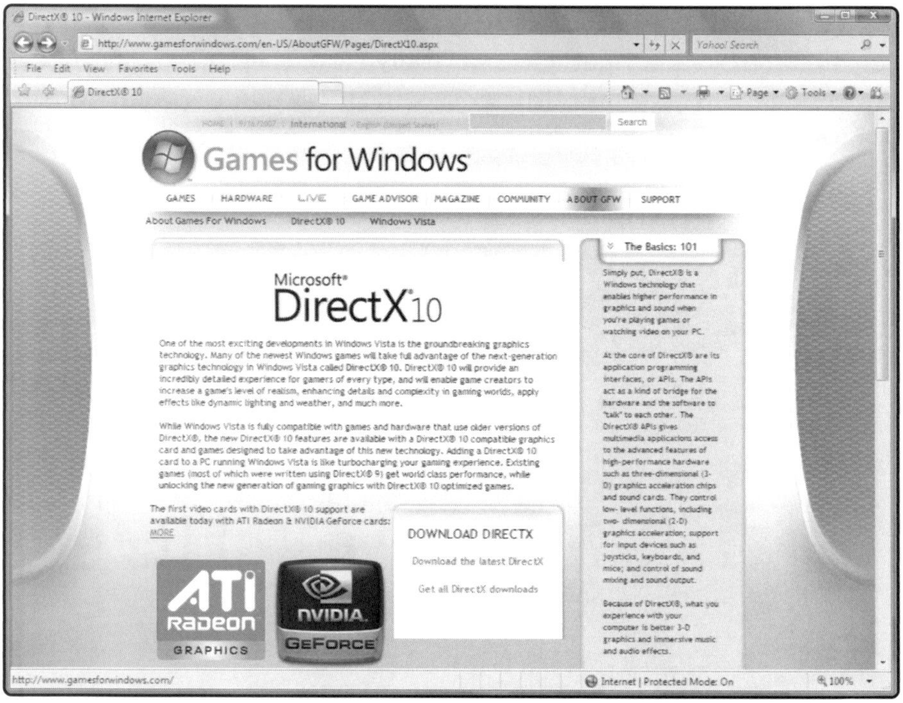


**FIGURE B.9**

The DirectX 10 home page is Microsoft's official DirectX site.

The DirectX web page provides an overview of DirectX and provides information on current and previous versions of DirectX. It also provides information about DirectX-compatible hardware as well as new DirectX games. Current and previous DirectX downloads are also available directly from this website.

## The Wikipedia DirectX Page

The Wikipedia DirectX web page, located at http://en.wikipedia.org/wiki/Direct_x as shown in Figure B.10, provides an excellent overview of DirectX and a detailed historical timeline of every version of DirectX.

The Wikipedia DirectX page discusses different DirectX components like Direct3D and DirectDraw and the application of DirectX on personal computers as well as Xbox and Xbox 360. Also provided is a collection of links where you can go to get additional information on DirectX.

## The DirectX Resource Center Page

Another website worth checking out is the DirectX Resource Center located at http://msdn2.microsoft.com/en-us/xna/aa937781.aspx, as shown in Figure B.11.

FIGURE B.10 Wikipedia's DirectX web page provides an excellent high-level overview of DirectX.

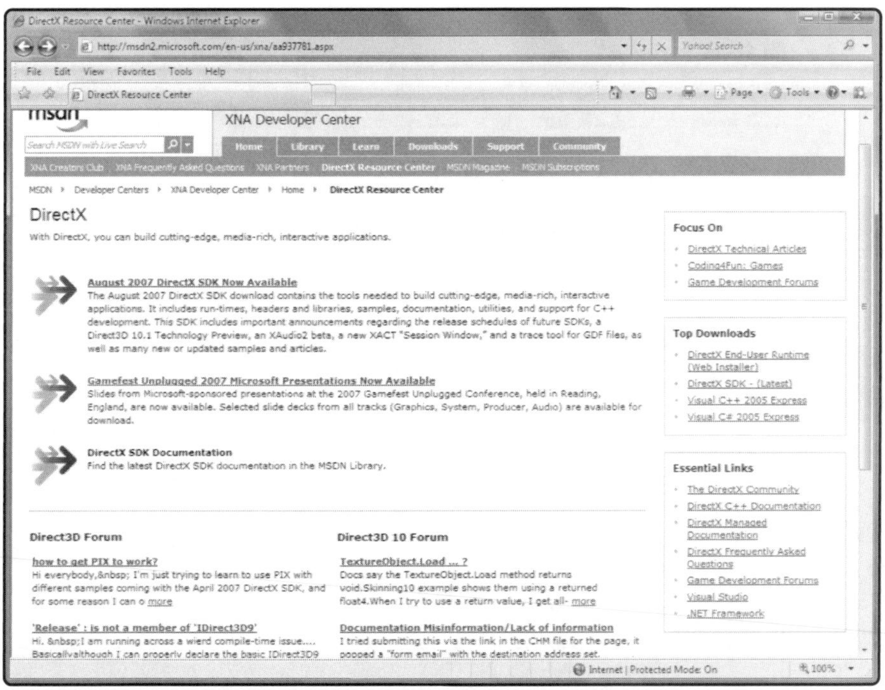

FIGURE B.11 The DirectX Resource Center website is a great technical resource.

The DirectX Resource Center website addresses DirectX from a developer's point of view and provides access to forums where developers can ask questions and exchange information with one another. You will also find plenty of technical articles and get easy access to different game development forums.

## Other Phrogram Resources

In addition to all of the Phrogram, DirectX, and .NET resources already covered in this appendix, you can also find some extremely helpful information on internet forums and blogs. Two particularly informative websites include:

- The Phrogram Company Forums
- Jon Schwartz's Got Schwartz? Blog

### The Phrogram Company Forums

The Phrogram Company website hosts a number of different forums (http://phrogram.com/forums/default.aspx) where Phrogram programmers, new and experienced, can congregate and discuss Phrogram, as shown in Figure B.12. By reading messages posted on these forums, you can learn what other Phrogram programmers are up to. By posting your questions on one of these forums, you can ask for help from other Phrogram community members.

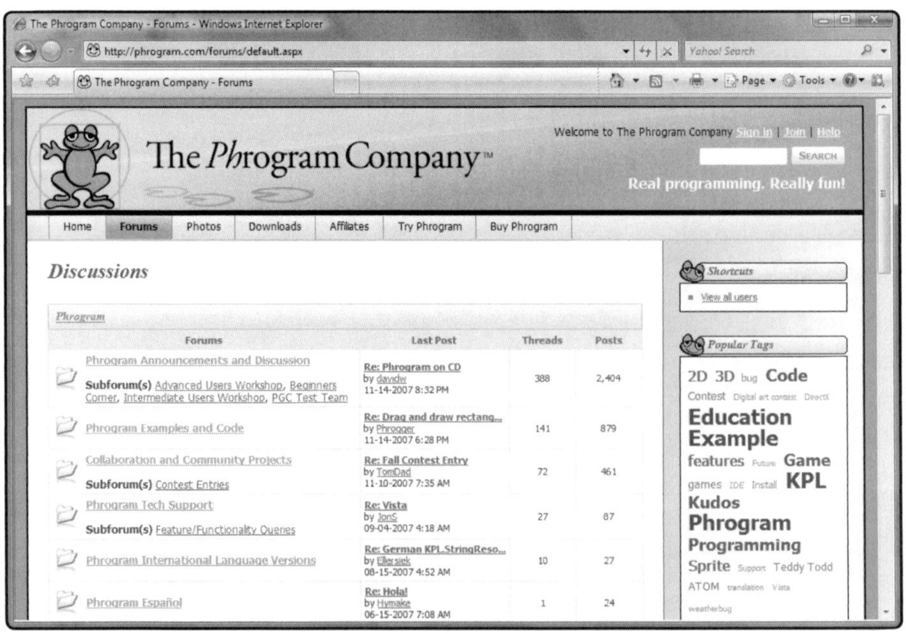


**Figure B.12**

Accessing the forums located on the Phrogram Company website.

Figure B.13 only shows a small number of the forums available at the Phrogram Company website. A complete list of the forums that you will find is shown in the following list. Many of these forums are organized into two or more sub forums, allowing for more granular organization of related subtopics.

- Phrogram Announcements and Discussion
- Phrogram Examples and Code
- Collaboration and Community Projects
- Phrogram Tech Support
- Phrogram International Language Versions
- Program Español
- Learn to Program with Phrogram
- Partners
- External Resources
- Curriculum
- KPL Questions and Answers
- KPL International Language Versions
- KPL Examples and Code
- Frogs and Phrogs
- Games, Toys, and other Fun Stuff

HINT

In order to post a message to one of these forums, you must first sign up for a free account. To sign up just click on the Sign in link at the top of the Phrogram Company web page.

## The Got Schwartz? Blog

Another great way to learn about new Phrogram developments is to regularly visit the Got Schwartz? blog located at http://theschwartz.wordpress.com, as shown in Figure B.13. This blog belongs to Jon Schwartz, one of the creators of the Phrogram programming language.

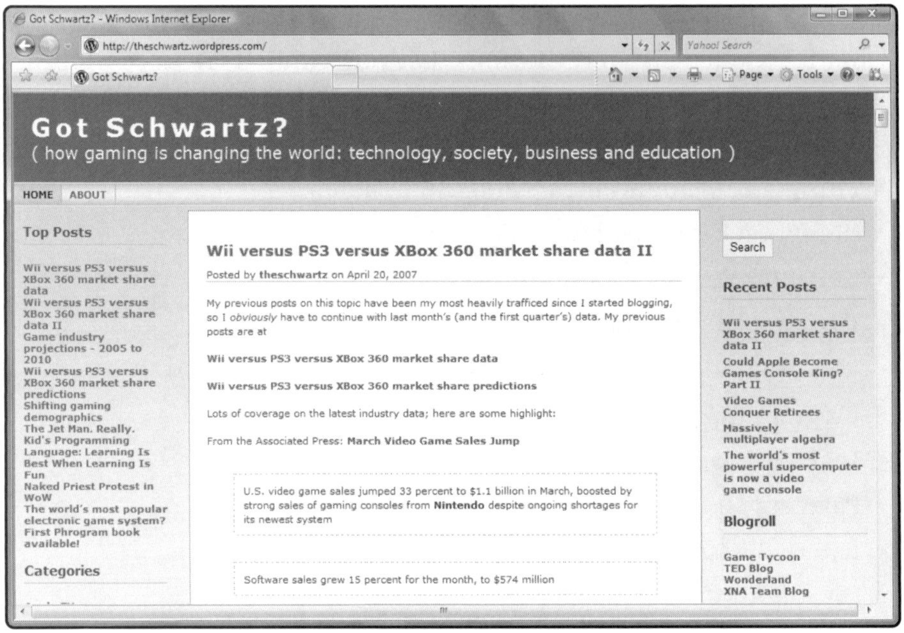


**FIGURE B.13**

The Got Schwartz? blog is a great source for learning about Phrogram and its developer's plans for its future.

## RECOMMENDED READING

In addition to all of the web pages and forums listed throughout this appendix, additional Phrogram documentation can also be found in the following electronic documents.

- **Beginner's Programming with Phrogram.** This 26-page PDF provides a brief high-level introduction to Phrogram and its overall capabilities. This document can be downloaded from the Downloads page at the Phrogram website (http://phrogram.com/files/default.aspx).
- **Let's Program with Phrogram.** This 46-page PDF is a Phrogram programming tutorial intended to provide the reader with a deeper dive into Phrogram programming than the Beginner's Programming with Phrogram guide. Although much of the material that is presented is also covered in the beginner's guide, this tutorial also includes a good introduction to sprites and data types and provides a number of additional coding examples. This document can be downloaded from the Downloads page at the Phrogram website (http://phrogram.com/files/default.aspx).
- **Phrogram v2.1 User Guide.** This 84-page PDF provides an overview of Phrogram and its IDE. It provides a brief overview of key language commands and briefly reviews the tutorial examples found in Phrogram's step-by-step tutorial folder. In addition, this file also provides a review of Phrogram's standard class library and its 3D game class library.

This document can be downloaded from the Downloads page at the Phrogram website (http://phrogram.com/files/default.aspx).

- *Learn to Program with Phrogram!*. ISBN 0321496833; Addison-Wesley, 2007. This e-book is designed to provide beginner programmers with a quick shortcut introduction to Phrogram. At just over 100 pages, it provides a quick read that provides a basic overview of the Phrogram language and its capabilities. This document can be purchased and downloaded from the online informIT bookstore located at http://www.informit.com.

# Glossary

**.NET Framework.** A software development and execution environment developed by Microsoft to support the execution of applications running on Microsoft Windows.

**Abstraction.** A term used to refer to a programming language's ability to define a logical representation of a real-world concept in the form of a class.

**Animated GIF.** A GIF file that is made up of two or more frames, each of which can be displayed in sequences when the GIF file is made visible.

**Argument.** A value, literal, or variable passed to a subroutine or function for processing.

**Array.** An indexed collection of related data, which is stored and processed as a unit.

**BASIC (Beginner's All-purpose Symbolic Instruction Code).** A programming language initially created to teach people the basics of computer programming.

**Boolean.** A value equaling either True or False.

**Break Point.** A marker within program files that temporarily halts program execution in order to facilitate debugging and the analysis of variable values and allow the programmer to exercise precise control over the application's execution.

**Camel Case.** A naming convention in which uppercase letters are used to format the beginning of words that are combined to create variable names.

**Class.** A definition or blueprint that outlines the variables, properties, methods, and functions that together form a template from which objects can be generated.

**Class Library.** A collection of constants, properties, methods, and functions, organized into a hierarchy that provides access to collections of predefined program code.

**Class Library Browser.** A Phrogram IDE window that allows programmers to browse the language's class hierarchy and view the syntax of all the language's methods and functions.

**Class Variable.** A variable defined within a class block and accessible only within the class in which it has been defined.

**CLR (Common Language Runtime).** A key component of .NET that is responsible for compiling applications into an executable format that the computer can understand and run.

**Code Block.** A collection of statements executed as a unit, which are enclosed within an opening and closing statement.

**Code Editor.** A specialized text editor designed to support the development of computer application source code.

**Collision.** An event that occurs whenever two sprites run into one another in a computer game.

**Comment.** A statement embedded inside a computer program for the purpose of documenting the development of the application.

**Compiler.** A computer program that translates program language statements into executable applications.

**Concatenation.** The process of joining together two or more strings to create a new larger string.

**Conditional Logic.** The process of executing sets of code statements based on whether a tested condition proves true.

**Console Window.** A term used to refer to the window in which Phrogram applications execute.

**Constant.** A descriptive name assigned to a known value that does not change during program execution.

**Data.** A piece of information collected, stored, modified, and processed during application execution.

**Debugger.** A program or utility that is used to compile and execute a program within a special environment that allows the programmer to exercise detailed control over the program as it runs.

**Decimal.** A floating point or real number.

**DirectX.** A Microsoft Windows technology designed to support the development of high-end graphics applications and games and is responsible for managing an application's interaction with graphics and audio hardware and game control devices.

**Distribution Package.** An application installation program that allows applications to be distributed to and executed on other computers.

**Encapsulation.** The process of simplifying application development by hiding as much as possible the complexity and inner workings of a class from the programs that use it.

**Endless loop.** A loop that does not have a means for terminating its execution.

**Explorer Pane.** A component of the Phrogram IDE, located by default on the right-hand side of the IDE, which is used to display Phrogram and application resources.

**Expression.** A program statement that is evaluated and produces a result.

**Extended I/O.** A free Phrogram add-in library that provides the ability to start and interact with external third-party applications.

**Flow Chart.** A tool used by programmers to graphically depict some or all of an application's logical flow.

**Folding.** A mechanism used within an IDE to conserve space when displaying a program file that collapses and temporarily hides program statements residing within functions, methods, loops, structures, and `If…Then` blocks from view.

**Function.** A named collection of program code statements that can be called upon to execute as a unit and which can return a value back to the statement that called upon the function to execute.

**Global Variable.** A variable defined within the program code block and accessible from any location within a program file.

**IDE (Integrated Development Environment).** A graphical application development environment designed to facilitate program development, which usually includes a code editor, compiler, and debugger.

**Identifier.** A term sometimes used in Phrogram documentation when referring to a variable.

**Inheritance.** An object-oriented programming concept in which one class is derived from another (parent) class.

**Instantiation.** The process of defining an object based on a class template.

**Integer.** An absolute or whole number.

**Intellisense.** An editor feature that assists programmers in writing program statements by monitoring programming statement input and displaying suggestions as to how to complete statements.

**Iterate.** The process of repeatedly executing the statements that make up a loop.

**Keyword.** A reserved word in a programming language that has a special meaning and which must be used in accordance with specific syntax rules.

**KPL (Kid's Programming Language).** The original name assigned to the Phrogram programming language when it was first released in August of 2005.

**Local Variable.** A variable that can be accessed only within the scope in which it is created.

**Logical Error.** An error created by a programmer mistake when developing the logic used to perform a given task.

**Loop.** A block of programming statements that are repeatedly executed.

**Method.** A named collection of one or more program code statements that can be called upon to execute as a unit.

**Method Variable.** A variable defined within a method or its parameter list, which is accessible only within the method in which it is defined.

**Nest.** The process of embedding one set of statements within another set of statements.

**Non-blocking Commands.** Commands that collect keyboard input without halting the execution of the application.

**Object.** A self-contained entity within a computer program that is made up of properties, methods, and functions.

**Object-Oriented Programming (OOP).** A form of application development based on the definition of objects, representing real-world concepts (like tanks, planes, and people), along with accompanying properties, methods, and functions required to interact with and control object operation.

**Order of Precedence.** A set of rules that specify the order in which a programming language evaluates a numeric expression.

**Parameter.** A variable defined as part of a method or function definition that identifies order and types of arguments that must be passed to the method or function for it to execute.

**Phrogram Academic.** A version of Phrogram Standard licensed for academic use by teachers and students.

**Phrogram Express.** A low-cost version of Phrogram that lacks the ability to develop stand-alone applications.

**Phrogram Standard.** A commercial version of Phrogram that provides access to all of the language's features and capabilities.

**PhrogramTalk.** A Phrogram add-in library that provides the ability to develop Phrogram applications that support chat and multi-player network gaming.

**Picture Browser.** A Phrogram window that allows you to preview graphic files within the Phrogram IDE.

**Pixel** (Picture Element). The smallest addressable area to which you can draw on the console.

**Polymorphism.** An object-oriented programming concept in which programmers define two or more like named methods or functions with different sets of parameter definitions to the same class definition.

**PrecisionMath.** A Phrogram add-in library that eliminates rounding errors that occur in complex mathematical calculations that was developed to assist with the creation of scientific and financial applications where precise calculations are required.

**Procedure.** A named collection of program code statements that can be called on to execute from any location within a Phrogram application.

**Process Queue.** A queue or buffer in which keystrokes are stored during application execution, allowing for their later retrieval.

**Program.** A file, sometimes referred to as a computer application, that contains statements that when executed tell the computer to do something.

**Property.** An object attribute that describes a characteristic of the object.

**Pseudo Code.** An English-like outline of all or part of the programming logic that makes up a computer application.

**Run-time Error.** An application error that occurs when an application attempts to perform an illegal action.

**Scope.** A term that refers to the area within an application where a variable can be accessed.

**Source Code.** The list of statements that make up a computer program.

**Sprite.** A 2D bitmap, drawn as an image on a transparent background that can be moved around the console window.

**Statements.** Instructions that make up a computer program.

**String.** A set of characters enclosed in a matching pair of double quotation marks.

**Structure.** A custom-defined collection of variables that can be managed together as a unit.

**Syntax.** Rules enforced by a programming language that specify how programming statements should be formulated.

**Syntax Error.** An error that occurs when a programmer does not formulate a program statement in accordance with the rules of the programming language.

**Variable.** A pointer to a location in memory where an individual piece of data is stored.

**Wave.** A file that supports the storage and playback of audio on personal computers.

**WeatherPro.** A Phrogram add-in library that provides access to real-time weather data.

# INDEX

## J



## K

## License Agreement/Notice of Limited Warranty

**By opening the sealed disc container in this book, you agree to the following terms and conditions. If, upon reading the following license agreement and notice of limited warranty, you cannot agree to the terms and conditions set forth, return the unused book with unopened disc to the place where you purchased it for a refund.**

### License:

The enclosed software is copyrighted by the copyright holder(s) indicated on the software disc. You are licensed to copy the software onto a single computer for use by a single user and to a backup disc. You may not reproduce, make copies, or distribute copies or rent or lease the software in whole or in part, except with written permission of the copyright holder(s). You may transfer the enclosed disc only together with this license, and only if you destroy all other copies of the software and the transferee agrees to the terms of the license. You may not decompile, reverse assemble, or reverse engineer the software.

### Notice of Limited Warranty:

The enclosed disc is warranted by Course Technology to be free of physical defects in materials and workmanship for a period of sixty (60) days from end user's purchase of the book/disc combination. During the sixty-day term of the limited warranty, Course Technology will provide a replacement disc upon the return of a defective disc.

### Limited Liability:

THE SOLE REMEDY FOR BREACH OF THIS LIMITED WARRANTY SHALL CONSIST ENTIRELY OF REPLACEMENT OF THE DEFECTIVE DISC. IN NO EVENT SHALL COURSE TECHNOLOGY OR THE AUTHOR BE LIABLE FOR ANY OTHER DAMAGES, INCLUDING LOSS OR CORRUPTION OF DATA, CHANGES IN THE FUNCTIONAL CHARACTERISTICS OF THE HARDWARE OR OPERATING SYSTEM, DELETERIOUS INTERACTION WITH OTHER SOFTWARE, OR ANY OTHER SPECIAL, INCIDENTAL, OR CONSEQUENTIAL DAMAGES THAT MAY ARISE, EVEN IF COURSE TECHNOLOGY AND/OR THE AUTHOR HAS PREVIOUSLY BEEN NOTIFIED THAT THE POSSIBILITY OF SUCH DAMAGES EXISTS.

### Disclaimer of Warranties:

COURSE TECHNOLOGY AND THE AUTHOR SPECIFICALLY DISCLAIM ANY AND ALL OTHER WARRANTIES, EITHER EXPRESS OR IMPLIED, INCLUDING WARRANTIES OF MERCHANTABILITY, SUITABILITY TO A PARTICULAR TASK OR PURPOSE, OR FREEDOM FROM ERRORS. SOME STATES DO NOT ALLOW FOR EXCLUSION OF IMPLIED WARRANTIES OR LIMITATION OF INCIDENTAL OR CONSEQUENTIAL DAMAGES, SO THESE LIMITATIONS MIGHT NOT APPLY TO YOU.

### Other:

This Agreement is governed by the laws of the State of Massachusetts without regard to choice of law principles. The United Convention of Contracts for the International Sale of Goods is specifically disclaimed. This Agreement constitutes the entire agreement between you and Course Technology regarding use of the software.